MW01044487

The Passion of Anne Hutchinson

The Passion of
Anne Hutchinson

*An Extraordinary Woman, the Puritan
Patriarchs, and the World They Made
and Lost*

MARILYN J. WESTERKAMP

OXFORD
UNIVERSITY PRESS

OXFORD
UNIVERSITY PRESS

Oxford University Press is a department of the University of Oxford. It furthers
the University's objective of excellence in research, scholarship, and education
by publishing worldwide. Oxford is a registered trademark of Oxford University
Press in the UK and certain other countries.

Published in the United States of America by Oxford University Press
198 Madison Avenue, New York, NY 10016, United States of America.

Library of Congress Cataloging-in-Publication Data
Names: Westerkamp, Marilyn J., author.
Title: The passion of Anne Hutchinson : an extraordinary woman, the Puritan
patriarchs, and the world they made and lost / Marilyn J. Westerkamp.
Description: New York, NY : Oxford University Press, [2021] |
Includes bibliographical references and index.
Identifiers: LCCN 2020046776 (print) | LCCN 2020046777 (ebook) |
ISBN 9780197506905 (hardcover) | ISBN 9780197506929 (epub)
Subjects: LCSH: Hutchinson, Anne, 1591–1643. |
Puritans—Massachusetts—Biography. | Women—Massachusetts—Biography. |
Social reformers—Massachusetts—Biography. |
Massachusetts—History—Colonial period, ca. 1600–1775. |
Freedom of religion—Massachusetts—History—17th century. |
Massachusetts—Biography.
Classification: LCC F67.H92 W47 2021 (print) | LCC F67.H92 (ebook) |
DDC 974.4/02092 [B]—dc23
LC record available at https://lccn.loc.gov/2020046776
LC ebook record available at https://lccn.loc.gov/2020046777

DOI: 10.1093/oso/9780197506905.001.0001

1 3 5 7 9 8 6 4 2

Printed by Sheridan Books, Inc., United States of America

Some material in Chapters 2 and 6 first appeared in a book published by Routledge.
Copyright © 1999 *Women and Religion in Early America, 1600–1850:
The Puritan and Evangelical Traditions* by Marilyn J. Westerkamp.
Reproduced by permission of Taylor and Francis Group, LLC, a division of Informa plc.

An earlier, shorter version of Chapter 7 first appeared as Marilyn J. Westerkamp,
"Engendering Puritan Religious Culture in Old and New England," *Pennsylvania History:
A Journal of Mid-Atlantic Studies,* Empire, Society, and Labor:
Essays in Honor of Richard S. Dunn, 64 (Special Supplemental Issue
Summer 1997), 105–122. Copyright © 1997 The Pennsylvania Historical Association.
This material is used by permission of The Pennsylvania State University Press.

For Cynthia, Claire, and Hugh
who have long lived with
Anne Hutchinson and the Puritans

Contents

Acknowledgments

This book has been at the center of my intellectual world for more years than I can fathom. My reading and my research have occupied me throughout these many years, and the entire structure of the project has been imagined, framed, and reinvented at least three times, benefiting from the developments in the history of gender and cultural studies. Of course, anything pursued over such a long time has been impacted by a significant number of people who have provided instruction, support, labor, and critique.

My research has taken me to a range of libraries and institutions on the East Coast, including the Massachusetts Historical Society, the Massachusetts State Archives, the Boston Public Library, and Harvard's Houghton Library, and I am indebted to the librarians and assistants who provided whatever help I needed. Although it is always important to drop into the British Library in London, my work in England was concentrated at the Bodleian Library and Worcester College Library of Oxford University, a veritable treasure trove of early print materials. These travels were supported by grants from the National Endowment for the Humanities. My research has also benefited from the time provided by a fellowship from the American Council of Learned Societies and University of California President's Fellowship in the Humanities. Additionally, over the years I have received many research grants from the University of California, Santa Cruz, that have provided travel funds but also support for research assistants, whose contributions have been invaluable.

I have found the University of California at Santa Cruz to be a personally supportive, generous, and intellectually invigorating home. When I found myself moving into early modern British history, my colleague Buchanan Sharp provided a primer and bibliography of the latest scholarship, which was particularly exciting since religion had begun to appear at the center of that universe. Moreover, as I became increasingly engaged in questions of gender and sexuality, fellow historians Gail Hershatter and Jon Beecher directed me to literatures that had nothing to do with early America or England, and everything to do with the possibilities inherent in gender studies and cultural history. Santa Cruz is an amazing community of scholars who seriously embrace interdisciplinarity with space and forums in which to explore eccentric connections across time and place. For a significant number of years, I worked within a feminist studies writing group, benefiting from the critical reading of Maria Elena Diaz, Dana Frank, Andrea Friedman, Beth Haas, Martha Hodes, Linda Lomperis Cindy Polecritti, and Alice Yang, and, more recently, I have benefited from the critical support of Kate Jones, Greg O'Malley, and Carla Freccero.

Pieces of this project have appeared at conferences, and I have always learned from the comments of colleagues. Dee Andrews, Ruth Bloch, Edith Gelles, Nancy Isenberg, Susan Juster, Ned Landsman, Ann M. Little, Mark Noll, Carla Gardina Pestana, Elizabeth Reis, and Robert Scribner have all shown interest in this project, and their ongoing support has been important to my thinking. Dwight Bozeman, Stephen Foster, Brooks Holifield, and Michael Winship, all exceptional intellectual historians of Puritanism, have provided key critical commentary, frequently in dispute, but always sharpening my own understanding of Puritan studies.

Several students have served as research assistants at various points along this journey, and their help has been much appreciated. I am indebted to Jennifer Cullison, Erika Falk, Jolie Katz, and Angela Redding, undergraduates who demonstrated intelligence and dedication as researchers. In the end, a significant portion of the development of this project was formulated in conversations with my graduate students, including Tiffany Wayne, Marta Bruner, Kevin McDonald, and Taylor Kirsch, who worked as excellent research assistants, but also Rebecca Hall, Megan Gudgeirsson, Benjamin Pietrenka, Noel Smyth, Lisa Jackson, and Danielle Kuehn. Living with a project for a long time requires new intellects to enliven, and sometimes destroy, old paths. As always, I am indebted to the staff of Oxford University Press, particularly Ponneelan Moorthy, attentive and relentless, working with me to ensure efficient production, and Cynthia Read, amazing editor who provided extensive advice on the construction of the book, assisting my efforts to enhance clarity and readability.

Finally, the support of my family has been unending despite provocation. I regret that my parents have died before they could see the final work, although I still recall exchanges I had with my father about my eccentric subjects. I daresay that my children are grateful that the end has come, although their support of my work and my fixation on the irrelevant past has brought its own satisfaction. Throughout these years, I have been blessed with a partner who reads widely in theology, with whom I can compare notes and argue about believers. She brings unending joy and inspiration into my life and work.

Introduction

Anne Hutchinson remains an iconic figure in early American history and women's history. American historians recognize Hutchinson as an influential religious leader ousted from Massachusetts Bay because of her outspoken criticism of the colony's clergy, and she remains one of the few women taught to schoolchildren and remembered from history lessons. In popular opinion she has been called a proto-feminist, a political dissident, a colonial reformer, and suffragette. Historians have proved slightly more sophisticated. From Perry Miller to Bryce Traister, more than eighty years of scholarship on New England theology and colonization have positioned Hutchinson and the controversy she provoked as a critical moment during the first decade of Massachusetts's settlement, although the importance of Hutchinson herself (rather than her male supporters) and the actual nature of her challenges have been matters of intense debate.[1]

John Winthrop, the first governor of Massachusetts, established the parameters that have limited historians' perceptions and interpretations. In his defensive response to theologians and clerics in Civil War England, *A Short Story of the Rise, Reign, and Ruine of the Antinomians, Familists, & Libertines*, Winthrop delineated the ideological afflictions of the independent churches of Massachusetts Bay as well as their ability to maintain order and orthodoxy.[2] In its very title, Winthrop framed the battle in terms of heretical sects, influencing not only English correspondents but future historians, who have labeled this the "Antinomian Controversy." From a purely technical standpoint, Massachusetts was afflicted neither by familists, who found the center of true religion to be love, nor by antinomians, who argued that faith abrogated the need to follow the law. Still, historians have produced an enormous collection of articles and books emphasizing the theological and political battles among men.[3]

If historians choose to read Winthrop at face value, they should note that despite all the characters wandering through its pages, *A Short Story* ends with the final church trial and excommunication of Hutchinson, the "*American Jesabel.*" The final three pages summarize her "entrance," "progress"—emphasizing her pride—and "downfall." He explains that because she seemed to repent her errors and confess that she had disrespected the ministers, she probably expected to regain her reputation. However, she

> kept open a back doore to have returned to her vomit again, by her paraphrasticall retractions, and denying any change in her judgement, yet such was the presence and blessing of God in his own Ordinance, that this subtilty of Satan was discovered to her utter shame and confusion, and to the setting at liberty of many godly hearts that had been captivated by her to that day.[4]

Hence, my decision to name the controversy Hutchinsonian, after its leading disrupter.

I have long been drawn to Hutchinson: her intellectual abilities and verbal jousting skills, her standing among Boston's men as well as women, her charisma, as both a magnetic leader and as a guide understood to be filled with *charis*, the extraordinary power of the Holy Spirit. Many years ago, I had hoped to craft a biography, but a traditional biography of Anne Hutchinson is impossible due to the scarcity of sources. (Those who have written biographies have frequently flirted with fiction.)[5] So I returned to the primary questions that energized my research, drove my curiosity.

The machinations—clerical conferences, correspondence, elections, trials—are interesting reflections of Winthrop's enormously skillful manipulations, although the end result, banishment and excommunication, was not surprising. Of course, she was going to lose; of course, leaders had vested interests in establishing order. This trajectory has been traced with sophistication and extraordinary subtlety. Social and cultural historians such as Ann Kibbey, Carol Karlsen, Mary Beth Norton, and Jane Kamensky have examined Hutchinson as emblematic of the status and limitations surrounding women in seventeenth-century New England.[6] Yes, this episode reveals an extensive, rich, illuminating cultural mandate integrated with political strategies. But this is old news.

My interest returns to the primary questions that many have forgotten. Why did Anne Hutchinson perform as she did? Why did she say she had received a revelation "by the voice of his own spirit to my soul"?[7] Perhaps she thought it was true, but this is only a partial answer. She had been called and charged before the General Court, the governing body of the colony. During the previous five months, Sir Henry Vane, supporter and governor, had lost his election and left the colony in disgust. Her friends and followers, including her brother-in-law, minister John Wheelwright, were disfranchised and banished. She was on trial. Why say that she had received a revelation if no one believed it possible? Winthrop claimed that she had thus condemned herself.[8] Surely a woman of her intelligence would have known the judgment her assertion would bring. Yet, in reading the transcripts of her trial and the writings of her friends, I discovered that, contrary to Winthrop's assertion, many believed that the revelation was possible. They believed her. Perhaps she was enjoying one last opportunity to prophesy.

This exploration of Anne Hutchinson as a charismatic leader has taken my research in two directions. First, I pursued the source of her theological knowledge and piety through her personal history, from her clerical father's checkered history to her own activities as recorded by supporters and eventual enemies. Although historians have the writings of a few New England women, including the correspondence of Margaret Winthrop, the poetry of Anne Bradstreet, and petitions of the incarcerated, Hutchinson left no writings of her own. Her voice is heard only through the mediation of recorders. Winthrop's *Short Story* includes some of her speech, a second transcript of her state trial, and transcripts of her two appearances before the church overlap and elaborate Winthrop's account. She was said to speak, however briefly, to Boston churchmen visiting the exiles, and a recorded statement appeared in a Quaker tract some forty years later. Yet out of these few pages of mediated writings, a voice of conviction and vitality, wit and intelligence can be heard.[9]

The second question moves beyond her own experiences to the power of her spiritual witness, her charismatic authority. The English women and men who colonized Massachusetts Bay were drawn from a deeply pious community. These English Christians had found the established Church of England to be significantly flawed and its clergymen uninspired, so they followed after pastors who preached acceptably and effectively and crafted for themselves private meetings of prayer, piety, and theological exploration. They carried this dedication across the ocean, and despite the fact that the churches now followed appropriate worship practices and the ministers preached the reformed gospel, these saints continued to meet in private prayer groups. In this world of bitter cold, food insecurity, and political uncertainty, where Indigenous residents were never quite out of sight or awareness, Anne Hutchinson gathered women to her Boston home to discuss sermons and pray; these weekly meetings attracted men as well, so she also hosted a second set of meetings with men and women. This may have been a struggling community in which people built new institutions and social structures, yet it remained a community permeated with joyous piety, where spiritual gifts were understood and holiness admired. Anne Hutchinson became a significant leader. How did that happen?

This book approaches Hutchinson from a position informed by cultural history and feminist theory, pushing into the intricate, competing, but sometimes complementary systems of Puritan religiosity and gender ideology.[10] The book takes up Puritanism as a religious culture over the long term, from its mid-sixteenth-century origins through the establishment of the New England colonies to the English Civil War, ending with the fragmentation of English Puritanism in the 1660s. Through Anne Hutchinson, her predecessors, her followers, and her fellow travelers, I explore the relationship between gender as an ideological system in flux during the early modern period and the radical religious community that arose during the sixteenth-century English Reformation and was transferred to New England.

Initially, informal networks of Puritan dissenters had challenged the newly established Church of England for its arbitrary hierarchies, lack of piety, and failure to adequately distance itself from the Roman Catholic Church. Puritans privileged piety and education as the two-pronged pathway to grace and authority. Intense piety, often realized in a deep, mystical communion with the divine, empowered ordinary individuals and directly challenged traditional birthright categories of status and authority, including monarchy and aristocracy. A rising class of men who would sit at the center of the new, godly societies of New England and Oliver Cromwell's Commonwealth envisioned themselves as biblical patriarchs and fortified their own claims through categories of "natural" difference: gender and class. Yet the equalizing principle inherent in Puritan religiosity not only destabilized the boundary between nobleman and commoner but also reached across to women and the lowest classes.[11]

From the earliest years of the English Reformation, women had played central roles as patrons, propagandists, and spiritual inspiration. Catherine Parr, sixth wife and widow of Henry VIII, lived at the center of one such community that furthered the work of reformation during Henry's final years. Foxe's Book of Martyrs includes many women in its pages, and figures such as martyr Anne Askew were enshrined in reformation hagiographies. Richard Hooker complained that Puritans labored most to convert women, for their judgments were "weakest by reason of their sex" and yet they were "propense and inclinable to holiness." More to the point, they were effective missioners to husbands, servants, children, and friends.[12]

Beyond the presence of devout female followers and patrons, Puritan radicalism was enhanced by the language through which Puritans constructed the believer's relationship with the divine. Theologians gendered both God (male) and the soul (female) and often employed erotic language to describe the soul's relationship with God. For women, this construction of the soul as bride of Christ enhanced their self-perception as they found a conduit promoting an intimate relationship with God, but reconstructing a man's spiritual self as female could undermine his masculinity. The result was a Puritan culture of intensified masculine activity operating alongside, and counteracting, a spirituality of feminine passivity.[13] When Puritans established their own societies free from interference of king and bishop, they frequently found themselves burdened with empowered women leaders. In response, political and clerical leaders invoked the natural hierarchy of gender to buttress their own patriarchal claims and disempower charismatic women.

Within a society that explained all relationships of power as the result of natural categories, gender became an obvious, defensible justification for existing structures of inequality as well as a rhetorical framework for explaining it. Seventeenth-century constructions of masculinity and femininity combined medical knowledge of the body with philosophical perceptions of the mind and theological beliefs about the soul to craft an argument for the subordination of female to male. This gendering of humanity connected women's biological experiences of menstruation and pregnancy to physical weakness, intellectual weakness, and ethical weakness. In other words, woman's inability to control her will and her mind was inscribed upon and evidenced by the uncontrolled female body. Her failure to discipline her desires was frequently translated into sexual behavior, and sexuality itself, especially deviant sexuality, fell primarily within the purview of woman. Additionally, this language was invoked as metaphor for other inequalities. Critiques of the lower classes, for example, frequently labeled the poor as physically and mentally weak, emotionally uncontrolled, and sexually deviant, that is, as women.[14]

Anne Hutchinson sits at the intersections of religious radicalism and gender, political power and spiritual charisma. The daughter of a cleric and wife of an affluent merchant, Hutchinson claimed the knowledge and status that placed her among Boston's leading women. She displayed the spiritual charisma that Puritan dissenters revered, and, following English Puritan practices, she held private religious meetings in her home and attracted a significant percentage of Boston's populace to her hearth. As she began to expound her vision of faith and salvation and to criticize most of New England's ministers for their failure to preach this vision, colonial magistrates and ministers discovered an urgent need to remove her from the community.

Hutchinson was not the first to challenge New England's nascent religious culture; a wide range of theologies and polities competed for predominance as the new orthodoxy.[15] Still, her enormous popularity across all social ranks, particularly leading residents such as magistrate William Coddington and aristocrat Henry Vane, her claim to direct communion with God, and her femaleness made her particularly problematic. Her opponents' use of every political and intellectual device available, from the disfranchisement and disarming of her male followers to veiled accusations of adultery, not only rationalized the political decision to banish her but also served to destroy her reputation among those supporters who remained in Massachusetts. Twenty years later, when Quakers, including Hutchinsonian Mary Dyer, arrived to preach their message of the equalizing power of the in-dwelling spirit, magistrates called upon the same ideological tools to harass Quakers and rationalize their brutal persecution of this group of manly women and effeminate men.

By incorporating the religious and cultural dimensions into this history of New England's women, this book parses the complicated system of gender hegemony and engages the peculiar happenstance of powerful, popular female leaders in a society that ostensibly had no space for women's authority. The instability inherent in the process of colonization, the absence of an institutionalized church, and a nurtured distrust of ordained clerics and government officials opened the way for controversy and provided opportunities for charismatic lay leaders, women as well as men. As some clerics and magistrates together struggled to establish religious orthodoxy, they grew committed to silencing all who disagreed with them. Those responsible for maintaining order turned to traditional hierarchies. The tools of gender were turned against sectarian dissenters whose membership, theology, and praxis were described as mostly female and lower class, heretical, and sexually deviant. If Puritans risked gendering the godly as feminine, they responded to this frightening possibility by gendering evil as feminine as well.

Finally, this book proffers a new answer to one of the oldest questions dominating Puritan studies. In his earliest work, Perry Miller identified the importance of an experiential, "Augustinian" conversion that defied rational explanation and sometimes grew into transcendent union with God. Yet in the construction of this text, he laid out what many historians have seen as the Puritan paradox: the centrality of Augustinian piety alongside the importance of learning.[16] What he did not perceive was the spiritual power that this radical religiosity had offered to the disfranchised. If women truly heard the voice of the Holy Spirit, then this power, this ultimate spiritual authority, would override the restrictions and rewards of patriarchal order. I find that Puritan efforts to undercut and, in some cases refute, that authority derailed the radical potential of Puritanism and further hardened evolving patriarchal boundaries. Clerical and political leaders strengthened their society's ideological commitment to rationalism and education, commitments that privileged men over women. They achieved this at the expense of joy, the ecstasy and power of mystical communion. They transmuted the unique character of their relationship with God and sacrificed their transformative piety.

In the final analysis, the seventeenth-century's culture of gender intersected with dissenters' theology and practice to structure a Puritan religiosity that in its very nature was gendered. When the unleashed power of spirituality, the charismatic authority, traveled among all believers, New England's magistrates and ministers had at hand the social and political structures of patriarchy to shut down access to all but the appropriate male figures. And while these legal and political systems served to silence women for more than a century, Puritan spirituality and practice empowered them.

1

Prologue

Anne Hutchinson and the Controversy

On March 22, 1638, the First Church of Boston excommunicated Anne Hutchinson; six days later she left the colony under sentence of banishment. Now despised and rejected of men, she had at one time commanded an enormous following among Boston's social and religious elite. Gifted with an extraordinary mind and an intense spiritual passion, Hutchinson, like many Puritans, had fled the degenerate English nation to seek the kingdom of God in Massachusetts Bay. Arriving in 1634, Hutchinson and her husband William quickly established themselves among the leadership of New England society. Scarcely three years later she was identified as the primary disturber of consensus and order, inspiring a large number of disciples who challenged the colony's political, social, and ideological foundations. Hutchinson led the last of several factions battling founding Governor John Winthrop for control of Massachusetts. Only with the Hutchinsonians' defeat did Winthrop become undisputed leader of the colony.

The very magnitude of the disruption had stunned the founding establishment, whose representatives would afterward write in an almost precious astonishment, a wide-eyed horror that any person, particularly any woman, could wreak the havoc that Hutchinson had wrought. She had gathered about her the overwhelming majority of the Boston church membership, captivated the leading merchants, and counted among her disciples the highest-ranking colonist of all, Henry Vane. With a speed that is, perhaps, possible only in a fluctuating, embryonic society, this woman had counted the majority of the city's social and economic leaders among her disciples and had mobilized them in opposition to the ranks of the colony's clergy. It took all the political skill and guile that Winthrop could muster to oust these enemies from government, return questions of religious orthodoxy to the deliberation of the clergy, and engineer the disintegration of the Hutchinsonian party and the downfall of its leader.

This story of what has become known as the "Antinomian Controversy" can be told in some detail because of the significant contemporary writings about Hutchinson and her following. By 1642, dangerous rumors and innuendoes had made their way across the Atlantic, and questions raised in Civil War England challenged Massachusetts's viability and orthodoxy. In their own defense, the Bay Colony leadership produced the historical reports, political vindications, and theological apologias, providing posterity with abundant, though generally hostile, accounts. These early writings revealed to the seventeenth century the fulfillment of divine providence, to the enlightened eighteenth century the intensity of intolerance, and to the romantic nineteenth the heroism of a pioneer for religious freedom; historians have consistently preserved the documents and re-examined previous interpretations.[1] The tremendous diversity of histories written over the past 350 years demonstrates that retrieving the narrative itself may be fairly complicated. John Winthrop's *Rise, Reign, and Ruine of the Antinomians* reveals a complex of political, theological, and social challenges arising amid the instability of the initial decade of Massachusetts colonization.[2]

The Hutchinsons left their Lincolnshire home in May 1634. Anne Hutchinson would later explain that she had followed her pastor, John Cotton, into the New England wilderness. Cotton, among the most highly respected of clerics, had for twenty years served the congregation of St. Botolph's in Boston, England. Although Hutchinson had lived twenty miles away in Alford, she had attended Cotton's ministry frequently enough to regard him as her pastor. Despite his strong identification with Cambridge University, that producer of Puritans, and his extensive popularity, even fame, among dissenters, Cotton had managed to maintain his pulpit and his freedom until 1633, when to escape arrest and imprisonment, he migrated to Boston, Massachusetts Bay, where he accepted the congregation's call as teacher. One year later Hutchinson arrived and became a member of the new world Boston church, gratified to be able to place herself directly under the spiritual care of Cotton.

When Hutchinson disembarked at Boston harbor, she found a colony scarcely four years old, the city of Boston little more than a village with great ambitions. Given its population of barely four or five hundred persons, the Hutchinson household must have represented a major addition to the town. Anne's eldest son, Edward, and William's younger brother and his wife, Edward and Sarah, had arrived the year before. They were now joined by Anne and William themselves, their other ten children, Anne's sister Katherine Marbury, and William's spinster cousins Anne and Frances

Freiston. William's sisters Susannah and Mary, along with Mary's husband
John Wheelwright, would arrive within the next two years. Add to these
the servants of the families (the elder Edward had at least two servants and
William four) and it is clear that the Hutchinsons, increasing the population of Boston by at least 5 percent, could claim influence through numbers
alone.[3]

Additionally, William's wealth and substance brought recognition and respect. With a gentry class that might have included thirty-five men, and an
upper corps of perhaps fifteen, one of those fifteen could not be insignifi-
cant. The Hutchinson family was granted a house lot near the meeting house
and directly across from John Winthrop himself. William was also allotted
six hundred acres, partly due to the necessity of supporting his enormous
family, but more in deference to his rank, for William's living was earned in
the merchant trade, not farming. Almost upon arrival William was elected
to represent Boston in the colony's assembly, the General Court; at other
times, he served on town committees and as church deacon.[4] William and
Anne, their five adult children, their in-laws Edward and Sarah, Mary and
John, and Susannah, and the Freiston cousins were all admitted as church
members. In a town of Boston's size and newness, the Hutchinsons made a
difference.[5]

As the wife of a prominent merchant, Anne Hutchinson would have
found a respectable position among Boston's women. Her skills and abilities soon enhanced her reputation, and her rise to prominence and ultimate downfall would inexorably tie her husband's stature to her own.
Apparently gifted in healing and midwifery, she was frequently found in the
sickroom or the birthing chamber. As the daughter of learned clergyman
Francis Marbury, she had been carefully educated in religion, and her scriptural knowledge and theological sophistication were soon greatly admired.
Testimony to Hutchinson's capabilities came in the first few months of her
arrival, when her admission to church membership was questioned by the
Reverend Zechariah Symmes, who had been one of her fellow passengers
on the crossing to New England. She had disagreed with him on points of
doctrine and scriptural exegesis, and when Symmes, diligently following
his pastoral duty, tried to correct "the corruptness and narrowness of her
opinions," she quoted to him, "I have many things to say but you cannot
bear them now." Whether this combative confidence was actually exhibited
in 1634 or simply remembered in 1637, Symmes did challenge her admission to the church, and she countered his objections successfully. The First

Church of Boston's pastor, John Wilson, as well as John Cotton, was satisfied with her responses to their questions, and she was accepted into the church.[6]

For a while there were no difficulties. In the same month that the Hutchinsons became church members, John Wilson sailed for England to fetch his wife to the colony. During the year of his absence, John Cotton served as primary pastor, and at some point, it is not known precisely when, Hutchinson began holding private religious meetings for the town's women. Such gatherings, a continuation of a practice common among English dissenters, were both devotional and educational, an opportunity for laypersons to continue their own religious explorations and improve their grasp of the week's sermons and lectures. Hutchinson's superior intellect and magnetic charisma made her the natural leader of these gatherings, and she quickly moved beyond explicating the ministers' sermons to delivering her own. Soon women brought their husbands along, and these meetings became so successful that Hutchinson began to hold, by popular request, two meetings each week, one for women only and one for both women and men. Hutchinson's enemies estimated the general attendance at sixty or more persons, at its peak as high as eighty.[7] Considering the population of Boston, this sounds as if most of the town gathered around her hearth. As late as the day of her excommunication, John Cotton agreed that Boston's women had "receaved much good from the Conference of [Hutchinson] and by Converse with her."[8]

Upon his return, John Wilson at first found very little to trouble him. He could not know that two notable men among his fellow passengers would, perhaps inadvertently, fuel rising contention through their support of opposing factions: cleric Thomas Shepard, whose reputation for piety and erudition equaled Cotton's, and layman Henry Vane, son of Sir Henry Vane, privy councilor.[9] By the following spring, 1636, word of the Hutchinsonians' aberrant theology had reached the colony's clergy; Shepard had begun to question Cotton's opinions and his involvement with the dissenters; and Vane, newly elected governor, had become an avid Hutchinson disciple. Rumors spread that, while Hutchinson attended and honored the spiritual preaching of Cotton, she severely criticized the "legal" preaching of Wilson and the other clergy.

The primary theological issue was the relationship between human endeavor and salvation. The Calvinist doctrines of predestination and divine omnipotence led to the obvious conclusion that one's salvation was completely in the hands of God. Individuals could have no responsibility for achieving salvation because they were powerless to effect it. Only faith, not works, could justify the innately depraved soul before God, and faith was possible only through divine grace. From the omnipotence of God Calvinists reasoned that when divine grace was offered, it could not be refused; grace was, in fact, irresistible, and the saint could no more fall from heaven than the sinner could escape hell. Once grace was offered and, perforce, accepted, however, this justification should be confirmed by the sanctification of the saint's daily conduct.

Given the unconditionality of Christ's gifts of grace and faith, the Hutchinsonians (and Cotton) stressed the futility of any action and the passivity of the believer in absolute dependence upon God. Deeds were of little import compared with the need to receive God's grace. In fact, one need hardly worry about conduct at all, since the sinner was irrevocably lost and the saint would just as inevitably do good. Most New England clerics, however, found such arguments dangerous, concluding that they would lead inevitably to heresy, irreligion, and anarchy. Although granting the absolutely arbitrary and unconditional nature of God's actions, these ministers understood the anxiety of believers desperately trying to discern some sign of their own salvation; so in their sermons, they emphasized the hope that lay in sanctification. Because behavior provided some evidence of salvation, then surely it was important to be able to recognize sanctified conduct. Lectures on behavior would also benefit the saint who, imperfect until the final triumph at death, must strive toward the glory of God.

The most intriguing direction this preaching took was the development of an idea that the potential saint could somehow prepare to receive God's grace. Still affirming that no human effort could affect God's ultimate action, ministers nevertheless encouraged hopeful believers to study scripture, attend sermons, guard their conduct, and pray so that they would be ready to receive grace when it came. Such preparatory efforts did, perhaps, keep believers from feeling so powerless in the face of arbitrary divine selection. The Hutchinsonians, however, found in preparationism hints of salvation through good works. The clergy had labeled Hutchinsonians fanatical and antinomian or anarchic; Hutchinson attacked the ministers for preaching a legalistic covenant of works.[10]

After six months of growing mistrust and animosity, open conflict commenced in October 1636 with the arrival of Mary and John Wheelwright, whose ideas echoed the spiritual emphases of Cotton and the Hutchinsonians. All of the clergy and Hutchinson met privately to reconcile apparent differences and, apparently, reached an amicable agreement. The Boston laity, however, were still dissatisfied. They voted to call Wheelwright as a third minister for the congregation, deliberately insulting their pastor, Wilson, in the process. By invoking a rule requiring unanimous consent to a call a minister, John Winthrop led a significant, though small, minority in derailing this effort. He was victorious, but he paid the hefty price of increased hostilities, clarified battle lines, and the alienation of the majority of church members from himself.

In December, Hutchinson, Cotton, and the colony ministers conferred again to address their theological differences. The "Sixteene Questions" asked of and answered by John Cotton, presumably as a result of this conference, indicate that the primary problem remained the issue of sanctification. Comparing himself to Jesus brought before the high priest, Cotton regretted the presumption and ill-founded hostility of his colleagues, but, "because you are much more deare and precious to me than the *High Priest* was to [Christ]," he agreed to answer their questions.[11] This time round, their disagreements remained unresolved as Cotton warned fellow clerics that in preaching sanctification they risked leading their listeners into a false comfort grounded in works. For her part, Hutchinson asserted that in emphasizing sanctification ministers preached a covenant of works. In the wake of increasing polarization, Henry Vane resigned as governor only to rescind that resignation when the Hutchinsonians, realizing that Winthrop as deputy governor would succeed Vane, convinced him that his duty lay in fulfilling his office. At this point, John Wilson delivered a speech on the sadly divided condition of the churches, pointing to the rise of new dangerous opinions and further irritating his congregation. The General Court voted to hold a fast day to beg forgiveness and attempt to heal the breaches in the church.

During the fast-day services at the Boston church, John Wheelwright, at the invitation of John Cotton, delivered a sermon that strengthened rather than reconciled divisions and deflected attention, briefly, away from Hutchinson. Taking advantage of this opportunity to add his own voice to the debate, Wheelwright devoted much of his sermon to denying that sanctification could be seen as evidence of growing justification:

> if men thinke to be saved, because they see some worke of sanctification in them, as hungring and thirsting and the like: if they be saved, they are saved without the Gospell. No, no, this is a covenant of works, for in the covenant of grace, nothing is revealed but Christ for our righteousnes; and so for the

Knowledge of our justification by faith, nothing is revealed to the soule but only Christ and his righteousnes freely given . . . .

Considering the current dissension, this line of reasoning would have been disruptive enough, but Wheelwright took his point far beyond the bounds of academic disputation. His sermon worked outward from the institution of the fast day itself, finding that in scripture the people of God fasted only in God's absence. Wheelwright threw down the gauntlet when he asserted that God was indeed absent from New England and that "those under a covenant of works, maketh [the saints] travaile under the burthen of that Covenant and so maketh the Lord absent himselfe from them . . . ." He noted that papists fasted more than anyone, identified as hypocrites those who strove to do God's work, and implied that those who disagreed with his vision of justification were the Antichrist. He encouraged the truly justified to stand with Jesus Christ and uphold this "light" against those who would return the nation to the darkness of good works and self-righteousness.[12] Encouraged by this call to battle, the Hutchinsonians grew more assertive, "and much offence was still given by her [Hutchinson], and others in going out of the ordinary assemblies, when Mr. *Wil*[*son*] began any exercise; and some of the messengers of the Church of *Boston*, had contemptuously withdrawn themselves from the generall Assembly, with professed dislike of their proceedings . . . ."[13] Some Hutchinsonians even refused to serve in the militia organized to assist Connecticut in its battle with the Pequots because the militia's chaplain was the questionable John Wilson.

Scarcely two months after the fast day, the General Court contemplated the strife within the colony. At this March session the magistrates and the towns' deputies revealed that, strong as the Hutchinsonians were in Boston, the movement was confined to that city. Most of the deputies represented outlying towns served by the besieged clergy, and they were weary of the hectoring behavior of the Hutchinsonians. They approved Wilson's December speech and found Wheelwright, in his attack upon the Massachusetts clergy, guilty of sedition and contempt. Of course, a minority in the assembly protested, and the Boston church sent a petition on Wheelwright's behalf, but neither challenge was admitted.

The Court also decided that in light of the disturbance in Boston, the next General Court, in May, would be held across the river in Newtown. At this session, the annual colony elections would be held; moving the elections out of the city would effectively disfranchise Boston, for the distance made it difficult for Bostonians to attend. The May session of the General Court followed the pattern that Winthrop had planned. Although a petition was presented on behalf of Wheelwright, and Governor Henry Vane ordered that it be read, Deputy Governor Winthrop and his party called for elections first. The order of business was put to a vote, and the majority voted to hold elections. Vane and his supporters refused to participate, so that same majority moved to one side and elected Winthrop governor. William Coddington and Richard Dummer, two Hutchinsonian assistants, were replaced, and Henry Vane was denied a colony office.[14]

Boston made its disapproval known. The town elected Henry Vane and William Coddington, among others, as deputies to the General Court, while the honor guard refused to provide an escort for the newly elected Winthrop. Nevertheless, despite such local disfavor, John Winthrop had demonstrated that after three years in a subordinate position he still commanded the colony-wide prestige and the political sophistication necessary to win back the colony's highest office.

Winthrop's political abilities stood him in good stead as he worked throughout the summer and autumn to solidify his position, destroy the Hutchinsonians, and reconstruct social and religious harmony. Against the voice of the Boston deputies, the General Court passed a law regarding strangers that forbade any person to stay in the colony for more than three weeks unless approved by the court. The government hoped that this law would keep the Hutchinsonians from adding to their numbers through immigration. Additionally, the General Court passed a series of resolutions that explicitly addressed the activities of the Hutchinsonians. They condemned congregants' efforts to dispute doctrine with the preacher and restricted questions to information, noting that such questions were rarely justified. Congregants were also forbidden to forsake their churches for any difference of opinions that was not fundamental. Of greatest importance, however, the court forbade Hutchinson's meetings. "That though women might meet (some few together) to pray and edify one another; yet such a set assembly (as was then in practice at Boston) where sixty or more did meet every week, and one woman (in a prophetical way, by resolving questions of doctrine, and expounding scripture) took upon her the whole exercise, was agreed to be disorderly, and without rule."[15]

The magistrates and clergy then organized a conference to address the wide-ranging doctrinal errors that were appearing in the colony, undoubtedly hoping to calm the dissent of Cotton, effect a theological consensus,

and bring the laity to acceptance of this orthodoxy. They identified and confuted eighty-two errors and nine unsavory phrases. Whether or not Cotton
and the ministers had worked out their differences regarding sanctification,
many of the "errors" named and phrases identified dealt explicitly with the
relationship between sanctification and justification. Many other errors
addressed the nature of faith, spiritual assurances, and revelation, pointing
up the hazardous undercurrents swirling amid the errors and arrogance of
the Hutchinsonians.

Having achieved a recognized orthodoxy among the clergy, and having
denied settlement to dangerous strangers (that is, Hutchinsonian sympathizers),
Winthrop needed to rid the colony of those dangerous persons already there.
Henry Vane gratifyingly departed from the colony in disillusionment, as did
several sympathetic merchants and their families, but a significant number
were left to the November session of the General Court. Wheelwright was
summoned to the court, where he was questioned concerning his contempt
for New England's clergy and his seditious encouragement of the Bostonians in
their obstreperous conduct. Wheelwright stood by his sermon, denied the contempt, and demanded that the court prove his involvement with the Bostonians'
political resistance. Self-righteous and unrepentant, he was banished from the
colony. Winthrop next brought the leading Hutchinsonians to account. They
were systematically interrogated and, in light of the content and tenor of their
responses, were disarmed, disfranchised, fined, and/or banished. Then and
only then was Winthrop prepared to turn to the source of the dissension. On
November 7, Mistress Hutchinson, "the head of all this faction . . . the breeder
and nourisher of all these distempers . . . a woman of haughty and fierce carriage,
of a nimble wit and active spirit," was brought to trial.[16]

It is noteworthy that Winthrop saved Hutchinson's trial for last. Reading
Winthrop's account in his *Journal* and his *Short Story*, one senses the
mounting tension as step by step Winthrop worked through supporters and
abettors. Even though Wheelwright was identified as "the instrument of our
troubles," and even though Winthrop judged Wheelwright author of his
own errors, Anne Hutchinson was recognized as the primary problem.[17] It
has been unendingly suggested that the problem was John Cotton, but this
simply doesn't ring true. Cotton was handled successfully, twice. In October
1636, following a clerical reconciliation that included Wheelwright, a dissatisfied Hutchinsonian laity continued to foster questions and raise objections,
inspiring another private meeting in December that ended less amicably.
In September 1637, a major synod involving the entire ministry addressed

eighty-two errors, and Cotton agreed with the synod's conclusions. Yet the problem remained. Not only did Wheelwright stand confident and unrepentant, but Hutchinsonians, when questioned about their seditious conduct, justified themselves and refused to acknowledge any error. Winthrop knew that such challenges would not end until the lay coalition was dismantled, its leader rooted out, and her authority completely destroyed.

The trial lasted scarcely two days, yet during those two days the essential nature of the conflict became startlingly clear. The intellectual mystification that had barely sprouted in the sixteen questions and reached full flower in eighty-two errors (and nine unsavory speeches) disintegrated before the purposeful charges of the court and Hutchinson's impressive self-defense. Unable to produce irrefutable evidence in support of their accusations or scriptural evidence in support of their opinions, the magistrates found themselves seeking help from the ranks of clergymen who had enjoyed private, pastoral conversations with her. This, in turn, threatened to replace theological mire with legal, procedural disputes. Yet suddenly, and unpredictably, Hutchinson told her own story to the General Court, providing the necessary evidence and justifying her own banishment.

The records of this incredible trial reveal Hutchinson in all her formidable intellectual prowess.[18] For one and a half days she ran exegetical circles around her opponents. They quoted scripture; she quoted back. They interpreted a verse against her; she responded with an alternative text and a valid interpretation. Winthrop began with a lengthy, condemnatory, rather frightening speech in which he accused her of generic disturbances, errors, and discord; he then demanded that she respond. Even at this stage she showed her mettle, asserting that she could not answer charges until she knew precisely what those charges were. She put Winthrop immediately on the defensive and made way for him to show the deep weaknesses of his case against her. In fact, he had very few specifics to lay against her, and those he did have were not supported by any but hearsay evidence.

He first charged her with breaking the fifth commandment because she countenanced those who had the previous March signed the seditious petition on behalf of Wheelwright. The petitioners, in challenging the General Court, had dishonored their parents, that is, their superiors. She responded that she might entertain the petitioners as children of God without countenancing their transgression. Of course, as a woman, Hutchinson had not explicitly joined this effort by signing the petition, so the court had no evidence of conspiracy on her part.[19] After a quick, verbal thrust and parry, a frustrated Winthrop asserted that she did adhere to the petitioners, she did endeavor to promote their faction, and thus she dishonored the magistrates, her parents, breaking the fifth commandment. Furthermore, the court did "not mean to discourse with those of your sex . . ."[20]

Perhaps seeking a more defensible position, Winthrop moved onto the painful and equally dangerous subject of the private meetings in her home. The scriptural rule clearly forbade women to teach publicly, but, answered Hutchinson, her home was not public. She produced biblical texts proclaiming the duty of elder women to instruct the younger; members of the court retorted that she was known to instruct men at her meetings. She responded that at the mixed meetings only men spoke, although she believed that if a man came to her, she was permitted to instruct him as Priscilla had guided Apollos (Acts 18:26). According to his own account, Winthrop began to attack the nature of her meetings, yet he could not prove the truth of his own description in the face of her denial. When Winthrop refused to acknowledge that her biblical citations provided a rule for her meetings, she asked whether she must "shew my name written therein?" In a second display of authority Winthrop announced that the meetings must end because he said so. "We are your judges, and not you ours and we must compel you to it."[21]

The General Court had achieved Hutchinson's acquiescence in the matter of her meetings: "If it please you by authority to put it down I will freely let you for I am subject to your authority."[22] However, it became clear that this would not be enough for the magistrates. As Deputy Governor Dudley complained, three years earlier the colony had been at peace, but from the moment that Hutchinson had landed in Boston, she had been the fount of great disturbances. Winthrop, Dudley, and their colleagues identified her as the primary source of unrest; they required weightier grievances in order to rid themselves of her presence in the colony. At this point they turned to the disruption caused by her criticism of the clergy. When she compared the clergy unfavorably to her mentor Cotton, she was attacking the primary arbiters of divine authority in Massachusetts. When she argued that the clergy were not preaching the true pathway to salvation, she implied that those who were recognized as the most spiritually fit were beneath the regard of the ordinary congregant. Obviously, such portrayals of the ministers had to be curtailed and condemned. Once again, though, Winthrop had to prove that Hutchinson had in fact delivered such derogatory opinions.[23]

The initial accusations came from the magistrates, and in their mouths the complaints sounded like what they must have been: hearsay and rumor.

Magistrates had certainly heard the uncomplimentary opinions that some Hutchinsonians had delivered on the subject of the clergy; in fact, one Stephen Greensmyth had been fined forty pounds for asserting that all but three of the ministers taught a covenant of works.[24] And the ministers had undoubtedly told Winthrop about some of Hutchinson's statements, not to mention the congregational heckling they had suffered. Nevertheless, the magistrates had apparently never heard Hutchinson so speak, for they did not testify against her. Nor could they expect her followers to so testify. Instead, Dudley and Winthrop opened a third potentially fruitless dialogue, accusing Hutchinson of making statements that she then denied. Finally, Hugh Peters, followed by other clergy, attempted to rescue the situation by reporting what Hutchinson had said at the conference held the previous December.

Here the court appeared to approach higher ground, for several clergymen were willing to give their own accounts. Hugh Peters, who hoped that he and other clerics "may not be thought to come as informers against the gentle-woman," proceeded to inform against her. He claimed that in her conference with the ministers Hutchinson had described wide differences between most of the clergy and Cotton, that "he preaches the covenant of grace and you the covenant of works." Throughout the conference, Peters asserted, she had discounted their abilities and spirituality, arguing that such preaching signified an absence of the seal of the Spirit and that they were not ministers of the New Testament. One after another minister present at the conference rose and spoke to his own memory of her statements, and while Thomas Shepard may have been relatively mild and hopeful while others seemed almost vindictive, their testimonies overlapped and reconfirmed each other. Throughout the afternoon, Hutchinson challenged those accounts, at one point asking John Wilson for the notes that he took of the conference. The day's proceedings ended amid yet another standoff.[25]

The following morning Hutchinson brilliantly redirected and enlivened the court by demanding that those clerics testifying against her swear an oath. Already this evidence did not sit easily with the court; after all, the conference had been private and protected, so that in speaking against her, the clergy were betraying a pastoral confidence. Now claiming that the ministers were both accusers and witnesses, she invoked standard legal procedure in order to reinforce her denial of their accounts. She had refreshed her memory through notes taken by Wilson, and she averred that she remembered the conversations differently and had witnesses to support her version.

First, however, the original testimony must be taken upon oath, a position that many court members seemed to support. The obvious affront to the veracity of the clergy had its predictable effect, and Winthrop and Dudley ardently defended the reliability and sincerity of the ministers. Yet amid the self-righteous furor were sown further seeds of doubt. The conference had occurred almost a year before, and, as Simon Bradstreet, a clerical supporter, argued, "Mrs. Hutchinson, these are but circumstances and adjuncts to the cause, admit they should mistake you in your speeches you would make them to sin if you urge them to swear." Although Bradstreet implied that his concern grew out of the possibility of minor errors concerning peripheral matters, the specter of major misremembrances appeared. Moreover, the clergy proved reluctant to swear, lending credence to Hutchinson's challenges.[26]

She asked that three witnesses be called in her behalf. However, supporter John Coggeshall was frightened into silence by Peters ("How dare you look into the court to say such a word"), and church elder Thomas Leverett proved able to utter only three sentences before he was challenged by Winthrop. A third witness delivered his extremely troublesome testimony in full. John Cotton had not wanted to testify, but his own memory of the conference agreed with Hutchinson's account. Sorry as he was that he and his colleagues should be compared at all, he did recall mild disagreements concerning the covenant of grace and the seal of the Spirit, and he gently reminded the others that he had instanced a story supporting Hutchinson's position. Moreover, the difference was not then "so ill taken as it is [now] and our brethren did say also that they would not so easily believe reports as they had done and withal mentioned that they would speak no more of it, some of them did; and afterwards some of them did say they were less satisfied than before." Finally, lest there be any doubt, he concluded that he "did not find her saying they were under a covenant of works, nor that she said they did preach a covenant of works." Despite further challenges, questions, and objections, Cotton did not countermand his testimony.[27]

By this point the trial was proving a disaster for Winthrop's party. Hutchinson had responded to the initial charges with skill and finesse, outwitting her opponents in scriptural argument and then graciously bowing to their commands because they were magistrates. By this means she retained the higher biblical ground while removing cause for their complaints. The latter, more serious charges of sedition against the ministry held great promise, but they were substantiated only through ministers' reports of a private conference held a year before. Ministers seethed in outrage as they made speeches and fed each other lines; the hostility grew apace. Just as the momentum seemed strongest, Hutchinson derailed the prosecution with the procedural demand for sworn testimony, a demand that many court members found eminently reasonable, a demand that pointed up the weakness of the prosecution's evidence. In the midst of these legal arguments three witnesses challenged the clerical version of the conference, and while two were easily silenced, John Cotton's personal authority and prestige required the court to attend and credit his reluctant testimony. At this moment Winthrop undoubtedly blessed the political wisdom that had led him to disempower so many of her followers beforehand, but he was fast running out of arguments by which he could bring the court to vote his verdict. Hoping to invoke the law to legitimize proceedings against the Hutchinsonians, Winthrop found that their leader could better use the law to expose him and his government.[28]

Hutchinson chose this moment, this outflowing of chaos, to proclaim her vision. Turning to her own spiritual conversion, Hutchinson told the court of her early religious concerns and doubts, of her ultimate dependence upon God, and of God's response to her prayerful pleas. She granted that she had become "more choice" in selecting a minister, for God had led her to distinguish the voices of truth.

MR. NOWELL: How do you know that that was the spirit?
MRS. H: How did Abraham know that it was God that bid him offer his son, being a breach of the sixth commandment?
DEP. GOV.: By an immediate voice.
MRS. H.: So to me by an immediate revelation.
DEP. GOV.: How! an immediate revelation.
MRS. H: By the voice of his own spirit to my soul.[29]

As she continued to recount her spiritual history, Hutchinson compared herself to the prophet Daniel. As God had delivered Daniel from the lion's den, so had God promised that he would protect and deliver her from her adversaries. Pouncing upon her testimony, Winthrop and other accusers pursued this question of revelation. They believed that any claim to a miraculous deliverance was blasphemy, for the age of miracles had long past. By the end of the proceedings, the overwhelming majority of the court would agree with Winthrop's disingenuous conclusion: "Pass by all that hath been said formerly and her own speeches have been ground enough for us to proceed upon."[30]

The intelligence demonstrated by Hutchinson throughout the early stages of her trial lead one to conclude that she must have known that her speech could conceivably end, as it did, in her conviction. Historians, not unnaturally, have wondered why this woman, who had run such brilliant circles around her accusers, would provide such damning evidence. Yet in accepting this exchange as the crucial moment of the examination, have not scholars allowed the prosecution to interpret the documents? Apparently, they have left unchallenged the cause-and-effect relationship that Winthrop posited between Hutchinson's testimony and the court's "easy" condemnation.[31]

If she really had condemned herself, why did the examination continue? After she had proclaimed her revelations, new indictments began, and witnesses testified to previous prophetic declarations. Nevertheless, the weight and character of these testimonies precipitated not an immediate censure, but a prolonged, extraordinary debate upon the nature of revelation itself. Perhaps the equation of claiming revelation with blasphemy was neither automatic nor obvious. When asked to contribute his own severe denunciation of Hutchinson, John Cotton refused. He chose, instead, to present an abstract discourse upon the two sorts of revelation: miraculous and providential. While an expectation of the miraculous would represent a delusion, he argued, any soul might have a justifiable faith in special providence. Therefore, before he would judge her, Cotton needed to know the nature of the divine deliverance Hutchinson expected, and he insisted upon this position until a frustrated Winthrop proceeded without his support. Hutchinson reiterated throughout this discussion her conviction in a special providence while her opponents accused her of prophesying the miraculous. At this point in his account, Winthrop gloated over her self-destruction, yet clearly the trial was not over. There remained discomfort concerning procedures; court delegates returned to the earlier charges and the lack of sworn testimony or substantial evidence against her. In the end, three clergymen did testify under oath; only then was she convicted and banished. When, in a final moment of defiance, Hutchinson demanded to know why she was banished, Winthrop responded with an echo of the previous day's exasperation: "Say no more, the court knows wherefore and is satisfied."[32] Winthrop declared the matter closed, having achieved his ends by the skin of his teeth.

While most scholars have judged her declarations as weakness, one might as easily see this as a moment of exceptional strength. The critical exchange was preceded by her warning, "Now if you do condemn me for speaking what in my conscience I know to be truth I must commit myself unto the Lord."[33] Hutchinson seemed to revel in her prophetic moment, for the court and its observers stood riveted upon her words, her revelations. The magistrates and the clergy wanted, needed these revelations to be discounted, and several witnesses spoke critically of her previous invocations of revelations. The accusers tried to rally Cotton against her, but he would not follow them. I suspect that rather than providing the evidence against her, the power gathered in her speech frightened Winthrop, warning him of just how necessary it was for evidence to be found. He unwittingly revealed such anxiety in his own analysis of this moment:

> Mistris *Hutchison* having thus freely and fully discovered her selfe, the Court and all the rest of the Assembly (except those of her owne party) did observe a speciall providence of God, that (while shee went about to cover such offences as were laid to her charge, by putting matters upon proofe, and then quarrelling with the evidence) her owne mouth should deliver her into the power of the Court, as guilty of that which all suspected her for, but were not furnished with proofe sufficient to proceed against her, for here she hath manifested, that her opinions and practice have been the cause of al our disturbances, & that she walked by such a rule as cannot stand with the peace of any State; *for such bottomlesse revelations . . . if they be allowed in one thing, must be admitted a rule in all things; for they being above reason and Scripture, they are not subject to controll.*[34]

Hutchinson undermined the authority of secular and sacred officers with her own spiritual power. At last she had openly claimed that power, for which her opponents were profoundly grateful, but they remained unable to convince Cotton or all the observers that her claims were blasphemous. Winthrop and the clergy returned in the end to charges of sedition and procedural rules of evidence, winning her banishment with the acquiescence of all but three participants. Winthrop must indeed have been satisfied.

At the end of this, the last of the trials, the Hutchinsonian community began to sort itself out. Some followed Wheelwright to a new colony in what would become New Hampshire; others, including the Hutchinson family, proceeded to organize their removal to a new settlement near Roger Williams's Providence Plantation.[35] Because she was sentenced at the beginning of winter, the court extended a questionable mercy in permitting

Hutchinson to remain in the colony until the spring, but demanded that she spend this time under house arrest in the home of an unsympathetic clergyman. While many of her followers, including her husband and her minor children, moved on to the business of constructing the new colony, Hutchinson became the unhappy focus of extensive clerical counsel. Supposedly in the interest of her conviction, repentance, and ultimate salvation, the clergy engaged in an emotional and intellectual barrage that explored a range and variety of theological questions and dicta that had been raised in neither of the 1636 conferences nor in her examination before the General Court. All of this material was brought forward to her final examinations before the church.

On March 15, 1638, the church at Boston heard charges against Hutchinson. The investigation focused upon her beliefs concerning the soul's immortality, the body's resurrection, and the union of the individual spirit to Christ. None of these questions had been raised the previous November, as Hutchinson insistently noted, but they became the center of this examination. The preliminary church trial ended in dissatisfaction with her responses and a sentence of admonition. Interestingly, the church elders requested that Cotton deliver the verbal chastisement "as one whose Wordes by the Blessinge of God may be of more Respect and sinke deeper and soe was likely to doe more good upon the partie offendinge than any of theas." Unspoken but of greater importance would be the effect of Cotton's denunciation upon the congregation. As the instrument of the clergy and elders, Cotton's alignment with their position was now fixed.[36]

The following week, having seriously reconsidered the theological questions, Hutchinson seemed to acknowledge her errors. She explained that at some points she was guilty of false or extravagant expressions and that her beliefs were actually opposite to the implications of those expressions.[37] At this second hearing she also sought to accept responsibility for her errors and to admit that she had slighted the ministers. Despite this promising start, the caliber and sincerity of her repentance were challenged by clergy and laymen (i.e., magistrates) alike. Noting that she repented only those errors discovered after November and left untouched those doctrines raised at her state trial, Thomas Dudley found that "her Repentance is not in her Countenance." Having judged her repentance insincere, the congregation had no problem reaching its judgment. The theological issues were murky, her continued adherence to her revelations was troubling, but, gratifyingly, Hutchinson's "insincerity" made her a liar. Because she had troubled the church with her errors, upheld her revelations, and had "made a Lye," she was excommunicated.[38] As she left the congregation for the last time, she was accompanied by one person, her longtime follower, Mary Dyer.[39]

Soon after her final confrontation with Boston's leadership, Hutchinson joined her family in Rhode Island. William was elected to the leadership of an infant community soon embroiled in political battles of its own. The couple lived in the colony for three years and grew increasingly frustrated at the lack of godliness among the residents. After William died in 1640, Hutchinson and her seven younger children moved to Long Island, where, in August 1643, all but the youngest were killed during the conflict between the Wappingers and the Dutch colonizers, thus hopefully putting an end to the entire episode. In this bloody, violent finale to the Hutchisonian crisis, some New Englanders found the divine vindication of Winthrop's work and judgment. "I never heard that the Indians in those parts did ever before this, commit the like outrage upon any one family, or families, and therefore Gods hand is the more apparently seene herein, to pick out this wofull woman, to make her and those belonging to her, an unheard of heavie example of their cruelty above al others."[40]

One may well say hopefully, for at about this time English Puritans, engaged in their own revolution and attempts to reconstruct civil and church order, began to examine closely the example of New England. In their general astonishment at the Hutchinsonian crisis, English clerics called upon New England colleagues to explain and justify Massachusetts's civil government and church polity in light of the fact that such an enormous challenge could rise up within a seemingly godly society. As competing factions vied for control of the new religious establishment in England, they looked toward the lessons to be learned from the Massachusetts experiment. Those who favored structured church governance would use the Hutchinsonian crisis as an example of the catastrophe that loomed when a church society, organized congregationally, lacked proper hierarchical controls. Those favoring congregational autonomy would see the resolution of the crisis as proof that orthodoxy could triumph without a more structured establishment. In other words, at the very moment that Winthrop ought to have been fully victorious, he and his clergy found themselves engaged in defensive expositions and rationalizations over and over again.[41] Even in death, Anne Hutchinson was not silent.

2

The Puritan Experiment

Errors and Trials

For all his power and stature, Thomas Dudley, an authoritarian, irascible, righteous magistrate, was an essentially simple man. Gifted with neither the wisdom of the serpent nor the harmlessness of the dove, Dudley displayed the intuitive instinct that often accompanies an uncomplicated mind. When describing the rise of the Hutchinsonian conflict, he pointed straight to the eye of the swirling cyclone of political and theological disarray. The troubles, he said with remarkable hindsight, began in the autumn of 1634: "About three years ago we were all in peace. Mrs. Hutchinson from that time she came hath made a disturbance, and some that came over with her in the ship did inform me what she was as soon as she was landed." Had he been less simple or, perhaps, more honest with himself, he might have argued that the problems began with the arrival of John Cotton, since "Mr. Cotton and Mr. Vane were of her judgment." However, "Mr. Cotton hath cleared himself that he was not of that mind," and, to remove any reservations, Governor Winthrop had declared that Cotton was "not called to answer to any thing but we are to deal with the party [Hutchinson] standing before us."[1]

While Dudley could without prejudice begin his story with Hutchinson's arrival in 1634, more sophisticated participants and scholars could not and do not dismiss John Cotton so easily. Winthrop's very efforts to distance Cotton from Hutchinson indicate Winthrop's knowledge of the fundamental role that Cotton played in Boston's religious and political disputes. Cotton stood as a renowned cleric and theologian, a spiritual prize attracted to the colony, and he found much wanting in the preaching of his new colleagues. The extensive correspondence between Cotton and a number of New England ministers, especially Thomas Shepard and Peter Bulkeley, and the 1636 and 1637 conferences at which clerics questioned Cotton's theology as well as Hutchinson's preaching, argue that this crisis might have begun with Cotton's acceptance of the call as teacher at the Boston Church. Cotton clearly established his influence over Boston congregants almost a full year before Hutchinson's arrival, cementing their devotion and loyalty during the year of John Wilson's absence. In key ways, this crisis represented a political battle over clerical orthodoxy, and intellectual historians, from Perry Miller through Philip Gura to Michael Winship, have seen in the seductive theological wrangling the center of the controversy.[2]

Still, with all the challenges that colonization brought to its leaders— concrete problems of food and shelter, negotiations with the Indigenous residents, the establishment of local and colony governments—why should they have concerned themselves with theological orthodoxy at all? Certainly, there had been no religious consensus before the colonists embarked. They were dedicated, in principle, to the reform and purification of the corrupt Church of England, to the eradication of all vestiges of Roman Catholicism within it, but theological unity broke down as soon as the methods and goals of that reformation were debated. Dissenters disagreed upon such disparate issues as infant baptism, clerical qualifications, congregational membership, and church polity.[3] Some extremists believed unwaveringly in the complete corruption of the Church of England and separated themselves from it as irredeemably lost; most continued to consider themselves members, planning to reform the church from within. Yet even these non-separating dissenters disagreed as to the appropriate sacred authority. Some argued that the congregation ought to be the primary and only unit of organization and authority, ordaining its own ministers and judging doctrine for itself. Others looked toward a kind of ministerial association, a presbytery, where clergymen evaluated and ordained prospective ministers and advised congregations in matters of church doctrine and discipline. Although most New England colonials saw themselves as Church of England members, separatists did claim some adherents among the settlers, particularly in Salem. So, too, on a personal level, settlers demonstrated commitments to a range of reformist sentiments. When in 1635 John Endicott, a magistrate, tore the cross out of the English flag as a graven image, his zeal, applauded by some, appalled most of the residents as well as the other magistrates.[4]

For many Puritans, the knowledge that such differences flourished among sincere, God-fearing individuals inspired tolerance of honest dissent. Roger Williams, for example, established an all-inclusive policy of religious toleration in Rhode Island even as he vehemently attacked in his writings certain religious sects. (His writings on the sect called, disparagingly, Quakers, would be particularly dismissive.) Moreover, twenty years after the initial Massachusetts settlement, Oliver Cromwell and his Parliament tolerated all dissenting Protestants who supported the Commonwealth government. For the Massachusetts's leadership, however, the diverse opinions represented so many errors to be condemned and heretics to be silenced. This leadership believed spiritual health and orthodoxy to be the cornerstone of the colony's future success and happiness; political loyalty that did not embrace religious truth was no loyalty at all.

The significance of the challenges brought by Hutchinson and the Bostonians as well as the responses of political and clerical leaders should be approached through the realities of this peculiar colonial environment. Too often, religious disputes, whether judged as serious or trivial, have been seen as upheavals within an otherwise stable community. Scholars must recognize that cultural problems were not layered on top of physical insecurities, uneasy relations with the Indigenous residents, and disagreements about power and political process. Far from disrupting a smoothly developing society, religious problems were part of the disarray, another venue through which disorder appeared, dissatisfaction was expressed, and quarrels were resolved. Most of the English people who migrated to New England during these early decades were convinced religious believers. As Virginia DeJohn Anderson has persuasively argued, these migrants were driven not by economic despair, or even need, but by the desire to pursue their religious practices and craft an ideal spiritual community, a godly space. Every town founded in these early years distributed land and built the church congregation at the same time.[5] In fact, because of who these migrants were, religious belief and praxis sat at the center of their society and culture.

This inability of a colony of dissenters to tolerate dissent lay at the heart of Massachusetts's early political struggles. In order to untangle the Hutchinsonian controversy, this drive for religious homogeneity must be recognized in terms of the colonizers' own construction of their exile settlement. Before the first wave of settlers disembarked on the forbidding coast, John Winthrop had reminded them of their mission:

> wee are entered into Covenant with [God] for this worke. . . . Now if the Lord shall please to heare us, and bring us in peace to the place wee desire, then hath hee ratified this Covenant and sealed our Commission, [and] will expect a strickt performance of the Articles contained in it, but if wee shall neglect the observacion of these Articles . . . embrace this present world and prosecute our carnall intencions seekeing great things for our selves and our posterity, the Lord will surely breake out in wrathe against us be

revenged of such a perjured people and make us knowe the price of the breach of such a Covenant.[6]

God had made a special, federal covenant with these, his chosen people in exile. Like the Israelites of the Old Testament, the colonists believed that God had called them for a special purpose, placing them under special responsibilities. Within this unique relationship, God promised extraordinary prosperity if they followed divine law and total destruction if they fell short. Consequently, the magistrates grounded their community upon obedience to God's law, sometimes voluntary and sometimes forced. Fortunately, considering the evil nature of humanity, it did not matter if individuals obeyed unwillingly as long as they obeyed. Mere formal adherence to scriptural law, along with suitable controls and punishments designed for those who refused even this much, would satisfy God and guarantee the new colony success in this world.[7] This construction of the community's covenant with God precluded any simple bifurcation of civil and sacred, of law and theology, for God demanded obedience in both secular and spiritual matters. Therefore, in its responsibility to maintain stability and promote prosperity, the government had to oversee all facets of community behavior, including its spiritual affairs. The religious was political.

Any exploration of the Hutchinsonian controversy must begin with this drive for orthodoxy among people who differed on points of theology, piety, polity, and praxis. The problems were formidable. No formal creed or directory of church government existed to provide guidance, so that before religious conformity could be enforced, a standard had to be established. In working toward this goal, the government had to gain popular acceptance of its involvement in religious affairs among dissenters who had shunned government interference and despised their own state church. Further, ministers needed to win the trust of those who came to spiritual maturity within a public religious climate infected by bishops, rituals, and frippery. Civil and religious leaders had to promote a public religiosity among believers who were accustomed to, even privileged, private devotional meetings. In other words, the roots of this controversy lay in the nature of English reformed Christianity and the circumstances of its birth, the movement's growth from a diverse collection of dissenters to a united political society, and the process by which this extraordinarily pious community of reformers adjusted a private culture of dissent to meet the demands of establishing a structured church institution.

By the end of the sixteenth century, the social, political, and ideological forces that would unite English dissenters into a self-conscious religious and political coalition were in place.[8] During its first twenty-five years, the English Reformation had produced inconsistency, institutional insecurity, even chaos under the reigns of barely Protestant Henry VIII, committed reformer child-king Edward VI, and Roman Catholic Mary. However, following Mary's death in 1558, Elizabeth and her religious counselors firmly established the Church of England as the state church, a *via media* between closeted Roman Catholics and the less well-hidden Puritans who struggled to continue the work of reformation. Initially, Puritans were set apart by their opposition to the relics of Roman Catholicism that continued, in their minds, to corrupt the English church. Formal rituals, music, vestments, holy days, even church architecture and decor were denounced as superstitious, idolatrous, sometimes pagan. Puritans called for a return to the plain preaching and plain worship outlined in the Scriptures.

Like other reformers, Puritans rejoiced in the priesthood of all believers, rejecting the notion of special priestly powers of mediation. Ministers were called to provide intellectual and moral guidance, that is, to interpret the Scriptures and exhort their congregations, tasks that required extensive learning and moral piety. Thus, while Puritans denied that clerics were particularly holy or endowed with an elevated sacred status, they denounced the Church of England for failing to demand of its clergy a respectable standard of behavior and, especially, erudition. Many practitioners were also deeply spiritual, and, increasingly disgusted with the legalism and formal emptiness of Anglican services, they felt justified turning to private religious meetings to satisfy their spiritual cravings. Laypersons gathered weekly, and sometimes more frequently, to pray, to study, and to preach, finding among themselves the piety, inspiration, and even knowledge absent on Sundays. They also spread word of reliable, reformed ministers, graduates of Cambridge, known for their learning and piety as well as their criticism of the established church.[9]

The same decade that saw England's naval victory over the Spanish Armada also witnessed the births of those who would play the primary roles in the Hutchinsonian drama. John Cotton was born in 1585, Anne Marbury Hutchinson in 1591, while John Winthrop was born the year of the Armada, 1588. Together, these three represent the varied backgrounds and interests that would be found among the colonizers, along with the commonalities they shared. All three hailed from East Anglia, although before her marriage

Hutchinson had spent some years in London, a second base of colonizers. John Cotton seemed the quintessential Puritan divine, graduate of Trinity College and fellow of Emmanuel College, Cambridge. There his scholastic abilities were rewarded with expeditious promotions through academic ranks until his spiritual awakening led him to leave the university for the pastorate. He was ordained to serve at Boston's St. Botolph's in Lincolnshire, a benefice that he held without too much government interference for twenty years. John Winthrop's background reflected the Puritan presence among the new landed gentry, successful men like his grandfather Adam, a merchant who had acquired land by purchasing confiscated monastery property. Having spent a couple of years at Cambridge, John Winthrop returned to manage the Lincolnshire estate he inherited, rising to the rank of esquire and justice of the peace. Wealthy, but newly wealthy, his wealth founded in trade, he represented the highest rank or class that would be found in New England.[10] William, Anne Hutchinson's husband, represented the other primary possessors of wealth and status among the colonists. An Alford merchant of rising economic and social importance, he stood among those whose mercantile activities expanded their worldviews beyond the confines of village life and local government.[11] William's high rank and sterling reputation carried prestige that came with him to the new colony. Hutchinson herself stood as an excellent example of the well-informed layperson, one with a preference in ministers and services. Obviously, she had made efforts to attend a gifted preacher, John Cotton, although his church was some twenty miles away from her home in Alford; she even followed him to Massachusetts Bay.[12]

The daughter of a dissenting cleric, Anne Hutchinson boasted an incontestable Lincolnshire pedigree. Her father, Francis Marbury, was the son of William, a gentleman of Lincoln and a matriculant at Cambridge. As a younger son destined for the clergy, Marbury also matriculated at Cambridge in 1571, although he never received his degree. He moved to Northampton, was ordained deacon in 1578, and was almost immediately imprisoned for his preaching. Released soon afterward, he was forbidden to preach further in the shire, but he disobeyed the order. In November 1578, he was summoned before the London Consistory Court, where he defied the bishops, publicly accused them of ordaining unfit men, and was thence imprisoned at Marshalsea. Seven years later, Marbury was found as the curate and schoolmaster in Alford, and while he complained in 1590 that he had been silenced and deprived of his living and his license to preach, within four years he was preaching again. His primary crime appears to have been his criticism of Anglican priests and his call for an ably educated clergy. By the time James I had ascended the throne, the magisterium found this grievance a minor one. At a time when pastoral vacancies multiplied as more than three hundred ministers were silenced or defrocked in an effort to curtail rising Puritan strength, a man who simply wanted clerics to attain higher intellectual standards was a godsend. Still known to the city's bishops, Marbury held a series of London rectorships between 1605 and his death in 1611.[13]

That bishops found him a safe choice does not necessarily mean that Marbury lacked reforming zeal. Perhaps because he had been relatively silent for so many years, or perhaps because he had concentrated upon clerical competence as the one battle he would fight, Marbury was not perceived to be a threat.[14] To be sure, with his support of the state, both monarch and magistrates, and his adherence to the Church of England, he had distanced himself from the more radical sectarians. Still, Puritanism was less a clearly defined community than a broad ideological umbrella that covered a range of purifying reformers, and in his call for high standards in clerical education, his unyielding criticism of unfit ministers, and his outspoken defiance of the magisterium, unto imprisonment, Marbury revealed himself a reformed cleric of the Puritan persuasion.[15]

Marbury's writings reflected a Puritan bias both theologically and politically, and these texts include several themes and insights that streak through Puritans' writings and controversies. In his preface to a *Treatise of Gods Effectual Calling*, he complained that "the greater part of both authors and translators of bookes may be taxed of officiousnes." Such writers needed to remember that they were "but candlestickes, for the light is Gods."[16] Here Marbury echoed a common complaint among Puritans: writers' (and preachers') devotion to eloquence above substance. Such artificial eloquence confused rather than enlightened the reader and revealed the conceit of the writer, who acted as if he were the author of truth. In fact, "God is in the spirit of the Preacher to deliver the word. . . ."[17] Among the many sins against reason outlined in his discourse on repentance, Marbury noted the sins of curiosity, including "delight in shelves of learning, eloquence, pleasant phrases and wordes which have no substance in them: and herein doe offende both speakers and hearers." A plain style not only edified the listener, it protected the preacher from the sins of vanity, curiosity, and intellectual conceit.[18]

As a reformer, Marbury was a moderate. He lamented that the turn of the century was proving verie enticing to corruption in religion, as [times] were before the floud.... And if ever there were a time for those that ... have carried themselves loosely & doubtfully in the matter of religion to fasten upon a resolution, it is now. It concerneth our freehold to embrace the religion, which by the gracious benefit of her majesties lawes hath been now so many yeeres and is still (and that exclusively) afforded and authorized unto us.[19]

Marbury observed that the primary religious threat still came from the papists, and that the Church of England, under Elizabeth, was pursuing righteous reformation. He further warned his listeners that the growing dissension among Protestants simply enabled the Roman Catholics to grow stronger.[20] He dedicated an entire sermon to the common duty of loyalty to sovereign and magistrates: "Let us bethinke us conscionably how much we are bound to our gratious Queene, and not be unthankefull, but thankfull." He urged obedience to magistrates and, reflecting Puritan outrage against flagrant immorality, defended the harshness of their decisions. "When sin is growne to an head (as among us) it is time for the magistrate to make head against it. He must punish extraordinarie wickednesses with extraordinarie severitie."[21]

With such praise for Elizabeth, such support for the magistrate, such affirmation of rank and estate, and such a call to unity, it is no wonder that Marbury was able to win a few livings after fifteen years doing without.[22] His extravagant praise of Elizabeth foreshadowed the writings of a later generation who would long for a return to the halcyon days of the great queen. Marbury applauded Elizabeth for England's successful diplomacy, political stability, and religious reform, and he decried the warnings of his more extreme colleagues. His conviction that reform would continue reflected the fact that his words were written at the end of Elizabeth's reign. He might have changed his tune, as did many, had he lived many years under the rule of James, much less Charles, though this is speculation. Marbury foreshadowed Anne Bradstreet's celebration of womanhood in Elizabeth's power and wisdom when he expanded his praise to all women: "Her sex is ligitimated with this honour by the fift commandement...."[23] Some Puritans, including Anne Hutchinson's father, were willing (or perhaps forced) to grant the intellectual and spiritual powers of women by the example of their remarkable monarch.

Theologically, Marbury emphasized justification through faith, not works, and he granted all spiritual success to God's grace and nothing to man's efforts, including that act of faith itself. Marbury warned that worldly wisdom must be shunned, and believers should be ruled "wholly by the grace of the Spirit, which must mortifie . . . enlighten and quicken us." God might use the natural powers of humanity in the work of salvation, but "it is God which worketh both the will and the deed. . . . "[24] His writing carried the conviction that an individual's conversion, like that of Japheth, "is determined to be by the onely power of God, it is therefore required of necessitie that the Lord himselfe by his spirit performe it."[25]

In this brief corpus of three sermons Marbury displayed the tension between his conviction of humanity's utter dependence upon God and the preacher's need to urge his hearers toward salvation. In his *Doctrine of Repentance*, amid continuously flowing acclamations that true repentance comes through grace alone, Marbury asserted the need for all persons to educate themselves on the pathway of salvation and not shun labor and study. "But every Christian is to bee a student and he that can reade, must reade though it be painful."[26] Marbury warned his listeners that the Holy Spirit "worketh not effectually in us if our affection be cold in turning unto him."[27] If a man did not turn fully away from sin and embrace godliness, it could only be judged as that man's resistance to the grace of God. A person who has received God's grace, yet moves slowly and imperfectly toward sanctification, might well be urged to strive to follow the divine way. However, Marbury suggests that one who was "in the flesh" and had "no true grace . . . at all" should and could deliberately follow a course of action that would lead to God. This seems to contradict his conviction that humanity was utterly dependent upon God's grace. This contradiction was echoed in his diatribe against the London masses. "For these wildmen, these Faunes and Satyrs (as I may say) are a kind of demoniacks, and are not so much as capable of the Spirit of God, till they have submitted themselves to bee members of Gods Church." Odd that God's Spirit appears dependent upon church membership.[28]

What remained unclear was the point at which the spark of grace began its regenerative work. A first step toward humiliation could be understood as the first sign of God's grace, just as a person's "resistance" to grace could be read as an indication that the work of salvation was not complete. Puritan writers who emphasized such human efforts gave serious attention to the process of regeneration, and Marbury was no exception.[29] His *Doctrine of Repentance* engaged the nature of the spiritual change reflected in the true repentance of the saved sinner. As the grace of God came to the individual, godly sorrow and angry self-loathing would rise; one could not escape such deeply felt emotions once filled with the Spirit. Yet through the regenerative process, which began with true repentance, a person would be completely transformed. The heart and the mind—the affections, imagination and understanding—were reclaimed, and the image of God in the human creature was again clearly visible. Like other theologians of his generation, Marbury described this conversion as a process rather than an immediate moment, but the magnitude of the transformation appeared no less astounding for that.[30]

In a mere three sermons and a two-page preface to another's work, Marbury showed himself a theological antecedent of many New Englanders. He emphasized the need for learning as well as simplicity of style, and he recognized the usefulness of the church and encouraged church membership. He also insisted on humanity's utter dependence upon God even as he exhorted his listeners to godliness. He gloried in the expectation of spiritual transformation, when believers would "be changed into the image of God from glory to glory, as by the Spirit of the Lord."[31]

During the final decades of the sixteenth century, Marbury had obviously irritated the establishment with his ringing accusations of clerical incompetence (an interesting foreshadowing of his daughter's acts), yet he remained a moderate, apparently silent upon the issue of ceremonies, challenging neither the authority of bishops nor the rights of the Church of England in disciplinary matters. His criticism of the church placed him among Puritan sympathizers, while his theology of grace and personal regeneration, increasingly common among Puritan divines, would soon be out of fashion among Anglican prelates. Marbury died in 1611, scarcely eight years after the death of Elizabeth, too early to indicate where he would have stood when the next generation confronted the Anglican zeal of the Stuart kings James and Charles and their chaplain William Laud.

In the first wave of Anglican efforts to curtail the Puritan movement, following the accession of James I, the bishops removed hundreds of clerics from their livings for their refusal to follow the prescribed ceremonies of the Church of England. These years saw the Brownists, a radical, separatist community, flee to Leyden to escape persecution. As the Anglican Church, with the support of the monarch, tightened its restrictions upon clergy and congregational practices, Puritans, lay as well as clerical, grew increasingly hostile to bishops. Power battles in the religious realm soon overlapped battles in the civil arena, and many Puritans and their sympathizers found themselves bound by political interests. Generally members of the rising bourgeoisie, either merchants or lesser landed gentry, they opposed not only bishops but also aristocracy and king as they struggled to establish their own economic and political power base within Parliament, especially the House of Commons. As the seventeenth century progressed, the king, first James and then his son Charles, had greater difficulty maintaining authority as religious and political tensions continued to increase. The Puritan/parliamentary party grew so strong, and so angry, that within forty years of the death of Elizabeth, England plunged into civil war.

When James became King of England in 1603, he faced a heavy disadvantage in his predecessor: Elizabeth had been remarkably successful, extremely popular, and exceptionally long-lived. Only the most gifted of politicians could have comfortably followed a reign noted for domestic stability, economic prosperity, and, of course, the imperial victory over the Armada. Yet James proved able to maintain an uneasy truce with nation and Parliament, although he could not master the houses and slowly lost power to them. To a certain extent, he carried forward Elizabeth's religious policies. He was not well liked, and his demand that the Scottish church accept Anglican ceremonies and bishops seriously irritated the strictly reforming Scots, but he still managed to keep the domestic political peace.

Not so his son and heir. While James was, inevitably, an inadequate successor to Elizabeth, Charles proved a thoroughly inadequate successor to James. He assumed an extensive royal prerogative, justifiable by law but unwise in practice, dismissing Parliament when the assembly would not accede to his demands. Under the direction of his chaplain, William Laud, he worked to make the Anglican Church more ritualistic and less plain. It became more difficult for dissenters to remain silent on Anglican ceremonies that became more complex, formalized, and, to Puritans, artificial. They also grew leery of theological modifications that moved away from humanity's complete depravity and dependence upon God toward a posture that encouraged individuals to work toward their salvation. On the other side, Charles was increasingly less willing to tolerate Puritan-style clerics and congregants, and he began an initially haphazard but soon systematic effort to force conformity to the progressively "catholic" Church of England. Ministers lost their livings; some were defrocked; congregants were fined for not attending Anglican services; and many influential Puritans, especially clerics, were arrested and imprisoned.

When Charles appointed William Laud Archbishop of Canterbury in 1633, the persecution of dissenters increased in severity and frequency and further strengthened the battle lines between Puritan critics and Anglican supporters of the monarch. The Puritan community found itself able to gather adequate resources for a colonizing enterprise, and the great migration to New England that had begun in 1630 escalated rapidly as the decade progressed. Dissatisfied and troubled by the growing estrangement between Parliament and king as well as the rising power of Laud, many sought to escape the monarch's control and Laud's influence in an overseas colony. Others perceived increased decadence, corruption, and the "popishness" of Laud and read these signs as harbingers of the impending apocalypse foretold in Revelation. Envisioning themselves as the saved remnant, they followed a millennialist impulse to flee God's terrible vengeance upon England and build a godly commonwealth that would continue the necessary work of reformation. Still others who were focused upon secular affairs found that the seventeenth century had brought a decline in the quality of life, including decreased economic opportunity, increased criminality, taxation without parliamentary approval, and a surfeit of corrupt bureaucrats, court officers, and lawyers driving people into deeper want and poverty.[32] Yet whether fleeing persecution, escaping divine wrath, embracing the responsibility and rewards of the saved remnant, or seeking the mundane goal of economic opportunity, a significant number of Englishmen and women embarked upon a holy experiment to build a godly community in the wilderness, under royal sponsorship but beyond royal interference.

Thus in 1628 a small group of merchants organized the New England Company and received from the New England Council a grant of territory in North America just north of Plymouth Plantation (which had been established by Puritan separatists eight years before). This tract included a seaport village, Salem, that had been settled for several years, and the company sent scouts ahead to take charge of the town. By spring of 1629 the company had recruited a large number of colonizers and investors, including Winthrop, whom they elected governor. The investors received a reconfirmation of their colonial grant from Charles and changed their name to the Governor and Company of Massachusetts Bay in New England. The following year the first voyage was organized, and on April 7, 1630, the small fleet carrying the first wave of seven hundred company settlers embarked for the new colony.

During the next twelve years, New England annually absorbed hundreds, sometimes thousands of immigrants fleeing economic and political instability and seeking prosperity, peace, and piety. During this "great migration," between fifteen and twenty thousand men, women, and children risked the crossing, uprooting families and livelihoods. Most, about thirteen thousand, remained in Massachusetts Bay, but many others, finding opportunities limited or the government unsatisfactory, moved onward to other settlements, including Plymouth, founded in 1620, or Providence, Portsmouth and Newport Island, New Haven, Connecticut, and New Hampshire, all founded between 1634 and 1637 by dissatisfied Massachusetts residents.

Unlike the other British colonial enterprises of Virginia and Barbados, where most settlers were young unmarried men, New England immigrants arrived in families. In her study of the migrants, Virginia DeJohn Anderson found that although there were a few more men, close to half the immigrants were female, and almost a third of the passengers were under fifteen years. Although the majority of adult men were artisans, most men took advantage of land availability, settled in small towns, and became farmers and, more importantly, landholders. Many who continued to practice their craft happily augmented their income with agriculture, embracing the opportunity to become landed themselves. These were not, by and large, adventurers seeking great fortunes but husbands and fathers with their wives, children, and servants, planning to settle permanently and build godly, thriving communities.[33]

Winthrop's primary challenge was to organize the colonists and their settlements so that the somewhat unprepared pioneers could withstand the first year. While many expected that the previously settled Salem would serve as the center of the colony, this idea was rejected almost immediately, though it is unclear whether this decision was due to its geographic position, a dangerous and depressing openness to the sea, its smallness, or the fact that it was already inhabited. For whatever reason, Winthrop moved the primary settlement to the sheltered harbor of what is now Boston, divided up the inhabitants among seven towns, including the port city, and made preparations for the winter. While the arrivals proceeded to dig out shelters and gather seafood to withstand the winter, Winthrop conducted essential negotiations with the Indigenous communities for land and food. The first winter was harsh, residents grew discouraged, and supplies, purchased by Winthrop himself, came almost too late, yet within a year farms were planted, towns were organized, negotiations succeeded, and the colony was on its way toward self-sufficiency.

As the colony developed, so did the town of Boston. Initially one of seven, Boston soon outgrew the other towns as the primary population center in the new colony. Within ten years, almost two thousand settlers lived in Boston, representing close to 15 percent of the Bay Colony's population. During the great migration, Boston became the primary port of entry, absorbing a significant proportion of the new arrivals, to be sure, but also providing initial goods and services to prospective residents who arrived with cash in hand (and little else) to purchase necessary food, building supplies, seed, and cattle before they moved out to other towns. Boston headquartered the import of goods into Massachusetts and, naturally, became the centralized point of distribution of those imports and, by extension, domestic products to the rest of the colony. As early as 1634 Boston held a weekly market day that coincided with John Cotton's weekly lecture. And while early efforts to import and resell goods met with a range of problems resulting from regulations and efforts to avoid regulations, by 1637 a community of merchants had established itself in Boston, providing the organization, skills, and credit that the market exchange required.[34] The commercial business of Boston required a substantial support population, and within the first decade, the Boston population was dominated by artisans, laborers, and merchants, the workers of port cities, along with a few tavern keepers and clerics; many outlying inhabitants were attracted to Boston precisely because of the opportunities that a burgeoning city offered to craftsmen or shopkeepers. Certainly by 1637, the families of artisans and laborers associated with shipping were among the majority in Boston, and the early predominance of the landed gentry was quickly giving way to the superior numbers and economic power of a rising merchant community.[35]

In fewer than ten years, Massachusetts Bay had established a stable government within an economically self-sufficient, even prospering colony.[36] These years did not always progress smoothly, politically or religiously. The fact that stability was achieved so quickly should not be taken as evidence of a homogeneous vision against which occasional deviants struggled. Individual founders may have had clear plans for the colony, but even among themselves they did not share one political vision. During his first four years as governor, Winthrop's struggles with the views of the two top magistrates, Dudley and Endicott, left palpable traces in the company's records. The extreme reformed sentiments of Endicott and the critical legalism of Dudley, who apparently believed that laws were meant to be rigidly imposed, forced Winthrop to devote time and energy to defending his actions as governor. Dudley accused him of leniency, a word that raised frightful specters among a people fleeing the "leniency" of fashionable hedonism and corruption in

English society, while Winthrop claimed that he was accommodating the needs of individuals meeting the strains of colonization.[37] As early as 1636, the large community that had immigrated together with minister Thomas Hooker only two years before relocated beyond the boundaries of the Bay Colony, in part to acquire additional land, but also in order to move beyond Massachusetts's political and religious government.[38]

Not only did the General Court, initially comprising colony officers and magistrates, have difficulties achieving consensus among themselves, but they experienced problems governing the settlers and gaining their trust. It might be supposed that with a relatively small population schooled for generations in deference, people who had known each other in England and shared the rigors of transatlantic voyages and initial settlement would be moved toward obedience. Instead, it seemed as if the smallness of the group and their personal knowledge of each other and the magistrates empowered people to challenge the status quo. People criticized the arbitrary, "despotic" power of officials even as Winthrop and the magistrates worked to extend political power throughout the colony. After expanding the freemanship of the company beyond company shareholders to include all free men who were church members, Winthrop found the freemen demanding a legislative forum in which to exercise their charter rights to enact laws. When Winthrop opposed this program as unworkable, he was voted out of the governorship in favor of Dudley. Although he continued as a magistrate, Winthrop remained displaced as governor for three years. In 1637 he was again chosen governor, an election that reflected the experiential knowledge and finely honed political skills of one who had since learned to navigate the dangerous shoals of a politics characterized more by interpersonal disputes, prejudices, and loyalties than by general principles of good government. After all, this was an embryonic political system so enmeshed in personalities that a questionable lawsuit over a pig, and the resulting popular outrage against the magistrates' decision, could bring the General Court to separate into two houses so that the people's voice would not be silenced.[39]

Religiously, the same confusion reigned, with competing opinions on polity and salvation vying for dominance. New England Puritans have been known for restricting church membership to the elect and, therefore, requiring potential congregation members to demonstrate their visible sainthood. Since this practice can be traced back only to 1634, those first congregations must have experienced some early controversy.[40] In 1629, the initial colonists scouting New England were refused communion by the church established at Salem because they were not members of the congregation and they did not bring testimonials of membership from an acceptable congregation. This decision was condemned by John Cotton as narrow minded and unjust, yet five years later he supported a similar program of exclusive church membership as necessary to protect the purity of the congregation. As early as 1639, at least one settler would take the concept of visible sainthood to one logical conclusion and refuse to accept the baptism of infants. By the mid-1640s, several Anabaptists would appear in the colony, most in Salem and the neighboring Lynn.[41] Yet even before the rise of the Baptists, Salem's self-sufficient spirit and its status as first settlement and port in the colony combined with the separatist impulses of its residents to create the first major religious dispute.

The charming, ever-persuasive Roger Williams had arrived in Massachusetts in winter 1631, just in time to join John Wilson's ministry and pastor for him during his coming absence in England. However, when Williams learned that the Boston congregation refused to repent for "haveing Communion with the Churches of Englande, while they lived there," he refused the call to this "unseparated" people and moved to Salem.[42] The Salem congregation was, apparently, willing to so repent. Enamored of Williams's rhetoric and holiness, they had determined to call him as teacher until a timely letter from Winthrop warned Endicott of Williams's dangerous, separatist opinions. Williams turned, one might say naturally, to Plymouth, where he found the avowedly separatist congregations more to his liking. They too, however, displayed a fatal weakness when they welcomed back, without censure, church members who had visited England and participated in church services in the unregenerate congregations there.[43] And so, in 1633, Williams returned to Salem, where he served the people in an unofficial pastoral capacity.

Not content with attacking the purity of the congregations, Williams dangerously extended his separatism into politics, attacking the validity of New England's charter. He declared that it was blasphemy to refer to Europe as Christendom and that King James had told a lie in calling himself a Christian prince; he also applied three (unflattering) references from Revelation to King Charles. When questioned by the magistrates, Williams seemed to capitulate to corrective arguments, offering submission and apologies, but over the next two years, he was again called to account for preaching against regenerate magistrates "worshipping" with the unregenerate when they tendered oaths, using arguments that persuaded many residents, including the ever-impressionable Endicott. Williams was later brought to court for denying that the civil magistracy had authority to restrict religion, even to the extent of punishing Sabbath breaking. He had also extended his separatism to forbid regenerate individuals praying among the unregenerate, even if those unregenerate were husband, wife, or children. All his opinions were condemned, and Williams was instructed to give satisfaction or expect a sentence. The Salem church, having tendered an official call to Williams as teacher, was judged in contempt of civil authority.[44]

The conflict came to crisis when the Salem congregation refused to remove Williams and instead solicited the support of other Massachusetts congregations in upholding congregational authority in such matters as the selection of officers and church discipline. When the other churches failed to rally to Salem's cause, Williams called upon his own people to renounce all the churches of Massachusetts. This far Salem would not go. Even without the support of the congregation, Williams remained recalcitrant to the end and, in October 1635, was banished. Although the court offered him the option to remain in Salem, silenced, until the following spring, he continued actively to draw supporters. In response, the magistrates made arrangements to have Williams apprehended and shipped to England, only to discover that he had left the colony for Narragansett Bay.[45]

The resolution of the Williams controversy displayed with startling clarity the methods available to and processes utilized by the colony's leadership. That much was accomplished through informal channels could be seen as reflecting the inability of the government to resolve conflict, but it might as easily be interpreted as the sly machinations of rulers hoping to discredit separatism and suppress dissent while maintaining the support of the populace and protecting their reputations overseas. For example, the General Court refused to acknowledge Salem's claim to a specific tract of land until the congregation capitulated to the magistrate's decision and dismissed Williams. When the church, outraged by this interference with congregational authority, called upon other churches to rally behind its cause and censure the magistrates for their abuse of power, the pastors who received the letters simply refused to communicate the contents to their churches, thus ending any hope of church support for Salem's efforts.[46]

Beyond such blatant manipulation, consider the many informal channels that were used to keep the dispute quiet as long as possible, avoiding a power battle that magistrates could not be certain of winning. From his first interactions with the Boston congregation, Winthrop found that Williams held dangerous opinions, yet during the first year of settlement Winthrop could not risk such a public confrontation with anyone as well known and well liked as Williams. When Williams voluntarily refused to serve Boston as an unfit congregation, Winthrop used his private influence with Endicott to keep Salem from extending a call. After Williams returned to Salem, speaking out against the king, Winthrop continued to work, successfully, through private persuasion. As late as March 1635, with Winthrop out of power and Dudley crying for investigation, John Cotton persuaded the General Court to allow the ministers to intervene. Following upon this clerical conference, Williams left the charter question alone, although his remaining time in Massachusetts was so short he may simply have had no time to return to that question.

Even after formal action had been taken against him, with the civil and clerical leadership carefully fragmenting any popular support Salem might have gathered, a shrewd undercurrent of extralegal activity was at work. Learning that Williams continued to attract followers, and fearing that when banished he would move beyond the bounds of Massachusetts and lead a movement subverting their authority, the impulsive court ordered him arrested and shipped off to England. Yet when they arrived, the military escort discovered Williams had left for Narragansett Bay just three days before; many disciples did indeed follow him. Why Narragansett Bay? This location had been recommended to him by Winthrop as a possible settlement site outside the charter boundaries of Massachusetts. Why had he left so soon? He had received word from Winthrop that arrest was imminent. Perhaps Winthrop liked and respected Williams despite the trouble caused; he said he did. Nevertheless, Winthrop was also frightened at the thought of Williams in England, earning royal disfavor by publicly denouncing the king and destroying the colony's credibility by denouncing the colony government. Surely in his attack on the charter, his denial of civil authority over religion, and the discord sown between Salem and the rest of the colony, Williams represented a major political threat. Yet he was handled delicately, secretly, out of the public eye as much as possible.

Massachusetts could little afford a religious confrontation. In their efforts to stifle the separatist impulse within the colony, however, the leaders were faced not only with Williams's popularity and prominence, but also with the absence of religious consensus among themselves. Probably even before Williams began spreading his views, a significant number favored separatist practices. Certainly, Williams was able to convert many to his positions, to the extent, for example, that in response to popular protest, magistrates stopped tendering oaths. Moreover, in this colony where the new freemen became so quickly jealous of their charter rights, any governmental effort to challenge congregational autonomy was likely to rouse freemen to action. How was orthodoxy enforced within a culture of dissent? The leadership consulted with clergy, developed an orthodox position on the questions at hand, assumed consensus, mobilized clerical support, kept the debates within the private arena, and delayed any public confrontation until the government was strong enough, or at least respectable enough, to win. When a potentially disastrous spectacle, such as a government show of force, appeared inevitable, an official quietly warned Williams, who fled the colony. With Williams still in New England, Massachusetts's reputation was safe, but since he and his most obstreperous followers were gone, the battle ended without dividing the countryside, alienating the general populace, or testing the ability of the new government to maintain order.

It is within this cauldron of religious heterodoxy, social volatility, and political instability that the Hutchinsonian controversy must be understood. At one level, Hutchinson was one of several leaders who threatened the ability of the clergy to establish their own authority. However, the composition of the parties of her supporters and opponents revealed many layers of personal, social, theological, and political battles engaged for control of the colony. John Winthrop had been excluded from the governorship for three years. Chosen governor even before the colony was settled, he had invested not only his time and energy, but his estate and his future in the colony. In 1634 he found himself rejected by the freemen, first in favor of Thomas Dudley and then John Haynes, a man who would leave for Connecticut the following year. In 1636, Winthrop's return to power began with his election as deputy governor under Henry Vane, the highest-ranking gentleman in the colony, to be sure, but also a new arrival and extremely young.

The election of Henry Vane underlined the importance of Boston to colony politics. The General Court was headquartered in Boston, and while all freemen could vote, the annual meeting for elections was usually held in Boston, and Boston freemen would therefore dominate the elections. Winthrop may have been revered and respected by clerics, civil leaders, and citizens throughout the colony, but he exemplified the biblical byword of a prophet unappreciated in his own town. Remember that when Winthrop was again chosen governor in 1637, the election had been held in Newtown, not Boston, and when he returned to Boston, the city's honor guard refused to escort him. Vane represented a personal symbol of Boston's rejection of

Winthrop, and while his rank justified that election, his youth and inexperience played out the insult.

The political struggle between the Hutchinsonians and John Winthrop
also reflected a growing division in the colony between the Bostonians and
the hinterlands, between the merchants and the husbandmen/farmers. Of
the nearly two hundred men who supported Wheelwright and Hutchinson,
almost half lived in Boston itself.[47] The petition condemning the action taken
against Wheelwright, the unmet demand of the deputies to be included in
Wheelwright's examination, and the behavior of Bostonians during the 1637
elections all reflected popular anger directed at arbitrary magistracy. The
meeting and election at Newtown were the response against Boston.

A significant majority of Bostonians of wealth and status, almost 75 percent, were Hutchinsonians, while 81 percent of the richest merchants and
craftsmen identified with the movement.[48] Bailyn has noted that the
merchants, "with striking uniformity," backed the Hutchinsonian cause.[49]
The appeal of the Hutchinsonian movement to wealthy Bostonians, particularly merchants, underlined a nascent division in the society that would
afflict the colony for years to come. Certainly the Hutchinson family's position among the leading merchants was one factor attracting them to the
cause. In addition to the general grievances that the freemen had against
the government, the economic realities of colonization had endangered any
political consensus that the leadership itself might attempt. The majority of
Hutchinson supporters worked in trades that the government tried to control through wage and price regulation.[50] Foodstuffs were prevalent and
cheap, while imports and labor were scarce and dear. In this cash-poor society merchants used their credit lines to acquire imports, and they expected
to sell goods at market prices. The very few skilled craftsmen able to perform the extensive labor required by colonists expected to sell their labor
for a high return. Consumers became outraged at what they labeled exorbi-
tant profits and wages, and the General Court, with the support of the clergy,
passed a series of laws regulating wages, markets, trade, and profit margins.
Such debates would continue through the seventeenth century. In the end
the merchants and craftsmen, by virtue of the market and their economic
power, would win, but at this early stage conflict raged.

Louise Breen, in *Transgressing the Bounds*, has argued that as early as this
first decade of settlement, Massachusetts society was divided between those
colonists focused inwardly upon the development of a godly society and
those who, while committed to godly community, also looked outward. Those

"cosmopolitan" men whose mercantile investments and military callings placed them in active relationship with the world around frequently expressed impatience with the narrow, parochial vision of Winthrop and the majority of colonists. It was not only that the government tried to restrict wages and profits. Such men of the world could not understand the strident intolerance that characterized most colonists, nor did they sympathize with the drive to silence dissent. Israel Stoughton, for example, supported Hutchinson in her demand that clerical witnesses take oaths not because he accepted her theology, for he did not, but because he judged the General Court's summary efforts to condemn her unwarranted and offensive. Men who regularly dealt with people outside the small, tribal community, men whose experiences had produced a worldview far more sophisticated than the rest, had learned the need to accept difference with forbearance. Though quite young, the well-connected Henry Vane understood that individuality did not necessarily undermine community purity, and he dismissed the idea that dissent brought social fragmentation. The government's efforts at social and ideological control may well have been the final straw pushing the most successful resident merchants to Portsmouth and Newport.[51]

Nevertheless, economics and politics notwithstanding, this was, in the end, a religious crisis. The spiritual trajectories of several well-known supporters who would later join the Baptists, Fifth Monarchists, and Quakers argue for their sincere espousal of Hutchinson's radical spirituality.[52] Even if most Bostonians did not understand the theological issues at stake, the more mundane problems and religious disagreements were having an impact. Undoubtedly many of the Hutchinsonians were drawn by the preaching and charisma (and fame) of John Cotton and, by extension, his self-identified disciple. The government was not the only political arena; the institutional church, even less stable than the state, served as an extraordinarily volatile venue for personal power struggles.

By virtue of his early arrival, John Wilson, relatively unknown in Puritan circles, was called to pastor the premier Massachusetts congregation at Boston; three years later he found himself working alongside John Cotton, one of the most famous Puritan clerics to migrate during this first decade. As Wilson left Boston soon after Cotton's arrival in order to bring his wife to the colony, Cotton had ample opportunity to extend his influence over the established residents as well as the new arrivals. A gifted theologian, persuasive preacher, and mild, tactful person, Cotton quickly became a favorite, and his Thursday lectures attracted crowds from far beyond Boston. Upon his return, Wilson initially faded into the background despite resuming his pastorate. Since he was neither gifted, nor persuasive, nor mild, however, he soon moved off the sidelines, reeling from a new antagonism and acrimony manifested by his congregation, most pointedly the subversive effort to call John Wheelwright to serve the Boston congregation.

Although Wilson stands out as the minister who suffered the greatest disrespect from his congregants, Cotton clearly inspired envy and distrust among other New England clerics as well. Clerical discussions may have focused upon Cotton's emphasis upon free grace and his colleagues' commitment to preaching preparation and sanctification, but in conferences the angriest ministers spoke not about orthodoxy but in defense of their own status. These debates placed Cotton in an awkward position that demanded all the persuasive and placatory tact that he could muster. He distrusted his colleagues' position and, privately, was exceptionally critical of the opinions and preaching of many. Yet while he, not surprisingly, found his theology more strongly allied with the opinions of his own congregants, including Hutchinson herself, Cotton maintained that he was involved in no effort or popular movement to displace the New England clergy. Throughout these difficult months he insisted upon the ability of the clergy to resolve their differences among themselves, and he defended clerical authority against the attacks of laypersons who espoused his own views.[53]

Perhaps the primary political struggle was not among the individual ministers, or even parties of ministers, but between clergy and laity. The Hutchinsonians may have invoked Cotton's name and teachings, but even after Cotton publicly distanced himself from such attacks, the challenges continued. It was a lay majority, without the support of any cleric, that almost succeeded in calling John Wheelwright as a third pastor to the Boston congregation, a movement that was defeated by Winthrop and a tiny minority of laypersons who invoked a technicality that called for a unanimous vote before sanctioning a ministerial call. Laypersons traveling beyond the bounds of their own congregations, were, with their cross-questioning, creating problems for ministers outside of Boston. In fact, the laity made it almost impossible for the clergy to resolve their theological differences. No matter that peaceful resolutions had been achieved through clerical conference; no matter that some differences were erased and others accepted as tolerable; no matter that their clerical mentor, Cotton, sought peace. The laity kept pointing up disagreements and feeding the distress, "pinching & excepting ag[ains]t the Proceedings of the Synod...."[54]

The Hutchinsonian crisis represented a real threat to the colony's stability, not primarily as a powerful challenge to the status quo, but more as a reflection of the unsettled questions that still plagued the new colony. Although clerical personalities and jealousies were important, the key church political battles were fought by the clergy and laity struggling for congregational control. The reverence due the erudition of the minister had to be balanced against the authority lodged within the congregation to ordain that minister—an extremely difficult task for a society that had yet to solidify the power of the state over the church, or, for that matter, to provide any internal institutional controls to establish, much less maintain, orthodoxy. Secular politics had revealed the same instability. With the election of Vane, whose adherence to the Hutchinsonian party was well established, many colonists, including the out-of-power magistrates, perceived a serious threat from the cosmopolitan-merchant culture of Boston to force its vision on the rest of the colony. While personalities must have been important, it could easily be argued that the conflict between Winthrop and Vane symbolized two competing colonial political visions: the organic rule of a few elite over an acquiescent, consensual, homogeneous populace and a politics of conflict resolution growing out of the diversity and dissension of a people struggling for godliness in the world. Within Winthrop's world, it was absolutely essential that he curtail this uprising and re-establish his magistracy and orthodox vision. That his magistracy had yet to be established or that this vision was his own construction of the ideal Christian state was less important to Winthrop than his assumption of authority and his right to govern. And Winthrop did pursue his agenda: systematically, quickly, decisively, and effectively.

If Thomas Dudley was the uncomplicated leader of the country party, believing in the need to enforce rigorous conformity to an unspecified orthodoxy, ousting Winthrop as governor in 1634 because he was too lenient and identified, perhaps, too strongly with John Cotton, Dudley lacked the abilities to govern Massachusetts during the turmoil of 1635, 1636, and 1637. Following the arrival of Henry Vane and the rise of the Hutchinsonian party, Winthrop appeared as the one founder politician able to re-establish order. Dudley may have resented Winthrop's resumption of authority, people's deference to that authority, and his extraordinary skill in political manipulation, but those factors enabled Winthrop to return the colony's control to the founders. Undoubtedly earning initial favor by lenient enforcement of charter requirements, Winthrop was attacked for this leniency. He survived the initial challenge, but the label "lenient" returned to haunt him during his three years out of power. In January 1636, Winthrop explained the reasons for his laxity and then graciously acknowledged his faults and promised amendment, all in the name of magisterial harmony. The following spring, when that harmony was again disturbed by Vane's election, the electors signaled their acceptance of Winthrop's political repentance by voting him deputy governor. Additionally, the methods through which Winthrop managed his own return to the governorship and, in the process, silenced the dissenters were worthy of Machiavelli. Relinquishing all hope of convincing Boston, Winthrop moved the general election to Newtown, insisted upon an election before most Bostonians arrived, refused to read the petition of Bostonians who were present, took advantage of the Bostonians' refusal to participate under such circumstances by holding elections anyway, and then used his newly acquired office to close the meeting.

Winthrop's actions through the summer of 1637 continued to point up his acumen. The new law against receiving "aliens" without a magistrate's approval served to bar several newly arrived friends and relatives of the Hutchinsons from remaining in the colony. Vane, amazed at such a parochial law and outmaneuvered by the master politician, left the colony in disgust. The trials and penalties meted out to Hutchinson and her supporters were a central feature of Winthrop's final resolution of the crisis, and even here, the order and expedition of the examinations and trials demonstrated consummate skill. The wisdom of moving against Wheelwright, Coggeshall, and Aspinwall first was thoroughly justified by the results, for when Hutchinson came to trial, most of her supporters had been awed by the brutal efficiency of a General Court that could condemn a clergyman and two such substantial citizens. And while the trial of Hutchinson appeared several times on the point of exploding against him, Winthrop, as in the case of Wheelwright and the others, had in fact managed the process and outcome with considerable skill and expedition. For example, when he summarily dismissed her arguments with a general invocation of magisterial authority, he was merely applying a formula that had served so well in the cases of the men.

Following the triumphant conclusion of Hutchinson's trial, Winthrop moved with an impressive speed against the Hutchinsonians. Considering the rank, wealth, and sheer number of those supporters, it was important to disempower them before they could gather their forces in a major political challenge. One week after Hutchinson's trial, seven particularly troublesome supporters were disfranchised, and ten Hutchinsonians from Charlestown appeared before the General Court to beg (and receive) pardon. Then the decisive punitive step was taken: seventy-five men, including fifty-eight Bostonians, were cited by the court to be disarmed. There were no summonses to appear before the court, no trials, no due process. Unless they voluntarily appeared before the court and acknowledged their sin, they were required by court order to turn over all weapons and ammunition. Taken by surprise, many Hutchinsonians proved unable to withstand their threatened loss, and over the course of the next few days, some thirty men came to acknowledge (or in five cases deny) their guilt. The others refused to repent and made preparation to leave the colony, departures that were unlooked for and frequently unwanted. Winthrop had sought capitulation, not expatriation, and over the next ten years he attempted, with limited success, to persuade the most worthy to return. Still, although Boston had lost many of its most notable citizens, the political attack upon Winthrop's rule was ended.

In his efforts against the Hutchinsonian party, Winthrop successfully met and curtailed the strongest popular protest against the colonial government during its first decade. The strength of this movement lay not only in the numbers but in the high rank of many of the protesters. Yet he identified Hutchinson, the religious activist, as the source of the trouble, and he remained determined to rid the colony of her. His skilled maneuvering against her was awe-inspiring, his perceptive comprehension of the problem even more so. Winthrop realized that the religious was political, and he understood that attacks against ministers were attacks against the colonial leadership. In order to solidify his own power and the power of the magistracy, he needed to maintain an alliance with the clergy. By staunchly defending the ministers against the aspersions and humiliation inflicted by the laity, he earned clerical support for a political agenda that included state control over the church, for order and stability mandated not only social and political order but also religious order. The Hutchinsonian challenge had brought reluctant ministers, nurtured in a religious climate of dissent, to fully recognize the need for an established, enforceable religious orthodoxy.

Winthrop's difficulty was John Cotton. Winthrop could afford neither to alienate Cotton nor to have him identified as a dissenter and a source of disharmony, or even a disaffected clergyman. His support of the Massachusetts experiment was essential to its credibility at home, all the more since Thomas Hooker, another illustrious cleric, had already left the colony. Placating the generality of the clergy without forcing Cotton to compromise his positions was a particularly delicate task, especially when considering some of the less-gifted, defensively postured clergy who struggled for self-justification.

However, Winthrop, along with clerical allies Shepard and Hooker, was assisted by Cotton's amiability, his willingness to acknowledge the soundness of his colleagues despite their differences, and his frequently expressed regret that these differences had become a public cause for dispute.

Hutchinson's trial required all the skill and patience Winthrop could muster to maintain the momentum against her without indicting or even criticizing Cotton. Although Cotton had agreed during the conferences of 1637 that private meetings held among the laity were dangerous, he refused throughout the trial to condemn Hutchinson and, in fact, testified in her favor. Still, Winthrop seemed determined to overlook Cotton's position and, if necessary (and it was), proceed without his support. As mildly as possible Cotton corroborated Hutchinson's own memory of the 1636 conference rather than the versions his colleagues brought forth against her. When his testimony on the conference, despite helpful "reminders," continued to gently countermand that of others, Winthrop dismissed the entire discussion: "I do not see that we need their testimony any further. Mr. Cotton hath expressed what he remembered, and what took impression upon him, and so I think the other elders also did remember that which took impression on them." Even after Hutchinson had asserted her claim to revelation, Cotton refused to judge her without further inquiry. In his abstract discourse on the nature of divine revelation, he drove Dudley to exasperation: "Sir, you weary me and do not satisfy me." Winthrop could not have been far behind. Yet Winthrop did not make the mistake of fellow magistrates in demanding that Cotton declare her revelations satanic or delusional. When it became clear that Cotton would not speak out against them, and a hitherto silent representative from Dorchester anxiously demanded that Cotton justify his position, Winthrop blocked that dangerous pathway with a single sentence: "Mr. Cotton is not called to answer to any thing but we are to deal with the party here standing before us."[55] The hint was well taken, and Hutchinson was witnessed against and sentenced to banishment without any further interruption.

Nonetheless, the problem of Cotton continued. During the subsequent winter, he learned that under the alien act several immigrants had been turned away from Massachusetts because of views that resembled his own, and, as he later explained, he feared "wee should receive no more Members into our Church, but such as must professe themselves of a contrary judgment to what I beleeved to bee a Truth." He had also heard that many people had concluded that doctrines put forth by him were the cause of all the disturbances in the colony. Determined not to bring further disruption to the

churches, Cotton decided to remove to Connecticut. He was further encouraged by the receipt of a lengthy subscription of persons ready to accompany
him. This potentially disastrous loss was averted by Winthrop, who assured
Cotton that the new arrivals has been rejected on other grounds, and that
while the magistrates did not agree with Cotton's positions, they did not find
them "of such Fundamentall concernment either to civill or Church-Peace,
as needed to occasion any distance in heart, (much lesse in place) amongst
godly brethren."[56]

Although, in hindsight, both Winthrop and Cotton claimed otherwise,
the contemporary records reveal that it was not until Hutchinson's church
trial the following March that Cotton completely withdrew his protection over her.[57] Having been kept under house arrest in the home of an
unsympathetic minister, Hutchinson was subjected to almost constant
interrogations, conferences, and counsels from a variety of clerics, all supposedly concerned with her salvation. As they probed her theology, they
developed a list of sixteen errors that they later read against her at her initial
trial before the church, and Hutchinson was again to be held publicly accountable for private conversation. What was most intriguing was that with
perhaps three exceptions, the list had moved away from the points debated
at the conferences and the accusations of November and onto a host of other
esoteric questions hitherto undiscussed, such as the immortality of the
soul and the resurrection of the body.[58] Her opinions as expressed on those
points were so far outside anyone's theological orthodoxy that Winthrop
and the clergy now had no problem gaining Cotton's support. As he delivered the admonition at the end of that first examination, he could assuredly
condemn Hutchinson without compromising his adherence to free grace
over preparationism.

Perhaps taken by surprise at the direction her church trial took,
Hutchinson protested that she had not held "any of thease Thinges before
my Imprisonment."[59] To be banished for one set of beliefs but tried in church
for another must have been exceptionally frustrating, but this complaint
against the clergy set the stage for the following week's trial and final excommunication. It was no longer necessary for the clerics to demonstrate
her heretical beliefs. After she had repented and recanted many of the errors
laid to her charge, John Wilson turned the church's attention to that proud
speech of protest. Thomas Shepard was joined by several others in doubting
the sincerity of her repentance; the more she tried to explain herself and her
positions, the stronger the advantage of her opponents. In the end, she was

excommunicated not merely for her heresies, but for her pride and her lies in her attempts to distance herself from those errors.

Thomas Dudley, apparently missing the entire thrust of this examination, unerringly pointed to the simple dynamic at work here.

> Mrs. Hutchisons Repentance is only for Opinions held since her Imprisonment, but befor her Imprisonment she was in a good Condition, and held no Error, but did a great deale of Good to many. Now I know no Harme that Mrs. Hutchison hath done since her Confinement, therfor I think her Repentance will be worse than her Errors . . . suer *her Repentance is not in her Countenance*, none cane see it thear I thinke. Therfor I speak this only to put the Elders in minde to speake to this whether she did not hould errors before her Imprissonment.

Like Hutchinson, Dudley was exasperated with the failure to engage the original errors that led to her examination and banishment. Consequent efforts to respond to Dudley's question led, inevitably, to his further remembrance that "whan she was examined, about the six Questions or Articles, about Revelations etc., that she held nothinge but what Mr. Cotten held."[60] In a final swirl of activity aimed at protectively distancing Cotton from Hutchinson, attending clerics returned forcefully to her attitude, which, Dudley agreed, seemed proud and unrepentant.

Despite this final impulse to derail the direction of the trial, I believe that with Hutchinson's excommunication, the primary purposes for "allowing" her to winter in the colony were achieved. First, in exhibiting to the Boston congregation the scandalous direction her heresies had taken along with her pride and arrogance, and in publicly denouncing and excommunicating her, the clergy and magistrates put a final, absolute period to her influence among the many church members who had admired and supported her. Second, the trial served to distance Cotton from Hutchinson and thus alleviate the misgivings of laypersons who had recently learned to distrust the great theologian. Finally, the examinations demonstrated to Cotton, if he needed proof, the dangerous nature of Hutchinson's opinions and the perils inherent in allowing the laity to hold and lead private religious meetings. In his condemnation of Hutchinson, Cotton cemented his alliance with the colony's leadership.

Historians have long been fascinated by what appeared to be Cotton's change of heart. He might have served as her advocate because he didn't thoroughly know her views, or Hutchinson's theology may have taken this astonishing direction, or Cotton might have submitted to his fellow clerics and betrayed his follower. Yet whether for this or some other combination of reasons, I think that, truly, Cotton was an easy mark. As a learned theologian and pious pastor, he identified with and had a founding interest in the New England experiment. Hutchinson had no such compelling commitment. Like many other lay immigrants, she had followed a noted divine and the religious community in search of religious purity, piety, and truth. When she didn't find it, she had no problems denouncing what she did find. This may have been less a question of personality than of the limitations of her experience as a layperson. Clergy were probably more willing to tolerate differences in religious style and theological emphases.[61] A shared culture of scriptural erudition and theological lore had made ministers aware of the difficulties inherent in constructing an absolute, unambiguous, inerrant interpretation or credo, with the best and the brightest often the most open-minded. Moreover, they shared a political interest in espousing the cause of religious reform for the greater glory of God, and they knew that they risked credibility in pursuing esoteric theological battles. Consider, again, the determination of the clerics to deal privately with Roger Williams about so weighty a subject as the legality of the charter and their ability to silence him on this issue. Lay magistrates, not clerics, had forced Williams's dissent into a crisis.

So, too, it was the Hutchinsonian laity on the one side, with their heckling, their complaints against Wilson and demands for Wheelwright, and the opposing laity on the other who brought the crisis to a head. The clergy attempted several times, with varying degrees of success, to put the disputes behind them, but the Hutchinsonians, granted with an assist from John Wheelwright, would not let the ministers work out those differences. Whether Winthrop might have persuaded Hutchinson to accommodate magistrates and ministers and step back from her unwavering criticism is an unanswerable question. For unlike his dealings with Cotton or Hooker or even Wheelwright, Winthrop never tried with Hutchinson. A close reading of both state and church trials reveals that even as Hutchinson capitulated on points one by one, her capitulation was not sufficient. Winthrop wanted her banished and excommunicated unrepentant rather than repentant and chidden and still in Boston.[62]

Why? The question of Winthrop's personality comes forward again. He may have resented her influence so much, particularly in terms of its disruptive impact upon his career, that he sought revenge. Yet Winthrop was not out of power at the moment of Hutchinson's defeat, and he had demonstrated that at the height of the organized uprising, with the weight of a Henry Vane and much of the Boston elite against him, he could still recapture control of the colony. Or perhaps he knew the Hutchinsons well, having lived across the street from them for three years, and he knew that she would never capitulate. Even if she pretended to agree with the clergy, problems would continue. Perhaps there is some justice here, considering that the conferences of 1636 ended more or less amicably but still were unable to resolve the problems within the colony. Yet this could have been due as much to the political motives of her followers as any assertive leadership on her part.

Something more was happening in Boston. Simple, single-minded Thomas Dudley saw this from the outset, though it is doubtful that he understood what he saw. The colony had not been problem-free before the Hutchinsons landed, and all of the disagreements inherent in the nature of reformed theology as well as the problems that rose with colonization provided obstacles to be overcome. There is no question but that the first decade of settlement was dedicated to surmounting problems in order to construct economic viability, political stability, and religious orthodoxy. Nevertheless, Hutchinson's arrival and religious activism seemed to escalate the crisis to a new intensity. She and her followers appeared to have destroyed not the peace of the developing society so much as the ability of the colony to resolve its conflicts peacefully.

True, her challenge was religious rather than simply political, and thus more complex than the noisy but successful demands of the expanding freemanship. Even so, her charisma appeared to inspire a crisis and response qualitatively different from that brought by the theological disputes of Hooker, Cotton, or even Williams. Winthrop continued to correspond with Hooker, seeking his advice and involvement in church affairs when problems arose, and he actively sought to appease Cotton and retain his presence in Boston. Moreover, Winthrop had dealt gently, if surreptitiously, with Williams and continued a correspondence that resulted in Williams's assistance to the New England colonies in future negotiations with Indigenous communities. He would even allow John Wheelwright to acknowledge his error and return to the colony.[63]

Winthrop may have been outraged at Hutchinson's presumptuousness as a layperson in claiming spiritual independence and scriptural knowledge, but his treatment of other lay dissenters was gentler. John Endicott, for example, destroyer of the king's flag and ardent follower of Williams, was handled privately over and over again. Even the many laymen who followed Hutchinson to Portsmouth and, later, Newport, were treated with care. Having failed to bluff many of the leading Hutchinsonians to bow to the magistrates' authority, in fact, having banished several, Winthrop expressed manifest regret as he made occasional sorties to attract some of the highly ranked laymen back into the Massachusetts fold. In 1639, the Boston congregation sent commissioners to check on the spiritual state of the exiles, hopefully opening the way for their return. They even made it clear to William Hutchinson that no one had any complaint against him, and he was welcome to come back to Boston and rejoin the church, though William had said that "he was more nearly tied to his wife than to the church, he thought her to be a dear saint and servant of god."[64]

Winthrop's hostility cannot be fully explained by Hutchinson's lay status; the very language of his condemnation pointed to the root of his scorn, anger, and real dismay. She was "a woman of A haughty and fierce carriage," "a very voluble tongue, more bold then a man, though in understanding and judgement, inferiour to many women." She had "cunningly dissembled and coloured her opinions" to gain admission to the church. As a skilled healer and birthing assistant, she "easily insinuated her selfe into the affections of many." At the moment of her trial, she sported "the impudent boldnesse of a proud dame, that *Athaliah*-like makes havocke of all that stand in the way of her ambitious spirit."[65] She had presumed not merely above her subordinate status as congregant, subject, and layperson, but above her subordinate status as female.

That femaleness certainly helped Winthrop in his efforts to win her condemnation, for her arrogance and subversive pride threatened the basic order of the society. Several charges brought against her directly focused upon her leadership and activities as inappropriate for a woman. Her house meetings were disruptive not in and of themselves, but because a woman led them. She had broken the fifth commandment in refusing obedience to her superiors: ministers, magistrates, husband. As Hugh Peter summarized, she had "rather bine a Husband than a Wife and a preacher than a Hearer; and a Magistrate than a Subject."[66] After her resettlement in Portsmouth, word came to Massachusetts that she had given birth to some thirty monsters. The actual nature and cause of these "births" has been avidly discussed by historians, but for the Puritan leadership there was no doubt. The monsters represented the monstrous opinions that Hutchinson had founded upon the colony, evidence that nature itself had rebelled against her sin. Not only was Hutchinson a woman, but in her unwomanly sins she had become a repugnant, unnatural woman. Her biology had turned on her; she could not even give birth to a natural child.[67]

Anne Hutchinson had not only fomented class conflict, intracolony conflict, and political conflict: she was also at the base of gender conflict. She threatened the social order by having male followers: Dudley seemed especially troubled by the possibility of a woman leading men in preaching and prayer. Even more disturbing, however, was the number of women who might (and did) follow her example. Winthrop had complained that she insinuated herself in the birthing chamber and had drawn many women after her. Thomas Shepard called her "a most dayngerous Spirit and likely with her fluent Tounge and forwardnes in Expressions to seduce and draw away many, Espetially simple Weomen of her owne sex." He remained particularly concerned for "all those Weomen and others that have bine led by her and doted soe much upon her and her Opinions."[68] Both magistrates and ministers saw before them a woman who refused to accept passively the restrictions that the society placed upon her, one leading other women to move beyond their roles of wife, housekeeper, and mother. Hutchinson offered women an alternative vision of independent, self-sufficient womanhood, threatening the very base of New England's social hierarchy.

3

Helpmeets, Mothers, and Midwives
among the Patriarchs

Puritan leaders longed to be patriarchs—rulers of an ordered society, their own society established according to their own vision of the commandments and the expectations of God. For decades, they had suffered the scorn and, at times, brutal persecutions of the English religious and political establishments as they struggled against a class structure that, in their view, valued unctuous bishops and noble birth above learned ministers and intrinsic worth. All through Elizabeth's prosperous reign, Puritans had hoped not only to purify the Church of England but also to establish themselves as a powerful force for good in the country. The uncertain years of James's kingship had brought even higher expectations along with increased anxiety, for in the face of James's hostility toward further religious reform, Parliament, the center of Puritans' political ambitions, was gaining power. His son Charles, with religious adviser William Laud, escalated the battle. The new government actively silenced dissenting ministers and enforced conformity, and the king met the rising intransigence of Parliament by dismissing its houses. Frustrated and embittered, Puritans feared for their families, their nation, and their lives. Yet in their distress Puritans found opportunities; the colonization of Massachusetts Bay enabled Puritan leaders to realize their vision of a Bible commonwealth.

When they landed in New England in 1630, these English Christians saw themselves as the New Israel, the chosen people, the antitype of the ancient Hebrews. They looked to the Scriptures for guidance and found rules for church organization, principles of civil government, even a criminal code. The Gospels, Revelation, and especially Paul's epistles grounded theological beliefs concerning God, humanity, salvation, and cosmology. But with respect to their day-to-day lives, New Englanders found much more assistance in the Old Testament. Leviticus provided lists of crimes along with suitable punishments, the prophets demanded holiness with an appealing urgency, while the history of the Hebrew people was pointed by important lessons on divine reward and punishment. The great patriarchs and kings became role models for leaders, and their recorded wisdom, reinforced by Pauline pronouncements, guided the pious toward an ordered, godly society. Puritan leaders recognized and embraced this patriarchy with pleasure, envisioning themselves as the new Abrahams and Isaacs, Samuels and Davids.

While some few persons were called to exercise power as magistrates and ministers, and many more as husbands and fathers, most, and certainly all women, were called to subject themselves to the authority of others. The Holy Scriptures had ordained a clear, ordered family system that arranged all members of society into dichotomous power relationships: master-servant, parent-child, husband-wife.[1] Within this domestic system the father assumed the central role as head of household. Their God was a God of order, and out of their religious convictions and experiences ministers and magistrates found divine sanction for a firm, clear hierarchy. Of course, it would be wrong to credit religion alone, for this ordered, biblical worldview was reinforced by other authorities, including social tradition and the English common law. Together, religion, law, and custom constructed and upheld an ostensibly scriptural, but certainly English, patriarchy.

In key respects, Anne Hutchinson's career can be understood only through the lens of the patriarchal ideology and social realities of the society that produced and nurtured her. Her life in England had been divided between London and Lincolnshire as the daughter of a clergyman, the wife of a successful market town merchant, and the mother of fourteen children. These forty-four years mirrored the lives of many Englishwomen who, whether married to ministers, merchants, or, as most found themselves, farmers, filled pivotal roles in their households. From earliest girlhood women had expected and were prepared to assume the social subservience and economic responsibilities of the housewife. Custom and practice, reinforced by erudite sermons and protracted domestic manuals, provided a concrete agenda of labors and attitudes necessary to the economic viability and emotional comfort and stability of every family. Moreover, the common law and chancery courts carefully constructed a complex of institutions and processes that defined a woman's status with each change of domestic situation. The English common law, augmented in Massachusetts by statutory clarifications and revisions, set restrictions, established protections, and guaranteed rights. The social circumstances and legal boundaries were further buttressed by an ideological construction of woman, gender, and humanity that combined scientific perceptions of female anatomy and sexuality with more general psychological and moral understandings of the female character.

Still, while women could not render legal decisions or enact laws, their responses to their situation did, at times, qualify the meaning, reconstruct the application, or undermine the effects of those legal rules. In addition, women were as active as their male relatives in defining the traditions that provided the primary boundaries surrounding their lives, sometimes accepting custom and at others transforming practices within their own sector of efficacy and control. Among the most prized and lauded achievements of a woman was motherhood, not the raising but the bearing of children. More than any other sphere, reproduction signified women's autonomy, and the politics of reproduction and midwifery provided ample evidence throughout the seventeenth century of the covert, although sometimes explicit, power located and contested within the home.[2] Women did not always envision themselves as men saw them; within the house, garden, and birthing chamber, women functioned within a separate female community that excluded women from spheres of public power but reinforced their control over their own domestic world and provided space in which women's voices could be heard. Throughout the late sixteenth and seventeenth centuries, men were generally content to allow women such domestic authority. However, when a woman like Anne Hutchinson grew too strong or undermined the leadership too directly, men could invoke the prescriptions that mandated complete, absolute male control and female subservience. Haphazard logic but consistent politics provided ministers and magistrates alike with extensive justifications for the complex hierarchical system that served their own interests and silenced women. At the same time, in its explicit identification of the domestic arena as a closed feminine space, this systemic hierarchical structure included places in which women, whether passive and weak or aggressive and authoritative, could speak and be heard.

When historians first explored the experiences of women in old and New England during the early seventeenth century, some argued that, in this precapitalist age, the economic and social primacy of the family and the mother's role as primary producer of food served to place a significant value on women despite legal and social disabilities. Their labor was necessary and valued.[3] But care must be taken not to confuse the value ascribed to the work with the value placed upon the worker. For it can be argued that in an effort to assure themselves the benefits of housewifery, men supported a system that not only legally bound women to this role, but also rendered them ec-onomically and psychologically dependent even as they were honored for their material contributions.

Scholars have recently focused attention upon these more patriarchal, re-strictive aspects of seventeenth-century society, finding that in wills, church records, and court proceedings the prescriptions were frequently imposed upon women. In Massachusetts Bay, a woman was less an individual than an element in a functioning system, and the civil law protected the system more than the individual. For example, although the law granted some agency to unmarried or widowed women, the purpose of such laws seems to have been the protection of property for male descendants of the original male pro-perty owner. Society, and the widows themselves, looked toward adult chil-dren, sons and sons-in-law, to provide for their widowed mothers, and, as Carol Karlsen has so persuasively demonstrated, Puritan women who did assume agency on their own behalf found themselves alienated from their community and, sometimes, facing criminal proceedings.[4] Only against the nature and structure of this legal, social, and ideological patriarchy can the full strength of Hutchinson's challenge be measured. Matriarch and mid-wife, Anne Hutchinson's power was, to some extent, a natural outgrowth of her status as an experienced, skillful, gentry-class matron. However, as she extended her charismatic authority over the residents of Boston, she chal-lenged the authority of her natural rulers and earned the condemnation she ultimately received.

Hutchinson threatened a powerful system grounded in the religious reforms of Calvin and his English followers. True, the turbulent years of the sixteenth century had brought very little perceptible change to the lives of Englishmen and women. In 1600 as in 1500, most adults in all classes married, bore children, and supported their families as best they could with their own labor and the luck of their circumstances. Nevertheless, the Reformation did mark a primary change in domestic relations, not so much in the social reality as in the ideology grounding that reality. Protestant reformers attacked the Roman Catholic Church for the premium that it placed upon celibacy. Reformers did not merely reject the superior spiritual status that had been attributed to the celibate; they contended that voluntary celibacy was hardly acceptable in any believer. "*Marriage*, saith the Apostle, *is honourable among all men*: and no disgrace then to any man. So are we to esteeme of it, and not to contemne what God hath graced, or to dishonour what he hath honoured. We shall but wrong the giver in debasing his gift."

William Gouge was even more outspoken: "it is accounted *a Doctrine of devils to forbid to marie.*"[5]

Reformed clerics agreed that it was the duty of man to marry, following the example of the patriarchs (though stopping short of multiple wives). Even the New Testament caveats invoked by Catholics were explained away. For example, following a discourse on the illegality of divorce except in cases of adultery, and his disciples' conclusion that "if the matter be so betwene man and wife, it is not good to marie," Jesus elaborated upon the difficult teaching of chastity. "All men cannot receive this thing, save they to whome it is given. For there are some chaste, which were so borne of *their* mothers bellie; and there be some chaste, which be made chaste by men: & there be some chaste, which have made them selves chaste for the kingdome of heaven. He that is able to receive *thus*, let him receive it." From this exhortation, the Calvinist commentator concluded that marriage was commanded. "This gift [chastity] is not commune for all men, but is verie rare, and given to fewe: Therefore men may not rashly absteine from mariage."[6] So, too, Paul's assertive preference for celibacy, "It were good for a man not to touche a woman," was clarified with equal vigor: "Or, expedient because mariage, through mans corruption, and not by Gods institution, bringeth cares and troubles." Later in the same chapter, Paul, though permitting marriage, argued with vehemence for the spiritual superiority of virginity, leading the commentator to explain that "he doeth not preferre singleness as a thing more holie than mariage, but by reason of incommodities, which the one hathe more than the other."[7]

English reformers went far beyond acknowledging the necessity of marriage; they encouraged it, praised it, wallowed in the bliss that was to reward family life. The turn of the century saw the publication of extensively detailed domestic manuals that filled hundreds of pages with descriptions of the utopian household along with instructions to householder, housewife, and, by extension, children and servants in the ways that such utopia could be achieved.[8] Miles Coverdale had already translated Henry Bullinger's *Christian State of Matrimonye* in 1541, but it was not until the third or even fourth generation of English reformers that the publications began in earnest.[9] *A Godly Forme of Household Government* was among the first, published in 1598, reinforced in later decades by such treatises as *Bathshebaes Instructions to Her Sonne Lemuel*.[10] As late as the 1640s, Daniel Rogers produced the weighty *Matrimonial Honour*, but the weightiest prize, quite literally, must be awarded to Gouge's eight-part, seven-hundred-page

Of Domesticall Duties.[11] Of course, those clerics who had no time to compose major treatises still delivered sermons, and weddings and espousals served as excellent opportunities for discourses on domestic life. In fact, the climate of the times so greedily absorbed such publications that clerics like Thomas Gataker could initiate prosperous writing careers publishing such occasional sermons.[12]

This literature went beyond permitting all to marry, even beyond celebrating the blessings of raising a family. A new spiritual elevation was attached to the calling of spouse and parent. The family became the most sacred of human institutions, a metaphor for all blessed associations within society. Gouge declared that "the familie is a little Church, and a little commonwealth," Thomas Taylor urged every householder to "maketh his house a little Church," while Francis Cheynell turned the analogy about and urged Parliament to remember that the commonwealth was its household.[13] The new vision not only allowed or encouraged each man to marry; it required him to do so. Rogers ranted against the superstitious notion that marriage was wrong and celibacy correct, while Alexander Niccholes found such chastity an entirely inadequate spiritual substitute for marriage. "But to go further, to equall [marriage] with the best commended Virginity, where is the man this day living whose virginity may be compared with Abrahams mariage, in whom all the nations of the earth were blessed."[14] Undoubtedly many aspiring young clerics were pleased that the unhappy demands of the chaste life would no longer be required. In place of the special spiritual status granted to a few by virtue of their celibacy and consecration, the mandate for wiving gratified all men. Each became a patriarch, to follow in Abraham's footprints, he who "was a King, a priest, a Prophet in his owne Family."[15]

But what of women? The reconfiguration of the Roman Catholic Church to a Protestant Church of England was followed by the destruction of those few institutions that provided some opportunities, however limited, for female independence. The anchoress, bricked into her hermitage, nevertheless lived autonomously, sharing her space with only one servant. If she was not free to move about the countryside, she was also not required to attend to the demands of male protectors. As Julian of Norwich had demonstrated, such a holy woman might exercise extraordinary influence over her patrons and social superiors. Also gone were the convents, sneered at by men of distinction, but nonetheless a haven from male restriction and interference. Medieval convents did require male priests to perform sacramental rituals, but these were female communities, governed by women for the comfort and encouragement of women.[16] Protestant women were destined to be married, to labor in the household, and to subject themselves to the rule of their husbands.

Still, as in the case of men, most women, before as well as after the Reformation, had married, so the new emphasis upon the domestic establishment must have changed very little in the lives of most women. Women continued to provide the central domestic labor for the household, exercising authority and influence within the home. Literally responsible for feeding and clothing her family, the seventeenth-century housewife was, like her spouse, tied to a seasonal work schedule mandated by climate, crops, and family needs. Such cyclical tasks as the production of cloth and clothing, gardening, and the preservation of food were inserted within daily and weekly routines that fed the family, cared for young children, and nursed the sick. Moreover, the excellent housewife might find herself trusted with complete control over the household stores and expenditures, and such trust would reward the householder with comfort and freedom from anxiety. Puritan authors greatly admired housewifery skills: they lamented a general decline in women's expertise and encouraged parents to educate daughters (and suitors to select wives) with these abilities in mind. Far from taking such labors for granted, these writers agreed that the price of a virtuous woman was "farre above the pearles. The heart of her husband trusteth in her. . . . She wil do him good, and not evil all the daies of her life."[17]

All writers emphasized the importance of a wife's piety, but, even among the most religious of preachers, industry was not far behind. "She is a *Wife* then indeed, and none but shee, in whom these two concurre, that shee is both *a good Hous-wife*, and *a good Wife* too *to him that hath her*." Parents were often remiss in preparing their daughters for courtship, emphasizing ephemeral accomplishments that might attract the desirable suitor rather than the significant virtues that would bring happiness in marriage. "Whereof also it is, that the chiefe care of parents is, to make [daughters] most beautiful, & most rich; altogether neglecting pietie and good huswiferie." The spiritual Elizabeth Jocelin, providing instructions for the rearing of her yet unborn child, recognized the need for a daughter's practical training. "I desire her bringing up may bee learning the Bible, as my sisters doe, good houswifery, writing, and good workes."[18] Even the beauteous, biblical Susanna, honored for becoming modesty and stalwart chastity under extreme provocation, could not escape notice as a housewife. Aylett adhered strictly to the apocryphal story of rape attempted and frustrated and virtue vindicated, yet his description of her character went far beyond her piety (and the original story). She directed her servants gently but effectively, excelled in the practice of physic, spun quantities of thread, and produced intricate needlework. She fed the poor and clothed her household,

> Who did him *good* not *evill* all her days,
> Industrious with her mind and hand always.[19]

The thirty-first chapter of Proverbs may have been describing the "virtuous" woman, but the details pointed less to modesty and charity than efficiency, diligence, and frugality.

The domestic manuals owed an extraordinary debt to the wife of Proverbs 31, as much for language as for content. Thomas Taylor warned that a wife's "pride, prodigality, wastfulnes" could weaken her husband's estate. The good wife ought "to help his outward estate, by honest sparing and improving the means and comforts of this life; as the vertuous woman doth her husband good and not evil all her dayes."[20] John Dod and William Hinde went further in such reliance, and the title of their treatise, "Bathshebaes Instructions," accurately reflected the structure and content of their advice for wives. They insisted that a wife labor in the family, no matter her rank, as "she setteth her maides and waiting servants their taske: where is to be noted, that shee is carefull for foode for the whole family . . ." She should also, like the wife of Proverbs, rise earlier and labor longer than the rest of the family.

> Many women there are, which although they give themselves much sleep, being notwithstanding once wakened and raised, they do with great readines & diligence dispatch business of the house, and in that respect they are praiseworthy. But . . . the holy Ghost requireth this even in the mother of a family, that shee should rise before the night be spent.[21]

The texts provided only sketchy details of the labor demanded of women, and when they did identify tasks, their authors' imaginations seemed limited to biblical injunctions fleshed out by products they had seen themselves. All waxed vague but glorious upon the generalities of housewifely offices; most elaborated upon the conservator virtues of frugality, efficiency, and effective servant direction; and all mentioned food and clothing. Particular eloquence was dedicated to the dual tasks of spinning and sewing, perhaps because such labor depended upon skills foreign to men, or because men found the fruits of this labor attractive or enticing. Notwithstanding the occasional mention of a specific labor, it may well have been that the authors, happy to leave such details to women's specialized knowledge, chose merely to emphasize the virtues of and rewards awaiting the excellent wife. In so modeling herself after Solomon's mother, Bathsheba, a woman was fulfilling her calling.

> It is no shame or staine therefore for a woman to be housewifely, be she never so well borne, be she never so wealthy.
>
> For it is the *womans trade* so to be: it is the *end* of her *creation*; it is that that she was made for. She was made for man, and given to man, not to be *a play-fellow*, or *a bed-fellow*, or *a table-mate*, onely with him, (and yet to be all these too), but to be *a yoake-fellow, a worke-fellow, a fellow-labourer* with him, to be *an assistant* and *an helper* unto him, in the managing of such *domesticall and houshold offacies.*[22]

Any effort to uncover the realities of women's daily lives must overcome the elusiveness of those details of housewifery. Diarists and correspondents apparently had little interest in such labors, either because the work was unremarkable or because it was not understood. Nevertheless, there does exist another, more helpful collection of "prescriptive" texts: housewifery books. Some women did keep their own recipe collections that they would hand down to daughters and their daughters' daughters until the pages finally disintegrated from use.[23] However, it was inevitable that some writers, almost all men, would not be content to trust the continuation of such knowledge to women. This was not only the era of the generalized, religious domestic manual; it was also the era of the practical guides that instructed housewives in all aspects of their work. Richard Gardiner instructed housewives on the best ways to plant, fertilize, and harvest their kitchen gardens.[24] Several helpful physicians, healers, and entrepreneurs provided extensive compendia of medicinal recipes for the treatment of every ailment from generalized headache to localized infection, from acute fever to overall fatigue.[25] Yet while such specialized texts must have held some appeal, by far the most popular publications were the general directories on housewifery. "Complete Housewives" and "Cookery Dictionaries" abounded, including Gervase Markham's compendia, the very title of which revealed the vast scope of women's regular labors:

> *The English Hus-wife, Contayning, The inward and outward vertues which ought to be in a compleat woman. As, her skill in Physicke, Cookery,*

Banqueting-stuffe, Distillation, Perfumes, Wooll, Hemp, Flax, Dayries, Brewing, Baking, and all other things belonging to an Houshold. A Worke very profitable and necessarie, gathered for the generall good of this kingdome.

Probably the most widely read and frequently reprinted English housewifery book of the seventeenth century, Markham's guide could be found among the earliest English settlers in New England.[26]

Clearly, more than half of a wife's labor was devoted to food, including daily cooking, weekly baking, and the seasonal tasks that produced and preserved meat, dairy products, fruits, and vegetables. The remaining time would be divided among the production of household stores such as tallow and lye; the brewing of beer, cider, and medicines; and the home manufacture of cloth and clothing. Textile manufacture required skills and equipment available only to a segment of colonial housewives, and that generally not until the latter half of the century. However, all women were able seamstresses, mending and altering clothing still usable, crafting new apparel when shirts or gowns were past mending, and ornamenting clothing and linens with decorative needlework. As both housewifery books and probate inventories indicate, colonial women spent most of their time in the kitchen.[27] And in New England during the first decades of settlement, the roughness of early houses and the scarcity of cooking equipment must have tried the ingenuity of the housewife.

The abilities required in the seventeenth-century kitchen were as diverse as Markham's recipes. The good housewife could butcher a pig, smoke a ham, and "recover venison when it stinks."[28] She could roast meat on a spit before an open fire while she baked bread in a brick oven off the same fireplace, and she ought to be able to produce an array of brews and potions to treat the common headache, fever, and cold. She had the strength to lift the huge kettles, as much as sixty pounds empty, and the flexibility (and courage) to walk around, beside, and behind the fires in her hearth. Her knowledge of crop cultivation probably equaled that of any farmer; and while her husband would have cultivated a few grains, she was raising many varieties of fruits, vegetables, and herbs. As the poet Aylett noted, the result was complete provision for her husband.

> A married life's a hav'n of blisse,
> Which who wants half himself doth misse;
> My veins now freshen blouds do breed,
> I with a better stomack feed.[29]

Still, no household was completely self-sufficient, and in this respect the frontier environment placed a further burden upon its housewives. While the English countryside had a variety of traditional resources that had developed through the centuries, New England, at least during the first decades of settlement, lacked the markets, fairs, traveling artisans, and peddlers that eased work in English villages. Here women found that trading for food and other necessities—knowing where to find the goods, how to judge them, and how to bargain—required an additional collection of skills.[30] Yet in her ability to adapt and provide, the Massachusetts wife proved her value to her family and the society, frequently earning the complete trust of her husband and her peers. Englishwomen had often been entrusted with the family stores, much to the dismay of clerics who had condemned as lazy or weak husbands who turned over the administration of such household property to their wives.[31] But in the colonies, where men pursuing business in neighboring colonies, England, and the Caribbean needed to absent themselves from their families for weeks or months at a time, wives had to be trusted not only with the household affairs, but with their spouse's public business as well.[32]

With the rising importance of the family as a spiritual unit, and the central role played in the home by the housewife, it might well be argued that the status of women improved.[33] While the anchoress or nun may have enjoyed greater autonomy than her married peer, might even have exercised some power or, at least, influence, this independence and authority grew out of a holiness possible only in her celibacy. In other words, by denying her sexuality and, thus, overcoming her femaleness, a "genderless individual" would arise and claim spiritual power.[34] But after the Reformation, this argument continues, women were honored in their fulfillment of their femaleness as essential participants in that sacred association, the family. This vision articulated in the domestic manuals was also reflected in countless eulogies and memorials.

> Here lies,
> A worthy matron of unspotted life,
> A loving mother and obedient wife,
> A friendly neighbor, pitiful to poor,
> Whom oft she fed and clothed with her store;
> To servants wisely awful, but yet kind,
> And as they did so reward did find.
> A true instructor of her family,
> The which she orderd with dexterity.[35]

So Anne Bradstreet praised her late mother Dorothy Dudley, praise that would be echoed across the seventeenth century as sons, husbands, and clerics lauded mothers, wives, and widows. Loving, charitable, kind, and wise, she ordered her family.

On the other hand, this argument seems rather shortsighted. Seclusion and celibacy may today seem an extraordinary price to pay for what many scholars in this post-Freudian age would judge to be an extremely limited power through religion. Yet in medieval eyes, the price may not have been as dear nor the power so limited. In disbelieving the satisfaction that some women claimed to find within monastic lives, twentieth-century scholars are accepting Protestant reformers' limited definition of female fulfillment.[36] So, too, a second look at the exalted status of the housewife raises questions about women's improved status. Consider what was meant by housewife: a superior laborer, a manager, a woman who, in the best circumstances, governed her female servants and young children under the headship of her spouse. A wife may have been honored for her sterling character and valued for her skill and industry, and some wives certainly exercised considerable influence over their households. Yet however great the honor and value, honor did not grant autonomy. The worthy Dorothy Dudley was also obedient wife, and women were required to submit themselves to their husbands. So Margaret Newcastle mourned: "Men, that are not only our Tyrants, but our Devils, keep us in the Hell of Subjection, from whence I cannot Perceive any Redemption . . . our Words to Men are as Empty Sounds, our Sighs as Puffs of Wind, and our Tears as Fruitless Showres, and our Power is so Inconsiderable, as Men Laugh at our Weakness."[37]

When Puritan clerics devised their manuals and wrote their sermons, delineating the ideal character and responsibilities of family members, they devoted thousands of words to the wifely duty of submission. Little may have been said concerning the heavy demands and complexities of household labor, but the nature of a good wife's subjection to her husband was fully developed. Gouge's third treatise on wives' particular duties was actually dedicated to one particular duty: subjection. A woman owed her husband outward reverence in gesture and speech; she should behave toward him with courtesy, mildness, sobriety, modesty, neither lightness nor wantonness. She would obey his commands, come when she was called, eschewing "Vashtie-like stoutness," and take meekly any reproofs. "Her husbands presence must somewhat restraine her tongue, and so will her verie silence testifie a reverend respect." He even listed appropriate titles to be used by a wife toward her husband: Lord, Husband, or perhaps Master with his surname. She ought not to call him Brother or Friend, nor Sweet or Love, nor by his Christian name, as all these implied an equality between them.[38] Gataker agreed that a wife was "one that is *subject to her Husband as Her Head*," while Rogers sought inward as well as outward submission. "Nor artificiall respectivenesse of the eye, the curtesie of body, the silence or composure of the tongue, or the like, can secure an husband of subjection, except all these be acted from an heart of subjection, through the conscience of the duty."[39]

Moreover, in contrast to the vague discussion of housewifery, the nature of this submission was elaborated and teased out to its most delicate nuances. In his reminder to husbands, Rogers recalled that a wife "hath done for thy sake, which thou wouldst not have done for her: for she hath not only equalled thee in forsaking her father and mother, and family, that she might be one flesh with thine, but she hath forgone her name, and put all her state and livelyhood into thine hand." Subjection meant more than appropriate dress, modest eyes, and blushing speech, more than quiet and sober behavior with and away from her spouse.[40] It involved property, with the entire estate, whether real or personal property, whether brought to the marriage by husband or wife, to be placed under the husband's management. She had sacrificed everything in her trust of her husband. If he became ill or profligate, a wife might consider taking charge, or a man might allow his wife to administer some portion, although this was deemed a dangerous, slothful practice that would weaken a husband's headship. This subjection of all worldly goods extended to charity: a woman should not give alms to the poor without her husband's consent.[41]

Subjection also involved religion. Several writers agreed that virtuous, pious wives were, of course, expected to take an active role in the spiritual life of the household, especially in the instruction of children and female servants. Even as he admonished her, John Cotton noted that God had given Hutchinson "good parts and gifts fitt to instruct your Children and Servants and to be helpfull to your husband in the Government of the famely."[42] However, they were also careful to add that the wife was expected to follow her husband's spiritual guidance and to ask him to clarify any theological dilemma or biblical passage that she had difficulty understanding. Thomas Dudley was deeply concerned to get clear the question whether Hutchinson in her home meetings had taught men. He would have agreed that "though her own gifts be more then ordinary, yet [she should] conceale & supress them in this kind . . . and enjoy them to her self in subjection." Rogers wrote quite elegantly of his own duty toward his wife's soul, "how to mould it unto true lowlynesse & meeknesse for God . . . to instill the principles of Christ and selfdeniall into her . . . to cause her to see into that scope and view of Religion, which, is the change and subduing of her will to God." Gouge expanded this concept further, noting that "the end why an husband is appointed to be the head of his wife, namely, that by his provident care he may be as a saviour to her." Here the husband is not merely a wife's legal but her spiritual guardian, mediating her pathway to salvation.[43]

While some husbands may have lacked the knowledge or piety to serve in such an exalted role, a wife had to submit regardless of her spouse's intellectual, civil, or spiritual merits. Most authors asserted that no one could be forced to follow a husband who sinned against the will of God, but they were also hesitant to describe or validate any specific situation.[44] Certainly no question of personal worth alone would suffice. However wealthy, intelligent, learned, or religious a woman was, however superior to her husband, she must still accept his rule and guidance. Certainly, no superiority of birth could countermand the hierarchy of gender in the marital relationship. Even a husband's base character and gross immorality did not justify a woman's failure to subject herself to his government. "Whereas God hath appointed the husbands will to be the rule & square of the wives will, not the wives of his . . . so here though the husbands will shall be crooked, so it be not wicked, the wives will is not straight in Gods sight, if it be not pliable to his." And while Gataker stopped just short of ordering a woman to follow in her husband's wickedness, Gouge provided even less hope of escape. "For the evill qualitie and disposition of his heart and life, doth not deprive a man of that civill honour with God hath given unto him. Though an husband in regard of evill qualities may carrie the Image of the devill, yet in regard of his place and office he beareth the Image of God."[45] The divine right of kings apparently applied to husbands as well.

Many writers lamented that women were loath to accept their natural inferiority, among family members the "most backward in yeelding subjection to their husbands."[46] Nevertheless, Puritan divines never doubted that God demanded a wife's submission. Theologians grounded their arguments for this gendered hierarchy in their conviction that man more closely than woman reflected God's image. Like so many patriarchs before and after, they found support for their position in the second and third chapters of Genesis. Some pointed to Eve's failure to resist the serpent, her obedience to Satan before God, and her subsequent temptation of Adam. Thus did she merit the punishment "that her appetite should be to her husband." Yet Rogers's denunciations of Eve's seduction should not be misread. The problem was not only her refusal to obey God's command, but the audacity and arrogance with which she embarked upon her sinful career. "For, since she would take upon her as a woman without respect to the order, dependance, and use of her creation, to enterprise so sad a business, as to jangle and demurre with the divell about so waighty a point as her husbands freehold, and of her owne braine to lay him and it under foot, without the least parlee and consent of his."[47] Eve had usurped the authority of her husband Adam, an authority that was reaffirmed following the original seduction and sin, but which predated the disaster. Woman was not subordinate to her husband as penalty for her sin; her status was inherent in the very order of creation. She had not been created first, nor at the same instant as man, but after all other creatures had come into being. The dominion over all creatures, the "freehold," was Adam's, not hers. Eve was made for man's benefit, as a helpmeet, because no other creature would serve. Moreover, she was created not independently but out of the man. Finally, she was formed from his rib:

1. To shew, that the rib receiveth strength from the breast, so the wifes power and strength is from her husband, by whose light she shineth as the Moon by the Sunnes light.
2. To shew and teach her humility; not to pride her selfe, as if she had been made of the head; subjection, not superiority belongeth to her.
3. To shew her dependance on the man for strength and protection, as the rib is safe under the shoulder.[48]

In other words, while God had explicitly demanded the subjection of wives to husbands, such subjection was grounded in the natural order of a gendered humanity.

Such exhortations went beyond the exegesis of the fifth commandment; honor to mother and father was extended to all superiors, including husband in relation to wife. Here, writers instructed a wife to hear the voice of God in the commands of her spouse. The marital relation was a type of God's relationship with his people. As the ancient Hebrew or the contemporary Puritan turned to God for guidance, protection, and sustenance, so the wife ought to turn toward her husband. Failure to obey one's husband was "to reject Gods Ordinance," and a disrespectful wife risked eternal damnation. A wife must remember that "when the husband admonisheth, God admonisheth in him; and hearkning to him, she hearkeneth to God in him: as on the other side contemning him, shee contemneth God and Gods ordinance in him." Stopping just short of claiming the husband's divinity, Rogers argued that a wife beheld "yet more manifest steppes of Gods image then in herself," and that "the husband [was] the voice of God when they [were] both together."[49]

In constructing ideal family relations according to the guidelines derived from the Holy Scriptures, clerics were greatly assisted by English common law and custom. Protecting male power and privilege against all challenges, English lawmakers developed a complex of procedures and statutes founded upon assumptions of marital unity and male superiority. The abstract ideal of female subjection was partially realized in the concept of coverture, through which the legal personhood of a woman was completely subsumed under her husband's identity. Before the law, a married woman ceased to exist independently of her spouse. She could not enter into contracts with other persons; she could not sue or be sued; she could not alone serve as a legal guardian or the executor of an estate. Any action at law must be engaged in tandem with her husband, while a man could act individually or with his wife. Upon marriage, a man's legal abilities expanded while a woman's were sharply curtailed. Furthermore, any property that a woman brought into the marriage came under her husband's control, and it was common for a man to bequeath to his wife her bed linens, cooking pots, jewelry, even her apparel, since, during his lifetime, she owned nothing. A wife's dependence was here not only a matter of religious, social, and legal restrictions, but necessarily of concrete economics. As one author so neatly summarized, "The common laws here shaketh hand with divinitye."[50]

Of course, Puritan clerics did grant that a woman had an abiding interest in the family property. The conservative Gouge explained that a wife, by necessity, made use of the property in her household role, that she was expected to be a "helpe in providing such a sufficiencie of the goods of this world, as are needful," and that she might survive her husband, and therefore ought to "have such a portion of those goods as are meet for her place and charge."[51] So, too, within the common law a wife was understood to have rights in the family's real property. A wife retained dower rights in the estate guaranteeing her livelihood after her husband's death. A widow was guaranteed a third of her husband's estate during her widowhood, with the property reverting to his children or heirs (or creditors) after her death. The goal seemed less a recognition of women's rights than fear that the widow would become a drain upon public charity, a conclusion reinforced by the court's willingness to award her a larger portion of the estate should a third prove inadequate and by the fact that the dower was taken before debts were paid. Nevertheless, whatever the primary end, a wife was recognized as having a primary interest in the family property, and a man was expected to gain his wife's consent before selling any real estate. Moreover, although a woman's husband administered all property owned by his wife before marriage as well as any she had obtained during the marriage, he could not sell that property without her consent. In both cases, this consent might be granted in private examinations, as it was in England, or it might be represented by a wife's signature to a conveyance, as it came to be in Massachusetts. Without such formal consent, a widow could challenge the sale of any family property claiming ownership or dower rights.

While this process recognized a wife's legitimate interests in property and supposedly protected that interest, the protection was more theoretical than otherwise. A woman who did not consent to action taken by her husband could file no counterclaim until after his death, automatically entailing legal battles. And while the common law's demand for private examination seemed to acknowledge the possibility of coercion, the understanding of coercion did not extend beyond the present moment in legal chambers. The law did not recognize that a woman might consent in response to threats of future punishment by her husband if she challenged the transaction. In other words, while the common law acknowledged that a husband might abuse his power as guardian of the household and his wife's property, the structures and processes of the law functioned within an idealized vision of the household in which a man always acted with the best intentions, and a wife's subjection served her and her family's best interest. This was particularly apparent in New England. In Connecticut, a wife's rights in family property were not even tacitly acknowledged until the eighteenth century, while, in Massachusetts, an unsupported signature to a conveyance was understood as proof of a wife's consent.[52]

It may be that such faith was justified. Most Massachusetts husbands leaving wills demonstrated extraordinary concern for the support of their widows. In a sample of seventeenth-century wills probated in Essex County, Massachusetts, 85 percent bequeathed their wives one third or more of their real property; 91 percent left their spouses one-third or more of the movable property; and the others allotted some other means of support, usually an annuity.[53] Moreover, many husbands took additional steps to ensure comfortable livelihoods for their widows. John Balch requested that "soe long as my said wife shall live my said sonnes shall sowe or plant 2 akres . . . for my said wife for the term of seven years and after thatt son Benjamin shall doe all himselfe." Joseph Parker demanded more from his children; he left his entire estate to his wife for her use during her lifetime, but it would pass on to his sons only if they had been obedient to their mother and had provided for her.[54] Some men expressed fear for their wives' future, like John Legg, who left his whole estate to his wife "to be at her dispossing Continuing her life soe that noe Children of ours shall disturbe or Mollest her in the time of her Life." Others demonstrated their faith in family harmony by requiring their children to share their home with their mother.[55] In many cases these wills reflected anxiety that property alone would not satisfactorily support a widow. Women could not farm land or maintain a shop without assistance, and many believed that women could not manage property for their own best interest.

The law certainly recognized a widow as an individual able to make decisions and take legal actions to profit from or protect her property, but widows often displayed little enthusiasm for their newly established legal personhood. Many depended upon adult sons, brothers, or even fathers and uncles to provide guidance and advice. When widow Mary Gibbs agreed to marry widower Samuel Sewall, the prenuptial contract was negotiated by her son Henry. During the early years of settlement, John Wilson had written of a widow who depended upon her aged father. There was even the case of Dorothy Symonds, whose ox was kept for her by her uncle, John Winthrop Jr. She offered to sell the ox to Winthrop for whatever he thought it worth, to be paid in commodities as he felt she needed them.[56]

Some women undoubtedly lacked the skills necessary to manage their property; others may have been psychologically unable to assert independence after decades of trained reliance upon fathers and husbands. Women were told from the pulpit and by the press that they were inferior; girls were raised to lives of marital dependence. Dorothy Leigh, author of the 270-page *Mother's Blessing*, wrote that women should not "bee ashamed to shew their infirmities, but to give men the first and chief place." And when Elizabeth Jocelin outlined her expectations and plans for her unborn child, she hoped that if the child were female, her husband would not overeducate the girl, making her unfit for a poor husband.[57]

Whatever her psychological profile, a woman's acceptance of male guidance and assistance must have been reinforced by the open hostility the community directed at independent women. In 1640, Ann Hibbens found herself excommunicated by the Boston church when she refused to settle her claim against a Boston carpenter at the behest of male arbiters; sixteen years later, after the death of her magistrate husband, she was convicted and executed as a witch. Anne Hutchinson was banished for her independent religious leadership, for acting more a husband than a wife, for exhibiting a "pride of Harte," and her adult sons and son-in-law were admonished by the church for supporting her rather than leading her away from her heresies and challenging her insubordinate practices.[58] Women who aggressively insisted upon their own property rights, without male protection or intercession, often found themselves in serious trouble. For example, widow Katherine Harrison, who had in 1666 inherited an estate of nearly £1,000 from her husband, found herself fighting a losing battle to protect her estate from vandalism. Efforts to challenge her neighbor's actions ended in her own conviction for slander and an outrageous fine. At one point she had survived a jury's conviction for witchcraft (the magistrates were unsure) with a sentence of banishment. When the accusations followed her to New York, the intervention of her daughter's father-in-law-to-be enabled her to live there peacefully. And although she had resisted remarriage, she finally turned the property over to the guardianship of two male relatives to be held in trust for her daughters.[59]

The strictures of the law, the harshness with which the courts met challenges from assertive women, and the inflexibility of clerical remonstrances all point to a social and ideological structure that rendered women powerless. As Newcastle lamented, "Yet howsoever, were she the Best Wife that could be, and he the Worst Husband, the Law hath no Power to Mend him, and Help her, for the Law ought not to intermeddle in their Quarrel, as having no more Power to take away the Prerogative of a Husband, than the Prerogative of Parents and Masters."[60] Still, the importance that Puritans placed upon the domestic unit did provide a legal benefit for women. English law and custom were particularly adamant upon the indissolubility of marriage, constructing the relationship as a spiritual permanency. English courts allowed legal separation from bed and board for adultery, desertion, and cruelty, but not the right to remarry. New England Puritan thinkers objected to both this theological construction of marriage as well as the arrangements. Although the family was a little church, marriage was a civil contract, not a sacred bond, and like all civil contracts it could, upon serious consideration, be dissolved. Furthermore, since the family *was* a little church, and marriage ought to produce a shared, stable domestic arrangement, if husband and wife lived separately, what possible end was served by maintaining the marriage?

For spouses unable to live in peace, both Massachusetts and Connecticut were prepared to consider granting a divorce and permission for the inno- cent party to remarry. Connecticut in fact refused to grant any other kind of legal separation. This is not to say that divorces were granted frivolously or even easily. Puritan magistrates and ministers did devote significant efforts toward helping couples make the best of a bad bargain. Nevertheless, ab- solute divorce was available to husbands and wives who, for reasons of de- sertion, adultery, cruelty, or hatred, could no longer live together. For these Puritans, a bad marriage was destructive of the common good, and divorce provided the opportunity to replace disastrous partnerships with more suc- cessful families.[61]

While tales of dissatisfied spouses rise out of court records throughout this era, how representative such complaints were is uncertain. Clearly, many couples seemed happy, although the scant evidence generally, though not al- ways, reflects men's rather than women's experiences and attitudes. It is per- haps more accurate to note that most marriages created stable household units, and that either because of love, contentment, lack of alternatives, or so- cial and legal pressures reinforcing marriage permanency, the overwhelming majority of women did not consider divorce. In fact, in New England, many of the women who sued for divorce did so on grounds of desertion, indi- cating that their husbands actually initiated the legal dissolution.

When considering prescription, legal structures, and social and eco- nomic realities all together, it becomes difficult to assess accurately the bal- ance of power within the household. With very little relief the law left wives dependent upon the care, protection, skills, and goodwill of their spouses. Puritan clerics and moralists mandated a wife's complete subjection to her husband, but domestic manuals also acknowledged that within the family hierarchy, a wife and mother exercised extensive control over children and servants. Supposedly she ruled under her husband's direction, but the ability and authority of a woman to rule her household remained. In other words, while a woman was expected to defer to her husband in every particular, practice probably left many women running their households without any male interference. Surely colonial wives often found themselves standing in for husbands who were away for weeks or months at a time, while a small but significant number of deserted wives proved able to manage their households and property over the long term without male assistance. Some men, like Samuel Sewall, may have liked a release from household cares and recognized in their wives excellent administrative and organizational skills. Daniel Rogers's criticism of husbands' allowing their wives to administer portions of their estates probably reflected his own observations. "I am not ignorant that many husbands some for sloth, others to avoid their wives discontents, supposing to allay their fiercenesse of spirit by resigning their right, others, under the color of ministeriall, or burdensome service, have, and do, put the bridle of providence into their wyves hand."[62]

Legal restrictions placed around the feme covert may be clear, and the prescriptive literature is awesomely consistent, but social practice remains difficult to fix and interpret. Impressions gleaned from the personal diaries and correspondence of a few men combined with the evidence of court cases and legal archives reveal a complicated picture. Wives, denied legal and moral authority in their households, sometimes assumed it from husbands who granted it willingly. On the other hand, widows, who were granted access to authority and autonomy through the courts, often exercised their rights only under the protection of an adult male relative. The social climate surrounding women's actions valued a woman's labor and praised her strength of character but punished her autonomy. The intransigence of this patriarchal ideology should have produced women thoroughly dominated and controlled by men, but the social realities of women's experience demonstrate that within this system women realized some status and power.

Although a few women have been heard either embracing or resenting the subservience demanded of them, the voices addressing the question of women's autonomy, influence, and power have been overwhelmingly male. Where, then, can women's voices be heard? There must have been moments in every woman's life when she was free of male interference, a social sphere in which women lived and worked among women, an ideological world they shared. The language of this world and the behavior of women within it might furnish a useful counterpoint to the monotonic male vision found in law and prescription.

It makes sense to return to the point where women appeared to exercise authority and merit honor: work. A comparison of men's and women's labor and access to the realm beyond the home does suggest a framework within which to pursue the question of female autonomy and strength. While the concept of a division between the private and public spheres may be more relevant after industrialization, even in the seventeenth century one can see that some roles were played entirely within the family and others took one outside the household into increasingly out-of-family contacts: village and church, then government and the world beyond the familiar. Women's labor kept them almost entirely within the family, with the exception of a few contacts with village craftsmen and cooperative work parties in which women joined with other women. This level of cooperation generally would not go beyond the village; even the midwife was not likely to travel beyond its limits. Women were completely excluded from participation in government at any level, even as party to a lawsuit or in a contract, and in this they were sheltered from any unmediated contact with the world beyond the familiar. In outlining the mutual duties of husbands and wives, the *Godly Forme of Household Government* paired a series of matched virtues that concluded with the predictable "The dutie of the husband is, to be Lord of all: and of the wife to give account of all." Leading to this conclusion lay a series of comparisons that separated husband and wife into two political and spatial spheres.

> The dutie of the husband is, to travell abroad to seeke living and the wives dutie to keepe the house. The dutie of the husband is, to get mony and provision: and of the wives, not vainely to spend it. The dutie of the husband is, to deale with many men: and of the wives, to talke with fewe. The dutie of the husband is, to be entermedling: and of the wife, to bee solitarie and withdrawne.[63]

Women may have been restricted to the world of the household and village, but within this world women assumed great risks, fulfilled a most dangerous duty, and therefore came to realize an enormous personal power, the power that lay in the most private of all worlds, the birthing chamber. In their utopian vision of marriage, an institution of love between man and woman that reflected, however imperfectly, God's love for humanity, Puritan men never forgot that the primary goal and natural outcome of marriage was reproduction. Marital love brought a "neare conjunction, even in regard of their bodies, for an holy procreation . . . ." Gataker, exhorting wives toward amiability and obedience, noted that "without *a Woman, issue* cannot at all, without *a Wife* it cannot *lawfully*, without *such a Wife* it cannot *comfortably* bee had." Niccholes, in his advice to young men seeking a wife, devoted a significant number of pages to the demands of childbearing. Virtue was certainly valued above riches, but so was fitness above beauty; a man should choose a wife who would "breed" decent children.[64]

Although these writers acknowledged the need for women to bear the next generation, the language and structure of their discourse undermined female power. In their portrayal of procreation as primary and natural, with the husbandry language of breeding used repeatedly, clerics demystified reproduction and reconstructed women as simple biological tools. Sometimes women could be inadequate tools, reflected in worries about breeding fitness and barrenness. Whether unfit or sound, however, they were tools of and for male procreators. Even Gataker, in his acknowledgment that children cannot be had without women, spent his time exhorting women to behave themselves so that men did not feel discomfort in the production of offspring. "And indeed what *comfort* can a man have . . . of *issue* by such an one who when shee should be *the light of his eyes*, and the *joy of his heart*, is as *a thorne continually in his eyes*, and *a sting at his* verie *heart*?"[65] There was even the suggestion that women, wayward and uneducated, required guidance and protection in order to bring their pregnancies to successful conclusions. One writer reminded women that a mother's duties began in the womb, and he urged husbands to take special pains to protect the unborn from their wives' follies.

> They who through violence of passion, whether of grief or anger, or through violent motion of the body, as by dancing, striving, running, galloping on horseback, or the like: or through distemper of the bodie, by eating things hurtfull, by eating too much, by too much abstinence, by too much bashfulnesse in concealing their desires and longings (as we speak) cause any abortion or miscariage, fall into the offence contrary to the forenamed dutie.[66]

Perhaps the best example of these attempts at demystification was the Protestant effort to eliminate rituals of purification for postpartum women. The churching of women had been constructed by the pre-Reformation church ostensibly to purify women polluted by the bloodshed of childbirth, a ritual that resonated every Candlemas when the church community celebrated the purification of Mary following the birth of Jesus. Reformers deemed such rituals absurd, if not blasphemous, in their negative commentary upon creation. Anyone who believed women to be polluted by childbirth, reformers argued, was ignorant and superstitious, for sexuality (as expressed in conjugal love) and childbirth were natural and godly aspects of divine creation.[67] I would argue, however, that these rituals, ostensibly concerned with pollution and filth, were actually performed at least in part to alleviate men's fear of women's incomprehensible powers. The strength of women was already apparent in their monthly loss of blood, the fluid of life, without ill effect. Women's ability to nurture within and birth a human being, to create and channel life, may have awed men who could only watch the external signs of internal power. Perhaps the new mother was feared as a person through whom the extraordinary power of nature pulsed, and the churching of women served to exorcise that power, to render women safe to men again. In their scorn of the churching rituals, reformers asserted that women as childbearers had no special abilities, that reproduction was not mysterious but natural.

Protestant reformers were supported by recent medical discoveries and the popularization of medical science. To the reasonable man of this new, scientific age, natural processes could be both understood and controlled. By the end of the seventeenth century, several medical texts, with anatomical illustrations, were available in English to the educated public. Nicholas Culpeper's *Directory for Midwives*, for example, went through several printings. Although illuminatingly and aggressively ignorant of recent developments in medical research, this text nonetheless provided explicit, detailed discussions of reproductive anatomy, male as well as female.[68] Medicine's ability to explain methodically and scientifically the mechanics of conception, gestation, and childbearing further naturalized reproduction.

Since, with the assistance of science, women's reproductive powers were no longer beyond the realm of male understanding, women should have become more comprehensible and, therefore, less threatening to men. Medical science might also have expected to further increase women's dependence upon men, due to men's superior scientific knowledge. But seventeenth-century England and its colonies were not yet scientific societies. It must be remembered that science has not always held its present privileged position in the world of ideas.[69] The seventeenth century was a transitional time, bridging a medieval society's cosmology of folk magic, religion, and apothecaries' potions with an enlightened age that would discount religion and the supernatural in favor of scientifically researched facts and theories.

The educated elite may have thrilled to the comprehension and power that the new scientific knowledge brought, but in the popular mind this knowledge competed, often unsuccessfully, against folk wisdom as the primary authority on matters relating to the human body. Thus while some writers explored the natural processes of procreation as explained by medical science and emphasized women's duties to nurture their husbands' children, the general community, and women especially, continued to credit women with the primary procreative abilities and to understand reproduction as the purview, responsibility, and gift of women. When Massachusetts resident Tristram Coffin died in 1704, his epitaph honored his twenty years' service as a church deacon. His wife Judith, however, was praised for piety, loyalty to spouse, and fertility, "having lived to see 177 of her children and children's children to the 3d generation."[70] And as late as 1710, cleric Cotton Mather would assure women that "it is to be esteemed a Mercy of God, that [procreation], One principal End of Marriage, is thus far in an Honourable way answered with you."[71]

Of course, a woman's duty and honor did not end with giving birth. As Rogers proclaimed, "[N]o sooner doth the infant which she hath warmed in her wombe, and given life to, in her wombe, behold the light, but it whimpers, and cries for the brest, as if it said, I am thine, nurse mee . . . the subject wife stops not her eare to this call: Shee seekes not brest in her husbands purse, but in her own bosome." Nursing her infant stood as a new mother's prime responsibility, and clerics in old and New England throughout the seventeenth century railed at the current fashion of wet nursing and called upon women to do their duty and suckle their own children. More than sixty years after Rogers's pleas, Cotton Mather was berating women who failed to nurse. "You will Suckle your Infant your Self if you can; Be not such an Ostrich as to Decline it merely because you would be One of the Careless Women Living at Ease. Of such we read, they are Dead while they Live. But if you have the Calamity of Dry Breasts, or your Health will not permit you to give suck; Entertain it with Submission to the will of God; but as a Calamity."[72] Dod and Cleaver explicitly tied this responsibility, again, to female biology. They declared that "as God hath given [woman], not onely the wombe to beare, but also the breasts and milke to nourish her child, so let her bee thankfull to God for these blessings, and use them to that end that hee have them." So, too, did Mather find a biological mandate: "If God have granted her Bottles of Milk on her Breast . . . her children have a Claim unto them."[73]

One of the strongest calls to nursing mothers came from a woman who had long repented of her failure to nurse her own children. *The Countess of Lincolnes Nurserie* delineated every argument in favor of nursing one's own child, including biology and nature, duty toward God, biblical example, and duty toward one's child. In this rehearsal of obligations she echoed the male writers, but a closer look also reveals a peculiarly female voice piercing through and overshadowing the list of duties. A woman's voice could be heard when she spoke eloquently of maternal affection and the love that should inspire a mother to suckle her children at her own breast. And it was neither preacher nor judge but a mother who grieved the death of one child, blamed her child's death upon the wet nurse's neglect and thus upon her failure to nurture her own child. As the author repeated, no one cares for a child better than its mother; if a mother refuses to nurse, how can she expect more of a woman who was stranger to the child? She drew an intriguing analogy between piety and nursing. "Indeed, I see some, if the weather be wet, or cold; if the way be fowle; if the Church be far off, I see they are so coy, so nice, so luke-warme, they will not take paines for their *own soules*. Alas, no marvell if these will not bee at trouble, and paine to nourish their *children's bodies* . . . ."[74] As a woman cared for her soul, so she cared for her child.

Here and among other female voices, women claimed childbearing and nurturing as their own, perhaps because they alone fully appreciated and accepted the risks.[75] Margaret Newcastle wrote that women's

> Lives are more profitable than men's Lives are, for they Increase Life, when Men for the most part Destroy Life, as witness Warrs, wherein Thousands of Lives are Destroyed, Men Fighting and Killing each other, and yet Men think all Women neer Cowards, although they do not only Venture and Indanger their Lives more than they do, but indure greater Pains with greater Patience than Men usually do.

Yet she also noted that "Nature hath made her Male Creatures, especially Mankind, only for Pleasure, and her Female Creatures for Misery: Men are made for Liberty, Women for Slavery . . . Slaves to Sickness, Pains, and Troubles, in Breeding, Bearing, and Bringing up their Children . . . ."[76] The female community was thoroughly familiar with the pains of travail, and folk remedies of herbs and charms were passed down through female generations along with birthing stools and childbed linens. Anne Bradstreet memorialized women's sufferings in her *Four Ages of Man*:

> My mother's breeding sickness I will spare,
> Her Nine months weary burthen not declare.
> To show her bearing pains, I should do wrong,
> To tell those pangs which can't be told by tongue:
> With tears into the world I did arrive;
> My mother still did waste as I did thrive,
> Who yet with love and all alacrity,
> Spending, was willing to be spent for me.[77]

Women were united not only by the pains of childbirth, but by the specter of death that hovered. Every woman knew that her pregnancy could well end in death, her infant's or her own. During the seventeenth century, infant mortality was high in England, and even within the relatively healthy environment of New England, the infant mortality rate was high. Hutchinson's health and strength were remarkable in that she lost only one child of the fifteen that she bore. Many women lost half their children in infancy, and most women had experienced the death of at least one baby.[78] Additionally, mothers had reason to fear for their own lives. A woman might die giving birth to her first child, and a woman who had survived the birth of eight children might die giving birth to the ninth. Precisely what proportion of women died in childbed during the seventeenth century remains unknown, with suggestions as high as 20 percent for New England and as low as 7 percent in the English countryside.[79]

While some might argue that this represented a low risk among villages and towns threatened with infectious diseases, it is important to remember that the risk necessarily dwelt in the mind of the expectant mother. Roger Schofield notes that in a village of a thousand persons, residents were likely to observe the death of a woman in childbed once every three years. He suggests that this may not have been especially threatening to women, particularly when they observed so many women and men dying from other causes.[80] It could also be argued, however, that this figure indicates that a woman facing childbirth was likely to have known more than one woman who had died giving birth. How many deaths need a woman have witnessed before becoming frightened? While the onset of life-threatening disease was unpredictable, childbirth was not. Healthy Puritans frequently spoke in general terms about death looming over everyone, but expectant women confronted directly their own mortality.

Those few women who wrote revealed a preoccupation with death in childbirth. A woman who accepted pregnancy automatically assumed mortal risks. As she neared the end of one pregnancy, Bradstreet bid farewell to her husband.

> All things within this fading world hath end,
> Adversity doth still our joys attend;
> No ties so strong, no friends so dear and sweet,
> But with death's parting blow is sure to meet.
> The sentence past is most irrevocable,
> A common thing, yet oh, inevitable.[81]

Sixty years later, Jerusha Oliver displayed the same fears, noting in her diary that she would use her time to "prepare for my Lying in, and would therefore prepare for Death."[82] For a pious woman, the possibility of death could transport her to an intense spiritual awareness. In her ninth pregnancy, Sarah Goodhue grew convinced that she would die in childbirth, and she wrote the pious *Valedictory and Monitory Writing*, which she hoped would help her husband and children cope with her death. She did in fact die in childbirth, as did Elizabeth Jocelin, who had worked feverishly to complete a letter to her unborn child. When Jocelin found herself pregnant,

> she secretly tooke order for the buying a new winding sheet: thus preparing and consecrating her selfe to him, who rested in *a new Sepulcher wherein was never man yet layd*. And about that time, undauntedly looking death in the face, privately in her Closet betweene God and her, shee wrote these pious Meditations; whereof her selfe strangely speaketh to her owne bowels in this manner, *It may seeme strange to thee to receive these lines from a mother, that died when thou wert born*.[83]

Together women shared the fears and pains as well as the joys and rewards of childbearing. Childbirths were major social events that gathered all women within the community to support and celebrate with the new mother. Although a man occasionally appeared there, throughout the seventeenth century the New England birthing chamber remained the purview of women. Young women worked under and learned through the guidance of older, experienced women, while a midwife presided over the labor and delivery.[84]

Among the most highly skilled of professional healers, a good midwife equaled and usually surpassed the available physician within her own sphere. True, during the sixteenth and seventeenth centuries, physicians had begun to be jealous of their own prerogatives, claiming a superior scientific knowledge grounded in chemistry and anatomy. Many skilled practitioners felt driven to establish professional standards, establish centers of medical education, and, in the process, restrict access to the healing profession. In these efforts to improve the quality of medical treatment (and their own status as physicians), midwives came under severe attack. Physician Thomas Willis claimed that childbed fever often developed because new mothers took some remedies from some "local woman." An equally noted medical man, Thomas Sydenham, also faulted midwives; their mistakes were often corrected only by a physician's intervention.

The Midwife, whether rude and unskilful, or Vainglorious, to shew how well he [sic] has performed her business, advises that her Women shou'd rise a few days after she has been Delivered, and that she should keep up a while; the Woman does so, and is presently seixed [sic] upon the first motion of her Body, with an Hysterick indisposition, and according as the Disease increases, the *Lochia* are first lessened, then quite stopped, whose untimely suppression a long Train of symptoms follow, which soon destroys the Sick, unless great Diligence and Skilfulness intercede.[85]

Yet while medical science had made great strides in the knowledge of physiology, physicians still adhered to the theory that balanced bodily humors promised health. Technical skill among surgeons and the new man-midwives increased as the seventeenth century progressed, while physicians still blistered, purged, and bled their patients using poisons and herbs, lances and leeches. There were major gaps in their knowledge of the female reproductive organs. Physicians had begun to diagnose many of women's illnesses as hysteria. Discussions of childbed fever revealed both an ignorance of the process of pregnancy and a preoccupation with bodily humors. For example, Willis claimed that after conception, the menses continued to flow into the womb, collecting and fermenting for nine months, and that fever resulted when, after birth, the woman's body failed to release all that pent-up menstrual fluid. Seen in this light, the experience and skill of the midwife more than matched the imperfect scientific knowledge of the physician.[86]

Midwives themselves were not exempt from the desire to increase their knowledge or set professional standards. The accomplished French midwife Louise Bourgeois published a text for fellow practitioners in 1609. Highly skilled and in great demand on the continent, Bourgeois's practice and text illustrated the level of technical skill that grew with experience. The seventeenth century saw the publication of at least eight more medical texts explicitly directed toward midwives, one written by a woman.[87] Some professional midwives in England, acknowledging the uneven skill and knowledge of practitioners, began a drive to establish a registry or college of midwifery in order to establish standards and protect their positions and reputations. This century also saw the rise of man-midwives, who sought not only to join what had been an all-female practice but to dominate that practice through the development and monopoly of a new, secret delivery tool, the forceps. Although many people may have agreed that men were intellectually superior to and more highly skilled than women, their concern for female modesty and their regard for female practitioners weakened support for male intervention in childbirth. In New England at least, men were expected to leave women's reproductive health to women. A man in York County, Massachusetts, was fined fifty shillings for "presumeing to act the part of a Midwife."[88]

The society and governments of New England colonies accepted midwives as the experts on female health and pregnancy, and the courts frequently called upon them to deliver expert opinions and advice, to be the legal guardians over the birthing chamber. Midwives examined accused witches for the telltale marks or witch's teats; they served as examiners of women suspected of premarital pregnancy or infanticide. The Suffolk County Court ordered that all women must have a midwife present at childbirth, threatening that a stillborn child, if the mother gave birth alone, could bring an accusation, conviction, and execution for murder. In cases of suspected fornication, a midwife's evidence could be the difference between conviction and acquittal. John and Elizabeth Garland had been convicted of fornication because their child was born less than eight months after the wedding. On appeal, they were released, for the midwife had testified, "I, being at ye house of John Garland about a fortnight after his wife was brought a bed: I tooke good notes of ye child, & I never saw so little a child in my life & So think it came before tyme taking of it into my lapp & it 'was to my apprehention nothing but skin & bones."[89] Occasionally, midwives would save women from corporal punishment, as in the case of Seaborn Cromwell, who had been sentenced to be whipped. The opinion of eleven women, including four midwives, was that she was pregnant and that "if Seaborn have any bodily correction at present it may prove dangerous and hurtfull to her." Although the magistrates wanted to go forward, they were challenged by the deputies, who, considering the women's evidence, did not consent to the magistrates' decision but recommended that the penalty be deferred.[90] So, too, when the convicted witch Elizabeth Proctor was acknowledged to be pregnant, her execution at Salem was postponed until after the birth, by which time the executions had ended.

The best of the midwives demonstrated abilities to untangle an umbilical cord before it strangled the infant, to turn a breech baby in the womb, even to hasten the progress of labor. Outside the sphere of childbirth, midwives often served as healers, custodians of particularly efficacious herbs and potions. Their capacity to channel the extraordinary power of birthing must have amazed; it certainly threatened the personal confidence and sense of well-being of many New England residents. A woman who could assist at birth and the sickbed could also cause sickness and death. Of all the women accused of witchcraft in seventeenth-century New England, twenty-two were known midwives and healers said to put their skills toward malignant ends. That almost all women gave birth, assisted at births, and served as nurses in family and community merely underscored the mysterious, if not devilish, potential of all women. Society's insecurity was revealed in the fact that while midwives were used to examine accused witches for marks, the courts and clerics relied upon male physicians to diagnose possession or bewitchment. In this century of transformation from the magical to the scientific world, community members, especially male leaders, seemed locked in a conflict between dependence upon women for birthing and general healthcare and their respect and fear of women's medical successes and failures.[91]

Thus in this century of transformation, a political battle was engaged over questions of reproduction, health, and nature. Karlsen has argued that, among other gender power plays, the frequent appearance of doctors in witchcraft investigations suggests that one function of the accusation of witchcraft was "to discredit women's medical knowledge in favor of their male counterparts."[92] Such an effort was obvious in John Winthrop's discussion of the Hutchinsonian controversy. When describing Hutchinson's early success among Boston's women, Winthrop credited/blamed her proficiency in the birthing chamber: "being a woman very helpfull in the times of childbirth, and other occasions of bodily infirmities, and well furnished with means for those purposes, shee easily insinuated her selfe into the affections of many . . . ."[93] One of Hutchinson's staunch followers, Jane Hawkins, was also suspect as not only heretic but midwife, "for it was known, that she used to give young women oil of mandrakes and other stuff to cause conception; and she grew into great suspicion to be a witch, for it was credibly reported, that, when she gave any medicines, (for she practised physic,) she would ask the party, if she did believe, she could help her, etc."[94]

A less sensational venue revealed a similar struggle for power. At some point before March 1649, the magistrates of Massachusetts Bay arrested and imprisoned Alice Tilly, a midwife of Dorchester. Apparently, she had been called to account for a run of unsuccessful confinements at which she had presided, although the exact charges against her are not known. One petition acknowledged that "mistris Tilly stands now charged before this honorable Court for the miscarrying of many wimen and children under hand"; others referred in general terms to "discouragements," "the black side of her actions," and "crimes writ upon her forehead." Little did the magistrates

realize that Tilly's arrest would antagonize and mobilize the female community. Despite what must have seemed to the court clear and certain evidence
of egregious incompetence, women were demanding that Tilly be available
to assist them. Eight petitions were presented in her behalf, the first in March
1649, the others in May 1650. Although many women signed more than one
petition, nearly two hundred women of Dorchester and Boston went on record in Tilly's support. One petition alone was subscribed by 130 women.
Initially, the women simply asked that Tilly be permitted to continue to serve
them when needed, returning to prison afterward. This request was granted.
Later, husband William Tilly convinced his wife that she was foolish to serve
the commonwealth from prison; she should demand complete freedom. The
petitioning women joined their voices with the Tillys', a "proud" request that
incensed the magistrates, and the last heard in the records was the court's refusal of Tilly's request.[95]

In the language of the petitions and the response of the General Court,
the boundaries of knowledge, experience, and power grow quite clear. The
most explicit discussion of the charges lay in the petition presented by Lydia
Williams. Refuting the charges one by one, Williams spoke from her own experience and in consultations with other midwives. While some comments
simply noted that such things happened—"I my self have had a child allive
just cominge at the birth, & yeat dead born"—others displayed the esoteric,
experiential learning of the midwife. If the magistrates were uneasy with
reports of Tilly's practice, it was only because they didn't know. "About putting back of a child in the womb I had a child putt back in after the midwife
hath had the knowledge of it, because she might have the main & greater
advantage to bringe it fourth." A bit later, Williams carefully explained,
"Concerninge the increasing of a woaman's paines by reason of the mother
lyinge in the childes way, when the midwife comes to putt it upp, it increases
the woamans paine, & it is a cause why the midwife cannott pluck out her
hand out of the womans body many times before the child be delivered . . ." In
her petition, Williams speaks as one who had given birth to several children,
one who had given birth with the assistance of Tilly, one who had attended
many births, and one who could refer the court to several witnesses, including midwives. She spoke from an authority that no man could possibly
assume or achieve.[96]

The petitions indicate that Tilly was among the most valued midwives in
Boston and Dorchester. In their statements accepting the misfortunes that
recently had attended her, the women nevertheless express desire for her

attendance and confidence in her skills. She was of great help to women, "especially in cases of extremity in hir office of midwifferye"; she seems to have succeeded when "nothing but death was to be expected." Many women, the petitioners lamented, would not feel safe in their confinements without her. Even the governor, Thomas Dudley, said that Tilly was the ablest midwife in the colony, but while the petitioners were gratified by the magistrate's ratification of the women's judgment, they also pointed out that "whereas the honored magistrates and many men more can speak but by hearesay; wee and many more of us can speake by experience and some by hearesay, and who have bin the witnesses that have bin with her in times of distresse." Men may have believed in her abilities, but the women knew. In one plea for Tilly's liberty, the rhetoric was obsequious but the demand assertive.

> we dare nott assume above our lien to direct, but leave the composure thereof to God & the wisedome given of God to you, who wee doubt nott butt will direct your worships therein, so as if his owne honour may be preserved, the security of your children, those of the weakest sexe provided for, as the humble requests of your poore petitioners granted, in opening the doore of sure liberty to our wombes way of instrumentall helpefulness by her, of whom our experiences are great, and necessity is greater.[97]

These women may have been the weaker sex, but they made their request with authority. Their experience was great and their need greater, and they were certain that God would direct the magistrates in their release of Tilly.

The men were impressed against their will. They claimed that they had effected justice, but their response to early petitions indicated otherwise. If Tilly had been as incompetent or wicked as she had been judged, how could the Court have allowed her to continue in her calling? The record noted that such connivance "at hir disobedience, so farr as they might, without betraying all authoritie into hir hands" was due to the respect which the magistrates had for the petitioners, but with one small qualifier. The governors revealed the nexus of the problem: magistrates needed both to believe in their own justice and to retain authority, a difficult task when individuals with no right to raise questions assumed to themselves, and demonstrated through technical knowledge and exclusive experience, the power and ability to challenge a judgment. The Court rather elegantly transformed the problem into a simple power battle, declaring that "it plainely appeares, by hir carriage and speeches, and hir urging others thus still to petition for hir, that nothing but a compleate victory over magistracy will satisfy hir excessive pride . . ." Reducing the charge to pride may have comforted the governors, but they only sounded doubtful and self-righteous in their obstinate assertion that there was "as much neede to uphold magistracy in their authoritye as Mrs Tilly in hir midwivery."[98]

The brief struggle between the Massachusetts government and Alice Tilly and her many supporters revealed in one slice the political and cultural battle between men, whose rightful authority was established by law, custom, and the Bible, and women, who discovered power within the exclusive experience and knowledge gleaned within their segregated community. Men seemed content to allow women to exercise the limited authority that housewifery and healing allowed. After all, since women were restricted to the household as submissive wives and daughters, they could claim no legal status, no public knowledges or skills, and therefore no ability to exercise direct influence over the outside world. In other words, from a male perspective, women had no access to any recognizable pathway to social or political power.

Women could be excluded justifiably from the public sphere because they were understood to be adjuncts to and under the protection of the male community. However, within this exclusion women found strength and exhibited a surprising authority through their experience as household managers and mothers and their identification with natural forces as healers and reproducers. In other words, although the ideological construction of private/public seemed designed to deny women power by withholding access to public paths of influence and authority, within the private world women discovered power. When, from this unanswerable position of domestic experience women challenged men in the political arena, as they did over Alice Tilly, men seemed flustered and frustrated by an incomprehensible strength centered in the private sector. The logical, defensible, well-buttressed codes of legal evidence and government structure were useless in the face of women's amorphous experiential knowledge. After all manner of reasonable, legal argument, the magistrates, in a move reminiscent of Winthrop's summary dismissal of Hutchinson's superior arguments, "We are your judges and not you ours," settled the matter with a unilateral invocation of natural hierarchy and the explicit authority of magistrates to govern.

On the other hand, perhaps restricting women to the home sphere was a response to women's power, an effort to contain women as well as retain power for the divinely appointed governors. If some women knew they held a limited but concentrated power, many men feared that this was so. At least they wrote and behaved as if women were potent forces that needed to be restrained and restricted lest they destroy themselves, their families, and the society. Domestic manuals, sermons, broadsides, even medical texts all displayed the paradoxical convictions that women were weak and in great need of male protection and that women were dangerous and able to drag men into the storm. Women were naturally passive yet dangerously active, innocent yet seductive, submissive yet controlling, pious yet frivolous, weak yet obstinate, sacrificing yet petty and demanding. In one sense these contradictions matched the commonplace dualism of madonna and whore, but with a decidedly Elizabethan emphasis upon sexuality and a conviction that the most honorable of women had strong whorish tendencies. The best women followed in the lines of Eve and Bathsheba—two legendary mothers, to be sure, but who had brought the sexual temptations that seduced Adam, father of the race, and David, the favored king, into sin. One writer reminded women that they were "all the Daughters of *Eve*, who was the Author of much more evil to mankinde, in seducing her Husband to eat of the forbidden Fruit, [than] *Judas* was in betraying our Saviour . . . ." However, such transgressions could be forgotten, and these two women could be justly honored because each had submitted herself to marriage and the restrictive control of a great patriarch.[99]

Throughout the didactic literature a few female biblical figures who appeared again and again personified both the glorious and the wicked potential of women. Those women meant to be imitated and honored exemplified not some idealistic, unattainable standard that no women could meet, but the true, achievable potential of women who lived up to their womanhood. So, too, the quintessentially evil women served as possibilities, warnings of what would happen should the naturally evil character traits of women overrun the good. For "we must acknowledge that women (in their natural inclinations) are all in extreams, for they that are good are really good indeed, and they that are bad are usually extreamly evill."[100] The authors neither simplified the types nor ignored the ambiguity latent in these women's intentions and behaviors, so that through such images and their interpretations of them, they presented both their hopeful prescriptions for female holiness and their complex deductions concerning women's real nature.

The chastity of Susanna, the loyalty and love of Ruth toward her mother-in-law Naomi, and the loyalty and subservience of Abigail to King David were all praised and, in Ruth's and Abigail's case, rewarded with marriage.

Piety, too, was celebrated, particularly if accompanied by an extraordinary surrender to the will of God, as in the cases of Hannah, Elizabeth, and Anna, all of whom had accepted the blight of barrenness. Paradoxically, God rewarded such submission with children: in Anna's case, sight of the Christ child, and the sons born to Hannah and Elizabeth. Mothering was honored in Mary, Sarah, and Rebecca, acclaimed for tricking Esau out of the blessing of his father Isaac in order to benefit younger son Jacob. As docility and submission were demanded of all women regardless of rank, the writers took particular pleasure in the humility of the Queen of Sheba. Among the most popular biblical women was Queen Esther, delicate and beautiful, courageous and pious. Exploiting her own beauty to achieve her goals, Esther followed her uncle's guidance and exhibited a gratifyingly feminine cunning. Yet she neither led individuals into sin nor insisted upon her own judgment. She came before her husband to defend her people, fainted at his expression of displeasure, and triumphed over her enemy by submitting her own views to her husband's decision.[101] In effect, the glory that was woman could predictably be summarized in two characteristics: pliable acquiescence and extraordinary love and devotion. In his elegy to women, Charles Gerbier devoted a chapter to women's love. They sacrificed themselves for husbands, fathers, sons, and brothers; they died upon hearing of a son's death, or a son's survival. As William Hill explained,

> the Lord hath made choice of your weak Sex, to be instrumental in these particular eminent and remarkable things following.
> 1. As when he was pleased to set forth the excellent grace of *Love*, he compares it far surpassing the love, not of Men but of Women, who are most apt and prone to abound therein.
> 2. Likewise, when he would express matter of Sorrow and Lamentation, he also compares that to Women, thus, *As a Woman mourning for the Husband of her youth*; as if there were no greater mourning.

Joseph Swetnam, on the other hand, focused less on devotion than simple submission, and he took great pleasure in the hope that "a young woman of tender years is flexible and bending, obedient and subject to doe anything, according to the will and pleasure of her husband."[102]

The most revealing feature of this moralistic typology may have been the notable silence about several glorious biblical heroines. Jael and Judith, who seduced and killed enemy generals, and Deborah, the one female judge of Israel, were scarcely mentioned. Jael and Judith both stepped out of their female roles to attack a man, and while both, like Esther, used the feminine wiles of beauty, hospitality, and sex, neither depended upon or even used male assistance. Both women killed their victims themselves. And while Deborah's military campaigns were, in fact, led by a man, Baruch, she alone was prophet and judge of Israel. Gerbier named all three in his discourse as exemplars of courage, but in his praise of the late Queen Elizabeth, he went beyond his colleagues in his witness to women's ability to govern. For most, the bravery of Jael, wisdom of Deborah, and self-sufficiency of Judith threatened the simple dichotomy that defined gender and established place in this era.[103]

In their independence the biblical heroines rather closely resembled the Bible's evil women in their dangerous strength. While the temptations posed by Bathsheba, Solomon's many foreign wives, and Samson's Delilah served as warnings to men, the lust of Potiphar's wife and of Lot's daughters was despicable. Of equal wickedness were the disrespectful Michal, who scolded husband David, and Job's wife, who berated her husband for his acceptance of fate. And if Esther's compliance proved a popular lesson, it was well balanced against the obstinacy of Vashti in her refusal to obey her husband's command. Of course, the arch-villainess of the Bible was the proud Jezebel, idol-worshipper, unrepentant queen. She seduced her husband into her idolatry and took upon herself the prerogatives of his rule, bringing murder and mayhem into the kingdom and ignoble death and destruction onto herself. Just before her death, she had painted her face and dressed her hair and was therefore marked by her own vanity and arrogance when she fell to her death.[104]

The evil of women provided much more material for discussion than did women's goodness. "Then for Wives, Ther's scarce one good of twenty, if I should say Forty, I thinke I should not lye, for one Scoulds, another Powts, one is Lazy, another Sluttish, a third proud, a fourth a downe right Drunkert, a fift a Title-tatle Goshopp, and so from one to a Hundred, from a Hundred to a Thousand, from a Thousand to many Thousands."[105] The female mouth was indeed corrupt, as nagging and gossiping were particularly feminine sins, for "scolding is the manner of Shrewes," and "their tongues vindicate themselves and scold, abuse, and disparage others; their lips utter lies & deceits."[106] Women showed themselves to be fickle, inconstant, and sly. They manipulated and nagged because they were frivolous, greedy, and selfish, and they exploited, sometimes robbed, their husbands in order to satisfy vanity with rich foods, elaborate clothes, and fine jewels. Such vanity

signaled the stubborn pride at the heart of every woman's being, a pride reflected in a wife's obstinacy against her husband.[107]

Some granted that men and women were created in equality.

> [Woman] hath the same prerogative of creation with man: For as he is
> endowed with a free, willing, immortal soul, so is she also; and as Man was
> put into a state of dominion and happinesse, so likewise was Woman.
>   The soul knows no difference of sex; the woman hath the same desires and
> appetites as Man; she is as well an heir unto the grace of life as he is . . .[108]

Most, however, were unwilling to offer such an unqualified endorsement of
female personhood and humanity. Thomas Taylor grants that woman was
made in the image of God and that she had similar qualities of mind and
soul: "she had perspicuity of understanding, she had purity of will, she had
correspondency of holy and chaste affections, both to God and her husband." Still, continues Taylor, "all the parts of Gods image were more cleare in
Adam then in Eve; and the woman was then the weaker vessel, as the Serpent
knew."[109] Similarly, the *Godly Forme of Household Government* acknowledged that women were as reasonable as men, with flexible wits capable of
both good and evil. Moreover, a husband and wife were equal in the chief
aspect of their identities, "that gracious and free benefit wherby they have everlasting life given them." Otherwise, said the authors, they were unequal.[110]

In the end, women were simply weak—morally, intellectually, and emotionally weak. Husbands were advised to "connive and conceale with wisdome
those invincible defects, ignorances, yea though it be uncapablenesse, which
either the frailty of her sex, or the speciall frame of her minde, or perhaps
the inexperience of one untrained in some business, may produce." A wife
should be treated carefully because of her weakness, "as the more britle a
Venice glasse is, the more gingerly we handle it, and the more tender-edged
a knife is, the more charily we use it." One of the angrier authors claimed
that women themselves recognized their own weakness and used it as a
defense when accused of sinful behavior. "Likewise a [woman] gives her
Verdict . . . you know that Women are the weaker Vessells, & men ought to
beare with our infirmities (as we beare them)."[111] And while pious women
would not invoke their inherent sinfulness as a defense of sin, some certainly
did echo this conviction of women's weakness. Elizabeth Jocelin advised her
unborn child to shun vanity and pride in dress, granting that "if a daughter,
I confesse thy taske is harder because thou art weaker, and thy temptations

to this vice greater," while Dorothy Leigh counseled her son to guide his wife with care and gentleness. "Beare with the woman, as with the weaker vessell. Heere God Sheweth that it is her imperfection that honoureth thee, and that it is thy perfection that maketh thee to beare with her."[112]

That women were weak and men strong was one of the facts of life, a natural difference reinforcing the moral imperative. Any man or woman acting otherwise transgressed against the natural order. "For what is more loathed by a discreet man than a woman mannishly qualified? And, what is more yrksome to a loving woman, then a man effeminate?" A man should avoid all uxoriousness, softness, and "nice affection for his wife," while a woman should be wary of "uncomely boldnesse." Men and women may not have always maintained their ideal gender characters; in fact, the rather frequent exhortations to manly strength and feminine meekness indicate irritation at the failure of many to adhere to a rigid gender dichotomy. Crossing these ostensible gender lines could and did bring criticism, scorn, ostracism, and legal punishment. Gataker argued that "a man-kinde woman or a masterly wife is even a monster in nature," and the violation of the natural gender order brought

> disgrace and contempt upon both parties, yea utter ruine oft of the family and of their whole estate. For howsoever women may thinke it an honour to them, yet it is indeede rather a dishonour. A masterly wife is as much despised and derided for taking rule over husband, as he for yeelding it to her, and that not onely among those that be godly and religious, but even among those that be but meere naturall men and women. Yea it is the next way to bring all to wrack.[113]

Surely, many of the accusations leveled against Hutchinson involved her assertive, "masculine" behavior in conducting private religious meetings, challenging ministers, and arguing points of doctrine, while her husband was privately criticized as "a man of a very mild temper and weak parts, and wholly guided by his wife."[114]

Seventeenth-century Puritans believed the weakness of women to be grounded in their physical being, an essentialist argument invoked without apology and ostensibly supported by science. The strength of men was attested by their obviously superior physical strength as well as the conviction that men's vigor lasted longer than women's.[115] The weakening affliction of hysteria, characterized by convulsions, fainting, unusual swellings, fits, melancholia, as well as headaches, rapid heartbeat, congestion, stomach and back pains, had been clearly established as a woman's disease. The cause, however, lay not mainly in the uterus as once thought but in an explosion of animal spirits in the body. Again, refusing to see female reproductive organs as special, faulty, or in any way less than ordinary and natural, physicians identified the true source of hysteria and provided explanations for its preponderance among women. Thomas Willis argued that

> The cause of these Symptoms must not be imputed to the Ascent of the Womb, and to vapours rais'd from the same. . . . But we say that the affect call'd Hysterical, chiefly and primarily is Convulsive, and depends principally on the Brain and *Genus nervosum* being affected, and is produc't wholly by the explosions of the Animal Spirits, as other Convulsive Motions. . . . for the Origine of this, as of many other Convulsive affects sometimes resides in the head, the Womb being wholly without fault: Though sometimes this affect happens through the fault of the Womb, and sometimes through that of other parts.[116]

Thomas Sydenham agreed with this analysis, noting that "women are much more inclined to this Disease than Men," but hastening to add that this was "not because the womb is more Faulty than any other Region of the Body . . ." He also diagnosed the cause as violent dispersal of "Animal Spirits forcing themselves violently upon the Organs," and claimed that such spirits were far more likely to wreak havoc in women.

> Wherefore this disease seizes many more women than Men, because kind nature has bestowed on them a more delicate and fine Habit of Body, having designed them only for an easie Life, and to perform the tender Offices of Love: But she gave to Men robust Bodies that they might be able to delve and manure the Earth, to kill wild Beasts for Food and the like.

Not surprisingly, men who lived "sedentary Lives," studied hard, and did little manual labor, effeminate men, might also be afflicted with hysteric symptoms.[117]

As physicians discussed the symptoms and causes of hysteria, they described a class of persons subject to the overwhelming influence and vagaries of bodily fluids and humors. The specter of menstrual blood continued to influence such analyses, and much weakness and sickness, including

smallpox and childbed fever, was attributed to its pollutions.[118] Their explanation of menstruation implied that this process provided women with a
means to expel turgid, fermented humors from the body, necessary because
women's bodies overflowed with putrifying fluids without any sure means
of relief. Unfortunately, the very character of woman showed that menses itself was less than adequate. Female emotionalism and passion demonstrated
this saturation, for emotions rose out of the coursing of fluids throughout
the body. The picture develops of femininity as cool, wet, and yielding, while
masculinity was dry, hot, and hard.[119]

This anatomical construction of gender difference seems bound up in
humor theory: women were frequently overwhelmed by humors because
their bodies provided little means of escape for excess fluids, and, consequently, women became emotional, enthusiastic, and ill. The presence
of such excess fluid weakened not only women's constitutions, but also
their characters, for within the damp swampy atmosphere of their bodies,
reason, the mind, and the soul were often unable to exert control over
feelings and urges. Why humors were more trapped in women than men
was not explained, merely observed, and this scientific fact of female biology
replaced the mysteries of the reproductive organs as the determinative, essential difference between the genders. Anatomists in fact described ovaries
and testicles as mirror images of each other, performing the very same function, creation of reproductive seed, in the very same way. Men and women
may have fulfilled different biological functions in the natural process of reproduction in that women carried the fetus from conception to birth and
nursed the newborn, but these functions, and the anatomy that supported
them, were not the foundation of masculinity and femininity. Instead, men
and women thought and behaved differently because of the chemical composition of their bodies; one might say that women were simply spongy men.

In their focus upon the movement of humors and their rejection of the
primacy of the reproductive organs as determining basic gender difference, it may appear that clerics and scientists rejected sexuality as the definitive factor. Such an interpretation, however, misreads reproduction as
sexuality, a misunderstanding that the Elizabethans had certainly avoided.
In grounding their definitions of masculinity and femininity within the
basic empirical evidence of human physiology, sexuality moved from the
periphery to the center of their definitions. Writers had replaced the fruits
of heterosexual relations with the evidence gleaned from the experience itself. In addition to observed differences in men's and women's musculature,

for example, the softness of women's breasts compared to the sturdiness of men's chests, ordinary sexual relations between men and women would have reinforced, if not inspired, these physiological conclusions. Surely the unyielding hardness of the erect penis was matched against the wet pliability of the vagina.

By positing the sexual relation itself as the ideological center of perceived gender difference, assumptions about and prescriptions for men and women become more comprehensible. Within the narrow boundaries of acceptable, "natural" sexual intercourse, man was active but reasonable; woman passive but passionate. Woman could only tempt; she could not perform; yet the temptations might be strong enough to overwhelm male reason. And while it would be wrong to say that active men never sexually attacked women without provocation, most male writers believed and argued that passionate women, like Eve, were the enticing initiators of most sexual exchanges. With passions growing out of the movement of fluids and spirits in the body, and women's bodies containing a superfluity of such humors, it is not surprising that men concluded that the wetness of women rendered them not only weak but passionate, seductive, and oversexed beings constantly seeking relief in men's beds.

Every aspect of her physical appearance revealed woman's corrupt, sexual nature. Her beauty, described by one author as "the Image of the Creator, and the Rhetorick of heaven," became for others testimony of her carnality. Young men were warned of marrying for ephemeral beauty; beauty would fade, since "diseases blast it, age devoures it, discontent doth wither it." Yet until that time, the beautiful woman would have greater acquaintance among society and was more likely to stray. "The golden tresses of their amorous hair . . . doth manifestly express the true performance of their dutie to their great Lord and master Lucifer," their rolling eyes ensnared, and their lips uttered lies and deceptions. "Their neck and breasts are left bare unto the open view of the world to signifie that nature hath fairly acted her part without, although their remain no grace within." Arms and hands were ready to assist the rest of the body, and legs and feet carried women to vanity. "Their Thighs are the ascent unto this frail fabrick of corruption . . . so that from the crown of the head to the sole of the foot there is not a good member, no not one."[120] Culpeper found that even the location of a woman's vagina testified to the corruption of woman's sexuality: "the neck of the womb is seated between the passage of Urin and the right Gut, to shew fond man what little reason he hath to be proud and domineer, being conceived between the places ordained to cast out excrements, the very sinks of the body, and in such a manner that his Mother was ashamed to tell him how."[121]

Every writer extolling the glory of the chaste woman was matched by another complaining, or sometimes simply describing, just how rare a chaste woman was. Frankly, women were generally "sluttish," and, as one such woman was quoted, "the uprightest man falls Seven times a DAY, Then we Woman may very well fall Fourteene times a Night." The angry Swetnam developed this theme further, explicitly tying sexuality to beauty.

> if a womans face glisten, and her gesture pierce the Marbel wall; or if her tongue be so smooth as Oyle, and so soft as silke, and her words so sweet as Honey . . . or if her personage have stolne away all that nature can afford, and shee be deckt up in gorgious apparell: then a thousand to one but she will love to walke where she may get acquaintance, and acquaintance bringeth familiaritie and familiaritie sitteth all follies abroad; and twenty to one, that if a woman love gadding, but that she will pawne her honesty to please her fantasie.

Even the gentler clerics found no escaping or hiding the reality of women's lustful character. The best behaved of woman could be, and probably was, harboring dangerous, lascivious inclinations. "For you see many women, which although sometimes they be farre from the crime of adultery, not onely in act, but also in consent; notwithstanding by reason of their gesture and behaviour, they are not free from all markes and notes of immodestie."[122]

The softly pornographic literature of the era thoroughly developed women's sexual charms and appetites. In the early years of the English civil wars, there appeared several pamphlets claiming to express the grievances of women. *The Virgins Complaint*, for example, decried "the losse of their Sweet-hearts, by these present Wars, And their owne long solitude and keeping their Virginities against their wills," while a *Widows Lamentation* regretted not only the "the Absence of their deare Children" and "Divers of their Deaths in these fatall Civill Warres," but also the absence of their "Suitors."[123] The "virgins" complained that they were now left with only the old men, "cold in their constitutions and performance." And in a singular testimony to women's sexual insatiability, they complained that

> surely this is a lamentable matter, when men shall be so scarce, that women must be confined to their husbands, and glad they can get them too; and

when before one woman, (by report) would have served twenty men, one man must be faine to serve twenty women, and yet all they can do not suficient to content us maids . . .[124]

A more explicit series was published in order to shut down brothels and root out prostitutes; at least that was the somewhat suspect, but assertively proclaimed intention. In fact, the anonymous author of *The Wandering Whore* pamphlets provided titillating, graphic descriptions of prostitutes' wide-ranging efforts to satisfy their customers. Such profligacy was here associated with disease and crime, with the frequent refrain warning un-suspecting men that while "their left hand [is] in his Cod-piece, the right hand [is] in his Pocket." Men in these descriptions appeared primarily as the pawns, cuckolds, and seduced victims of vicious creatures. One prostitute paid a portion of her earnings to her husband for his sufferance. Granting that economics drove women to prostitution, the author argued that "pov-erty, which together with idlenes, makes so many whores and dishonest women amongst us." Busy women were good women, but women with nothing to do would immediately succumb to their base natures. While most of these women were identified as members of the laboring classes, the au-thor moved beyond class to attack all women in his notice of a man soliciting a virgin, "a pure untoucht Maiden-head, for I am even surfeited with Citizen's wives, who are eager after S——."[125]

Women did not easily accept such judgments. Following the publica-tion of Swetnam's *Arraignment* (and each edition thereafter), female voices rose to defend women's honor. "Ester Sowerman" argued that women were known to be superior to men, as demonstrated by the fact that women's faults were always more scandalously remarked. A drunken man was merely drunk; a promiscuous young man was a bit wild. A drunken woman, however, was a social disgrace, and an erring young woman was a ruined whore. Women did not tempt men; men sought women. "As *Eve* did not offend without the temptation of a Serpent; so women doe seldome offend, but it is by provocation by [*sic*] of men." "Men," reminded this writer, "are the Serpents."[126] In a later response, "Mary Tattle-well" and "Joan Hit-him-home" reiterated these points while emphasizing the lasciviousness and vi-olence of men. "Nay many times when you [men] are denied the game, you have offered Fees; and by rape to hazard the Gallowes." Women, on the other hand, had very little interest in sex aside from procreation, and they mar-ried only for children. "Thus good and modest Women have been content to have none, or one man (at the most) all their whole life time, but men have bin so addicted to incontinency, that no bounds of Law or reason could restraine them."[127] These comments echoed in the writings of the famously pious Dorothy Leigh.

> Man sayd once, *The woman which thou gavest mee*, beguiled me, and I *did eate*. But wee women may now say, that men lye in waite every where to deceive us, as the Elders did to deceive *Susanna*. Wherefore let us bee, as she was, watchfull, and wary, keeping company with maides. Once *Judas* betrayed his Master with a Kisse, & repented it: but now men, like *Judas*, betray their Mistresses with a kisse &, repent it not: but laugh and rejoyce, that they have brought sinne and shame to her that trusted them.[128]

An extremely angry screed, all the more remarkable in that she wrote these passages to guide her children, all sons.

The experiences of New England women reflected the ambiguity surrounding women's sexuality, responsibility, and power. Initially, for the minor sexual offense of fornication before marriage, Massachusetts tended to forgive women if they married the child's father. Yet within fifteen years of settlement, women came to dominate the lists of sexual miscreants, reflecting men's construction of sexuality as grounded within the female.[129] Massachusetts law recognized the crime of rape as well as a range of male sexual offenses, and court records do reveal trials and convictions. Yet when a woman began such a process, claiming that an attack had occurred, she placed her own reputation in jeopardy. In a society where some believed that "there never comes Conception upon Rapes," the very fact that a woman was pregnant was possible evidence of licentiousness.[130] Had a woman been unwilling, had she not been provocative or sexually available, she would have been protected. When Henry Greenland attacked young Mary Rolfe, whose husband was away at sea, she feared accusing him because he was a creditable gentleman while she was merely a woman. A similar lament was heard from Jane Bond, who said she dared not reveal that Robert Collins had raped her. Both of these women were eventually vindicated; this vindication came largely through the intervention of other women who respected the victims, believed their stories, and were outraged by the men's conduct. Other women were not so fortunate, and if a woman told her story "incorrectly," or had already given cause for doubt by her amiability or merriness, she might well find herself whipped for her sluttish carriage.[131]

Within the political, social, and ideological boundaries of the world of sexuality, the ambivalence in the way the idea of woman was constructed and the ambiguity of woman's actual status came to the fore. Adultery was defined according to the status of the female transgressor: if she was married, she and her illicit lover committed adultery; if she was not, regardless of the man's marital status, they were guilty of simple fornication. Grounded in a husband's property rights to his wife's body, adultery law emphasized woman's dependence, subservient status, and legal nonexistence. In recognizing that women were sometimes physically forced into adultery or fornication, rape law supposedly defended them, upholding society's need to provide some protection for its weaker members. In dealing with sexual infractions, however, the courts avoided a charge of rape if at all possible, since a conviction would result in the execution of the male perpetrator. Lesser charges were often filed, and women were as likely as men, perhaps more likely, to bear the guilt and, consequently, the punishment. While the ostensible purpose of these laws was the protection of female chastity, the underlying goal, often successfully achieved, was the punishment of female "licentiousness": the control of women whose sexuality was so powerful that it overwhelmed both themselves and men. In other words, although the statute expressed a protective esteem of women, the enforcement of the law spoke of men's fears of being destroyed through falling victim to the sexual powers of women. Within this fearful, increasingly controlled political environment, the only moments of actualized female power occurred, again, in the community of women, when women stood together, defended each other, and forced the male establishment to live up to the paternalism of its criminal codes regarding sexual behavior.

Of course, clergymen and magistrates believed that they were maintaining the social and political order, fulfilling women's needs and restricting their behaviors in light of contemporary knowledge about the female character. From the literature, medical, theological, and humorous, the female character emerged as sexual, overly emotional, and intellectually weak. A woman was capable of obstinacy toward her father and her husband, but she lacked the strength of will necessary to exercise true virtue. Dependent, childlike, and dangerously innocent, she was easily deluded and led astray. Obviously in urgent need of protection, woman was yet troublesome to man in her passions and her potential willfulness. These thinkers emphasized that woman's sexuality grew out of her biology, reflecting weakness, silliness, and hypocrisy as well as presenting a danger for man as seductress.

The ideal role for woman was that of wife and helpmeet, subject to a strong husband who would control his wife's behavior out of his love for her. A wife's submission to her husband was reinforced by her economic dependence as well as a political system that ignored female voices and a legal system that denied a married woman existence before the law. Protected and controlled, woman supposedly benefited economically, socially, and spiritually from the institution of marriage. If she found the protection abusive and the control tyranny, the brutality of her spouse, though heartily lamented and condemned, did not diminish her duty to him.

Yet while a woman's status and rights were subsumed under her husband's person, her labor was economically crucial to the running of the household. The exclusively female role of mother/reproducer was also recognized as central to the maintenance and prosperity of society. That the role of housewife overlapped the role of reproducer/healer was apparent in housewifery manuals and cookery books, where medical recipes easily coexisted with cheese-making and butchering instructions. Undergirding woman's domestic prowess was an acknowledgment that in bearing children she exhibited significant natural power, and that midwives demonstrated even greater abilities. The seventeenth century saw the beginnings of challenges to women's control over birthing––male midwives, licensing battles, and physician interference––but at this point men had made little progress with respect to entering the birthing chamber. The primary means through which these female powers were minimized and controlled was the normalization of heterosexual sexual relations and procreation. The Protestant/Calvinist condemnation of the churching of women denied the mysterious nature of female reproductive power. So, too, toppling celibacy off its moral pedestal gave expression to a reformation faith that men's spiritual power was no longer at risk from women, a vision more hopeful but less influential than the demystification of reproduction. The society continued its sexualization of woman. Woman's essential biology no longer involved reproduction, a frightening but glorious power that had to be revered; it was now entirely about sexuality, still frightening, but a disgusting, dangerous seductive power that had to be controlled—through heterosexual marriage.

Turn-of-the-century Puritan society reflected the contradictions and enigmas of a transitional world. Transforming English faith and religiosity as they reconstructed their understanding of reformation, transforming English politics in their drive for reform, Puritan activism also unsettled, perhaps inadvertently, basic social institutions and gender hierarchies that grounded English society. Many religious and political radicals initially missed the social implications of their systemic challenges, but most rallied to a new, "reformed" vision of woman that claimed to elevate her status through a glorification of marriage, yet regretfully required her subservience as necessary to her prosperity and salvation. Writers continued to compartmentalize and commodify woman within the domestic sphere. Woman was valued for her labor (as husband's housekeeper), her sexuality (as husband's sexual relief), and her reproductive health (as breeder of husband's children).

Although women could exercise some authority within their domestic sphere, when a woman grew too powerful, unequivocal and uncomplicated prescriptions were available. Ideological absolutes defining gender differentiation and an inflexible legal system of gender hierarchy inspired and supported patriarch John Winthrop and the clergy of New England, and justified the political and social boundaries that would establish order in the nascent colony. They buttressed the male leadership when faced with the challenges posed by Anne Hutchinson. Yet the puzzle remains. If everyone agreed that woman was to be subsumed under man, and that in all ways woman was inferior to man, how was it possible for Hutchinson to gather such a large coterie of followers? The Hutchinsonian crisis stands as a stark reminder of the blurred lines of gender demarcation that characterized this transitional society. Had she merely challenged the status quo, there would have been no crisis. Despite Dudley's conclusions, Hutchinson's rising influence and power did not bring social and political chaos; they reflected a confusion that had already infiltrated English society and threatened (or promised, depending upon the point of view) a social revolution. The Hutchinsonian story began not with Puritan patriarchy per se, but with the conflict inherent within a culture that considered women an inferior class of humanity and yet had space for a prophesying female.

4

Sectarian Mysticism and
Spiritual Power

When historians tell the tale of Anne Hutchinson in Massachusetts Bay, they seem to begin in the middle of the story. Many have noted that she was born of an outspoken clerical father, a Cambridge graduate, who if he hadn't explicitly identified with the Puritan cause had certainly exhibited Puritan sympathies in his writings and behavior. They have also recorded that although she lived briefly in London, she was raised and nurtured in Lincolnshire, a center of Puritan activism, and returned there with her new merchant husband upon their marriage in 1612. There she lived for twenty-two years unremarkably, that is, unnoticed by church or civil courts. According to her own account, she participated in the religious life of the countryside and, like so many devoted Christians, sought after exceptional clerical guidance. Like many Lincoln Puritans, she found her mentor in John Cotton and sometimes traveled as much as twenty miles to attend his services. When Cotton left Lincolnshire for the new colony, Hutchinson and her family joined the throng that followed him across the ocean. She arrived in Massachusetts one year after Cotton had landed, settled in Boston, and joined the Boston church.

The Boston church records reveal that while William Hutchinson was accepted into membership upon presentation, his wife's application was challenged by several individuals, notably Zechariah Symmes, who had traveled with her from England. This official hesitation lasted scarcely two weeks, however, and having satisfied all questioners, she too was accepted into the church. Thomas Dudley would claim that the problems started immediately upon her arrival in 1634, but aside from this brief challenge to her application for church membership, there is no record of any trouble. Historians know almost nothing about her New England career until October 1636, when a conference was called among ministers to establish some theological consensus. At first glance, this conference appeared to involve John Cotton's disagreement with his clerical colleagues, and this was indeed an issue.

However, the fact that Hutchinson was present reveals that this was an effort to deal with the preaching of a laywoman and to discover whether Cotton was the source of her objectionable opinions.

From this point onward Hutchinson's history has been told and retold; a significant body of public and private documents have revealed the theological, congregational, and political issues involved. Yet what is fascinating is that when Hutchinson first emerged in the public record, even in retrospective accounts, she was already holding private weekly meetings with sixty to eighty persons present. During her examination before the General Court, Winthrop initially charged Hutchinson with holding those meetings, as if their very existence were the problem. The meetings did not begin only in the summer or autumn of 1636, however, but some unspecified time before. By the time they were discussed as a problem, their attendance had grown exponentially. Apparently, Hutchinson invited women to her house, the number of such invitations offered and accepted expanded and multiplied, and she even began holding a separate meeting that included men as well as women; yet she heard no public outcry or criticism. In fact, there is no evidence for such meetings until some critical commentary supposedly heard at her home was repeated outside the meeting, undermining the authority and reputations of the ministers of the colony.

In other words, in the midst of this patriarchal society, buttressed by law and theology, a godly woman actively gathered other women, and soon men, to meetings at her home (a home, incidentally, directly across from Winthrop's own house). Among those who attended were two elders and three deacons of the Boston congregation, at least nine selectmen of Boston, five deputies representing Boston in the General Court, magistrate William Coddington, and Governor Henry Vane.[1] John Winthrop claimed that "the whole Church of *Boston* (some few excepted) were become her new converts, and infected with her opinions . . ."[2] Even in the midst of delivering his admonition against her after the first segment of her church trial, John Cotton noted that Hutchinson's meetings had greatly benefited the women of the community. "I doubt not but some of you [congregational sisters] have allsoe receaved much good from the Conference of this our Sister and by your Converse with her: and from her it may be you have reaceved [*sic*] helpes in your spirituall Estates . . ."[3] With twenty-first-century hindsight, whether informed by antipathy or sympathy for Winthrop, it is easy to see why Hutchinson was silenced. Her early months of tolerated speech, however, present far more interesting questions. What was her appeal? From whence came her authority? More to the point, when this woman began to speak, gathered a following, and demonstrated spiritual power, why was she not immediately silenced? Was it simply that "the great respect she had at first in the hearts of all, and the profitable and sober carriage of matters, for a time, made this her practise lesse suspected by the godly Magistrates, and Elders of the Church there, so that it was winked at"?[4]

The resolution of this question of gender politics lies, again, in the nature of Puritanism itself: its social and cultural inheritance and its intensely religious quality. If the outpouring of domestic manuals was any indicator, both religious and secular leaders were deeply concerned with familial relations, including those of husbands and wives, fathers and daughters, and mothers and sons. As writers constructed a rigidly patriarchal system of gender relations, they also mapped out their own model of female virtue, determined, in part, by their particular comprehension of women's weaknesses as well as their desire and need to sustain male authority from the household outward. Predictably, New England moralists looked to the Bible to provide all the materials necessary to their argument. They praised Bathsheba's housekeeping, Susannah's chastity, Esther's feminine wiles, and Mary's devoted submission; they condemned with equal fervor Michal's disrespect and Jezebel's arrogance and conceit. They ignored the less traditionally feminine biblical women such as Judith and Jael, and although the rigors of frontier warfare at the end of the seventeenth century would bring New England ministers to honor one English woman for fighting the enemy, as did Jael, for the most part the heroics of such courageous, self-sufficient women remained uncelebrated.[5]

There was yet one other group of biblical women whose names and example had garnered only limited attention from theologians. Throughout the book of Acts and Paul's epistles, female preachers and community leaders are identified and honored. In Romans alone, Paul commends, among his disciples, Phebe, Priscilla, Junia, Julias, Nereas's sister, Rufus's mother, "Tryphena and Tryphose, which *women* labour in the Lord . . . [and] Persis, which *woman* hathe laboured muche in the Lord."[6] Hutchinson herself invoked such figures in her defense. She referred to Titus's statement that older women should instruct the younger, and at one point she cited Priscilla's and her husband Aquila's instruction of Apollo as a precedent allowing for a woman to instruct a man. The magistrates denied the validity of her examples as scriptural rules governing her situation, leading Hutchinson to ask, "Must I shew my name written therein?" In those terse exchanges, Winthrop never denied the texts, only Hutchinson's interpretation. His refusal to argue the point at any length, ordering an end to her meetings with the assertion, "We are your judges, and not you ours and we must compel you to it," reflected the weakness of his position.[7] While Puritan men may have redefined these gospel women and reinterpreted their stories, they did not deny that at one time some women had exercised extraordinary spiritual authority. "The gifts of miracles and tongues were common to many as well as the gift of Prophecy."[8]

Despite efforts to relegate prophesying women to the miraculous years of the early Christian church, the years during which God actively revealed his scriptural word, Puritans were deeply interested in the strength of such seemingly ordinary women and men. They searched out the source of their *charis*, their spiritual authority, and they marveled at the power of their speech. Fascinated with this powerful spirituality, Puritan religionists found themselves turning toward these disturbing, less readily comprehensible biblical lessons, which appeared to contradict simpler ones about hierarchy and order. In such stories Puritans found promise of the ability of ordinary persons like themselves to see God, to reach God, and they reveled in the hope of that astonishing moment when God would touch them in return.

This conviction in the mystical ability of the individual soul to touch God stood at the center of Puritans' strength: their self-confidence and their willingness to stand against and resist the powers of a corrupt church and a cunning, degenerate monarch. Their conviction of their ability to reach God and their achievement of communion with the divine provided a sense of spiritual superiority that supported the overthrow of governments and the building of colonies. Yet this conviction was also the source of ideological confusion in the face of the New Englanders' struggle to create the perfect patriarchal community. Puritan leaders had to grant, foster, but harness the power women realized through their highly valued labor as well as their reproductive ability, for they believed that women—physically, intellectually, and emotionally inferior to men—had to be controlled for the good of the community as well as of the women themselves. However, in this essentially religious culture, the community's leadership confronted and necessarily embraced the sacred potential of all individuals, women as well as men, to discover God and the joy of election.

Within Puritan religiosity was embedded this source of power for the powerless. The Hutchinsonian crisis arose at the intersection of English patriarchy and Puritan religiosity, a conflict between the spiritual authority of individuals and the demands of a godly social order. On the one side, theology and devotional practice applied and reinforced patriarchal goals and assumptions within and through religious ideas and institutions. Men, with their superior intellect and strength of will, far surpassed women in their ability to pursue godliness. In support of the effort to entrench men's control of religious practice, theologians explored the nature of the female soul, a debate that reflected beliefs about the female character and personality as the natural outgrowth of woman's biology. Many ministers and magistrates had concluded that women were not merely inferior to men, but were, in essence, evil, or at least burdened with a congenital inclination toward evil; such propensities even led some to become witches. Despite these intellectual efforts, and evidence of widespread female witchcraft, believers found themselves and their arguments confronted by the spiritual foundations of Puritan religiosity. They recognized that within these spiritual connections with God lay sources of charismatic power not only for the patriarchs, but also for Anne Hutchinson and her followers, male and female, those very inferiors that patriarchs had hoped to control.[9]

Among the challenges brought by reformation was a revolt against the privileges of priests and bishops, privileges grounded in the false, according to Protestants, cornerstones of spiritual precedence and sacred class. Within Roman Catholic theology, priests held a special, sacred status as individuals whose ordination and priestly office placed them above the ordinary believer and closer to God. When he celebrated mass, granted absolution, performed a marriage, or anointed the dying, the priest stood as a mediator between God and believer, perhaps the channel through which prayers could be heard, but certainly the voice of God to the congregation and the instrument through which God's grace and blessing flowed. Bishops, with the sole power to perform the sacrament of priestly ordination, held even loftier positions as the authorities over priests, mediating between God and humanity on a grander scale.

The medieval Catholic clergy had consolidated its power and authority in part through its domination of learning. The Bible, the writings of the church fathers, even many of the arts lay within the domain of priests, bishops, and members of religious orders, though not all priests were, by any means, educated. By the fifteenth century, however, as learning had increased among the upper classes, priestly status became focused in the almost magically constructed powers associated with their sacramental functions. The clergy remained the only ones permitted to read the Bible and interpret Christian faith for others (in fact, the pope had listed the Bible on the index of literature forbidden to the laity). But it was the sacred power to forgive sins and consecrate bread and wine that continued to set the priest apart as mediator of human souls.

Sixteenth-century Protestant reformers denied that the priest held any special sacred status by virtue of his ordination. Citing the Bible as their authority, they agreed that some individuals might be specially called to preach and pastor individual believers, to lead congregations, to assist the poor, all offices that they found named and described in New Testament texts. Reformers also granted that some officers were set apart to those offices through ordination. Although they disagreed as to the qualifications for each office, which offices required ordination, and who had the authority to ordain, most reformers acknowledged an ordained clerical officer, pastor, whose duties included preaching, catechizing, baptizing, and leading the congregation in communion celebrations. That some men were called to the pastorate—the ministry—did not, however, relieve laypersons from their spiritual responsibilities to educate themselves, to pray, to study, and to follow Christ. In their understanding of the believer's spiritual quest, reformers posited a direct relationship between God and the soul. God offered grace, the soul was transformed, and salvation was realized. Among reformed congregations, a clergyman might have assisted individuals on their spiritual quest through teaching, counseling, and exhortation, but he could not intervene with God on the soul's behalf. In the end, each person was his or her own priest, requiring no magical, mediating force.

Proclaiming "the priesthood of all believers," reformers used both positive and negative arguments to buttress their rejection of an especially holy religious class. They attacked the ignorance and immorality of many priests, asserting that most were not fit for such superior regard. Beyond their belief that the esteem bestowed upon celibacy was, at best, misguided or, from another perspective, a wickedly arrogant denial of God's gifts of love and children to humanity and a rejection of the divine command to procreate, many reformers also noted that celibacy did not always equal chastity, and that some priests and bishops hypocritically maintained sexual relations with women. Added to this was a conviction of the general corruption of the church, along with what was perceived as the unearned and undeserved wealth of bishops and religious orders. That some church property holders were exploitative landholders underlined the corruption of a system that conflated spiritual worth with material value.[10]

Puritan reformers were also unimpressed with the educational achievements of the Catholic clergy, education that supposedly set them apart as the only appropriate readers and interpreters of scripture, tradition, and theology. On the individual level, some priests had little education beyond a rote knowledge of the Latin mass and were unfit for any teaching office. Moreover, the church's insistence upon Latin as the language of religious services, scripture, and theological discourse doomed all but the clergy and a very few highly educated men to learn about God, sin, and salvation through an intermediary whose primary intellectual qualification was the ability to read Latin (and even this was suspect). If scripture and other devotional writings were available in the vernacular, believers and seekers, as sophisticated as most priests, could read for themselves. The idea that the rite of ordination elevated the office, and therefore its holder, to a superior sacred status reformers found superstitious and absurd. While ordination was the mark of a call to an important office of spiritual trust, the guidance of souls, it could not alter the character of the individual officeholder nor guarantee him special access to the divine.

Reformers not only attacked the abstract theory of an elite, priestly class along with the occupants of that class, they also actively supported the idea that all believers could interpret scripture for themselves, pray directly to God, and struggle with their own souls on the pathway to salvation. All persons were held to high moral standards of chastity, justice, honor, industriousness, and all were equally likely to fail. Men of rank or office might be held accountable for the work, life, and faith of others as well as themselves, but the fact remained that regardless of class or education all people, descendants of Adam, were born in sin and constantly falling into temptation through inevitable human weakness. Yet despite their conviction of human depravity, these Christians embraced an optimistic faith in the ability of all individuals to understand scripture and grasp basic theological truths.

Like all Protestants, Puritans called for the translation of scripture into the vernacular and urged all believers toward literacy as a necessary condition for following their pathway to God. They knew that the Bible, as the word of God, was a difficult text, and they believed that most laypersons, lacking formal education, were unable to grasp without (or even with!) assistance many abstruse points of theology. Nonetheless, with the guidance of a highly educated ministry, reformers argued, all were able to approach the unknowable. In addition to their faith in ordinary human reason, many reformers, and certainly Puritans, discovered in scripture ample evidence that God engaged the individual soul directly. God may have been a God of majesty and power, but through grace and the Holy Spirit he was also accessible to the least of his children. For the Puritans, therefore, an individual did not need a priest; he stood as his own priest. Every person was able to interpret God's word as revealed in the Bible, and each was spiritually capable of forming a relationship with God independently, that is, without mediation.

Although Puritans expressed extensively divergent opinions on a wide range of theological and polity issues, there were two ideological convictions shared in common by these English dissenters, principles that reinforced their commitment to the priesthood of all believers. The first was the emphasis placed upon learning. In part a reaction against both Roman Catholicism and the Church of England, this focus on learning questioned the capabilities of priests and argued for the opening of orders along lines of merit, not class, transforming the ministry from a sacred stratum to a respectable profession. Additionally, reformers encouraged literacy and learning among the laity, perceiving individual believers as thinking Christians responsible for their own knowledge and behavior. The second commonality was the Puritans' certainty that each person realized a direct, personal, soteriological relationship with God. This relationship would be reflected in the conversion experience expected of every believer, and taken much further by some. It provided a mystical counterpoint to the emphasis upon learning, and stood, I would argue, as the more important common thread tying Puritan dissenters together.[11]

For many Puritans, particularly in New England, the focus upon learning joined with a common understanding of the conversion experience to fulfill the need of faithful individuals to control their own spiritual destinies, or at least to provide some direction to their spiritual careers. Coming to religious maturity in a theological climate characterized by election and, by extension, predestination, many reformed believers found themselves anxiously traversing a dangerous spiritual landscape. Calvinists risked fatalism and depression, or, alternatively, arrogance and hedonism. The problem lay in an understanding of sin, damnation, and salvation grounded in the total depravity of humanity and the omnipotence and omniscience of God. "All the works and doings of God are wonderful, but none more awful than His great work of election and reprobation . . . [God] will not be tied to time nor place, nor yet to persons, but takes and chooses, when and where and whom he pleases. . . ."[12] The human soul, naturally depraved, could achieve salvation only through faith made possible by divine grace. God offered this grace only to a few whom he chose for arbitrary, unpredictable reasons. Those elected had been predestined for salvation (and the rest of humanity for damnation) from the beginning of time. If only a small number of persons could count themselves among the elect, and if the membership of the elect had been predetermined, then why should anyone attempt holiness? Upon what grounds could a pastor encourage scriptural study and holy behavior if one's spiritual fate was predetermined? In a world that had so recently looked toward the afterlife to counterbalance the unfairness and suffering on earth, what encouragement could there be when salvation rewarded the elect and eluded others despite their actions, whether benevolent or sinful? Physical force and earthly penalties to one side, Puritan governors also needed ideological means to convince the citizenry to control their behavior.

Of course, the truly elect did not require rewards for godly behavior; buoyed by their own gracious states, they moved naturally toward goodness. Although Puritan believers had no doubts that a soul was "justified," or saved, by faith and not works, and although they knew that such faith was possible only through the intervention of God's grace, they were also certain that once justified, a believer was sanctified. Sanctification meant the transformation of behavior, manner, and attitudes. Hitherto a slave to sin and hypocrisy, the saved soul engaged in the pursuit of perfection in order to glorify God.[13] By preaching about sanctification, ministers could refocus their hearers upon the visible fruits of the Spirit, reinforcing individual and community commitment to holiness and strengthening the government's efforts to keep the federal covenant with God. Sanctification, like justification, was understood to be in the hands of God, but because it was expressed in visible behavior, sermons on sanctification might have given believers some sense of controlling their destiny. The language of sanctification was language of action. "For in every act of Sanctification we are but turning from sin and from our selves, and returning to the Lord."[14]

For those who were anxious about their election, sanctification could serve as reassuring evidence of salvation. "Hence a mans primitive consolation may arise from his Sanctification, supposing it to be such as accompanieth Salvation." Ideally, sanctification was accompanied by a conviction of one's justification, but many theologians argued that even when faith was weak, sanctification still stood as evidence to be trusted.

... suppose a man savingly sanctified, we thus conceive,

(1) That when Justification is hid from the eye, Sanctification and faith are there in the heart and oftimes effectually working. ... (2) That when

Sanctification is working it may be seen; because others may see . . . (3) That when God hides his face most, there is oft in a justified soul . . . very close and humble walking before the Lord.[15]

This position was not accepted by all. Cotton argued that when sanctification became the primary, or even the sole, evidence of justification, believers were building their salvation upon works. "If my Justification lyeth prostrate (that is, altogether dark and hidden from me) I cannot prove my selfe in a state of Grace by my Sanctification. For while I cannot beleeve that my Person is accepted in Justification, I cannot beleeve that my Works are accepted of God, as any true Sanctification." Accepting sanctification as adequate evidence, Cotton continued, would encourage believers to do good works in order to reassure themselves, and this would be a covenant of works.[16] Peter Bulkeley claimed otherwise: "The same covenant of grace which promiseth justification promiseth sanctification also, and so to evidence one of these by the other, is noe turning aside to another covenant, but an evidencing of one parte of the covenant of grace by another . . ."[17] Bulkeley and most of his New England colleagues found sanctification a reliable index of justification, even if unaccompanied by the immediate witness of faith; Cotton considered such reliance suspect.

Had the clerical majority in Massachusetts been content with this basic premise of sanctification as an adequate pointer toward justification, their disagreements with Cotton, a peace-loving divine, might have been acceptable, even reconcilable. However, many insisted that sanctification was crucial to discerning an individual's gracious state. John Cotton may have believed that the "Testimony of the Spirit [it self] is so cleare, as that it may witnesse immediately," but others needed to see sanctification to ratify such testimony. In fact, saints were not just encouraged to follow pathways of righteousness, they were required to do so: "the covenant of grace requires works not as a part of our righteousness, but that thereby we should glorifie God, and manifest it that we are made righteous by Christ." Cotton believed that without the witness of the Spirit the evidence of sanctification was suspect; his colleagues demanded godly behavior to buttress any claim of justifying faith. "And yet where faith is discerned it will give little evidence in sad houres, for it will be suspected to be but a dead faith, unless the presence of Sanctification be seen with it; and then it may give stronger evidence."[18]

Cotton feared that such an emphasis would inspire simpler, unsophisticated believers to think that they could somehow bring about their own

salvation through holiness, and he warned his colleagues of excessive dependence upon "works." Nevertheless, he did grant the presence of holiness
in most saints, and he acknowledged the potential import of sanctification.
"If this [true Christian] Sanctification be evidently discerned, it is a true evidence of Justification, a Posteriori; as Justification is likewise a true Evidence
of Sanctification, a Priori."[19] Neither spiritual process was independent of
the other, but the order of experiences was plain. The New England clergy
generally agreed that justification preceded sanctification, although signs of
sanctification were sometimes visible before a person's justification was apparent. All agreed that while a striving Christian might be encouraged by
personal holiness, no one could be certain of election on this basis alone. The
worst hypocrites could read scripture, follow the law, and model their behavior after a gospel example. For this reason, Puritans looked toward the additional, some would say superior, evidence of the witness of the Spirit.

Cotton may have emphasized this witness more than other clerics, but
all acknowledged the testimony of gracious workings in the soul, an intense
conversion experience that transformed mind and will. This conversion was
not a momentary event, but an exhaustive, never-ending process recognized
by all believers, from the most highly educated theologian to the least lay
congregant. The nature of this experiential conversion was discussed and
debated, chronicled in diaries, and related in church testimonies with such
monotonous consistency that scholars have long been able to reconstruct
its morphology in minute detail. Essentially, elect saints traversed three
dimensions in their spiritual careers, with each dimension incorporating two
or more developmental stages. In the early stages, the struggling soul, morti-
fied by his or her own sins, was terrified by the specter of eternal punishment
that awaited, grew desperate in the knowledge that the penalty was deserved,
and became humiliated by the inability to follow God's law. During the
middle, climactic, stage the saint, finally acknowledging complete dependence upon God, opened the self up to divine grace, came to hope in Christ's
atonement, and realized the assurance of salvation. In the final phase, the
saint's thoughts and actions were sanctified, and while ongoing doubts would
haunt the believer, if she or he were truly saved, divine grace would continue
to appear and reassure.[20]

Obviously, the question of evidence of election was not merely an abstract
theological exercise. Many believers sought and discovered profound spiritual comfort in such hopeful, recognizable signposts. Additionally, the New
England churches had an explicit organizational investment in this evidence.

Unlike the English parishes left behind, where all but the notoriously sinful were accepted as church members, Massachusetts strove to build a more perfect church by limiting its membership to the truly saved. While acknowledging that mistakes could happen (some reformers denounced even the possibility of distinguishing the saved from the damned), most New England church members held that the elect could be identified with a fair degree of certainty. Thus they demanded that candidates for admission to church membership demonstrate their election through evidence of both sanctification and conversion.

Observing and evaluating a person's behavior was relatively easy. Identifying specific behavior as sanctified may have required godly discrimination on the part of the observer, but at least the behavioral evidence was apparent to all. Hence the popularity of sanctification as evidence of justification despite the hypocrite's ability to ape holiness. Judging the evidence of spiritual experience, however, was far more difficult because a candidate's conversion was by nature intensely personal and private, the evidence hidden from common view. Still, the New England churches developed a solution to this problem as well: they asked candidates to testify to their meeting with grace. Since the nature of conversion was understood among knowledgeable Puritans, and since all current church members had, by definition, their own personal knowledge of conversion, congregations were deemed qualified to recognize a true conversion when they heard it described.

By requiring candidates for admission to church membership to articulate their convictions, New England churches subtly altered the meaning of the conversion experience for many believers. If the original experience was private and personal, an emotional confrontation between soul and Spirit, witnessing to this confrontation seems an excruciating public test of spirituality. Such testimony became an expressive performance that pastor, elders, and congregants could judge and, perhaps more importantly, manipulate. If the narrative was initially unconvincing due to its brevity, even if its "plot" was unrecognizable to most listeners, the narrator need not fear, for a series of clarifying questions could elaborate the briefest account or wrest the most puzzling tale into a comfortable pattern. "How did the Lord bring you out of that estate of security into a state of fear and spirit of bondage? . . . How hath the Lord brought you out of this estate unto the Lord Jesus? . . . How came you to assurance?" asked the Newtown elders of Robert Daniel. In another case, despite an extensive and elaborate testimony replete with biblical quotations, elders found it necessary to force Mary Angier's confession into the mold. They asked "whether she had closed with the person of Christ," and later "whether she had assurance."[21] Such leading questions worked beautifully to benefit both applicant and congregation. Clearly, if able to answer the questions, the candidate would be accepted into membership. But beyond this, the congregation would hear reinforced the normative construction of conversion. By reconstructing the narrative and delineating the paradigm, pastors and elders transmuted what may have been diverse human/divine encounters into homogeneous tales of terror and redemption.[22]

As they further dissected the character of these stages of conversion, the New England clerics encountered their deepest difficulties. John Cotton believed that the human soul was merely an empty vessel to be filled with the oil of divine grace, completely passive in the face of God. Only after receiving grace could the believer actively follow God's will.

> A Christian is more active after *Regeneration* then before, before *Regeneration* we are not active at all in any spirituall Christian [work], no nor in *Proxima Potentia*, Passive to receive helpe from God to doe it, but after *Regeneration*, *Acti Agimus*. If we act and goe forth in the strength of our own spirituall *Giftes* ... we fall as *Peter* did, *Matth.* 26.33.39. etc.[23]

Acti Agimus: once the Spirit has acted upon the soul, the soul can act. Cotton's colleagues, on the other hand, encouraged their hearers to prepare for that moment when the Spirit would arrive. In fact, their descriptions of conversion preparation became entwined with the initial stages of spiritual transformation. That is, human preparation became part of the Spirit's witness.

The very word "preparation," used by many New England theologians in their discourses, pointed up the paradoxical nature of the relationship between God and humanity. While agreeing with Cotton that a sinner could not move a single step toward faith and salvation without grace, most insisted that believers needed to prepare for that grace. "Nay, there is no faith can be infused into the soule, before the heart be thus fitted and prepared: no preparation, no perfection. Never humbled, never exalted." So argued Thomas Hooker, author of numerous, long, elaborate, and redundant essays on the need and method of preparation. He had sharp words for those skeptics who, begging the individual's total inability to effect his or her salvation, questioned the need to follow God's law in preparation for grace: "howsoever thy good workes are not sufficient to save thee, yet thy evil workes are enough to damne thee. . . . Their sinne is become out of measure sinfull,

because mercy is revealed, and they have made a mocke of it."[24] Thomas
Shepard also urged preparedness, warning his readers, "If unready now, you
will be much more unready the next day . . . you will be more unfit the longer
you delay . . . thy heart will be harder every day than another." For, he continues, if you are unable to see your sin or Christ's grace, "thou shalt see the
gate shut upon thee hereafter."[25] Hooker agreed.

> Doe you thinke it fit, that grace, and mercy, and the spirit, should still
> stand and waite upon you, and strive, and alwayes be despised? Is it not
> marvailous just, that the word which you have despised, should never
> worke more; and that mercy you have refused, should never be offered to
> you any more? It is just, and you shall find it so in the end, and therfore take
> heede the termes of mercy be not out.[26]

The preparation required was described in the vaguest of terms. Hooker
counseled his readers to "come to him" and to "yeeld to the Lord Jesus Christ
to be at his disposing and carving." Others called upon sinners to seek out
God. If such evidences as prayer and brokenness of heart did not convince
a person that he was saved, "he is to lament his unbelief, and to seek to the
Lord to persuade his heart as the man in the Gospel did."[27] Somewhat more
explicitly, Hooker wrote again and again of humiliation and contrition, essentially the first two phases of the conversion experience. God must first
bring the sinner to a sense of the vileness of sin. Once convinced of the
need for change, the truly contrite sinner could then be led by grace into
the valley of humiliation, the realization that alone she or he is unable to
effect that change and must therefore place all in the hands of God: "yet he
is content, that God should dispose of him as he thinkes good, onely (if it
bee possible) he prayes, that the Lord would shew mercy to a poore forlorne
creature. Now the sinner is prepared . . ." Although Hooker implied that the
grace of God would bring these blessings to the soul, he instructed the individual to "cry and call for the spirit of humiliation and contrition . . . ."[28]
Peter Bulkeley carefully delineated the steps that any potential saint had to
take toward conversion.

> Break your covenant with your old sins, and your lusts, or else God will not
> enter into covenant with you . . .
>   Goe before the Lord as guilty of thy former rebellion, and unfaithfulnesse
> in breaking covenant with him, and judge thy selfe for it, lay downe thy selfe

and life before God, confessing and acknowledging, that it were just, if he should destroy thee . . .

Come with a humble submission to yeild up thy selfe to the obedience of the will of God.

Here believers were instructed not to await passively the Spirit's grace, but to act themselves—to desert old sins, confess, and yield to God's will.[29]

A variety of means were available to the believer hoping to prepare for grace: the Bible, prayer, sermons, the sacraments. These guaranteed neither salvation nor faith; they could not be read as evidence of election. Nevertheless, they were "guides to leade us to a Christ, so they are meanes to convey grace, mercy and comfort from Christ to our soules."[30] Sinners should strive in this preparation, avoid "vaine, joviall" company, and "labour to acquaint your selves throughly with God and with his law, and to see the compasse and breadth of it; the words of the Commandements are few, but there are many sinnes forbidden in them, and many duties required."[31]

Many believers recorded such efforts while they testified and were examined concerning their spiritual state. Again and again, petitioners recorded scriptural study, private prayer, listening to sermons, and attending ordinances. Sometimes they noted great struggles, sometimes failures to live up to their own high standards. Edward Collins, for example, "could not find God's presence in ordinances, being full of mixtures." Occasionally, a person like John Trumbull would tell of great efforts.

And reading *Poor Man's Pathway*, they told me the more I read the more I would delight in it but I read in it only to learn to read. And at last I heard he that read that book over and it should be a witness against him. And though [I] thought it a serious book, then reading book of repentance, learning some sins yet I lived in, so saw my misery.[32]

Hooker's ambiguity on the subject of preparation let him balance on the fence fairly carefully. In his essays he asserted at different points that the work of preparation was enacted by God's grace upon the soul. "First, the dispensation of the worke of Grace on Gods part, hee pulls a sinner from sinne to himselfe, and secondly, the frame and temper of spirit, that God workes in the hearts of those that he doth draw."[33] This in no way contradicted the Calvinist doctrine of human powerlessness; it might be argued that the New England clergy were merely delineating the steps taken by God to prepare the sinner.

On the other hand, several preachers, notably Bulkeley and Shepard, forcefully pushed struggling Christians toward human effort. Even Hooker employed language of action. The sinner should submit, yield, seek, labor, follow God's ordinances as guides to Christ. Whatever they intended to say, and in his correspondence with Cotton Shepard clearly acknowledged that all effective ability to move the sinner lay with God, many listeners, including the Hutchinsonians, heard themselves urged toward study, prayer, meditation and self-examination, and attendance at sermons. And while clerics claimed that they left all to the Spirit, their insistence upon preparatory works was so emphatic that Cotton distanced himself from their position. In other words, like their discussion of sanctification, whatever the intended theological meaning of the preparationist position, the general effect was one of urging people to action. This is what Cotton and the Hutchinsonians heard. Moreover, the horror with which Shepard and other ministers responded to Cotton's dictum of passivity in meeting God speaks to the point that, at some level, human endeavor is what the preparationists intended.[34]

In the end, these efforts to reassure anxious believers striving toward salvation served to provide them with some sense of control over their spiritual destiny. A concentration upon sanctification was profoundly helpful to New Englanders' commitment to order, for while Puritans knew that true sanctification could only follow upon justification, outward behavior could, in fact, be controlled and sanctified behavior emulated. Additionally, much of the fearsome mystery of the conversion experience was countered by a clear delineation of its development phase by phase, and the implication that at least the initial stages involved human activity. If discussion of sanctification stressed visible, controllable behaviors, the treatment of conversion and preparation transferred the attention of the believer from the inscrutable workings of grace to the tangible actions of preparation and the final performance of testifying to one's conversion.

While Puritans would have insisted, with Paul, "there is nether male nor female: for ye are all one in Christ Jesus," their intense engagement with sanctification and preparation belied this.[35] The means toward grace, the "ordinances," including sermons, catechizing, and the sacraments, were justifiably under the control of a male clergy. "Though the knowledge, and the fear of GOD are common to men and women (for women also are in the Covenant, and must not be ignorant of the Articles thereof, especially seeing GOD hath vouchsafed them to be spirituall both Kings and Priests) yet the administration of sacred things is the peculiar of men."[36] And while prayer was certainly available to all, only private prayer remained a genderless occupation. Women were expected to pray publicly along with the congregation, but they were not permitted to lead public prayer. Even in the private circle of friendship, women were permitted to lead prayers only for other women, and only if no men were present. So, too, within the family a woman could lead her children and female servants in prayer; only in her husband's absence ought a woman to conduct family prayers.[37]

The central importance of studying the Scriptures established a firmly gendered religious hierarchy. Puritan leaders insisted that all persons needed to be able to read, if only to peruse the Scriptures for themselves. As early as 1642 the government passed a law calling upon parents and masters to foster their children's "ability to read & understand the principles of religion & the capitall lawes of this country."[38] Within twenty years of settlement a series of laws required towns to provide a schoolmaster. The very popularity of books in New England, the successful establishment of a printing business in 1639, and the extensive publication of inexpensive popular pamphlets all speak to the high level of literacy of the society.[39]

While everyone was encouraged to learn to read the Bible for themselves, Puritans understood most people needed assistance interpreting the Scriptures, for the text was difficult, often abstruse and obscure. They established a high standard of erudition for the clergy, demanding a university baccalaureate of their ministers and encouraging other men to enjoy the benefits of a year or two at university. Only with serious training in languages, logic, rhetoric, and theology was a man truly prepared to engage the Scriptures, just as study in mathematics and physics (i.e., science) enabled him to comprehend better the workings of providence in the natural world as well as the human soul. The academic credentials of the first-generation clergy constitute an impressive list of Cambridge University colleges, degrees, and fellowships. The college was often the place of intense spiritual growth as well, and many clerics wrote of conversion experiences that occurred during their academic tenure.[40] The most obvious New England reflection of the value placed upon higher education was the establishment of Harvard College within the first decade of settlement, long before economic and social stability had been achieved, and, incidentally before the laws aimed at basic literacy had been passed.

The attainments of an Anne Bradstreet or Anne Hutchinson notwithstanding, women suffered from the educational imbalance.[41] It would, of course, be a mistake to assume that all New Englanders were able to read, although an extraordinary number could. Literacy was much higher among the wealthier classes. The literacy rate was also higher among men; it has been estimated that approximately half as many women as men could read.[42] Moreover, while the 1647 law required towns to provide schooling for all children, most towns were slow to accommodate themselves to the law, and among those that did, most educated boys only.[43] Additionally, women were absolutely excluded from formal, advanced education. Most New England residents did not enjoy the benefits of the university, and this was yet another means of differentiating leaders from the masses. No women were educated at the university; any woman interested in advanced study was dependent upon the determination, industry, and skills of her parents and herself. By privileging erudition as a primary source of secular and especially religious authority, Puritans effectively disfranchised women.

"These words (*and he is the Saviour of the body*) as they doe declare the office of Christ, and the benefit which the Church reapeth, so they note the end why an husband is appointed to be the head of his wife, namely that by his provident care he may be as a saviour to her." Did Puritans believe in the priesthood of all believers, or of all male believers? Did they grant that "the soul knows no difference of sex," or did Puritans believe that women required male mediation in their quest for salvation?[44] If learning was important, and women were denied formal schooling, then it would seem that women needed the intellectual guidance of men.

Even the centrality of the conversion experience had been somehow replaced by the preparatory steps of reading, study, and prayer, the sanctification following conversion, and the performance involved in testifying to the soul's conversion. While the conversion experience may have been available to all regardless of gender, the testimonial performances differed. Men witnessed publicly before the congregation and responded to questions asked by pastor, elder, or any male congregant. Women generally related their experiences privately before pastor and elders, answered questions posed in private session, and stood silently before the congregation as their testimonies were read out by a male church officer. As one minister explained, the churches had "such a tender respect [for] the weaker sex (who are usually more fearefull and bashfull) that we commit their triall to the Elders & some few others in private, who upon their testimony are admitted into the Church, without any more adoe."[45] While every believer's experience had already been impacted by the act of testifying, and while every believer was further manipulated by the questions posed, men, in the end, retained something of their own individual voices. Women's voices were completely subsumed under the male interlocutor's report, as if women were unable to understand or interpret the work of the Spirit in their own souls. Denied the power to articulate their experiences, women lost some of the power to determine their own religiosity. Moreover, beyond this effort to construct private spirituality, it seems that an emphasis upon sanctification and preparation would also favor men. Here the will and the intellect were of prime importance, and New England's leaders basically agreed with other Englishmen that men boasted superior strength of will and mind.

When considering the spiritual potential of women, Puritan theologians returned to the indisputable doctrine of natural female inferiority. Men and women were equally likely to find themselves among the elect, and both depended upon the efficacy of divine grace: souls remained on an equal footing before God. Nevertheless, to Puritans it was clear that men and women on earth were quite different, fulfilling different roles and following different pathways to salvation. All that was understood about female biology and the female character applied to the feminine soul. The common analogy was the head to heart, with the head justifiably ruling: "though the man be as the head, yet is the woman as the heart, which is the most excellent part of the body next the head, farre more excellent then any other member under the head, and almost equall to the head in many respects, and as necessary as the head."[46] Almost but not quite equal, this difference was grounded in biology. Weakness and strength were passed down from generation to generation in a sort of gendered natural selection. "The reason why sometimes a male is conceived, sometimes a female, is the strength of the Seed: for if the Mans Seed be strongest, a Male is conceived; if the Womans, a Female. The greater light obscures the lesser by the same rule, and thats the reason weekly Men get most Girls, if they get any Children at all."[47] Men were stronger, physically and mentally. Women were emotional to the point of hysteria, intellectually confused, gullible, and sexual.

Woman's general weakness of body and mind translated into weakness in her dealings with God and the Devil. Again, the prototype was Eve, so easily seduced by Satan. "As the first Woman was deceived at the first, so are many of that Sex deceived at this very day." Women were weak—credulous, ignorant, envious, vain—easy prey to the wiles of Satan.

Why *Satan* singles out *Woman*?

1. *A fitting object to work upon*: In as much as she was the *weaker Vessell*, less able to withstand the stroke of his Temptations. Had he encountred with

the Man, there might have been more probability of resistance, less hope of prevailing; Therefore he singles out the Woman, as apprehending more hopes of prevailing there, by reason of the natural infirmity of her Sex.[48]

All humanity may have been deeply depraved, but, due to her inherent inferiority, woman far outdistanced man in her wickedness. Not only was she more likely to sin, but her sinning took on an exaggerated, shameless character. When compared to man,

> the woman proves the worst. Its much what, in this sexe, as in the inferiour natures of creatures, the shee-Beare, Lyonesse, or Wolfe, is the most savage and fierce: so here, the impotency and unbridelednesse of the sexe, makes her more subject to rage, unrighteousnesse, revenge and wickednesse then a man.[49]

Compounding woman's original weakness was the aftermath of the fall. Woman's naivete, credulity, and pride led inevitably to humanity's fall from grace, and many believed that through the fall woman's weakness was magnified a hundredfold. She became "ignorant, shallow, proud, ambitious, fantastike, inconstant, passionate, and vaine-glorious, indiscreet, easily led into extreames, either in good or evill."[50]

Such weakness also characterized woman's intellect. She was unable to follow complex reasoning or judge intelligently the arguments of others. Woman simply lacked the mental capacity. One learned woman, wife of Governor Hopkins of Hartford, was said to have completely lost her understanding and reason because "of her givinge her selfe wholly to readinge & writinge, & had written many bookes." As Winthrop explained, "if she had attended her household affaires, & suche thinges as belonge to women, & not gone out of her waye & callinge, to meddle in suche thinges as are proper for men, whose mindes are stronger, &c: she had kept her wittes, & might have improved them usefully & honorably in the place God had Sett her."[51] It was not that woman lacked zeal or commitment, but that no matter how strenuously she searched, woman was intrinsically unable to recognize the truth unless it was pointed out to her. "Ever learning (like many of our female zelots) continually hearing all the Sermons they could come at; yet for all that he said, that they never came to the knowledge of the truth; they acquired a jangling knowledge, holding of opposition, a knowledge falsely so called."[52] Because of her feeble capacities, woman was destined to follow and learn of others. "In the Schools of CHRIST there are masters and Schollers; women are placed amongst Schollers, *they must learne*, yet so are they placed amongst Schollers, that they may never hope to be Masters...."[53] The proof of woman's incapacity lay in the obvious results of some women's misguided decisions to judge preachers, sermons, and theology for themselves. One writer noted "the *propension* and *proclivity* of that sexe to take up errors, that women are more easily seduced than men, and have their judgments first, and soonest poysoned." And once led into error, women became the leaders of factions and promoters of errors, unreachable by the calm voices of reason.

> As they are weak, so are they wilful, weak in capacity and judgment, less strength to resist, lesse judgement to discern errors from truth, not so able as men to reach the depths and mysteries of knowledge . . . as out of their credulous simplicity they are first, and easily seduced: so out of their peevish obstinacy they are last, & with more difficulty reclaimed; and I dare say, a man may sooner convert five men from the errors of their wayes, than one woman.[54]

The problem was not only that women were unsophisticated and gullible, but also emotional and willful: "Passion and Affection in [women] either in love or hatred, is much more extream and violent then in Men . . ." And contradictory though it may seem, the sex that could be so easily seduced into error was as likely to be obdurately dedicated to the heresy into which its members had fallen. "Women are commonly more wittie then wise, for wisdome requires the pondering of circumstances, but the forwardnesse of their affections will not suffer women to pause so long; whereupon it followes that their resolutions are rash and wilfull, which cannot prognosticate any good events."[55]

Actually, what may initially seem contradictory need not have been so. Woman could be seduced into error; she could not be persuaded from error. The notion of persuasion, an intellectual enterprise, brought to mind efforts to convince or influence the reason. A man's ability to be persuaded by theological discourse reflected his intellectual strength, while a woman's determination to stand by her errors, her refusal to "listen to reason," further demonstrated her weakness. Likewise, the language of seduction, with its sexual implications, reinforced the picture of women as foolishly led by passions, easily manipulated by evil forces. In fact, the language of seduction worked to move the construction of woman's soul beyond the condition of pitiable weakness toward a fearsome malevolence. Just as the passionate, emotional nature of women made them sexual prey and sexual predators, so, too, the feminine soul so easily led into temptation could transform a woman into a greedy, irresistible temptress.

Ever since Eve had lured Adam into sin, women had displayed a "naturall perswasivenesse of such incensing to evill forcibly." As John Brinsley had noted, Satan singled out women not only because of their weakness, but also because of their power. "As fit to *work upon*, so to *work by*; A fitting *Instrument*, being her self deceived, to deceive her Husband, by conveying the same suggestions unto him, who would the lesse suspect what came through her hands, of those cordiall and entire affection he was so fully perswaded." Seduction followed seduction naturally, reproducing wickedness and error across the landscape. "And silly women being thus seduced, seduce their husbands, as *Eve* did *Adam* . . . dangerous champions in a schism, and there be no such ensnaring attractives to errors & factions, as women are." This was the picture of a creature both in need of protection and in need of restriction, a creature at once threatened and threatening. "For when women beare rule over men, having catched and bewitched them in their subtill snares, what is it that they will not do for them?"[56]

While the beauty of Esther, the chastity of Susannah, and even the house-wifery of Bathsheba may have inspired hopes and praises of women's potential, the wretchedness of Michal, Delilah, and Jezebel fascinated and horrified. Eve may have been the mother of the human race, but it was as the tempted and tempting pawn of Satan that she was most frequently memorialized. Yes, woman was inclined toward frivolity, vanity, extravagance, sloth, scolding, scandal-mongering, pettiness, envy, stinginess, and pride. However, such small vices represented but the outer edge of a vast pit of corruption.

> And if we but seriously consider the nature and qualities of the generality of that sex, even in all ages from the fall of man unto this present, we may well perceive that they have not been onely extreamly evil in themselves; but have also been the main instruments and immediate causes of Murther, Idolatry, and a multitude of other hainous sins, in many high and eminent men.[57]

Evil flowed deeply in woman's body amid the excess fluids overbalancing her emotional stability and corrupting her ability to reason. Menstrual fluid, the

symbol of woman's faulty physiology, was believed to cause reproductive disaster. "But the greatest cause of womens bring [sic] forth Children imperfect,
or mutilated, or crook-back't, or with Issues or Leprosie, &c. I take to be, because the act of Copulation was done at that time when the woman had her
Menstruis upon her." And that female menstrual fluid became a symbol of
evil and pollution. Peter Bulkeley said about the damned: "they are to [God]
as the filthiness of a menstruous woman."[58]

Women's evil nature bore frightening fruit. The predilection of women
toward error, heresy, and blasphemy was matched biologically by the occasional production of monsters. Tales of "monstrous births" were a common
(and popular) form of sensational literature during the sixteenth and seventeenth centuries.[59] Based on the extremely graphic descriptions that were
a significant aspect of these stories, medical analysts today can recognize
severe birth defects such as spina bifida as well as the expulsion of tumors
from the body. However, early modern physicians and philosophers were
just beginning to understand such tragedies as natural, and they sought the
causes in nature. Nicholas Culpeper was the author of a popular "scientific"
directory on midwifery that demonstrated his ignorance of contemporary
medical developments. He presents an excellent example of this transition
from miraculous to natural explanations. He looked toward menstrual fluid
for the cause of slight deformities but believed that a monster might develop
from "humane seed, and the seed of a beast." He thought, however, that this
was far less likely than that a woman's imagination had been damaged, for
women looking at men in vizards (masks) had been known to bring forth
monsters with cloven feet, horns, and beaks. "It is seldome, for the forming
faculty doth not err of itself, but is seduced by the imagination, or frustrated
of its ends, from a fault of the Spirits, the health or matter. Therefore imagination is the cause of Monsters."[60] It is not surprising that many believers
saw such events as providential communications from God, sometimes
warnings, sometimes punishments, and sometimes the predictable fruit of
the sins of a woman.

Strange Newes from Scotland was typical of such tales. The pamphlet included a picture of the monster as well as a detailed description, but the primary text quoted the dying speech of the mother who claimed that this birth
was the judgment due her sinful opinions. She had been a sectarian and had
desired the ruin of the church and state government as well as the destruction of the established ministry. The monster, of course, represented the outward manifestation of her horrid opinions. Such tales were so common that a

humorous broadside, *Mrs RUMP Brought to Bed of a Monster*, used the monstrous birth (with Mrs. London as midwife) as a metaphor to criticize parliamentary actions.[61]

Predictably, when Mary Dyer and Anne Hutchinson both suffered childbirth tragedies, New England leaders had no difficulty interpreting such special providences as reflections upon their wickedness, although individual interpreters differed as to the final import of the message.[62] When called for advice following the stillbirth of Dyer's child, Cotton counseled that it be buried and the details concealed, because "God might intend only the instruction of the parents, and such other to whom it was known, etc.," and providence had managed to remove most of the witnesses before the birth. While Cotton saw the birth as a private rebuke, however, Winthrop discovered public evidence of divine displeasure of both parents and midwife. "The Father and Mother were of the highest forme of our refined Familists. . . . The Midwife, One *Hawkins* wife of St. *Ives*, was notorious for familiarity with the devill, and now a prime Familist."[63] Similarly, after her banishment to Rhode Island, Hutchinson was said to have given birth to some thirty monsters.

> Then God himselfe was pleased to step in which his casting voice, and bring in his owne vote and suffrage from heaven, by testifying his displeasure against their opinions and practises, as clearly as if he had pointed with his finger, in causing the two fomenting women in the time of the height of the Opinions to produce out of their wombs, as before they had out of their braines, such monstrous births as no Chronicle (I thinke) hardly ever recorded the like.[64]

Both Dyer's and Hutchinson's purported births were seen as judgments, clear, harsh expressions of divine displeasure. They were also punishments tied to, or perhaps one should say growing out of, their femaleness, illustrating the connection between mind and body.

> And see how the wisdome of God fitted this judgement to her sinne every way, for looke as she had vented mishapen opinions, so she must bring forth deformed monsters; and as about 30, Opinions in number, so many monsters; and as those were publike, and not in a corner mentioned, so this is now come to be knowne and famous over all these Churches, and a great part of the world.[65]

The clearest evidence of the intrinsic evil of women was found in the prevalence of women among Satan's human servants, witches. Wherever witches were hunted—the European continent, Scotland, England, or New England—communities, churches, and courts found that most witches were women. In Germany, France, and Scotland, where witch fever ran high, women represented about 80 percent of the accused, while in English counties, where far fewer witches had been sought and discovered, women constituted between 90 and 100 percent of persons identified as witches. In New England, approximately 78 percent of accused witches were women. This percentage jumps to 87 when one considers either those tried for witchcraft or those convicted. Such statistics reflected contemporary beliefs that most practitioners of witchery were female. Christina Larner records one story of a man in Scotland who claimed he was attacked by a witch in the form of an angry sheep. He asserted that if all the women in the vicinity were gathered into a sheep pen, his dog would be able to identify the witch. King James I had estimated that the proportion of female to male witches was twenty to one; a contemporary observer set it as high as a hundred to one. Men who were accused of witchcraft were frequently connected, by marriage or kinship, to a female witch.[66]

The sixteenth-century perception that most witches were women grew out of a complicated network of ideas that went beyond the simple conviction that women were evil. The nature of witchcraft as defined and understood during this era played upon contemporary knowledge of women's work, women's character, and the nature of evil. Witches were not merely wicked; their sins were the sins of women writ larger, baser, more destructive. Both theological and popular beliefs constructed a circle of meanings where the definition of a witch matched the definition of woman in so many particulars that no one could be surprised that most witches were women or that so many women were inclined toward witchcraft. In other words, the cultural construction of gender and the construction of witches worked symbiotically to further the depreciation of women and reinforce calls for women's protection and restriction.

Throughout the sixteenth and seventeenth centuries, there flourished two distinct conceptualizations of witchcraft, each grounded in a different ideological framework.[67] On one side was a definition shared by the common people and reflected in court proceedings. Most Englishmen and women identified witches by their maleficium, the harm that witches inflicted through magic. Methods included charms, potions, curses, and wax dolls, essentially magical manipulation through matter and speech. With such magic, a witch brought illness or death to her neighbors, disease to their cattle, destruction to their crops, or simply the mischief of cream that would not churn into butter or beer that would not brew. Generally, an individual would be accused of witchcraft because some unusual distress that afflicted a person, family, or neighborhood could be connected to the actions, speech, attitude, or mere presence of the suspected witch. Trials of witches always presented evidence of maleficium, including testimony to the initial prov- ocation of the witch, the magical means used by the witch, and the result of her efforts. In England and the colonies, almost all trials of witches were responses to popular accusations of maleficium, and it is unclear whether the populace ever accepted any definition of witchcraft not dependent upon evil magic.[68]

By the end of the sixteenth century, however, English theologians had begun to move beyond this definition, following their continental colleagues toward an understanding of the witch as one who had negotiated a contract with the Devil. This point of view was partially enacted into law in the witch- craft statute of 1604, an act that directly tied some forms of witchcraft to diabolical compacts, a crime punishable by death. Nevertheless, the law con- tinued to provide lesser penalties for lesser degrees of magic, reflecting the popular belief that not all sorcery was tied to the Devil.[69] Theologians came to reject absolutely any notion that sorcery existed except in league with the Devil. For them the nature of the witch had less to do with the way a witch behaved toward her neighbors than with the witch's relationship with Satan. While the church and the state had once condemned only "black" magic, the new definition served to condemn all sorcery. No longer was magic judged by the effected goal of its practitioner, or even by the methods used; now, by definition, magic was evil. The witch was a heretic, a blasphemer, in league with Satan.

This was a position that theologians found reasonable and especially powerful. Adhering to a perception of the natural world as a world ordered by divine law, religious leaders rejected the possibility of altering the nat- ural world without supernatural assistance. While one could pray to God for beneficence or vengeance, human prayers could not bind an omnip- otent God in the way that charms and incantations unfailingly manipu- lated nature. That such spells and potions achieved results demonstrated the involvement of another supernatural force: the Devil. Puritans knew that Satan walked the earth, seeking souls and bringing destruction. He might promise riches, health, status, or power, but one of his primary lures was the power to work magic. Spells and potions, therefore, were obviously the tools of Satan, and they could be given to anyone who signed a contract with him.[70] When individuals were tried for witchcraft under Puritan governments, courts found it essential to prove this diabolical contract. The successful English witch hunter Matthew Hopkins, a man committed to this understanding of witchcraft, was active during the late 1640s, years of Puritan domination. So, too, although juries sometimes convicted on maleficium alone, New England's judges sought proof of a devil's pact before condemning a witch.

In other words, these two perceptions of witchcraft flourished side by side, and, different though they may have been, these definitions came together in accusations leveled at the same individuals. Each described a malevolent figure to be feared, an individual more likely to be female. Women tilled the gardens where powerful herbs and roots could be cultivated; they had charge of the hearth and of cookery, where those herbs and roots could be brewed into potions and secreted in charms. Healing and medicine were also within women's domain, and the individual who could heal could also bring disease. Margaret Jones of Charlestown, convicted and executed for witchcraft in 1648, was known to practice physic, and her "medecines beinge suche things as (by her owne confession) were harmlesse, as Aniseed, liquoris, &c: yet had extraordinary violent effectes." Moreover, despite her claim that she was a healer, she actually brought on illness: "she was fonde to have suche a malignant touche, as many persons, (men, woemen, & children,) whom she stroked or touched (with any Affection [or] ... displeasur, or &c) were taken with deafnesse, or vomitinge, or other violent paynes or sicknesse."[71] Added to this special knowledge was woman's weakness of character. She was petty, jealous, impulsive; she boasted a short temper, held deep grudges, and nursed "a *secret dislike of, and discontentedness with her present condition*, the condition wherein God himself had set her."[72] Jones's behavior at her trial was "very intemperate, lyinge notoriously, & raylinge upon the Jury & wittnesses, &c. . . ."[73] A woman was an envious, vindictive person easily tempted to use magic against her neighbor, and as a good housewife she perhaps had the skills to do so.

Those intellectuals who defined a witch as one who had signed a compact with the Devil certainly appreciated the corroboratory evidence of maleficium; anyone engaged in sorcery must have been in league with

Satan. Their writings served to reinforce popular opinion, since theologians had already concluded independently that Satan would have better success in ensnaring women. Women were gullible, unsophisticated, easily controlled and manipulated by the unscrupulous. Moreover, a woman's envy and pettiness, her discontent with her present condition "letteth in a *Sea of Temptations* upon her, so making way for her seduction."[74]

Here, again, the sexual language of seduction pointed up the gendering of witchcraft. Medieval perceptions of witches—collected, organized, and published in 1486 in *Malleus Maleficarum* (The Hammer of Witches)— placed illicit sexuality at the center of the contract with the Devil. Engravings and woodcuts often portrayed women copulating with the Devil (or with demons) as part of witches' rituals.[75] As early as the twelfth century, the witch of Berkeley was depicted as "excessively gluttonous, perfectly lascivious, setting no bounds to her debaucheries."[76] Witches were known to have animal "familiars" that were thought to be either sexual partners or the products of sexual relations with demons, and the presence of an animal in the home was important evidence against an accused witch. All accused women were subjected to invasive body searches as court representatives sought out "witches' teats." These teats were supposedly sucked by demons or familiars, and they were variously understood to be either sources of nourishment for foul offspring or a locus of sexual pleasure. In fact, many such excrescences were found by evidence seekers near the breasts and genitals. Margaret Jones was discovered to have a teat "in her secrett partes, as freshe as if it had been newly sucked"; a later search revealed that it had withered, and "another beganne on the opposite side." Further, while she was in prison, she had been seen sitting on the floor, "her clothes up," and a small child, undoubtedly her familiar, was seen to run from her to another room, where it vanished.[77] Puritans were following a long and venerable tradition that individuals entered into demonic compacts out of spite, covetousness, and especially lust. The sexual construction of the witch in New England was revealed not only in writings about witchcraft but in the character of the accused witches themselves, for many had been previously convicted of sexual crimes.[78] Women were more likely than men to become witches not only because they were simple thinkers, vindictive and greedy, but because they were sexually depraved.

The gendering of witchcraft stands as the best evidence of the Puritan gendering of good and evil. Puritan men's experience bred bright hopes and deep suspicions (and their philosophy confirmed both) that men were more easily moved toward holiness and women toward sin. The human soul was obviously gendered; biology was destiny, spiritually as well as socially. The spiritual essence of woman differed significantly from the spiritual life of the normative believer (that is, man), and while the holy man was a spiritually active individual, the holy woman passively submitted her spirit to male guides. Women were intellectual inferiors unable to fathom the profound and complex knowledge necessary to approach the Bible, much less the providences and creative actions of God. When women did attempt to interpret the Scriptures, chaos reigned, as the case of Hutchinson so regrettably demonstrated. Added to their mental incapacity, women's weak character required not only guidance but restraint if they were to have any hope of attaining salvation. Even the godliest of women, when considered for church membership, were treated differently from men, as if women were incapable of understanding or interpreting their own spiritual experience.[79]

Puritan theologians were too sophisticated to subscribe to a simplistic dichotomy. Just as the Bible told stories of weak and evil men like Jezebel's husband Ahab and the traitor Judas, the Scriptures also recounted the virtues of Esther, Ruth, and Susannah. Indeed, all those domestic manuals had praised the usefulness and sanctity of the good, pious wife. If women were honored for their submission, their passivity, and their silence, at least they were still honored. Puritan theologians' understanding of humanity's spiritual journey, combined with their construction of gender difference, worked to place men upon a higher sacred plateau. Yet these theologians could not, after all, have been completely oblivious to the paradox inherent in their cosmology. While Puritans appeared to believe that women were more inclined toward evil than men, they also argued that all humanity was innately, totally depraved. What could have been worse than complete, inborn depravity? How could woman's will be weaker than man's when man's will was completely corrupt and, according to Augustinian and Calvinist (and, by extension, Puritan) theology, thoroughly enslaved to Satan?

This contradiction becomes striking when considering that man (and woman) could be saved from this innate depravity in only one way: through the direct intervention of God's irresistible grace. Despite their emphasis upon learning, preparation, and sanctification, Puritan clerics had to grant that God's grace came freely to each believer. God had a personal relationship with each individual, understood to be a direct communion between the believer and the Holy Spirit, unmediated by anyone. "To works of creation there needeth no preparation; the almighty power of God calleth them to be his people, that were not his people. 1 *Pet*.2.10. And by calling them to be so, hee maketh them to be so. *Rom*. 9.25, 26."[80] Cotton was not alone in emphasizing the free, arbitrary nature of God's grace and denying the believer's ability to take a single, unassisted step toward the grace of salvation. One English minister compared the unconverted soul to a dead man awaiting resurrection. "A dead man is a meer *patient* in the work of his own resurrection. . . . and so is a *sinner* in the *first act* of his own *Conversion*." Once called to God, the soul experienced an extraordinary transformation: "The *beleever* being once engrafted into *Christ* his *nature* is thereby changed. . . . Changed in his *Affections, Motions, dispositions*: having *divine nature*." Until that moment, the believer was passive and dependent: "But in the first act they are meerly passive; Onely *receiving* of Jesus Christ. . . . Neither can they do this of themselves; this being a work of the Spirit of God in them, which is to them a *Spirit of Revelation*, and a *Spirit of Faith*: Revealing Christ to them, and in them: inclining and perswading their hearts to close with Jesus Christ."[81]

Hope for this grace and anxiety concerning salvation had led New Englanders to seek out ways in which grace could be discovered within the soul. The one event that affirmed a person's spiritual journey was that moment of conversion, when the believer felt God's presence and was assured of his or her election. Because God offered grace freely and unconditionally and because, in the end, learning and preparation merited nothing, this gracious experience of conversion came to be recognized as the key sign of election and the centerpiece of the Puritan's spiritual journey. Whether clerical or lay, gentleman or laborer, male or female, Puritans looked forward (or back) to that point when they would know the grace of God in their lives. Divine grace brought spiritual gifts of faith and repentance, replaced the inevitability of damnation with the hope of paradise, and freed the will to embrace glad obedience to God's commands.

The core of Puritan religiosity was revealed most clearly not in the esoteric debates and discourses of theologians but in the words of the converts themselves. When she testified before the congregation, Alice Stedman reported that she had been convinced "not to build my faith on duties but on freeness of God's love in Christ." The examination of Nicholas Wyeth affirmed a belief in free grace with creed-like specificity.

Question. Do you remember nothing how God hath tendered Christ to you? Answer. In Ephesians 2 I heard when far off then made near and Lord let me see no way to be saved but by His own free grace. Question. What effects did it work? Answer. I saw it was His free grace to encourage me to go on. The Lord let me see I had nothing in myself. Question. Did the Lord ever give you any assurance of His love in Christ? Answer. The Lord let me see if not born again I could not enter into Kingdom of God. Question. What supports your heart with hope? Answer. Nothing but free grace in Christ.

Many applying for membership in the Newtown congregation testified that they had followed all the preparatory rules. They had studied, prayed, heard sermons, participated in private prayer meetings, and attended the ordinances. Over and over, they confessed the failure of such efforts.[82]

Here, self-reliance proved both fruitless and sinful. Anne Hutchinson had reported that she had been much troubled, and for twelve months she "begged" God for guidance with little success. However, control was finally taken from her as God revealed that in her activism she pursued "a Covenant of works, and did oppose Christ Jesus . . ." As soon as Hutchinson gave up agency, knowledge was brought and she was led to John Cotton, to New England, and to the God who revealed himself to her "sitting upon a Throne of Justice."[83] Until a believer had fallen into depths of despair, until she could say, as Barbary Cutter did, "[I] saw nothing but vileness. And could say nothing but—Lord I am vile," the struggling Christian would wander amid confusion and doubt. It was God who brought hope to sinners like Stedman: "by John 3:16—that whoever believes—the Lord was pleased by that word to overcome my heart and to show me the freeness of His love, not only to them that be in greater, but in a lesser measure humbled."[84]

Aspiring church members appeared as ambivalent toward preparatory means as the clergy, perhaps more so. They knew that they should be attending to means, and they condemned themselves when their determination and efforts grew weak. Stedman spoke for many when she declared her inability to discover God through duties or ordinances rather than looking toward divine grace; Christopher Cane had heard that "it was good to persist in use of means," and resolved to do so. Sister Crackbone found that "means did not profit me and so doubted of all Lord had done, yet hearing when Lord will do good He takes away all ornaments. And so thought of seeking after ordinances but I knew not whether I was fit." Likewise, Joanna Sill, "though she did not neglect duties, yet she found no presence of God there as at other times," while Elizabeth Olbon finally understood "how duties could not help her because a man in prison must be always paying his debts." Candidate

Sanders demonstrated a sound understanding of the problem, though, when he said, "I resolved to walk in a Christian course, but did it in my own strength and so I was by Satan put out of my bias and found Lord forsaking of me, thinking while I walked with God He would with me." Those depending upon such human means were often, perhaps unconsciously, hoping that they would be able to reach God through their own efforts. In laying claim to some self-sufficiency they were pretending to control God: "no duties can save soul, but only Christ." On the other hand, those open to the work of the Holy Spirit could find themselves blessed. When Edward Collins sought for direction from God to participate in church ordinances, "the Lord in His time, though not in mine," made way for him. "And I blessed God that he would not let me lie still but to show me my unthankfulness. And so at last I came to see need of all God's ordinances, watchfulness that I might answer the end for which He sent me." Utter dependence upon God was the key, and it was only after the coming of grace that the ordinances became meaningful and fruitful for the believer.[85]

The person who opened herself or himself to grace would reap an awesome reward. Swept up by the Spirit and carried into light, sinners captured by divine grace found joy in ordinances and sermons, duties and prayers, a joy that elevated the experience beyond comprehension. True, theologians had constructed a developmental morphology that delineated an individual's gracious progress and enabled preachers to explain the experience and lead their listeners through distinct, identifiable stages. Lay congregants could grasp and evaluate a convert's testimony and, if the narrative was unintelligible or puzzling, could elicit an orderly presentation by posing a logical series of questions. An extraordinary amount of reasoning and analysis had gone into these efforts to define, describe, and categorize the conversion experience. The language of conversion was not a rational language dissecting spiritual growth, however, but a rhapsodic outpouring struggling to express the incommensurable joy and strength felt in a union with God.

The conversion experience resisted the boxes imposed by preparations and stages. Thomas Hooker found that believers began "to be light headed, because they are so ravished therewith, they are always cleaving thereunto, insomuch that many times they are almost besides themselves."[86] Converts did not proceed through a logical, cumulative, intellectual exercise but were attacked, overwhelmed by the onrush of grace. Elizabeth Olbon "witnessed the Lord's love to her. Sometime a heart to run and sometime to sit still in the

Lord's way." Robert Holmes heard a sermon on "Zechariah 12:10—spirit of mourning—and hence heart melted and I had joy." Nathaniel Sparrowhawk seemed taken completely by surprise.

> But on the fast day morning, desiring to be alone and to bewail my condition and there entreating reconciliation, the Lord revealed Himself so as never before with abundance of sweetness of Himself, which rejoicing made me break out to weeping and hardly could I refrain from speaking to others to let them see what the Lord had done.

As Sister Moore so beautifully summarized, "when the Lord filled the temple I found Lord had filled my soul with glorious apprehensions of Himself."[87]

Preachers often turned to the metaphor of marriage in their attempts to elucidate that nature of God's love for his people; that was the way that many converts had experienced and interpreted their union with the Spirit. As one woman candidly explained, "Hosea 2—I'll betroth thee to me—and setting out spiritual marriage of a king, making suit to a poor silly maid do but give thy consent and then care not for other things and Christ would be better than earthly husband. No fear there of widowhood so I took Christ then upon His own terms." These were not intellectual exercises in analogical argument but deep, open struggles to grasp their feelings. "And hearing of the freeness of the love of the bridegroom and speaking that all things were ready in Christ," John Fessenden declared, "the Lord affected myself with it. And the Lord made me willing to take the Lord Jesus." This was a sensual, passionate love that aroused the soul in instinctive responses. Before her heart ran in the Lord's way, Olbon realized that "she must come to a naked Christ and that she found the hardest thing in the world to do. Yet by this Scripture out of Isaiah and Matthew He let her feel His love."[88] It was a passion that enflamed layperson and clergyman alike, drawing each convert into the loving whirlwind that was grace.

> Lord am I thine? Art thou, Lord, mine? So rich!
> How doth thy Wealthy bliss branch out thy sweets
> Through all things Present? These the Vent-holes which
> Let out those Ravishing Joys our Souls to greet?
> Impower my Powers sweet Lord till up they raise
> My 'Fections that thy glory on them blaze.[89]

As Hutchinson said, God had taught her to distinguish the voice of anti-christ, the voice of John the Baptist, the voice of Moses, and "the voice of my beloved."[90]

The importance of this mystical experience to Puritan religiosity cannot be overstated. All Puritans, even the most rational, believed in and sought out, or at least longed for, conversion. This experience represented God's struggle with one particular saint, a passionate exchange through which a sinner was brought into the warmth of divine love. In their understanding of conversion, many believers acknowledged the profound possibility of a divine–human relationship of great personal intimacy, almost a mystical, ec-static, transcendent union with God. "Here is a *spiritual Coalition* betwixt *Christ* and the Believer; an *union*, and that a very near one. Not only like that of the *Ivie* and the *Oake*, which are one by Adhesion, the one cleaving to the other; but like the *Graft* and the *Stock*, which are made by one *Insition*; both one *Body*, one *Tree*."[91] God was understood to have established a covenanted relationship with the community as a whole, mandating communal ide-ology and commitment. At the same time he had, paradoxically, developed a private, personal relationship with each individual believer. Conversion, much more than erudition or moral behavior, provided the powerful iden-tity and communal vindication; it became the cornerstone of Puritans' sense of chosenness, grounding their spiritual superiority. It justified the New England migration and creation of a saint-controlled government, justified a civil war and creation of the Commonwealth.[92]

Yet however glorious this vision, it came with a hefty, unrecognized com-munal price. This deep, personal relationship with God, offered by God, through his Spirit, because he arbitrarily chose to do so, was available to every elect individual, female as well as male. This concentration upon the conver-sion experience and the individual's relationship with God empowered indi-vidual believers to stand against the community. It was a leveling force with the potential to eradicate class and gender hierarchies, and while Puritan leaders may have liked the leveling influence as long as it granted them equal access to avenues of religious and political power, they grew uncomfort-able when it meant access for the underclasses. Nonetheless, as long as the Puritans embraced, or even acknowledged, the personal relationship with God, they would have to confront such challenges. When Joshua Verin's wife chose to follow her spiritual inclinations, she insisted upon attending reli-gious services far more frequently than her husband could tolerate. He for-bade her to attend, saying she was neglecting her housewifely duties, and beat her violently; her rights were upheld by Roger Williams, and the Providence government found Verin guilty of abridging her freedom of religion. In disgust Verin returned to Massachusetts, forcing his wife to come with him, where, despite an emphasis upon personal experience, the state recognized a man's right to control his wife.[93]

Access to institutions could be and was controlled, and magistrates devoted extensive efforts to strengthening those institutions against personal challenges. The restrictions placed around higher education served to limit access to one primary avenue of spiritual power. Access to God, however, could not be controlled, and a surprising array of persons, clerical and lay, upper and lower class, educated and illiterate, exhibited extraordinarily strong evidence of extraordinary grace. These were the men and women destined to become spiritual leaders of the community. Within a society that most valued holiness and intrinsic knowledge of the divine, a society in which piety was highly prized and devout men and women were striving toward godliness, those men and women most gifted in grace, those who appeared to have achieved an elevated spiritual plateau, became the models and guides. Many pious individuals, especially laypersons, had established such leadership while still in England, gathering together the true believers in private home meetings of prayer, scriptural study, and moral support. So many English Christians had found their pastors to be scripturally ignorant, theologically legalistic, spiritually "dead." Dissatisfied, sometimes disgusted, with uncaring and worldly pastors, they had turned to each other for spiritual guidance. These habits of mind and practice, fermented within the intense climate of dissent and persecution, accompanied the emigrants to their new Israel. That drive for self-realization and respect for lay piety would not disappear simply because the colonial ministers and magistrates espoused the reformed cause. That the colonial clergy was sound and sanctified did not discount the piety of gifted lay leaders.

Within this framework, Hutchinson's popularity becomes easier to understand. Puritan believers acknowledged that all persons, male and female, had equal access to God. Men and women joined the church membership rolls in fairly equal numbers, just as William and Anne Hutchinson had joined the Boston church upon their arrival. Hutchinson proved to be exceptionally knowledgeable and perceptive. Had she been a man, it was likely that this child of a minister would have attended Cambridge University. Yet being barred from the formal education of an ordained minister did not inhibit her spiritual progress or community influence. What is known of her pre-migration history reveals an exemplary believer who devoted singular efforts to discovering and attending the ministry of an exceptional, worthy clergyman.

Hutchinson's intelligence as well as her godliness, her determination to heed the voice of God in her life, set her apart from and above the average Puritan. Her home became the center of private weekly meetings like those held in England, and she easily rose to the leadership of those meetings. As a mature, pious, and wise midwife, Hutchinson first established her influence over Boston's women. She had initially organized her meetings as gatherings of women, for women were often better able to assist other women in spiritual as well as mundane affairs.[94] Even John Cotton noted, while delivering his admonition to her, that many women had been helped spiritually by her intervention. Yet within a few months Hutchinson's influence had quickly surpassed her gender. So many men began to attend her meetings that she organized a second weekly meeting attended by men as well as women. Wisely, she affirmed throughout her trial that women, including Hutchinson herself, never spoke at meetings at which men were present.[95] Nevertheless, the opinions and honors were hers.

In this conflict between hierarchical social and ideological structures and the radical impact of a powerful spirituality, it is not surprising that the battle was fought in the religious realm. A society that envisioned human experience and endeavor as sometimes public, sometimes private, and carefully prescribed and proscribed roles in each according to gender and rank, would see a clash of expectations in the spiritual arena.[96] The worlds of money and politics, marketplace and town meeting, that is, public arenas, remained the domain of man, while within the private circle of the household woman was granted some limited power. Religion, however, was a peculiar amalgam of public and private, and as such mandated male control even as it opened space and powerful opportunities to women. The institutionalization of the church created a public, male environment. Yet while church ordinances were experienced and, possibly, enjoyed as reassuring public affirmations of faith and grace, the spiritual journey remained a solitary business. Puritan spirituality placed an individual's struggles between the self and God at the center of its religiosity. Driven to their "closets," believers spent days, weeks, sometimes months or years agonizing over their salvation. However, despite the lonely nature of his travail, once a man had experienced the full flush of divine grace, he testified publicly to his conversion. Furthermore, the power of divine grace came privately to women as well as to men, and if women did testify privately, they still testified.

In these spiritual travels Puritans turned toward a circle of guides and supporters, often finding comfort and counsel in private conferences with their pastors or amid a small, intimate community of piety. The very existence and popularity of such conferences and prayer meetings blurred the boundaries between public and private. As the Hutchinsonian crisis demonstrated, the conduct and debates of people who met privately to study and pray could have an extraordinary impact upon the public climate. In hurling their new understandings against the clergy, the Hutchinsonians were partially to blame for this transformation of house meetings into a public problem. The ministers contributed to the conflagration when they took public offense at words uttered in private sessions. As Increase Nowell of Charlestown described the common talk, "I do hear it affirmed, that things which were spoken in private are carried abroad to the publick and thereupon they do undervalue the ministers of congregations."[97]

Surely, one of the more disconcerting moments for Hutchinson must have been the decision of several clerics to testify in court to statements she had made during a private conference. Before the General Court, this most visible and official of forums, the clerics' speech transformed what had been private conversation into public utterance, further forcing Hutchinson into the role of public nuisance. As William Coddington lamented, "She spake nothing to them [the elders] but in private, and I do not know what rule they had to make the thing publick, secret things ought to be spoken in secret and publick things in publick, therefore I think they have broken the rules of God's word."[98] Because she would not speak seditiously, or even critically, in public, they did it for her and then reacted as if she had done it herself. As Winthrop noted, "This speech was not spoken in a corner but in a public assembly, and though things were spoken in private yet now coming to us, we are to deal with them as public."[99] When Hutchinson treated their testimony as public speech, demanding that they swear oaths, she was pointing out their sleight of tongue. Unhappy about the responsibility of an oath, the clerical witnesses tried to retreat to the safety and imprecision of private dialogue, but the examination had proceeded too far. In the end, three ministers agreed to swear, thus confirming and validating their own reconfiguration of private speech into public discourse. Four months after her examination before the court, the clergy would again prosecute Hutchinson. Through intensive examination on a variety of theological topics, church officials would remake five months of spiritual explorations and private communications between believer and pastors into public heresy.

In light of this conflation of public and private and the new invocation of heretofore unidentified boundaries, the official response to Hutchinson can be explained, even in its early admiration of her piety, its later tolerance of her gatherings, and its final hostility and inflexible condemnation of her activities. As long as the private meetings remained private, that is, as long as nothing happened within those meetings to upset structures established and decisions made within the public spheres of church and state, church and state leaders did not care; in fact, Hutchinson was praised for assisting individuals in their private spiritual endeavors. However, when Hutchinson "moved" into that public sphere, when her opinions challenged the hierarchy and ethos of that sphere, she was excoriated—in large part for daring to enter public life. The entire sweep of the Hutchinsonian crisis suggests a new distinction between public and private spheres that explicitly engaged questions of power. Puritan leaders had come to realize that this was less an issue of experience of or participation in the public realm than a question of power within that world. In his many responses to Hutchinson's defense of her meetings, Winthrop confirmed this new construction in his refusal to approve the meetings in any way. At one point, when she argued that she did not teach in a public congregation, the court replied,

> You are gone from the nature of your meeting, to the kind of exercise, wee will follow you in this, and shew you your offence in them, for you do not as the *Bereans* search the Scriptures for their confirming in the truths delivered, but you open your teachers points, and declare his meaning, and correct wherein you think he hath failed, &c. and by this meanes you abase the honour and authority of the publick Ministery, and advance your own gifts, as if he could not deliver his matter so clearly to the hearers capacity as your self.[100]

As long as Hutchinson held sway in her own home only, her meetings were private and acceptable, even though everyone in the town knew that she was an active, leading participant. But when, through her followers, she began to challenge the governors and clergy, she had trespassed into the public arena and overstepped her place. Additionally, lest anyone doubted the public import of her private meetings, the clergy made certain that she was established as a public nuisance. It was a boundary drawn and held against women.

Yet this boundary was pushed again and again throughout the seventeenth century. For despite human efforts to keep women in line, the Holy Spirit could and did continue to empower female believers. And despite his own gendered ways of knowing, Winthrop had seen her authority take hold. "She had in a short time insinuated her selfe into the hearts of much of the people," and they saw her as "a Prophetesse, raised up of God."[101]

5

Prophesying Women and the Gifts of the Spirit

"It is said, I will poure my Spirit upon your Daughters, and they shall prophesie," quoted Hutchinson. "If God give me a gift of Prophecy, I may use it." So Hutchinson claimed her right to lead religious meetings in her home. During her trial, she spoke of the confusion that had characterized her spiritual journey in England. Unable to find her way out of the wilderness, she turned toward God with prayer and fasting. The Holy Spirit responded to her pleas and "by his prophetical office" opened scripture to her. She was brought to confront the atheism of her own heart and, eventually, was led to Christ, "from which time the Lord did discover to me all sorts of Ministers, and how they taught, and to know what voyce I heard, which was the voyce of *Moses*, which of *John Baptist*, and which of Christ; the voyce of my beloved, from the voyce of strangers." The Spirit had further revealed that she should go to New England and foretold her suffering there. Considering herself a prophet of God, she envisaged herself as Daniel in the lion's den, and with the power of a prophetic identity she warned the court:

> Therefore I desire you to look to it, for you see this scripture fulfilled this day. . . . You have power over my body but the Lord Jesus hath power over my body and soul, and assure yourselves thus much, you do as much as in you lies to put the Lord Jesus Christ from you, and if you go on in this course you begin you will bring a curse upon you and your posterity, and the mouth of the Lord hath spoken it.

The court accused her of conducting a public ministry; this she denied, for she did not preach in a public congregation. In fact, she denied her own voice and said that the Spirit spoke through her. "They must not take it as it comes from me, but as it comes from the Lord Jesus Christ, and if I tooke upon me a publick Ministery, I should break a rule, but not in exercising a gift of Prophecy . . ."[1]

Of course, Hutchinson's right, however disputed, and willingness to speak prophetically did not mean that everyone or anyone had to listen to her. Indeed, without an attentive and admiring audience, she would have posed no societal problem. The Boston church, concerned for the good of her soul, or for their own well-being in their covenanted relationship with God, might have disciplined her; but it is unlikely that the General Court would have been involved. In the first generation of settlement, spiritually outspoken women did occasionally appear, but they were effectively controlled by minimal corrective action. The Boston church admonished Sarah Keayne for her "irregular prophesying in mixt Assemblies and for Refusing ordinarily to heare in the Churches of Christ." Sister Hogg was admonished and later excommunicated for "disorderly singing" and "her refusing to labor and saing she is commanded of god soe to doe." These sanctions apparently silenced and disempowered Keayne and Hogg without any need to involve the state.[2] Even Lady Deborah Moody, "a wise and anciently religious woman," was fairly easily neutralized. Because she had taken a position against infant baptism, she was admonished and later excommunicated by the church at Salem. She maintained her views, but, like her cousin Henry Vane, she voluntarily left Massachusetts, moving to the Dutch colony of New Netherlands along with others "infected with anabaptism."[3]

A more troubling incident involved Mary Oliver of Salem, a woman who had already suffered in England for her dissenting posture in refusing to bow at the name of Jesus. She was angry that she was not admitted to communion unless she testified to her faith and joined in covenant with the congregation. On the day that the church celebrated the sacrament, she publicly demanded communion, argued her right to admission, and refused to be silent until the magistrate threatened to have the constable throw her out. She was brought up on charges of disturbing the peace of the church and, following a few days imprisonment, she acknowledged her fault. After her release, she was found to hold "dangerous" opinions, but there is no record of any action taken. Five years later, however, she was whipped for reproaching the magistrates, saying that the governor was unjust, corrupt, and a wretch, and at a later date she was again punished for reproaching the elders. Because she had publicly reviled church, state, magistracy, and church leaders, she was penalized by the state, but the sentences were relatively light, considering that she was a public dissenter. Winthrop provided the explanation. "She was (for ability of speech, and appearance of zeal and devotion) far before Mrs. Hutchinson, and so the fitter instrument to have done hurt, but that she was poor and had little acquaintance." Without an audience, Oliver posed no threat to church or state.[4]

Clearly, the problem was not that Hutchinson spoke but that people heard and heeded her words. Women and men sought her out, week after week, and apparently went on to promulgate what they heard in other congregations. What her followers heard appeared to challenge many clergymen at key points. In acting upon their new lessons, the Hutchinsonians extended her impact in the colony, undermined the ministry, and threatened the already tentative foundation of the government. Hutchinsonians almost succeeded in adding John Wheelwright to the pastorate of the Boston church. A few months later they refused to join the militia organized to assist the English settlers of Connecticut in their war with the Pequots because the chaplain was the questionable John Wilson.[5] Even before these public battles, the clergy complained of heckling from Hutchinsonian critics. In October 1636, the clergy, with the encouragement of the state, held a conference to reach some accord about problematic beliefs and preaching. Although all claimed to be satisfied with the outcome, the clergy again met in conference in December, with less amicable results. While these conferences were ostensibly called to establish some clerical consensus of orthodoxy, Anne Hutchinson sat as a primary participant at both, marking her importance as a religious leader and suggesting that the real purpose of the meeting was less clerical accord than the unofficial examination of and negotiation with her. Finally, in order to re-establish clerical hegemony, the governor found it necessary to disfranchise and disarm large numbers of her followers. In the end, many of her followers would accompany Hutchinson in her banishment.

In their sometimes overt, sometimes subtle maneuvers to disempower Hutchinson, the magistrates and clergy showed themselves as leaders of a less than stable church and state, struggling to legitimate their authority. The extraordinary popularity of Hutchinson, less a cause than a symptom of this instability, showed the strength of the challenges that could arise, almost accidentally, among people driven to search for spiritual satisfaction. Some historians have seen Hutchinson's popularity from the vantage point of the social and political conflicts raging among Boston's elite. Many merchants and artisans must have resented the government's application of a code of sanctified behavior to economics and trade, severely restricting profits and wages; some may have moved to Rhode Island to avoid such limitations. An alternative religious system that privileged human passivity in the expectation of grace might well have appealed to merchants, for this theology did not demand that men curtail their economic activities or shortchange their rewards in order to achieve godliness. Other scholars have seen the controversy as an enactment of the Boston-cosmopolitan/colony-provincial jealousies within the religious arena.[6] However, by placing a premium upon social identity and economic goals, they fail to credit the intense religious commitment of the community's members.

Yes, the Hutchinsonian controversy reflected early social and political conflicts, but at its center lay the cultural imperative to reach and experience the Holy Spirit in the soul. Massachusetts was a profoundly religious colony, though not in the sense of widespread, sophisticated understanding of theology. Many read the Scriptures for themselves and, as is frequently the case in aural cultures, were able to recall significant passages and huge blocks of text, yet their knowledge was often serendipitous and their understanding naive. This controversy was not only about beliefs and orthodoxy, although the clergy labored to reduce Hutchinson's charisma to a list of heresies. This conflict concerned pathways toward salvation and communion with God. As illustrated by the extremely long and defensive will of the notoriously wealthy Robert Keayne, even worldly merchants were deeply worried about their spiritual estate.[7]

Returning to the historical circumstances surrounding the rise of Puritanism in late sixteenth- and early seventeenth-century England, and looking at the common response of Puritans to those circumstances, the possibility and attractions of an Anne Hutchinson become clearer. These religious communities were in constant flux, adjustment, and transformation, in part as they developed their own cultural imperatives and strengthened their defenses, but also as they experienced their own spiritual inspiration and the empowerment conveyed by this inspiration. Many men, entrepreneurs, master craftsmen, merchants, and a rising lesser gentry developed a powerful sense of personal authority through connection with the divine. Authority was not limited to leading men; many women, some key supporters of these faith-filled leaders, as well as people of the middling classes, grasped at and exercised their own voices. As the reform movement grew in a society ordered by the Church of England as well as the state, those who were not permitted to use their voices were relegated to supporting their own leaders with faithful attendance and money. But as order broke down, or had yet to be formed, space opened for the socially disfranchised but spiritually empowered.

Historians have long depicted Anne Hutchinson as a unique figure, impressive in her daring and power. And I do not mean to argue that she was anything less than a charismatic woman who gathered followers and attracted their allegiance. Nevertheless, beyond the tiny province of Massachusetts Bay, or even the larger New England, to the sprawling reformed network, other women also began to appear. Just as the embryonic colony suffered initial, liminal years characterized by conflict and instability, Civil War England, with the destruction of establishment institutions of authority and the disintegration of unity and order among the reformers, saw women arise. Anne Hutchinson was one of many impressive women who came forward. Two locations in different times, responding to different pressures but equally urgent in their efforts, shared a common social and cultural disarray.

Those English Christians who emigrated to New England were religious seekers. All sought their own personal, eternal salvation, and many entertained hopes of constructing a godly society on earth. New Englanders had risked lives and property in a colonization project aimed at the creation of a biblical commonwealth. Yet before this search led families to leave England, these Puritans, grounded in the confidence and strength attained in their spiritual journeys, fought against religious structures and boundaries imposed by bishop and king. In other words, the founders of Massachusetts had reached spiritual maturity within a climate of dissent; many colonizers were second- or even third-generation dissenters.

Puritans' foundational experiences had led them almost reflexively to question the established church and the state. And while they were resisting the demands of the state, that is, while they were struggling against conformity, they pursued holiness. Because the established church offered no spiritual nourishment that satisfied them, Puritans provided their own sustenance. Learned, pious clerics were identified and attended by Puritan believers, but often too few right-thinking ministers were available. In the absence of pastoral care the laity themselves often provided the services they needed: prayer meetings, biblical study, spiritual counseling, and even preaching. Private house meetings became a well-established feature of Puritan culture, and such mini-congregations not only supplemented but sometimes supplanted regular religious exercises for participants.[8]

New England colonists carried such lay activism with them to the new settlement, which proved particularly useful during the early years when a dearth of ministers left communities without pastoral leadership. For example, when the leaders of Massachusetts instructed John Wilson to leave the Boston congregation in order to fetch his wife from England, he exhorted the congregation to love, and "comended to them the exercise of prophesey in his absence, & designed those whom he thought most fitt to it. viz. the Governor, mr dudley & mr Noell the elder . . . ." During Cotton's early years, "the Lord gave witnes to the exercise of prophecy, so as thereby some were converted and others much edified."[9] Even Thomas Weld, one of the strongest opponents of lay preaching, admitted that in difficult times the laity were called upon to speak. "For though wee deny not, but in some case, some able judicious experienced Christians, may humbly & soberly, when necessity requires, as in the want of Ministers & being invited thereunto, dispence now and then a word of exhortation to their brethren." Weld may have believed that such exhortation was a poor substitute for "Preaching in an ordinary way, *with all Authority*." His quotation of Cotton's numbered list of guidelines suggests firm efforts to control such speech. Cotton prescribes that there should be "2 no prophecy till Elders have done, 3 not unlesse the time permit, 4 and then also they must first be called thereunto by the Elders." Nevertheless, Cotton's first point, "prophecy must, 1 be allowed for Prophets" reveals that, contra Thomas Weld's denial of the lay exhorter's authority, the speaker was understood to speak from a position of spiritual power.[10]

While Weld portrayed lay exhorters as having to meet certain standards of learning, prudence, and decorum, Puritan spirituality, with its focus upon the mystical conversion experience, recognized the potential of all believers to achieve spiritual success regardless of learning, rank, or other worldly accomplishments. Conversion alone did not establish an individual as a leader; but by privileging the mystical side of their religiosity, Puritans implied that the primary qualifications for leadership could be intangibles—gifted by God rather than man. As deeply religious women and men seeking after the Spirit, Puritan believers might turn to any person who promised a pathway toward salvation, anyone who seemed especially gifted. Of course, the compelling example of personal holiness was not always accompanied by spiritual knowledge and charisma: not every righteous practitioner could provide hope and enlightenment to others. So, too, clerics, by definition, had the knowledge, but not always the inspiration. This combination of knowledge, charisma, and holiness that created disciples was apparent in several New England ministers, including John Cotton, Thomas Hooker, Thomas Shepard, and Roger Williams. It was also present in Anne Hutchinson. That she was included in the clerical conferences of 1636 reflects, at the very least, the clergy's tacit acknowledgment of Hutchinson's strength and spiritual authority among the populace.

Intense seekers after reformation, truth, and salvation, New England Puritans not only envisioned the reform enterprise differently but also embraced a number of alternative spiritual roads, many of which emphasized communion with God. The lack of religious support from the established church turned many individuals toward private meetings where laypersons provided preaching and spiritual counseling. Even when a pastor was available, such meetings continued. The lay appetite for spiritual experience seemed insatiable. New Englanders had, after all, requested a weekday lecture as well as two Sunday services. From this perspective, Hutchinson provided an important service when she opened her home to private religious gatherings, offering a forum for further exploration and experience of the spiritual realm.[11] Add to this the value that Puritans placed upon spiritual rather than humane gifts, and it becomes absurd to think that Anne Hutchinson could have been the only layperson, or even the only laywoman, in such a position of leadership. The uniqueness of Hutchinson is a historical myth that should be dispelled. Hutchinson was undoubtedly one of many women engaged by these alternative religiosities: women who led private meetings, preached at them, and found a spiritual justification for their leadership.

Within their tradition, English Puritans honored many women among their founders. In that earliest, almost sacred account of the origins of the English reformed movement, John Foxe's *Acts and Monuments*, pious women, as well as men, demonstrated courage and strength of faith when called upon to suffer. Foxe honored Anne Askew, executed in 1546 for her unwavering adherence to reformation ideals, for her courage as she faced the fire. She had left her husband and her home in order to maintain her religious principles; she had endured torture. At the stake, she brought to her three compatriots in death "greater comfort in that so painful and doleful kind of death; [they], beholding her invincible constancy, and also stirred up through her persuasions, did set apart all kind of fear." One of the few women who left their own accounts of their ordeals, Askew would be read by her religious descendants as a model of female strength, "a singular example of christian constancy for all men to follow."[12]

In his accounts of the Marian persecutions, Foxe listed, among the hundreds of sufferers, more than eighty women.[13] Here, too, he told their stories in some detail, recording examinations, details of particularly harsh tortures, and dying speeches that came to his hand. Gender politics were certainly acted out during the persecutions against these women. When Rose Allin refused to counsel her parents to recant their Protestantism, proclaiming that "they have a better instructor than I; for the Holy Ghost doth teach them, I hope, which I trust will not suffer them to err," the persecutor burned her hand with a candle, calling her "gossip." After she proved able to endure the pain, he "thrust her from him violently, and said, 'Ah! strong whore; thou shameless beast! thou beastly whore!'" Likewise, Elizabeth Young, during her early examinations, was called rebel whore and traitorous whore; she was later released, in part due to her "weakness." Among the more revealing tales was that of Alice Benden, imprisoned for refusing to attend the church, delivered into her husband Edward's care, and then turned over to the magistrate by her husband after she refused to accompany him to the church. The intertwining of marital politics with the heresy trial became even more apparent when Edward sought her release (again), and it was refused because she was obdurate in her heresy. Edward then recommended that the bishop isolate her from her brother. "If your lordship could keep him from her, she would turn; for he comforteth her, giveth her money, and persuadeth her not to return or relent."[14]

It cannot be denied that seventeenth-century Puritan theologians also thought that women frequently courted heresy and blasphemy; they, too, lamented women's intellectual weakness and pitied (and feared) them in their heretical seduction. However, the honor that Puritans accorded these female martyrs does seem to override traditional perceptions of women's inferiority. Or perhaps the female example was even more astounding and had greater impact because women were expected to be weak and easily led. Surely such women as Alice Benden, and even the popular Anne Askew, staunch in their faith and their refusals to submit to their husbands' religious headship, presented models of mixed messages. John Bale, Askew's publisher, had concluded that in Askew "the strength of God is here made perfyght by weakenesse."[15] And what could be more powerful than a story such as that of Joan Waste, poor, blind, and illiterate? Her physical weakness and low status undoubtedly worked to enrage readers against the brutality of the persecutors. Foxe points up the contrast between Waste's lowliness—her impairments, lack of erudition, and poverty—and her extensive scriptural knowledge and spiritual strength.[16] It was as if the Holy Ghost used her quintessential female weakness and class identity as a counterpoint against which to display his extraordinary power.

As the reform movement progressed, or failed to progress, during the reign of Elizabeth, the heroism of those memorialized by Foxe would continue to inspire clerics, and lay men and women. Certainly the sufferings and stoicism of Foxe's women taught important lessons on the strength of the weak, affirming for female believers the potential of feminine spirituality, and the dangers of spiritual pride. They served as a warning to men who, supposedly stronger in body and mind, had yet to be challenged to accept the pain and humiliation endured silently by these of the weaker sex. In addition to balancing his portrait of the spiritual community, in the hope that future believers might find inspiration and grace, Foxe intended to record the historical realities of persecutions. Less concerned with publishing the activities of women who supported those pastors imprisoned during the Marian persecutions, in this venue women provided central emotional and, sometimes, logistic and financial support to men awaiting execution.[17] The large number of women found in Foxe's account of the Marian years reflects the very real importance of women to the reform movement. In England, women were sufficiently important to be burned as heretics; in exile, women served as key lay leaders and valued participants within the English communities on the continent.[18]

In his *Practical and Polemical Commentary*, Thomas Hall wrote, "God doth great things usually by weake meanes. He can make weake women instrumental to spread the Gospel." He was, of course, speaking of female martyrs.[19] But he could as easily have been referring to the activities of living believers who supported reforming clerics and spread their message across city and countryside. Patrick Collinson has argued that the women of London "occupied the front line in defence of their preachers," rising up before bishops and demanding justifications for decisions. When John Gough and John Philpot were sent out of London to Winchester, their departure was attended by two or three hundred women bringing them provender for the journey and "animating them most earnestly to stand fast in the same their doctrine." In the wake of the suspension of lecturer John Bartlett, sixty women rose up and marched their complaint to Bishop Grindal, at his home. The bishop ordered them to depart; they could send a few representative husbands with whom he would talk. However, the women refused to leave until John Philpot made the request. A month later, Grindal found himself "hooted at," especially by the women who cried "ware horns."[20]

If the Marian years were the era of women's heroic accomplishments, the Elizabethan age observed many contributions that built and sustained the

Puritan movement. During the latter half of the sixteenth century, women seemed to become increasingly important to the reform movement as spiritual leaders, correspondents, and gatherers of private house meetings. Anne Locke temporarily left her husband for Geneva during the Marian persecutions, translated and published the song of Hezekiah from Isaiah 38, and corresponded with John Knox. After her return to England in 1559, she continued this correspondence, serving as conduit between her community and the reformer. Upon her husband's death she married a vibrant Puritan minister, standing at the center of a community of female worshipers, many of whom were devoted followers of her husband. Toward the end of her life, while married to her third husband, she is known to have furthered the reform movement by sharing unpublished Knox manuscripts with others and publishing her own translation of Jean Taffin's *Of the markes of the children of God*.[21]

The Puritan movement was also assisted by devout widows who were printers and booksellers. Some women of wealth and rank, such as Lady Anne Bacon and Lady Elizabeth Russell, became honored patrons of the Puritan clergy.[22] Even beyond the financial support (and courtly influence) that these noblewomen could provide, women served as "patrons" in the sense of bringing the movement to their community and hearthside. Many reformers believed that women had great persuasive powers that they could exercise over fathers, husbands, and sons. Richard Hooker complained that Puritans labored most to convert female members, for their judgments were "weakest by reason of their sex" and yet they were "propense and inclinable to holiness." "[T]he eagerness of their affection, that maketh them, which way soever they take, diligent in drawing their husbands, children, servants, friends and allies the same way," would lead pastors and propagandists to see women as invaluable personal spiritual resources.[23]

It is not surprising that the Puritan movement attracted large numbers of female participants. The Puritan criticism of the Anglican clergy, particularly the bishops, accompanied a broader ideological movement that challenged the unmerited and corrupting privileges of the upper classes and hinted at sympathetic leveling tendencies. Such inclinations were also evident in reformers' successful efforts to recruit among the yeomanry and artisan classes; Foxe's martyrs were mostly members of these groups. While these men and women were certainly people of substance, they were not gentry and had yet to come into their own as a class with power. Male dissenters risked their standing and livelihoods; women, however, by virtue of their

civil nonexistence and general exclusion from the public economic and political spheres were, unless they were public nuisances, often ignored. Within
a movement in which the traditional hierarchies were questioned and unmediated pathways were opened to all believers, women might well have
enjoyed the freedom that their invisibility provided. They could seek and
find avenues of spiritual power for themselves and, in the process, surmount
some of the social limitations imposed by their gender.

This dynamic can be observed in Anne Askew's accounts of her
examinations and imprisonment.[24] Bale and Foxe, her publisher and me-
morialist, emphasized her weakness and gentility as a canvas upon which
God's Spirit could display his power and goodness. Askew's own writings,
however, reveal independence and great personal strength. When cast out
as a heretic by her Catholic husband, Thomas Kyme, Askew sought a divorce, invoking scripture to justify her request. She moved to London where
a significant Protestant circle, dominated by women, revolved around
Catherine Parr. When she was brought before the London jury on charges
of heresy, she embraced the public forum, describing and analyzing the numerous and sundry examinations. These dialogues revealed a woman who
outmaneuvered her judges, corrected their use of scripture, turned questions
and accusations to her own advantage, and incorporated a subtly ironic,
witty commentary on the contemporary perceptions of female deficiencies.
She portrayed herself as quick and clever, learned in scripture, dignified in
stature as well as unflinching, a woman steady in her beliefs even in the face
of torture and threatened death. Askew had the option of recantation and
accusation of compatriots, but, in choosing to stand firm, the ultimate end
of her ordeal was never in doubt. In the skill with which Askew could turn
phrases, manipulate the examinations, and rise victorious, at least rhetorically, over her opponents, she stands as a foremother of Hutchinson. Despite
the ultimate futility of their efforts, both used the forum offered by public
examinations to justify themselves and promote their cause.

In addition to the welcoming invitations and the opportunities for self-
realization found among the reformers, their dedicated religiosity may have
held special appeal. By the turn of the century Puritans were known (and
often mocked) for intense piety, tortured spirituality, and painful introspec-
tion. It was a character destined for parody—men and women seeking a perfection that they knew, intellectually, was not possible. Yet failure to struggle
was failure in faith. Belief may have been grounded in knowledge of the scripture, but the center of true piety and faith lay in the experiential knowledge of

God, experience that transformed the mind, heart, and will. This experiential base, often bordering on the mystical, combined with a Puritan focus upon personal and family holiness may have been, as Hooker argued, particularly attractive to women.[25]

Women's inclination toward these mystical, perfectionist spiritualities were apparent in their predominance among English sectarians. In their parodies, many Anglicans tended to lump all Puritan dissenters together, accusing the most conventional with ridiculous excesses, from the reclusive and tribal to the frivolous and profligate. The commitment to theological, ritual, and moral reform did lead to confrontational and, sometimes, socially disruptive behaviors, but before 1640 these dissenters were a fairly decorous lot. Yet even in these early years, from 1580 onward, there were extremists who pushed the possibilities of politics, theology, and ritual praxis ever outward. Many women found honor as well as significant service among congregations attending the more conventional of the reformed clerics: those with Puritan sympathies who nevertheless managed to hold on to their benefices until the 1620s. Indeed, most identifiably dissenting women would have been found in these congregations. Still, some women flocked to those sectaries that were enthusiastically committed to the more radical, egalitarian, mystical spiritualities.

Among the most extreme of these early sectaries were the English followers of Hendrik Niclaes, an Anabaptist originally of Munster.[26] Following his imprisonment for heresy, Niclaes fled to Amsterdam in the 1530s and there founded his Familia Caritatis, or Family of Love. He visited England in the final years of the reign of Edward VI and attracted a significant following that, while remaining small, never really disappeared. His followers even managed to translate and publish several of his voluminous texts. While Niclaes did not return to England before his death in 1580, his small band of disciples persevered covertly until the upheaval of the Civil War allowed all sectaries to come above ground again. During the 1640s and 1650s, the Familist communities increased their membership, while the writings of Niclaes, reissued by radical printers, inspired a variety of sectaries.[27]

Niclaes experienced a series of divine visions, or revelations, that called him to prophesy and establish his Familia Caritatis. His published writings generally begin with a testimony to these revelations as the primary authority, as powerful as scripture itself, for his text.[28] Several of his texts incorporated long accounts of elaborate visions that appear to be allegories outlining the successful pathways toward salvation. His theology was constructed around the love of God and called upon his followers to open themselves up to the divine promise. In describing the possibility of mystical union with the divine, Niclaes employed the language of "godded with God, one beeing with Gods Beeing," a communion beyond the spiritual capabilities of most, if not all, of humanity. In fact, while the possibility was certainly there for all believers (witness Niclaes's own experiences), the subtext of the accounts of these visions and promises indicates that for many, spiritual pleasure would be found in the struggle itself, rather than the mystical achievement.[29]

In seeking this union with God, believers were encouraged to distinguish between spiritual enlightenment and ordinary learning. Niclaes warned of the temptations of humane learning and decried erudition in favor of spiritual knowledge. "It is true indeed that the truth ought not to give place, but betwixt the knowledge and the truth, there is a great difference: for much knowledge (which yet men call truth), can, easily arise out of the subtilty of wit; but the truth of God proceedeth out of the love, and is even of one being with the love."[30] While Niclaes understood that many found comfort and security in placing their faith in knowledge, or earthly wisdom, he wrote of the emptiness of such security and its failure to bring peace. Learning was not evil, but it was incomplete and useless in and of itself, for, as many a pedant had failed to notice, such learning was located within a mind unredeemed and therefore flawed. Misplaced pride in reason and theological knowledge had led to schisms throughout the Christian community, schisms that were frequently accompanied by vitriolic accusations and remonstrances, all working together to destroy God's kingdom. After embracing the spirit of God's love, a person was able to profit from learning through a mind reclaimed. In one long allegorical tale, "Testimony of Truth" came to earth to fetch "Mans Understanding," who, untrusting at first, finally embraced and was transformed by spiritual enlightenment.

> Then said *Testimony of Truth* to the *Mans* sanctified *Understanding*; behold, now understandest thou . . . that Gods Light and Wisdom, and his heavenly Riches (which are come unto thee out of his living Beeing) doth far excell the Light and Wisdom that proceedeth out of the riches of the Knowledg; and that thou before (the whilest thou soughtest the Wisdom in the Knowledg, and in the ingenious Prudencie) inheritedst not else, what, but great travell, heaviness, and the deadly beeing: but now (in this same Wisdom of God) the Rest, and the everlasting life.[31]

Although moderate Puritans would have denied any similarities, the Familists resembled them in many ways. They condemned church buildings, called by the people "Gods houses; and they use there many maner of foolishnesses of taken on Services, which they call Religions, or God-services, whereby to wave or hold forth something in shew, before the ignorant people . . ." In their perception of the need for reason to be enlightened through the believer's spiritual transformation, the Familists were not far from moderate reformers, who also judged reason to be flawed. The primary difference lay in degree. Most Puritans, and certainly the clergy, were prepared to accept human reason as a valuable, though flawed, gift, whereas the Familists, in their extreme emphasis upon divine love, had to forfeit all reliance upon learning, encouraging individuals toward a holy life rather than study and preparation with a pastor. In their rejection of games and gambling, theater, musical instruments, and foolish books, they also appeared to echo their moderate colleagues. In fact, they were more extreme here as well, condemning jewels, plate, and ornamental dress, not only feathers, silks and embroidery, but even "divers sorts of unprofitable colours upon Cloathes."[32]

Moderate reformers were willing to embrace the paradox of encouraging learning while crediting spiritual enlightenment, the counterpoint of the free offer of God's saving grace (or love) with the honor of the believer's struggle. The spiritual commitments of Niclaes and the Familists fell entirely on the side of passivity and light. While Puritans sought that mystical connection and believed, theoretically, in unmediated pathways to the divine, Familist theology and practice acted out the realities of mystical communion with God, encouraging (requiring) everyone to experience divine love for himself or herself. In the city of peace, declared Niclaes, all were equal and righteous. There was no need to urge people to religious learning or practice; all had achieved salvation. There was no private property, no discord, for all were perfect in the Spirit and kept the commandments. The result was an implied rejection of the law as unnecessary, and a truly egalitarian ethos that outraged most other religionists in England.

> Hereunto we are all called to one and in one, no man exempted, the Gentiles as well as the Jews, the Commons of the people as well as the Magistrates, the sinners as well as the wise, the wives as well as the husbands, the children as well as the parents, the bond as well as the free, the servants as well as the masters, and the handmaids as well as the Mistresses, God is no respecter of persons; for all those that turn them to God and love his Righteousnesse are acceptable unto him.[33]

The Familists were among the most extreme of the sectaries, often pro-mulgating their own revelations as equal if not superior to the Scriptures, but they were by no means the only community standing outside the bound-aries of respectable dissent. During the early decades of the seventeenth cen-tury, the Grindletonians appeared in Yorkshire. Followers of Roger Brearley, curate of Grindleton, they supposedly established a new religion founded entirely upon Brearley's teachings, believing that "the Arke of the covenant is shutt upp and pinned within the walls of Grindleton Chappell." They found it absolutely necessary for a believer to experience the Spirit person-ally, and they proceeded to judge the individual's experience by their own standards.[34] Another radical sect, the Eatonites, were convinced that through the Holy Spirit baptism created a new creature requiring neither the min-istry of the word nor the restrictions of the law.[35] Anabaptists, imported by Dutch practitioners, developed small but loyal congregations of individuals who refused to sanction infant baptism. Barrowists, Brownists, and other separatists completely rejected the Church of England as irredeemably cor-rupt and thus incapable of nurturing piety, guarding morality, or promoting the progress of the spirit.[36]

Although no sect matched the Familists in every particular (like the moderates, most would have been shocked at the suggestion), they did to some extent share limited trust in reason and erudition, perfectionist regimens, mystical intensity, and a practical realization of the heretofore theoretical concept of spiritual equality. These features all worked to attract women to the sectaries. Throughout the 1580s, sectarian women, as well as men, were called before the visitations to answer for their nonconformity. Helen Colman and Dorothy Fenning admitted their participation within a conventicle of separatists, while Margaret Colevill confessed to perfectionist convictions. During this era, the majority of those imprisoned at Bridewell as separatists were women, while several female separatists were known to have left their husbands for the haven of the Netherlands.[37]

Upon the death of Elizabeth and the accession of James I, the Church of England, supported by the monarch, grew less patient with moderate reformers and altogether intolerant of sectarians. Throughout the first decades of the Stuart reign, the repression of dissent increased almost ex-ponentially, and both moderates and sectarians appear to have moved un-derground into those conventicles and house meetings. I suspect that the relative silence of sectarian voices during these years reflected neither a loss of spiritual commitment nor the disappearance of these communities but the success of persecution as a damper upon public enthusiasm. The most moderate of Puritan clerics were deposed, defrocked, and silenced; presses were censored; laypersons were fined; and sectarians not in hiding were either in prison or, like the Brownists who fled in 1605, out of the country. In the face of an increasingly hostile officialdom, women continued to play significant roles in the dissenting communities. In the 1620s, for example, Arthur Lake, as Bishop of Bath and Wells, preached a sermon at St. Cuthbert's, Wells, "when certaine Persons did Penance for being at conventicles where a Woman Preached."[38] In Northumberland, historians have found a record of one Anne Fenwick who had built a reputation for godliness, spiritual charisma, and intellectual gifts. She was well known to Bishop Richard Neale, who summoned her to Durham in order to examine her, but she managed to escape into the underground. When Thomas Shepard stayed in Heddon prior to his migration to New England, he noted that he had spent several months in the home of a Mistress Fenwick.[39]

The continuing dissent and lay activism, male and female, were apparent in the events of the 1630s, 1640s, and 1650s, when the absence of effective monarchical or Anglican authority opened the way for Puritan dissenters to construct their own congregations. Clerics and laypersons alike publicly explored the meaning of the Scriptures, deciphered the true path toward salvation, and prophesied and proselytized among their neighbors.

The colonization of Massachusetts Bay and the English Civil War have, at first glance, little in common, save that both were prosecuted by Puritan reformers who were responding to increasingly difficult political conditions. The colonization of New England involved a socially homogeneous segment of the English population who removed themselves far from the persecuting rigors of the Laudian movement and from the daily comforts and demands of English life. Although there was frequent communication with England, the colonists enjoyed the protections and suffered the miseries of relative isolation from crown and homeland. Their goal was the construction of a self-sufficient, self-governing colony free from royal interference and yet under the ostensible authority of the king. They paid for this autonomy with struggles against unfamiliar terrain, primitive material conditions, and towns situated amid Indigenous communities whom they feared and despised, attacked and thus provoked. The parliamentary uprising involved a less homogeneous population who, far from isolated, acted amid the intensifying persecutions and increasing restrictions of the royal government. Willing to forfeit their own personal comforts, their goal was the destruction of the power of the monarch and the reformation of the government with Parliament at the center. The price of open warfare was paid not only by themselves but by England as a whole as well as Scotland and Ireland and, unlike the success of colonization, the Civil War failed to solidify a unified, reformed national church, much less establish a secure Commonwealth government that would endure beyond Oliver Cromwell's life.

Despite these obvious differences, the religious and cultural environment of the New England of the 1630s was comparable to that of the England of the 1640s and 1650s. The same political/cultural vacuum functioned in these two separate regions and decades, by virtue of the removal of the Church of England as a religious authority and the king as an effective governor. The New England leadership immediately confronted a diversity of religious beliefs and practices to be sifted and organized into an orthodox platform along with a panoply of experimenters who had to be discounted, disfranchised, or silenced. As one contemporary English commentator explained, "Some persons among those . . . that went to hence to New-England, being fraighted with many loose, and unsound opinions, which they durst not here, they there began to vent them . . ."[40]

The Commonwealth churches engaged a similar process of consensus construction that failed and experienced an even more explosive outbreak of sectaries, most of whom were tolerated by the state. The difference between the New England and English responses may have been the difference between peace and war; or between geographically tiny and large areas; or between small and large populations; or, still, between the complete absence and the limited presence, however disempowered, of the Anglican Church and the supporters of the king respectively. However the difference in response to dissent is interpreted, it remains noteworthy that, in the words of Stephen Foster, "representatives of most of the sectarian Puritan opinions that emerged in Interregnum England were to be found in some form in New England."[41] Parallel networks of sectaries, prophets, and competing congregations arose, phoenix-like in both regions, due to the breakdown of social and religious order.

The resemblances between these two phenomena—the shared cultural ancestry of the participants, the variety and multiplicity of dissenters, and the precondition of religious/cultural instability—become important in the effort to understand the nature of dissent within New England and the responses, official and otherwise, to that dissent. What happened in Massachusetts has been carefully documented: the extensive records of the three major, and many smaller, episodes provide a thorough account of the colony's religious disorder during its first two decades. In addition to the Hutchinsonians and the separatist followers of Roger Williams in Salem, Massachusetts's leaders battled against the charismatic Samuel Gorton. Envisioning himself a preacher of free grace, Gorton led a group of ambitious young followers out of the colony into territory unclaimed by any jurisdiction, thereby uniting Massachusetts and Rhode Island in a strange alliance against him in order to control a community both colonies considered anarchic.[42]

Among the many smaller episodes, Stephen Batchelor, leader of a group called the "Husbandmen," in 1632 founded a separate congregation at Lynn, and though enjoined to stop preaching, continued to do so in Saugus, then at Newbury and Hampton.[43] Baptists also had a serious following in Massachusetts. The most famous incident involved the arrest, imprisonment, and punishment of John Clarke, John Crandall, and Obadiah Holmes, three Baptists from Rhode Island. It must be remembered, however, that when they preached in the northern coastal towns in the late 1640s, they found many interested in their doctrine, including some who were immediately rebaptized. In fact, some Massachusetts residents had come to support the Baptist doctrine prior to and independently of these preachers, including Lady Deborah Moody; several clerics, including Thomas Lenthall and Hanserd Knollys; and two early presidents of Harvard College, Charles Chauncy and Henry Dunster.[44] Moreover, when several more sects, such as the Fifth Monarchists and the Quakers, rose up in England during the 1640s and 1650s, many New Englanders, including some who had returned to England and some who remained in the colonies, quickly joined their ranks.[45]

One of the best reflections of the disorder that flourished at the most mundane level involved the case of Welsh preacher Marmaduke Matthews. In 1649, Matthews, then minister at Hull, was called before the General Court of Massachusetts to answer for erroneous and unsafe expressions: expressions that to modern ears sound rather Hutchinsonian in tenor, although the court did not charge him with this connection. Admonished and officially separated from his congregation, Matthews still failed to satisfy objections raised by the magistrates, and he continued to preach. The court had warned the town of Malden "not to proceed to the ordination of Mr. Mathewes . . . yett, contrary to all advice, and the rule of Gods word, as also the peace of the churches, the church of Malden hath proceeded to the ordination of Mr Mathewes . . ." Because New England faced a shortage of ministers (yes, even Puritans had a shortage), congregants' spiritual hopes moved them to take risks. As the women of Malden had put it: "god in great mercie to our souls as we Trust hath after many prayers Indeavors & long wayting brought Mr. Mathews Among us & putt him into the worke of the Ministrie. . . . [By his] pious life & labour the Lord hath Afforded [us] Many Saving convictions . . . and Consolations." Two years later, he still refused to acknowledge his sin, and the court fined him ten pounds. The town of Malden, seemingly unrepentant, was fined fifty pounds. In the end, Matthews delivered some form of confession, not as complete as had been hoped, but accepted nonetheless.[46]

Incidents like the rebellious call to Matthews occurred frequently during the early decades of Massachusetts's development, but beyond listing the names of accused, the documents provide only haphazard, incomplete information. Even less is known about the ideological dynamics and social and cultural networks out of which these sectaries erupted, particularly the activities, inspiration, and ultimate authority of female dissenters and leaders. The limitations of such knowledge have led to the perception of Hutchinson as an exceptional, if not unique, figure among Puritan women. Historians cannot interpret New England documents and texts that don't exist, but the recorded behavior of women like Mary Oliver, Sarah Keayne, and the women of Malden who praised Matthews and berated the court for not providing spiritual leadership points toward a more complex interpretation of Puritanism's gender dynamics. Some women felt empowered. Whatever the limitations of the New England data, the materials from revolutionary England reveal the religious possibilities inherent within Puritan culture and patterns of participation and response. The upsurge of sectarianism during the 1640s and 1650s and the significant number of women who preached, prophesied, and organized congregations indicate that Hutchinson might be better understood as an early New England example of the kind of women empowered and voiced by the Spirit within a society enmeshed in political and religious chaos.[47]

By 1642, the English Parliament proved not only sufficiently exasperated with royal domestic and religious policy but also sufficiently strong to challenge Charles I and his advisers.[48] Parliament raised its own army and waged war against the king and his supporters. Within seven years, these revolutionaries had destroyed the power of the monarchy, cowed the Anglican Church, executed William Laud, Archbishop of Canterbury, and King Charles, and erected a new Commonwealth government under the Protectorate of Oliver Cromwell. Among the earliest, most difficult problems facing the parliamentary government was the establishment of a newly reformed state church. Like their colleagues in New England, the now powerful

Puritans found that they could not agree among themselves upon the doctrine and the structure of the new church.

In the battle for ecclesiastical control, the primary antagonists were the Presbyterians, favoring a highly educated clergy and church hierarchy that extended above the congregational level, and the Independents, supporting primary congregational authority and greater power for the laity. On the periphery of these battles some Puritans were exploring further possibilities of radical reform, and the old radicals like the Brownists, Familists, and Anabaptists were joined by such new communities as the Ranters, Seekers, Levellers, and Fifth Monarchists.[49] Presbyterians argued for purity of doctrine and the power of an established church, demanding that unseemly sectarians and heretics be controlled by the state. On the other side the pragmatic Independents, recognizing the need for political solidarity and the presence of a significant number of sectarians in the popular army, chose to tolerate those dissenters who did not challenge the legitimacy of the Commonwealth government. Clerics and laypersons in both camps contributed to a flourishing, furious pamphlet war (and the burgeoning print industry), with Independents calling Presbyterians legalistic, narrow-minded persecutors, and Presbyterians attacking Independents as sectarian, anarchistic schismatics. Not far behind, the sectarians found everybody lacking in civility and godliness and promoted their own spiritual causes in print.[50]

The sheer number of pamphlets and books published, not to mention the intensity, enthusiasm, and severity of many of the authors, reflected the partisans' zealous commitment to their causes. In particular the Presbyterians of England, like the leaders of Massachusetts, were deeply concerned with orthodoxy and order. And while many Presbyterian writers, from erudite clerics to sympathetic satirists, devoted a significant amount of ink to attacking the sectarians, these most decorous Puritans also found much fault with the doctrinal stance and practices of Independent ministers and congregations. Many Independents downplayed the rigors of the law and favored lay leadership, both organizational and spiritual. Presbyterian polemicists were most distressed at the number of laymen and laywomen who gathered new communities, led small groups in separating from their parish congregations, and served as lay exhorters. Moreover, they were extremely critical of the Independents' position on religious toleration, in essence blaming them for the proliferation of blasphemous, disorderly sectaries. Within this critical literature is an extraordinarily intriguing and complete, if one-sided, portrait of the religious radicalism of the age.

In his vitriolic and excruciatingly long and detailed *Gangraena*, Thomas Edwards opened his discussion with a jumbled list of 176 errors.[51] This list was a true hodgepodge, with no heresy assigned to any of the sixteen sectaries that he identified. Nevertheless, the list served as a rhetorical alarm, for Edwards's identification of sixteen sectaries, beginning with Independents, ending with Skeptics, and encompassing both known communities, like Brownists, and generic adjectival labels such as Enthusiasts, reflects his own conviction that all non-Presbyterians were alike.[52] One of the most grievous faults in his eyes was the leadership and preaching of women, and *Gangraena* was filled with dark hints of silly, ignorant women overwhelming and suppressing the more appropriate leadership of men. Women's preaching was understood as one predictable result of an iniquitous ideological framework that privileged extempore speech above prepared text, spiritual inspiration above erudition, and spiritual equality above earthly rank and stature. Some of the sectaries even justified their way with "miracles, revelations, [and] visions."[53] Edwards's 127th and 128th errors concerned sectarians' topsy-turvy approach to preaching. They believed

> that men ought to preach and exercise their gifts without study and premeditation, and not to think of what they are to say till they speak, because it shall be given them in that hour, and the Spirit shall teach them. . . .
>
> That there is no need of humane learning, nor of reading Authors for Preachers, but all books and learning must go down, it comes from the want of the Spirit, that men writ such great volumes, and make such adoe of learning.

Edwards discovered that out of this rejection of erudition and study and this trust in the personal inspiration of the Spirit, many had concluded that the pulpit should be open to all supposedly called by the Spirit. These sectarians believed (Error 124) that it was "lawfull for women to preach, and why should they not, having gifts as well as men? and some of them actually do preach, having great resort to them."[54]

Of course, Edwards was not the first to note that by placing a premium upon the work of the Spirit within believers, some religionists were empowering women. In the sermon against women preachers that he delivered at St. Cuthbert's, Arthur Lake pointed to the problem posed by Puritans' belief in the Holy Spirit. Amid a long disputation that reduced godly women to subservient, silent wives and sermon hearers, Lake acknowledged that in both Old and New Testaments, God "raysed up Prophetesses," citing the promise in the book of Joel: I will "power [sic] out my Spirit upon all flesh: and your sonnes and your daughters shal prophecie." Lake further noted, however, that God's use of women as prophets was "extraordinary." The Bishop gave it as his judgment that while God "by a silly woman gave entrance unto Christianitie in a whole Kingdome . . . such instances are rare, and they are workes wherein GOD shewed himselfe to have power to dispense with his owne Ordinance, and dispose at his pleasure of his owne gifts." Bishop Lake completed his indictment by positioning women prophets and priests among pagan polytheists of the past. "Ordinarie Women—Prophets and Priests, sprang up amongst the heathen with the corruption of Religion, who as they had female Gods, so had those Gods for their attendants suitable persons of their owne Sexe; yea, sometimes their He-Gods had She-Priests, in the Poets tales you shall find enough of such trash."[55]

John Elborow, Anglican critic of all Puritans, complained in 1637 that women were fomenting schisms within their parishes, declaiming against church government, against bishops, against the liturgy and vestments, against the ring at marriage and the cross at baptism. He regretted the power that congregations gave to such women and feared what would come.

> It is lamentable to consider, that abundance of knowledge should produce such ill effects; as rebellion, disunanimity, disuniformity: that every woman will be a *Bernice*, & dare to interpret Scripture, which is not of private interpretation; that every *Euodias* and *Syntyche* will busily intermeddle with the Rites and government of the Church, and teach the magistrate to rule, and the Minister to preach . . .[56]

Eight years later, the anonymous pamphlet *A Spirit moving in the Women-Preachers* attacked this "affronted, brazen-faced, strange new Feminine Brood." From the title page onward, the author questioned the women's personal character, calling them "rash, ignorant, ambitious, weake, vaineglorious, prophane and proud, moved onely by the spirit of error." Although women's personal weaknesses were the primary arguments against their assumption of such public roles, the position was reinforced by the observation that such women demonstrably brought disorder and fomented schism. The author was most outraged that these women claimed that their authority was lodged in the workings of the Spirit.

Puffed up with pride, divers of them have lately advanced themselves with vain-glorious arrogance, to preach in mixt Congregations of men and women, in an insolent way, so usurping authority over men, and assuming a calling unwarranted by the word of God for women to use, yet all under colour, they act as the Spirit moves them; wherein they highly wrong and abuse the motions of that blessed Spirit, to make him to be the Author of so much Schisme, disorder, and to contenance their ignorance, pride, and vain-glorie...

This anonymous critic noted that sectarians (unspecified) invoked a millennialist vision and argued that due to the lack of "good" men, virtuous women were needed in the pulpits. Men were "good for nothing, but to make their Texts good by expounding the language of the Beast, but [women] themselves would preach nothing, but such things as the spirit should move them."[57]

John Taylor complained of a similar attitude among the Brownists. He attributed to them a prayer of thanksgiving for "those blessed and fruit-bearing women, who are not only able to talk on any Text, but search into the deep sense of the Scripture, and preach both in their owne families and elsewhere" and complained that "in some families the women catechize and preach, making the backside of her groaning Chaire the Pulpit, their prayers being unpremeditate and without president." John Vicars was outraged to find "*saucie Boyes*," "bold botching Taylors," and "illiterate *mechanicks*" in the pulpit, and "to see bold impudent huswives, without al womanly modesty, to take upon them (in the natural volubility of their tongues, & quick wits, or strong memories onely) to prate (not preach or Prophesie) after a narrative or discoursing manner, an houre or more . . ." Here, as in much of this literature, women, children, and ignorant male laborers are classified together as the unfit.[58]

In many cases, diatribes against women preaching remained general, abstract indictments, but some publications named names. *A Discoverie of Six Women Preachers* identified all six: two women of London, three of Kent, and a woman preaching in Ely. The author reported that Anne Hemstall was inspired by a vision of the prophetess Anna, opening her preaching with "Now doth the holy Ghost descend downe upon you, wherefore give eare unto me." And although skeptical, the author noted that she did in fact attract a crowd, for some had come from miles away to hear her. Joan Bauford of Kent supposedly taught that wives were free to forsake unbelieving husbands, while Arabella Thomas, also of Kent, predicted doom for all ministers who failed to preach twice on the Sabbath. In his exposé of William Franklin, a man who claimed to be Christ, Humphry Ellis identified Mary Gadbury as "professing and asserting her self to be *The Spouse of Christ*, called *The Lady Mary, the Queen, and Bride, the lambs Wife*." Shocked as he was by Franklin's claims and activities, Humphry managed to lay the greatest blame upon Gadbury.[59]

Among the unsympathetic texts, the longest list of female preachers can be found in Edwards's *Gangraena*. Acting as an unofficial heresiographer for the Presbyterian party, Edwards had encouraged his colleagues across the nation to send him information on sectarian abuses. He printed everything he could verify (although his testimonials are often "unsigned") and much of what he could not substantiate. While he was angered by women who heckled ministers, he saved his greatest fury for those who preached. He reported that a Lincolnshire woman preached and, supposedly, baptized, although he was uncertain of the latter. He had learned of some women preachers in Hartfordshire who "take upon them at meetings to expound the Scriptures in Houses, and preach on Texts," of a woman preacher on the isle of Ely, "Island of Errors and Sectaries," and of some London "women who for some time together have preached weekly on every Tuesday about four of the clock, unto whose preaching many of resorted."[60] In Kent, he claimed, "there is a woman Preacher (one at least if not more) in which company besides Preaching, 'tis reported (as this Minister saith, very commonly) that they break bread also, and every one in their order."[61] Moreover, he discovered that even in the army the dangerous ranks of mechanic preachers and political levelers might be augmented by women. A lieutenant in the army of Thomas Fairfax had told Edwards that "women might preach, and would have had a gentlewoman in the house (this young mans sister) to have exercised her gifts, telling her he knew she had gifts and had been alone meditating."[62]

Edwards's citations of women preachers among the sectaries were mostly one-time references, anonymous except for the name of the town or county in which they appeared. Edwards expected his readers to assume, as he did, that these women were ridiculous, if not delusional or dangerous. Yet despite his hostile agenda, the two exceptions to the anonymous examples show the diversity of women who drew his ire. In London, Mrs. Attaway, a lace seller, joined forces with a gentlewoman, wife of a major in the army, and a third unnamed woman. Attaway began the meeting with the almost obligatory allusion to Joel, "that God would poure out his Spirit upon the handmaidens, and they should prophecy." She then prayed extemporaneously for half an hour and preached for forty-five minutes. The gentlewoman followed her, was flustered by heckling, and was defended by Attaway. Edwards further noted that they preached at least twice more. When one woman asked Mrs. Attaway by what warrant she preached, she cited four biblical texts and claimed authority under the gifts of the Spirit. Doubtless Edwards felt that the circumstance in which a gentlewoman required assistance from a lower-class woman further demonstrated the unsoundness and instability of the sectarians. His judgment was further supported by reports that Attaway had defended Milton's doctrine of divorce, left her husband and children, and run off with a preacher who had left his pregnant wife and children.[63]

The second woman Edwards mentioned by name was the famous Katherine Chidley, variously labeled as Brownist, Leveller, and, as she identified herself, Independent. She, too, was active in London, where she was described by Edwards as engaged in debate with William Greenhill, minister at Stepney. Chidley later moved from London to Suffolk, where she founded an Independent congregation. Edwards worked hard to make her ridiculous, describing the debate as an occasion during which Greenhill answered and confounded her, "but in stead of being satisfied or giving any answer, she was so talkative and clamorous, wearying him with her words, that he was glad to go away, and so left her." A later reference portrayed her as a "brasen-faced audacious old woman [who] resembled unto Jael." (This reference to Jael seems an unconscious slip of the pen, since Jael was on the side of the righteous and, as everyone would have known, killed the enemy general by driving a peg through his head.) Edwards failed to mention that she had, by this point, published two pamphlets that explicitly attacked his own treatises, pamphlets that reveal Chidley to be a thoughtful, knowledgeable, and well-spoken polemicist who easily outmaneuvered Edwards.[64]

In hundreds of pages attacking the theology, practices, and manners of Independents and sectarians, Edwards provided an extraordinary catalog of information concerning religious leaders who had risen from among the disfranchised, especially women and the lower classes. Yet the aura of intense hostility that surrounds this evidence undermines its credibility. The few opportunities that exist to interrogate Edwards's statements, for example by comparing his derogatory portrait of Katherine Chidley with the quality of her own writings, raise further concerns. Perhaps he overstated the numbers of women preachers in order to further his antisectarian cause, denigrating

sectarians as both attractive to and led by women. He might have exaggerated the numbers because he expected numbers to be high, or because, in
the mind of the polemicist, three or four became multitudes. Yet, as Ann
Hughes has so eloquently expressed, the blatant bias of a source does not
necessarily render it fiction,[65] and Edwards's account of extensive female religious leadership was well supported by other sources. In addition to hostile
pamphlets, there were a few anti-Presbyterian tracts written by sympathetic
men who knew of women preachers (as well as "mechanicks") and praised
their commitment, ability, and spirituality. More important, women left their
own texts. Some wrote brief accounts of their ministries; a few more had disciples who recorded their words and saw the speeches through publication;
but most wrote and published their own prophecies and revelations as they
had been inspired by the Spirit.

The pamphlet literature of the 1640s and 1650s, as well as scattered records
of sectarian communities, reveal the names of more than three hundred
women preachers, prophets, writers, and congregational leaders.[66] About
some of these women almost nothing is known but name and place. For example, Joan Bauford, Mary Bilbrowe, Anne Hempstall, Susan May, Arabella
Thomas, and Elizabeth Bancroft are named in *A Discoverie of Six Women
Preachers* with scarcely any details. The anonymous author located three
of these women, May, Bauford, and the Welsh Thomas, in or near Kent
and noted that Hempstall preached at St. Andrews, while Bilbrowe spoke
in the parish of St. Giles. Historians have found some interest in Bancroft,
who preached against Laudian ritual in Ely, Cambridgeshire, and may have
been the "woman of Ely" mentioned during Hutchinson's trial. But many
others, like Katherine Chidley, were authors in their own right. To be sure,
Chidley's work as a polemicist and defender of Independency marked her
as exceptional among women writers, although Elizabeth Warren's texts of
spiritual edification were also crafted within a polemical frame, such as her
Old and Good Way Vindicated, written as a defense of a minister.[67] However,
most published women wrote from a more personal position. Lady Eleanor
Audeley Davies Douglas produced a plethora of texts recounting her own
prophecies and denouncing her treatment at the hands of the state.[68] Anna
Trapnel traveled about to bring the truth of the gospel to all; as she fell into
trances, her utterances were transcribed and later published for the edification of her readers and the vindication of her prophetic work and words.[69]
Susanna Parr, on the other hand, published to defend herself against public
attacks by the pastor of the congregation that she founded.[70] The writings

of these women, as well as the publications of sympathetic friends and defenders, clarify and elaborate the opportunities that women found as participants and leaders within the multivocal crisis culture that Puritanism had become.

Women preachers and prophets appear throughout the two decades of the Commonwealth period, and their activities seem to have been concentrated in London, although that may be the illusionary byproduct of the position of the city's print industry as primary publishers of preachers/prophets and therefore a key resource for historians working to recover these actors. Quaker women, a group who published extensively, corresponded, and kept accounts of members and the travels of their missionaries, have been found by historians throughout Britain. Preaching women also represented a range of classes, including the aristocratic Eleanor Douglas, gentlewoman Margaret Fell of Lancashire, Mary Pope and Katherine Chidley, wives of a merchant and a haberdasher, respectively, and Elinor Channel, the wife of "a very poor man" with "many small children, three of them very young ones," who, failing to get an audience with Cromwell, traveled to London and managed to publish her words through the intervention of Arise Evans.[71]

While many were not directly concerned with the political order, others expressed views reflecting a range of positions. Eleanor Douglas had prophesied, with some pleasure, the downfall and death of Archbishop William Laud and of King Charles.[72] Mary Pope wrote in support of restoring Charles to the throne, denouncing the "unjust" Civil War, and Elizabeth Poole wrote in support of clemency for Charles. Although Poole supported the nascent Commonwealth, her three pamphlets, published before and after Charles's execution, become increasingly strident in their condemnation of the Commonwealth army's action.[73] Elinor Channel explicitly called on Cromwell to protect the king's elder son Charles so that he could return from exile in France and ascend the throne.[74] Moving leftward, Katherine Chidley wrote as a defender of Parliament as well as Independency and religious toleration; she was probably a supporter of John Lilburne, friend of her son Samuel, and the Levellers.[75] Many other preaching women, such as printer Mary Overton, were strong advocates of this radical parliamentarian party, which incorporated an egalitarian politics, spiritual and secular, that extended to women as well as the middling and lower classes.[76] Fifth Monarchist Mary Cary fully supported the Parliament's actions, asserting that she had long known that "Parliament should prevail over him, and at last destroy him."[77] Going further, fellow traveler Anna Trapnel denounced

Cromwell for his "great pomp, and revenue, whiles the poor are ready to starve," and she prophesied for Cromwell what Douglas had promised Charles, predicting the imminent downfall of the Commonwealth unless they moved toward creating Christ's kingdom on earth.[78]

These women arose from a variety of denominations and sectaries. In addition to the Presbyterians and Independents, there were Brownists, Fifth Monarchists, Baptists, a few Royalists like Channel who were, perhaps, Anglicans, and Eleanor Douglas, whose theology incorporated universal salvation.[79] Fifth Monarchists such as Trapnel were particularly prominent, in part because they were among the very few organized sectarian groups to offer continuous, vocal challenge to Cromwell's government and, therefore, among the few sectarians to be censured and, sometimes, imprisoned by the Commonwealth. Fifth Monarchists included many women among their prophets, and, as B. S. Capp notes, in the surviving church lists women outnumber men.[80] By far the largest number of women leaders who appear in the historical record during these decades can be identified as Seekers, later Quakers, which perhaps explains a contemporary observation that all Quakers were women.[81] In her definitive treatment of seventeenth-century Quaker women, *Visionary Women*, Phyllis Mack identified 120 active Quaker women, including 56 authors, and an additional 123 Quaker women who appear only once or twice in the record. More than 80 percent of women identified as preachers were Quakers.[82] The overwhelming predominance of Quakers among preaching women during the Civil War may well reflect the attraction that this movement held for women across Britain and Ireland. However, like the historical factors that lead historians to London, the predominance of Quakers among preaching women could also be a function of the longevity, organizational stability, and dedication to print and posterity that has characterized the Quaker community.

Many of the contemporary attacks on women preachers employed a rhetoric connecting these women with the lowest classes, "women and mechanick preachers," to mark their behavior as vulgar and their minds as untrained and uneducated. Katherine Chidley deeply resented Presbyterian accusations that Independent sectaries were led by illiterate preachers harboring contempt for authority.[83] The writings of a few of these women display astute critical skills and suggest some knowledge of the classics. Just as Anne Hutchinson's intellectual training was evident in the verbal exchanges reported by her detractors, Chidley's abilities came through in her sophisticated responses to Thomas Edwards's attacks on Independency. Her *Justification of the Independent Churches of Christ* cut through Edwards's profuse verbiage and layers of biblical and theological citations to focus directly upon the arguments for and against Independency. She challenged the applicability of his scriptural references, claimed that Edwards had "misread" John Robinson, and she denounced Calvin, as well as Edwards, for constructing their church organization out of "unwritten verities."[84] Elizabeth Warren, also an articulate and educated author, was less open to self-educated pastors. Warren's engagement with the question of intellectual achievement reads like a Puritan endorsement for the "plain" style. On the one hand, she warned that "wee may not think that such knowledge collected, and onely reserved for vain ostentation, will prove a fit antidote to preserve us from infection, or secure our souls from the snares of errour, wee must therefore with *David* hide the word in our hearts, as a means to keep us from such contagion." Yet on the other, she denounced the "meerly mechanick, who leap from the limits of their lawfull station, affecting a dignity transcending their desert, and feeding the Cameleons on the aire of popular applause," as well as those who asserted that "humane learning is needless, and that men are qualified by immediate inspiration, tacitly implying with the Jesuits, extraordinarie revelations by continued miracles."[85] Throughout her three publications, Warren makes frequent reference to classical mythology, ancient history, and classical philosophers. Her *Warning-Peece from Heaven*, an effective denunciation of the chaos and evil swirling about in 1649, incorporates marginalia in English and Latin throughout the published text, including occasional Latin citations from Calvin and Augustine.[86]

While most of the published women prophets did not exhibit Warren's knowledge of theology or the classics, their scriptural knowledge was impressive. Within the few speeches attributed to Anne Hutchinson during her examination, she cites texts as dispersed as Proverbs, Hebrews, 1 John, and notoriously referred to the story of Abraham and Isaac from Genesis. She invoked the epistle to Titus and the book of Acts in support of her meetings and efforts at instructing others; she found in Isaiah and Jeremiah passages that upheld her in her spiritual journey.[87] Hutchinson's scriptural recall is also in evidence in the transcript of her trial before the First Church of Boston. Much of the trial seems like exegetical debate incorporating texts from Genesis to the epistles; in his list of twenty-nine errors attributed to Hutchinson, Winthrop identified ten different biblical texts attached to various errors. The transcript incorporates many more textual references. Questions were posed, answered, elaborated, and challenged, with ministers and Hutchinson volleying verses back and forth, though Hutchinson's knowledge may, in part, reflect the fact that the exchange is between her and several formally educated clergymen.[88] Even so, the verbal exchanges at the trial show that Hutchinson and her inquisitors did not argue theology within an abstract philosophical or "systematic" theological framework. Rather, all debate in theology and ethics was tied directly to specific biblical references. These were generally not isolated, individual verses, but networks of citations/ideas gleaned from expansive readings of scripture.

This approach to religious polemic and spiritual proclamation characterizes the writings of most of the women prophets. The numerous pamphlets of Eleanor Davies Douglas generally focused upon one of two topics that reflected Douglas's self-absorption. Either she published or reiterated her prophecies concerning Charles I and William Laud, or else she wrote in self-defense, chronicling the abuses that she had suffered at the hands of her husband and the state. The state had fined her £3,000, committed her to the Gatehouse, and ordered her to make several public acknowledgments of, and penitence for, her sins. She was said to have proclaimed herself "a Prophetess, falsly pretending to have received certain Revelations from God; and had compiled certain Books of such her fictions and false Prophesies or Revelations, which she had in person carried with her beyond the Seas," and printed, and brought back to England. Amid the worries about her revelations and publication is found the note that "she took upon her (which much unbeseemed her Sex) not only to interpret the Scriptures, and withal the most intricate and hard places of the Prophet Daniel . . ." Her examiners were, in essence, shocked by her audacity, "as such bold attempts as those of hers, in taking upon her to interpret and expound the holy Scriptures, yea, and the most intricate and hard places therein, such as the gravest and most learned Divines would not slightly or easily undertake, without much study and deliberation."[89] Fifth Monarchist Elizabeth Avery referred to the prophetic books of Isaiah, Jeremiah, and Hosea, Psalms and Ecclesiastes, the Gospel of John, the first epistle of John, and the Revelation.[90] Elizabeth Poole used the story of Abigail and David as an exemplar of the appropriate response to an overly aggressive king, while Elizabeth Warren's references included Pauline epistles, 1 and 2 Samuel, and a pointed invocation of Athaliah (2 Kings) to represent her understanding of those who overthrew Charles I: "she being an usurper of royal dignity, a bloody tigresse, and a monster of her sex, expressing the height of all horrible cruelty, by paving her ingresse with the murther of Innocents, and teaching Intruders who have no just title, to take away all that may stand in their way . . ."[91] Even Susanna Parr, who was writing a self-defense against her accusers, incorporated extensive references that included Balaam's wish in Numbers, the sin of Dathan in Exodus, and citations from Lamentations, Zechariah, Colossians, 1 Corinthians, Psalms, Job, 2 Corinthians, Philippians, Ephesians, 1 Thessalonians, and Deuteronomy.[92]

Despite their emphasis upon listening to the spirit within, Quaker women wrote in the same vein, returning frequently to scripture to support their arguments. Margaret Fell, for example, used many of the standard texts cited by other women preachers in developing her arguments in support of women speaking. She referred to Old Testament figures such as Ruth, Hannah, the Queen of Sheba, Esther, and Judith, as well as gospel women such as Elizabeth and Mary the mother of Jesus, whose Magnificat the Church of England "put into your Common Prayer." Fell also provided lists of women named in the epistles and Acts and cited the text from the third chapter of 1 Corinthians instructing women to cover their heads while prophesying.[93] More impressive still was Fell's *Standard of the Lord Revealed*, in which she cited her way through the Bible to prove the Quakers' theology of the spirit to be true. She began with Genesis, Exodus, and Deuteronomy, then proceeded to the historical books of Joshua, Judges, Ruth, 1 and 2 Samuel and 1 and 2 Kings (the section on 2 Kings is almost twenty pages), continued with Ezra, Esther, the other prophets, and moved onto the New Testament through to Hebrews and the Revelation of John.[94]

The voluminous textual evidence of this facet of women prophets' knowledge and style of presentation is certainly impressive. Among the publications illustrating this knowledge and reliance upon biblical texts is Anna Trapnel's *Cry of a Stone*. Trapnel introduced herself as the daughter of William Trapnel, a shipwright, in Stepney parish. She was "trained up to my book and writing," possibly by the congregation that she had joined as an adult.[95] Such basic literacy can explain neither her facile eruption into verse (albeit doggerel verse) nor, especially, the fluency of her prose. She and her interlocutors argued that this was proof that her words were those of the Holy Spirit, but the very limitations of her literary education offer another possible explanation. The doggerel was similar to what might appear on any broadside, so that the rhythms and flow of such speech might well come easily to someone who had read widely in (or listened to) the cheap print of the penny press. Moreover, in her remarkable and illuminating analysis of *Cry of the Stone*, Hilary Hinds has demonstrated how the Bible served as a primary source of Trapnel's speech. Not only were Trapnel's visions and interpretations self-consciously elaborated through scriptural citation—the immense number and variety of the quotations is incredible, but turns of phrase and literary images incorporated brief (three- to ten-word) biblical quotations. For example, Trapnel states that Satan came to her as "an angel of light" (1 Corinthians 11:14), that "before the Protector was established, I had a glorious sight of a throne, angels winged flying before the throne, crying 'Holy, holy, holy' " (Isaiah 6:2–3), and that the "resurrection of Jesus was marvellous in our eyes" (Psalms 118:23). While such images and quotations were more frequent in the prose sections, even the verse included phrases like

> True prophets of the Lord
> Will live upon that pay which he
> Declared in his word, (Luke 10:7, I Timothy 5:18)
> O death, where is thy sting,
> O grave, where is thy victory (I Corinthians 15:55)
> Oh desire rather a dish of herbs,
> Than this thy stalled ox . . . (Proverbs 15:17).[96]

Hinds's skillful annotation of *Cry of a Stone* argues that Trapnel's verbatim knowledge of scripture was so broad and deep that in addition to quoting at will, she had unselfconsciously incorporated biblical words and phrases into her thought and speech.

The allusions and quotations did reflect, to varying degrees, the multiple texts of the Old and New Testaments, and these writers used scripture to ground major arguments, to support peripheral details, even to replace their own words. Verses could be enjoined at any point, and these women certainly pursued a range of subjects through scriptural argument and example. Elizabeth Warren promoted godly behavior along with her support of the established Presbyterian ministry, while Katherine Chidley defended Independency, and Margaret Fell promoted the Quaker way and the inner light as the biblically based model for godliness and piety. Among the more radical sectarians lay a concentration of allusions to the books of Daniel and Revelation, texts through which millennialist prophecies envisioned the imminent end of the world.

Hutchinson, in her spiritual autobiography as recorded by Winthrop, relied heavily upon the prophecies of Daniel. Most of what she said concerned her own situation as she warned her examiners of their impending doom.

> When the Presidents and princes could find nothing against him, because he was faithfull, they sought matter against him concerning the Law of his

God, to cast him into the Lions denne, so it was revealed to me that they should plot against me, but the Lord bid me not to feare, for he that delivered *Daniel*, and the three children, his hand was not shortened.[97]

She also spoke of the Antichrist, an archetype out of Revelation, and there was some evidence that she had been caught up in millennialist expectations. At her examination before the General Court, one witness noted that "when she came within sight of Boston and looking upon the meanness of the place . . . she uttered these words, if she had not a sure word that England should be destroyed her heart would shake. Now it seemed to me that time very strange that she should say so."[98] It may have seemed strange to her interrogator, but here Hutchinson showed herself one of many who would find in the coming political and social chaos the fulfillment of the apocalypse foretold in Revelation. When Anne Fenwick published a second edition of *The Saints legacies* with a new publisher in 1631, six pages were added to the text, marking the author as a radical millennialist who looked forward to the imminent day when God would establish the new Jerusalem.[99] In 1625 Eleanor Davies Douglas had, apparently, prophesied that William Laud, or the Beast of Revelation, would be destroyed in nineteen and a half years, that is, in 1644. Douglas would also claim that she foretold the death of Charles I four years later. She repeated these prophecies with various details in her publications. As noted above, these pamphlets all took the form of interpretations of the books of Daniel and Revelation.[100]

During the 1640s and 1650s, the Quakers and Fifth Monarchists stood among the most outspoken of the millennialists who believed that the apocalypse of Revelation had burst upon England.[101] Ann Gargill warned of coming destruction, prophesying the victory laid out in Revelation: "the subtil shall be confounded in their own snares, and the wisdom of the eternall God shall stand forever, and the Adulterous Woman shall be confounded: long hath the heritage of the Lord Layen wast, through the abomination of the Harlot; but now shall the innocent judge the Whore, her reward shall be doubled, and her pride brought to nought . . ."[102] Mary Cary interpreted the first fourteen verses in the eleventh chapter of Revelation as a prophecy of the English Civil War, including the early victories of the king's forces and then, how after three and a half years (days in the text), the witnesses, or saints, rose from the dead and the tide of battle turned. For "JESUS CHRIST did long since reveale to *John*, how that after the mysticall *Babylonians* had persecuted his Saints a long time, he would raise up his Saints out of their persecuted condition, and bring down those their *Babylonian* enemies." In her *Resurrection of the Witness*, Cary devoted an extraordinary number of pages to demonstrating that the "Babylonian enemies" and the saints to be raised were English.

> It is true that in other Kingdomes, as in *France*, and *Germany*, and *Scotland*, &c there are a vast number of such as are called Protestants, but they are exceeding formall, and luke-warme generally; they are professors, but few professors of Christ: but for sincere, reall Saints that walke close with God, in a pious & holy conversation; *England* exceeds all other Kingdomes in the world. Now the war being made against these, it was made against all the Witnesses, against all the Saints.[103]

While Cary saw corporeal persecutions and the destruction wreaked upon England as the fulfillment of the prophecy, Elizabeth Avery believed that the threat portrayed in Revelation was a spiritual one: "Babylon, concerning whose destruction the Prophets of old and *John* in the *Revelation* speak, that spiritual Babylon as it is a State and church, and mystically Babylon in our gathered Churches, and Antichrist rendered in a mystery in the Saints, all which, out of question is to be accomplished in this Island of *Great Britain* . . ." Avery believed that they would not be destroyed physically by the sword, but would implode spiritually through their own evil ways. "And so whereas it is said that Babylon did cause the slain of Israel to fall, it's Babylon in the Saints, that is, Confusion and Errour that have slain the Saints in a spiritual sense."[104]

This millennialist position placed women preachers within the mainstream of their own sectaries. While among the many who attended their prophesying, some may simply have come to watch, others actively sought them out or followed their leadership. Throughout the records of Trapnel's prophesying and preaching, particularly "Poetical Addresses," millennialist references abound, and in the visions recounted in the first twelve pages of *Cry of a Stone*, she spoke of the four horns, probably of Daniel, as the powers of bishops, gathering of representatives, and a false king like Absalom of 2 Samuel.[105] According to those who recorded her speech and described the events, Trapnel attracted a crowd wherever she spoke, a claim buttressed by the fact that the government felt the need to arrest and imprison her, sending her to Bridewell for a brief period of time.[106] Of course, the spectacle alone might have attracted a crowd—a woman in a trance-like state speaking in verse, but she was not unique. The extremely hostile Thomas Edwards reported that the preaching of Mrs. Attaway and her compatriots had attracted large numbers of hearers. Katherine Chidley was an active evangelist and Independency organizer in the outskirts of London, while a Baptist woman, Dorothy Hazzard, established a Baptist congregation in Bristol.[107] Susanna Parr not only established a separate Independent church in Exon, but her leadership, like that of Anne Hutchinson, was so strong that her growing dissatisfaction with the minister fractured the congregation.

James Cranford, in his epistle introducing Elizabeth Warren's *Spiritual Thrift*, called Warren "the Phoenix of this age, this rare and precious Gentlewoman, the envy and glory of her sex," but that was one man promoting a book and its author and making claims for her reputation.[108] Hutchinson's admirers certainly numbered more than one or two dedicated disciples. Even as he admonished her, John Cotton conceded that some of the women of Boston had received spiritual assistance from her. John Winthrop went further:

> she had in a short time insinuated her selfe into the hearts of much of the people (yea many of the most wise and godly) who grew into so reverent an esteeme of her godlinesse, and spirituall gifts, as they looked at her as a Prophetesse, raised up of God for some great worke now at hand, as the calling of the Jewes, &c. so as she had more resort to her for counsell about matter of conscience, and clearing up mens spirituall estates, then any Minister (I might say all the Elders) in the Country.[109]

Her situation was not unlike that of Susanna Parr, who, with other women, engaged in battle with Lewis Stucley, the congregation's new minister, at the outset of his pastorate. "Master Stucley required each one of us to consent likewise unto the agreement they made at *torrington*, without declaring what it was; which being done by all the men, he desired the sisters . . . to do the like," which they refused to do, "resolving that we would not act by an implicite faith." Stucley worked to change their minds, arguing that "what was done was a Church act, because they who went with him consented thereunto." Parr called this "serpentine subtilty," and she reproved him "to his face."[110]

Why didn't Stucley simply dismiss as unimportant or irrelevant the refusal of Parr and a faction of women to assent to the decision of male church members? If Bostonians, men and women, were attending Hutchinson's hearth for spiritual guidance, why did ministers not question their own effectiveness as pastors? From the earliest decades of reformers' activities, lay leaders had played crucial roles not only in supporting dissenting ministers, but also in fostering pious communities and building congregations. Women as well as men were involved in such work, and ministers not only accepted but applauded the efforts of gifted laypersons. Boston's clergy became defensive only after rumors began that Hutchinson was critical of their theology, preaching, and pastoral leadership, just as Stucley grew hostile to Parr only after she openly questioned his leadership. The problem was not that women assumed leadership roles. Conflict ensued because women used authority produced by their spiritual power to challenge when they should have supported, or deferred.

Congregational leadership and preaching, or prophesying, were tricky enough, but some of these women explicitly challenged men's traditional authority. No matter how much Puritan authors and clerics encouraged women to develop their spiritual lives and assist others to do the same (and not all of them did), lines were drawn. More and more, especially in the chaos of colonization, war, and fractured church establishment, these may have been lines in the sand; nevertheless, these were lines women were not to cross. Domestic manuals promoted roles for women as teachers of children and female servants, counselors guiding daughters toward godliness and feminine virtue. Elizabeth Warren's guide to a virtuous life, in which she called upon believers, particularly women, to avoid factionalism and place themselves under the guidance of scripture and a proper minister, was, after all, the work of a "Phoenix." In histories and martyrologies, readers found examples of women who achieved great things spiritually. However, women were not expected to, indeed were denounced for, questioning their traditional, subordinate position as husband's wife, minister's congregant, magistrate's subject. Yet these women did just that, most of them knew they were doing it, and some justified it.

As the sole woman, among several men, who established a separatist community of laypersons, Susanna Parr could claim a high degree of respectability and influence. She tells a tale of hesitant speech and reluctant leadership, reluctant to attend meetings because of Paul's words, "Let your women keep silence in the Church," but the minister said that "he would do nothing without the consent of the whole, and when I was present, he himself would constraine me to speak my opinion of things proposed." Yet Stucley complained that Parr was contentious and contumacious. "She did for a long time contend for womens speaking in the Church, and being admonished for practising accordingly, she did openly professe, that she would not be present at Church meetings, when matters were debated, unless she might have that liberty." This was, of course, the same story from different perspectives, told after the trouble erupted. The key to the dispute lay in Stucley's own account. He continued his story, noting that "being denied [that liberty], she ever since contemptuously neglected Church meetings, and slighted the officers of the Church."[111]

In her account, Parr recalled posing difficult problems for the congregation, questioning the acceptance of questionable individuals into full fellowship, or directly questioning a member's claims to assurance.[112] The unresolvable conflict arose when, in a crisis of faith following the death of her child, Parr began hearing another minister. She came to see separatism as a great evil and found comfort in attending the preaching of Ford, a Presbyterian minister. Her fellowship disallowed individuals from attending worship anywhere except within their own group; in response to their "prelatical spirit," as she framed it, Parr left the congregation. One congregational officer told her that "they were very much troubled at my leaving them, and that they would look on my *Returne* as a *Resurrection mercy* . . ." Parr also reported that several women asked her to return to the congregation for the sake of the community's reputation, pleading "what a dishonour it would be unto the Church, if I left them." The implication was that Parr held such a staunch regional reputation as a saint that by deserting this congregation she tarnished *their* reputation. In self-defense, they preemptively warned Parr's new community about her troublesomeness, but the ministers were convinced that the charges were unfounded and frivolous.[113] Interestingly, the original congregation linked Parr's sins and excommunication with that of Marie Allein, a woman who had at one point resisted her husband's authority, leaving her household without his consent or knowledge to stay with a friend/midwife. Toby Allein, who had been unhappy with his wife, turned on Stucley for interfering in his domestic affairs, declared his wife a godly woman, and eventually left the congregation in disgust.[114]

Such women did indeed threaten male authorities as great as John Winthrop and the General Court of Massachusetts, or even of Cromwell himself. Elizabeth Poole spoke out against the proceedings of Cromwell and Parliament against the king, for which she was excommunicated from her congregation.[115] However, the challenge was more frequently as basic as a wife's resistance to her husband's authority. Yet this was part of the tradition. Anne Askew had left her husband, traveled, and become a central member of the reformed community there. Eleanor Davies Douglas also refused to abide by her husband's restrictions. Had she respected them, she would not have published her words. Elinor Channel had been "three times hindered" by that very poor husband, and she says she left behind several small children. Thomas Parker chided his sister Elizabeth Avery about her conduct. "You will not come to Ordinances, nor willingly joyn in private Prayer, with your own Husband, but onely to condescend to his infirmities, for you say you are above Ordinances, above the Word and Sacraments, yea above the Blood of Christ himself, living as a glorified Saint, and taught immediately by the Spirit."[116] Katherine Chidley laid out the issue quite clearly:

> consider the text in I Cor.7 which plainly declares that the wife may be a
> beleever, & the husband an unbeleever but if you have considered this text,
> I pray you tell me, what authority this unbeleeving husband hath over the
> conscience of his beleeving wife; It is true he hath authority over her in
> bodily and civill respects, but not to be a Lord over her conscience . . .[117]

Even a preaching woman who did not verbally challenge her husband's headship might have done so by her actions. Phyllis Mack has argued that these women did not question traditional household roles; some, in fact, explicitly spoke in favor of women's fulfilling traditional expectations. Anna Trapnel went so far as to warn women against public speech.

> The Devil he to the woman came,
> And she would needs forward be;
> She had a mind the uttermost
> Of all to know and see.
> This should learn Female Sex that they
> Of speech should be very slow,
> And that in forwardness they should
> Not in such a manner go.[118]

Hutchinson herself was credited with her acceptance that "if I tooke upon me a publick Ministery, I should breake a rule." Yet these women wrote, spoke publicly, and, in some cases, left husbands and children to go to

London, tour the countryside, or cross the ocean to bring their message. The resolution of the paradox lies in a distinction that Hutchinson supposedly drew when she qualified her statement about public ministry by explaining that a rule would not be broken in her "exercising a gift of Prophecy."[119]

Many of these writings incorporated some texts or icons to justify women's public speech and missionizing actions. When asked who they were, these women placed themselves among specific women of the Bible. When Puritan men wrote of women, they often invoked the example of Mary and Elizabeth, Hannah, Sarah and Rebecca, even the paradoxical Bathsheba and Eve. Women preachers were as likely to invoke women warriors like Jael and Judith and, especially, those women who worked with Paul during the early years of Christianity. As Margaret Fell quoted Paul, "if he had stopt Womens praying or prophesying, why doth he say *Everyman praying or prophesying, having his head covered, dishonoureth his head; but every Woman that prayeth or prophesieth with her head uncovered dishonoureth her head?*"[120] Moreover, these women did not rest with justifying their speech by biblical example. Rather they spoke not only of hearing the words of the Spirit, like Anne Hutchinson, but of the obligation of men and women of the Spirit to speak. Trapnel explained that God "has not sent thy spirit to the Great, to the learned, to the high, to the rich; but to the poor, to the lame, and to the feeble; and thou dost it, that the strong may not glory in their strength, but in the Lord." She knew, however that following the way of Christ required open affirmation and attestation, praying that "those that are willing to follow thee, come how thou wilt, in Male, in Female: blessed are those that are not offended at matter or manner which carries to Christ, and makes profession of him."[121]

According to Thomas Edwards, Mrs. Attaway invoked five scriptural texts to justify her public speech; only the verses from Joel mentioned women explicitly, but all broached the gifts of the Spirit and the divine mandate attached to those gifts. She noted the discussions in the epistles to Titus and to the Hebrews on the gifts of the Spirit, and laid out the requirement to spread the words. In Malachi, God promises to "spare" those who spoke "that feared the Lord, everie one to his neighbour," while Peter urges, "Let everie man as he hathe received the gifts, minister the same one to another, as good disposers of the manifolde grace of God."[122] Elizabeth Warren had written spiritual guides for the virtuous Christian and Katherine Chidley had entered political debate, but most of these writers and speakers envisioned themselves, or were understood as, prophets. As a defender of Susanna Parr wrote, women "speak in the church *Where they have an Extraordinary Gift of Prayer and Prophecy:* (I say) *an Extraordinary Gift,* (as I Cor.11.5) *Every Woman that prayeth or Prophesieth &c.*" The writer pointed to Anna and the four daughters of Philip in Acts, adding that "where there are *Impulses Extraordinary from the Spirit of God, in cases Extraordinary falling out in a church,* there may be the same ground for their speaking now (*in such cases*) as there was then."[123]

Anna Trapnel proclaimed repeatedly that the Spirit of God filled and moved her.

> The souldiers slight thy hand maid, but she matters not, they shall and must consider in time; they say these Convulsion-fits, and Sickness, and diseases that make thy handmaid to be in weakness. But oh thy know not the pouring forth of thy Spirit for that makes the body to crumble, and weaken nature; In these extraordinary workings thou intendest to shew what is coming forth hereafter, & oh how does thy handmaid bless thee!"

Here, as in sixteenth-century texts, the power of the Spirit was placed in counterpoint against the weakness of the individual. Avery more explicitly discounted any strengths of her own: "because the power of God doth appear . . . in respect of the weaknesse and contemptiblenesse of the instrument whom he doth here employ, as formerly it hath been his course in doing great things by weakest means, and so by such foolishnesse he doth bring to nought the wisdom of the wise, that so no flesh may so glory in his presence."[124] Trapnel and Avery insisted on their human, and at other points female, incapacity to speak as if the "poorness" and "contemptiblenesse" of the instrument became proof that the Spirit was present. Trapnel's scribe further attested to the presence of the Spirit within her. "If any may be offended at her Songs; of such it is demanded, If they know what it is to be filled with the Spirit, to be in the Mount with God, to be gathered up into the Visions of God, then they may judge her; until then, let them wait in silence, and not judge in a matter that is above them."[125] The presence of the Spirit marked such a woman as not merely credible or holy but powerful, as if the listener could not help but hear and heed her words. In a tract that recounted her vision and interpretation, Elizabeth Poole included a letter from a supporter attesting to her spiritual legitimacy. "I have found a most divine spirit in her as far as I could discern, and that which comes to the spirit and life of things, and in this methinks you should rejoyce, for truly, I have heard many professors and professions, but to my knowledge I never heard one come so near the power."[126]

The power of the Spirit instructed these prophets, providing not only the words, but the means by which the words would be disseminated. Elinor Channel explained that her "heart was so directed, that she was given to understand *how that the Spirit of the Lord had called her*; to the end that she should be sent to our Highness: and by the same *Holy Spirit*, inwardly though she be but a weak woman in expression, she was taught in brief how to express her message from God to your Highness." Avery, on the other hand, found that in passivity the Spirit did everything and enabled her to be the vessel of communication. "And as it hath been the manner of God's proceedings heretofore, so likewise I finde the immediate acting of the Spirit in giving in, and so accordingly in carrying me forth to communicate it to others." The force of the Spirit was palpable, witnessed as unstoppable by the hearers of Anna Trapnel. "Since thy Handmaid is taken up to walk with thee, thy Handmaid always desired that she might be swift to hear, slow to speak; but now that thou hast taken her up into the Mount, who can keep in the rushing winde? Who can bind the influences of the Heavenly Orion, who can stop thy Spirit?"[127]

Mary Cary invited her readers to attend the Assemblies of Saints, where individuals "doe hold forth the word of truth; and by the Spirit of Prophesie doe speak unto men, to edification, exhortation and comfort." People were invited to hear the "glad tidings" of the gospel published by those empowered to do the work of an evangelist, to experience the mysteries of the gospel opened by those empowered to "teach and instruct the simple." "In a word," she concluded, "Come and partake of the Apostolicall, Propheticall and Pastorall gifts, of all the particular operations and manifestations of the Spirit of Christ in his Saints, which are given to profit withall." Along with many sectarians, Cary advised people to attend assemblies where the leaders were known for their spiritual gifts and where the power of those gifts overwhelmed any pretensions of humane circumstance, education, or accomplishment. For such assemblies to prosper, believers must answer the call of God. For Cary, the call to prophesy was less an allowance for the saint to speak than an obligation laid upon every church member. "And now, since the Scripture speaks but only of bishops and Deacons, that were ordained by the laying on of hands, and declares it is the duty of the rest of the brethren in the Church to prophesie, as I Cor. 14:31 . . . it is the duty of others in the church to doe the work of Evangelists, Pastors, and Teachers."[128]

The Spirit's gifts of words and abilities brought a mandate for men and women to bring God's words to the populace. As Margaret Fell so eloquently articulated:

> God hath said that his *Daughters* should Prophesie as well as his *Sons*. And where he hath poured forth his Spirit upon them, they must prophesie, though blind Priests say to the contrary, and will not permit holy women to speak.
> And whereas it is said, *I permit not a Woman to speak, as saith the Law,* but where Women are led by the Spirit of God, they are not under the Law, for Christ in the male and in the Female is one.[129]

However skilled or educated such women were, the right and the obligation to speak came not from man's recognition but from God's command. Not only did gifted women assert their claims, but many others, men as well as women, heard, admired, and believed. When Anne Hutchinson rose to influence in New England, promoting traditional piety and attracting the devotion of many, she, like Anne Fenwick of Heddon, was lauded and embraced as a model of the Puritan female leader and nurturer. But when she challenged the authority of ministers and magistrates, questions were suddenly raised about this woman's public speech, although her followers had, to that point, entertained no doubts about Hutchinson's spiritual witness. In the 1640s and 1650s, gifted women continued the tradition of prophetic speech, and some men continued the tradition of defending the right of such women to speak. Although Hutchinson left Rhode Island in 1641 and died in 1643, many of her followers continued in her spiritual tradition, joining with the Fifth Monarchists and the Quakers, heeding and celebrating the words of the Spirit wherever they were heard.

6

Gracious Disciples and
Frightened Magistrates

The English people in New England knew and were excited by the revolutionary challenges rising in England in the 1640s. A decade before, they had chosen to leave their homeland, fleeing the persecution inflicted by the established church, fleeing the possibility of divine wrath, and running toward the opportunity to build a new, godly community. Winthrop's "City on a Hill" took form, although progress toward godliness was less than peaceful. Colonizers disagreed about their relations with the Indigenous residents, appropriate workings of authority and subservience, the nature of theological orthodoxy, and the ultimate relationship between governmental institutions, congregational systems, social organization, and individual liberties. Still, communities in Massachusetts, Connecticut, New Hampshire, Plymouth, and Rhode Island formed themselves into deceptively homogenous colonial units, navigating their various ways forward. The colonizers appeared to have founded independent political units, focused upon their own efforts to reach perfection and earn earthly rewards through their federal covenant with God. Despite such intentions on the part of many colonial leaders, however, some residents, including some magisterial leaders and clerics, kept an eye on England and empire.[1] If the successful foundation of godly colonies spoke of divine blessings on parochial efforts, those cosmopolitans who were looking outward watched to see if the spiritual power of their movement would lead to a transformation of England. News traveled across the Atlantic: Henry Vane wrote of his excitement and expectations to colleagues in Rhode Island, while clergymen like Hugh Peters sailed back to England to join and support the efforts. If the New England colonies confirmed the strength of Puritan dissenters, an upset in England itself seemed possible.

English emigration to New England slowed to a trickle in the early 1640s, and some went back in hopes of forwarding the ultimate destiny of the nation. Those who did return, along with those who had remained in England, sent news of successful war, regicide, and the rise of Oliver Cromwell as leader of a new Commonwealth government. During the years of war and unrest, followed by years of relative tranquility, churchmen in England struggled to establish a united church along biblical lines. Significant disagreements roiled these aspiring leaders, and questions about orthodoxy, polity, and the nature of clerical authority creating sectional alliances. Some argued for stronger clerical authority. Consulting colleagues in Scotland, who had apparently navigated such questions in the late 1630s, they invited them to attend an assembly at Westminster.[2] Others fought for congregational authority. Both groups turned to New England for examples of the success (or failure) of congregational polity.[3] No major party was ultimately successful. Cromwell's government tolerated all religious groups that supported it, and throughout the 1640s and 1650s, sectaries flourished. Some old groups, like the Brownists and Familists, reappeared; others, like the Fifth Monarchists, arose and challenged the government.[4] Both factions disappeared. A very few worked through problems of authority and organization, and continued far beyond the brief decades of Cromwell's rule. Among these were the Quakers.

The excitement and chaotic activity in England were known throughout New England as individuals and news crossed the Atlantic. Before the first Quaker missionaries appeared in Massachusetts, magistrates, clerics, and ordinary colonials had heard about the Quakers and their scandalous behavior as these dedicated messengers, answering the call of the Spirit to spread the gospel light, voyaged throughout the empire and beyond. These new sectarians were understood to be religious fanatics, social and political anarchists, determined to overthrow orthodoxy, government, and order, the very core of the godly commonwealth. From their early communities in the north of England, these heretical missionaries carried the word across the ocean, established a foothold in Barbados, and then continued on to New England.

So anxious were the magistrates that, when Anne Austin and Mary Fisher, the first Quakers to land within Massachusetts's jurisdiction, arrived in 1656, they were immediately arrested and imprisoned. The magistrates seized and destroyed their books, held them incommunicado, and then shipped them out of the colony. The following year Anne Burden, a Quaker widow but not a preacher, landed in Boston to collect debts owed her late husband; the government ordered her to prison, despite the pragmatic, secular nature of her visit, her dower rights denied. Returning from England, Mary Dyer, sometime follower of Anne Hutchinson and resident of Newport, landed in Boston on her way home to Rhode Island. During her English sojourn, she had joined the Quaker community, and upon disembarking in Boston, she, too, was imprisoned. The General Court forced William Dyer to give bond to remove his wife from Massachusetts, "nor to lodge her in any Town in [the] Colony, nor to permit any to have speech with her (an unmanly thing) in her Journey." Apparently, Quakers so threatened the colony's leadership that their very presence, even for transient reasons of practical business or travel, could not be tolerated.[5] Still the Quakers came; still the colony forbade them. The Massachusetts General Court's persecution of Quakers grew so harsh and brutal that within six years King Charles II, himself no supporter of Quakers, intervened on their behalf. Four Quakers had already been hanged, while countless others were maimed, whipped, and imprisoned. Even after the royal warning, the Bay Colony continued for several years to escort Quakers to its borders whipped at the cart's tail.

The Quakers represented a central spiritual challenge to the ordered religious orthodoxy that clerics and magistrates had almost established. Magistrates saw themselves as the keepers of pure orthodoxy, doctrine and practice, and they initially responded as if the Quaker crime were blasphemy. Later, leaders argued that Quaker practices were anarchic and would undermine the moral fabric and political order. Throughout, magistrates vehemently insisted that the Quakers were peculiar and dangerous and that the citizenry supported state efforts to control them. Many historians have accepted this ideological paradigm, and, whether sympathetic to the Puritan or Quaker side, they have generally focused their investigations upon the nature and perception of the "Quaker" threat.[6] Scholars have also been seduced by those magistrates into seeing desperate, god-fearing men struggling against the persistent efforts of recalcitrant Quakers, and this perception is not entirely wrong. Unlike Hutchinsonians, who mostly stayed banished even when invited to return to Boston, the Quakers kept returning, no matter how forceful or violent their expulsion. The implication is that the Quaker invaders, foreigners, coming where they weren't wanted, brought this brutality on themselves. However, before the Quakers could be accused of returning, they had to be banished, and herein lies the conundrum.[7]

Anne Hutchinson, John Wheelwright, and their followers were charged with and convicted of specific acts before they were banished.[8] Quakers Anne Austin and Mary Fisher, on the other hand, were imprisoned before they had even disembarked, charged with an identity and planned disruption rather than any crime. And while Austin and Fisher were, in fact, missionaries, Anne Burden wanted only to collect debts; Mary Dyer originally intended to pass through Boston on her way to her home in Rhode Island. Later, Quakers would appear in Massachusetts to preach against dead religion and unjust treatment, but on the testimony of Puritans and Quakers alike, initially, Quakers did nothing except appear in New England with heretical books.[9] Why did magistrates contravene established criminal procedures and, in later years, develop special trial processes for Quakers? Magistrates granted themselves enormous power to handle Quakers, to ensure protection of the community against the pollution of the heretics. Why were such tactics necessary if the citizenry so thoroughly despised the intruders?[10]

Quakers did pose a serious threat to the hegemonic orthodoxy. Politically, Quakers denied the right of government to interfere with religion or worship, expressing early support for the separation of church and state. Socially, Quakers rejected hierarchy in all forms, affirming that the equality of souls before God countermanded artificial hierarchies of birth, wealth, and education. Theologically, Quakers carried this equality into spirituality and leadership, rejecting an elevated role for an educated, ordained clergy, asserting that divine revelation beyond the Scriptures continued down to the present day, and claiming that all believers had access to such revelation. As distressing as such challenges might have been, they were not foreign to Puritan society. Anne Hutchinson, after all, had said that she was responding to an "immediate voice" of the spirit, and many believed her. I argue, with Geoffrey Nuttall and Rufus Jones, that these challenges were inherent in Puritan culture itself and that this threat of disorder came from within.[11] This was less a foreign invasion than an internal insurrection, and *because* this threat came from within, the magistrates attacked with surprising intensity.

The radical potential latent in English Puritan dissent came to fruition among the sectaries during the English Civil War. With a growing tradition of resistance to the Anglican elite, Quakers mirrored the efforts of New Englanders to return to the simplicity of public prayer. Francis Howgill produced a detailed list of the rituals, ceremonies, objects, and ideas that detracted from the worship of God, including feasts, holy days, vestments, bells, book prayers, and "singing psalms in musical tunes."[12] Margaret Fell also objected to the music in churches "more like may-gaming then worshipping God, playing and piping of Organs, and setting a company of wilde, ungodly, light boyes to sing tunes to them, which is such a kind of Worship, as no Christians in the Primitive times exercised."[13] English nonconformists of the sixteenth and seventeenth centuries, including New Englanders and Quakers, had found their right to challenge authority in an identity based within election as revealed through conversion. It bears repeating: Puritans' conviction of their own superior godliness was founded upon a mystical experience available equally to, though not embraced by, all souls. Early New England leaders had believed in the possibility of a unifying orthodoxy, worked to establish its doctrines and enforce conformity, but then watched as individuals' dedication to a variety of theological and ecclesiastical positions challenged that assumption about a single orthodoxy and threatened the success of the experiment. So, too, while the Presbyterian party in Civil War England had hoped to maintain a similar order, their efforts were undermined by the failure of any party to establish political, religious, or social authority. Despite the best efforts to create religious order through traditional hierarchies of birth, wealth, and gender, the fact that God called and powerless humanity responded constantly undercut efforts to maintain order.

This mystical sensibility continued to sit at the heart of mid-seventeenth-century religiosity, and while the Presbyterians and Congregationalists wrapped around it restrictions and privileges grounded in education and markers of sanctification, Quakers threw those off as peripheral and irrelevant in a saint's relationship with God. George Fox proclaimed that "all people fear God, and give Glory to him, and worship the living God which made Heaven and Earth; and away with all such who call *Oxford* and *Cambridge* two Fountains, and so keep you from God who is the fountain of Mercy, which are old and rotten."[14] Priscilla Cotton and Mary Cole had explained that "Paul counted all his learning dung for the excellency of the knowledge of Christ . . . & the learned that studied curious Arts burnt their books that were of Great price, when they came to the knowledge of Christ." Learning was not merely irrelevant, but dangerous, for it prevented the believer from receiving the wisdom and grace of the Spirit. Rather, they warned, "Silly men and women may see more into the mystery of Christ Jesus then you: for the Apostles, that the Scribes called illiterate and *Mary* and *Susanna* (silly women, as you would be ready to call them, if they were here now) these know more of the Messiah then all the learned Priests and Rabbies; for it is the Spirit that searcheth all things, yea, the deep things of God . . . ."[15] Margaret Fell found learning a distraction, even a corrupting influence; her *Touch-stone* drips with scorn for the clergy who based their right to leadership on formal education. "Schooles and Colledges and Universities, and Nurseries of Learning, which they call their *Mothers*, with a heap of Stuffe, which are better known by them that exercise themselves in them, than the Revelation of Jesus Christ is."[16]

The Revelation of Jesus, through the Spirit, should be valued and sought, but too many seek God through church preachers and leaders, rather than through the spirit within themselves. In her testimony before the General Court in 1637, Anne Hutchinson had described her distraction, even spiritual insecurity, as she was "troubled to see the falseness of the constitution of the church of England." Having struggled to discern where the truth lay, she found that

> the Lord was pleased to bring this scripture out of Hebrews. He that denies the testament denies the testator, and in this did open unto me and give me to see that those which did not teach the new covenant had the spirit of antichrist, and upon this he did discover the ministry unto me ever since. I bless the Lord, he hath let me see which was the clear ministry and which the wrong.[17]

In similar fashion, Quakers, distracted by the noise, suffered in silence; Esther Biddle claimed that this was literally so, for God had taken "away my hearing that I was deaf to all Teachings of men for a year." Yet after a year "did the Lord carry me to a meeting of the People Called *Quakers*, where I was filled with the dread and Power of the Lord, and it raised my Soul to bear Testimony to the Truth."[18] From prison, Sarah Blackborow warned, "Wisdom hath uttered forth her voice to you, but the eye and ear which is a broad, waiting upon a sound of words without you, is that which keeps you from your Teaching within you," while Mary Dyer petitioned the General Court to take "counsel, search with the light of Christ in you, and it will shew you of answers as it hath done me . . . ."[19] Fell chimed in, asserting, "We received not this spirit of Man, nor by Man, but by the immediate power and revelation of Jesus Christ, according to the work and operation of it in us . . . ."[20] Christ could only be known through these gifts. "Now all that do succeed the Apostles and true Church in the fellowship, it must be by walking in the Light, as he is in the Light, and there they shall know cleansing by the Blood of Christ."[21] These spiritual gifts need not be hoarded, for they had been already given to all; one need only be open to receiving them.

> A Love there is which doth not cease, to the seed of God in you all; and therefore, doth invite you every one Priest and people to return to it, that into Wisdoms house you may come, where there is a feast provided of things well-refined, and the loving bread of God is known and fed upon,

and the fruit of the Vine drunk of, the unity of the spirit witnessed, the well-beloved of the Father is here.[22]

Quaker claims of divine revelation were well known, and feared; the General Court recognized this: "Whereas there is a cursed sect of haereticks lately risen up in the world, w[ch] are comonly called Quakers, who take uppon them to be immediately sent of God, and infallibly asisted by the spirit to speake & write blasphemouth opinions."[23]

For Quakers, hearing the voice of the Spirit did not displace but augmented the value of the Scriptures. Francis Howgill explained "Concerning the Scripture . . . that which gave them a being is greater then they, as he that Creates is greater then they that are Created . . . so the Spirit is greater above and before the words, and yet this doth not Diminish, neither Derogate from the Scripture."[24] Fox celebrated the working of the Spirit, for "the heavenly spiritual Man is known by the *Revelation of his Light and Spirit*, and the Revelation of the Faith (that is by the Gift of God) which Christ is the Author of, and *Mary* knew him by *Revelation*; and *Simeon* knew him by *Revelation*."[25] Quakers regularly spoke of apostles and travelers in Acts and the Pauline epistles, and they saw themselves as spiritual colleagues, people who, with open hearts, heard the voice of God just as their biblical predecessors had done. Francis Howgill challenged clerical leaders in Massachusetts who "ignorantly call the written Word, as though all the Scriptures were but one word; the Word is Christ." Howgill points to the error that marks so many learned believers whose spirituality is grounded in scripture. The center of their spirituality is texts, words, whereas the center should be Jesus, who is the Word. Howgill continues, this "was revealed in the Saints, which spake the Words forth; and he is the Way and the Rule of Life to them that believe, and his Spirit is the leader and guider into all Truth, and the Rule of Obedience."[26]

The Scriptures were indeed the revealed word of God, but they were not sufficient. As Fox explained, "None can Use the Scriptures aright, but with that Holy-Ghost, that leadeth into all the truth of them." Moreover, if one could only be saved through the Scriptures, "Then what Means had Abel, Enoch, Noah, Abraham, Isaac, Jacob, and Moses, before the Scripture was written, if the Scripture be the means of Faith?"[27] Jesus, through the indwelling Spirit, continues to speak to believers. As Hutchinson testified, she knew the truth "by the voice of his own spirit to my soul."[28] Mary Stout asked simply, "And is not his Spirit the Spirit of Truth, which he promised he would send, which should guide into all Truth?"[29] The Quakers pursued a relationship with God that pushed far beyond traditional dissenters' theology and praxis, and incorporated a complicated engagement with the Scriptures. Fell wrote that "though these *Scriptures* bear *testimony* to the truth of this, yet these *Scriptures* are not our *testimony* only, for we have *our testimony* in the same *spirit* as was *in them* that spoke forth the *Scriptures*; and these *Scriptures* bear *testimony* with *us*, and *we* to *them*, and so are *in unity* with the *same Spirit* which gave *them forth*.[30] This invocation of "unity" again suggests the mystical journeys of earlier Puritan believers. Through their language of Spirit, revelation, and especially "light," Quakers had developed an ability to unequivocally name, describe, and celebrate the mystical union that they experienced.

Knowing the Spirit went far beyond knowledge and thought, beyond emotions and feelings. This mystical connection caught up the believer in the exhilaration of the moment. Sarah Blackborow remembered that "the first time they spake to me, & my understanding was opened, and then I knew that that was Gods witnesse which had been working in me from my child-hood, and had begotten pure breathings and desires, and thirstings after God."[31] Breath, thirst, longings, expressed through the language of embodied physicality. "So that here is free love, and free grace, and free mercy, that everyone that thirsteth may come freely and buy Wine and milk without money and without price, without any respect of persons."[32] Here was a sensual thrill, and while Fell expressed her pleasure in the language of food, Fox turned toward an erotic corporeality, the marriage bed.

> So, in the *Power*, and in the *Bed of Purity*, in the Singleness of *Virginity*, and in the *Beauty* of *Holiness* live, where *Righteousness* and *Holiness* and *Truth* dwelleth together, and *Peace* in the Kingdom of Power, where is the Everlasting Joy, Peace and Dominion, and Victory, where the *Bed* is not defiled, but the *Marriage* that is honorable, is known.[33]

Embracing the reality of Spirit, of the light within, moved beyond the personal, internal experience of mystical union toward an awareness of spiritual understanding and the mandate to share that knowledge of the light. The Spirit roused Blackborow, even in prison, to preach the light. The "well beloved of the Father is here, and this is he who is the fairest of ten thousand, there is no spot nor wrinkle in him; long did my sol thirst after him." And again, "Oh! Love, truth and its Testimony, whether its Witness be to you, or against you, love it, that into my Mothers house you all may come and into the Chamber of her that conceived me, where you may embrace and be embraced of my dearly beloved one, love is his Name, Love is his nature, Love is his life, surelie he is the dearest and the fairest."[34] This light, once experienced, empowered, even impelled the believer to spread this gracious knowledge to others.

Women, supposedly characterized by the passivity and humility of their feminine nature, were particularly open and attracted to the light, and the deep connection with the Spirit. Fox provided explicit instructions: "Ye *Daughters*, to whom it is given to *Prophesie*, keep within your own *Measure*, seeing over that which is without, answering *that of God* in all."[35] The teaching's appeal to women was observed by sympathizers and enemies alike, and the large number of female Quakers, especially women preachers, had been noticed as a curiosity and the object of scorn and condemnation. When Sarah Tims said to a cleric in a graveyard, "Man, fear the Lord," she was assaulted by a mob, beaten, and then imprisoned. At the Assizes, she asked what law she had broken, and the mayor answered that "sweeping the house, and washing the dishes was the first point of law to her." Jane Waugh was imprisoned, called before the court, and although nothing was charged against her, was still required to give surety for good behavior; she refused to promise silence and was returned to prison. Anne Audland, an outspoken critic of the local minister, was, she explained, "unjustly imprisoned at the first in the town of *Banbury*, for no other thing but speaking the truth."[36]

The Quaker community justified the acceptance of grace-filled women called to speak, implicitly invoking scriptural support. Like Hutchinson, citing Joel's assertion that your daughters shall prophesy and Titus's instruction to the elder women to instruct the younger, Margret Killin and Barbara Patison proclaimed, "Thus saith the Lord, I have sent my sons and daughters from far. I have raised up Prophets amongst you, I have placed my witness in you." Margaret Vivers, a bit more direct, explained, "So was there women guided by the Spirit of the Lord, that were the Lords prophetesses, as wel as there were men that were his Prophets; and the Lord spoke his word by his own Spirit, in and through the one as wel as the other." Hutchinson had cited the example of Priscilla, but Vivers's list was more extensive. In addition to Priscilla, Vivers's list of female disciples included Phoebe, Tryphena, Tryphosa, and Persis, and she turned to the Hebrew Testament to reference Miriam, Moses's sister, "a Prophetess," Deborah, and Huldah.[37] References to Joel 2:28 can be found throughout writings by and about women. Both Fox and Fell, among others, found opportunities to engage Joel. "So mark, here is *Servants, Hand-maids, Young-men, Old-men, Sons and Daughters*, the Lord hath promised he would pour out his spirit upon them"; and again, "He spoke of his Spirit, which he was then going to pour forth, which he hath now largely manifested, which he is pouring upon all flesh, upon his *sons* and upon his *daughters*, upon his *servants*, and upon his *hand-maids*."[38]

Other writers incorporated allusions to theological concepts, prescriptive texts, and specific individuals. In her well-known *Women's Speaking Justified*, Margaret Fell gathered arguments *Proved and Allowed of by the Scriptures* responding to clerics who supported their objections to women's "medling in the things of God" by pointing to Paul's instructions for women to keep silent in churches, 1 Corinthians 14:34–35 and 1 Timothy 2:11–12. Fell argued that the clergy had misunderstood Paul. She supported her argument by reference to key moments and women prophets in the Old Testament, naming women who were identified as messengers of the gospel, and even engaging Revelation.[39] At the outset, Fell noted that in the first chapter of Genesis God created male and female with no distinction between them "as men do; for though they be weak, he is strong."[40] Here she has invoked the concept of weakness and turned it around, much as John Foxe had done in his discussions of women martyrs like Anne Askew more than a century before. Foxe and other male hagiographers, impressed with Askew's stalwart testimony and stoicism in the face of torture and fire, had maintained that God demonstrated his strength through the extraordinary performance of a weak woman. Fell, however, observes that both male and female are weak, and in their weakness God's strength is manifest.

Fell wrote of the Samaritan woman (John 4), of Martha's testimony following the resurrection of her brother Lazarus (John 11:25–26), and of the woman who washed and anointed Jesus's feet (Matthew 26, Mark 14:3, Luke 7). She reminded her readers that at the crucifixion the primary mourners were women, and that many, including Mary Magdalene, Mary mother of James, Salome, and Joanna, were the first witnesses of the resurrection of Jesus (Mark 16:1–4; Luke 24:1–2; John 20:16–17).[41] She cited the work of Aquila and Priscilla in Acts 18 and then, finally, picked up the prescriptions of 1 Corinthians. She argued that the women Paul ordered to be silent were those still needing instruction because they were in confusion, infected by malice and strife. Despite Paul's warning, her challenge held strong: "And what is all this to Womens Speaking? that have the Everlasting Gospel to preach, and upon whom the promise of the Lord is fulfilled, and his Spirit poured upon them according to his Word."[42] Fell offered a further, sophisticated contextualization of 1 Corinthians, reconciling the seeming contradiction of verses 11:5 and 14:34, which respectively direct that women who prophesy should have their heads covered and women should keep silent. She finished with a flourish, adding to her biblical catalog of speaking women Sarah, Deborah, Huldah, Anna, and the daughters of Philip from Acts 21. "God hath said, that his *Daughters* should Prophesie as well as his *Sons*; and where he hath poured forth his Spirit upon them, they must prophesie . . ."[43]

With this engagement with the Spirit, it is not surprising that many in New England were drawn to the Quakers. In the late 1650s Quakers did appear throughout New England, and over the next ten years, many were called to account in New Haven, Connecticut, and Plymouth as well as Massachusetts. Although generally not as harsh as Massachusetts in their treatment of nonconformists, New Haven, Connecticut, and Plymouth all struggled to maintain a degree of religious orthodoxy. New Haven and Connecticut were established by individuals, including clerics Thomas Hooker and John Davenport, who disagreed with the religious order in Massachusetts. They exemplify the continuing problems that arose when dissenters become the establishment. Providence Plantation was another such enterprise, although Roger Williams's departure from Massachusetts was less than voluntary. Still, Williams did move south, purchasing land from the Narragansets, bringing with him several of his followers from Salem. Williams had always upheld the separation of church and state and modeled this toleration.

In addition to those few who had accompanied Williams to Providence, including Katherine Marbury and Richard Scott, Hutchinson's sister and brother-in-law, many who left Massachusetts in the wake of their disfranchisement and disarmament in 1637 settled new towns next to Providence. In the spring of 1638, they gathered together in Boston, and led by William Coddington, William Hutchinson, John Coggeshall, and William Aspinwall, twenty men crafted and signed the Portsmouth Compact, establishing their government. Following the pattern of previous colonizers, they formulated their own efforts within an acknowledgment of fealty to God:

> We whose names are underwritten, do here solemnly, in the presence of Jehovah incorporat our selves into a Bodie Politick, & as he shall helpe, will submit our persons, lives, and eates unto our Lord Jesus Christ, the King of Kings & Lord of Lords and to all these perfect & most absolute laws of his,

given us in his holy word of truth, to be guided & judged thereby. Exod. Xxiv, 3, 4; 2 Chron., xi, 3; 2 Kings, xi., 17.[44]

Coddington purchased land from the Narragansets, and they built their settlement on Aquidneck Island. But within a year, the energy and competition within this community of strong and ambitious colonizers brought a division, and several leaders, notably Coddington, Coggeshall, Nicholas Easton, and William Dyer, moved on and established a second settlement, Newport, while others, including William and Anne Hutchinson, remained.

These two towns united their governments after two years, and Coddington, with others, set up civil governments that served the communities. Now they struggled to keep Portsmouth and Newport together but separate from Williams's control. Sometimes their efforts succeeded, and sometimes all of the towns, including Pawtuxet and Warwick, under Williams's government, were gathered into one colony. In an effort to gain the support of the Commonwealth government, both groups solicited Henry Vane, who clearly had more important things on his agenda. "How is it that there are such divisions amongst you? Such headiness, tumults, disorders and injustice? The noise echoes into the ears of all as well friends as enemies, by every returne of shipps of those parts." Vane wondered where the fear of God had gone, the love of Christ. "Are there no wise men amongst you?" he asked, warning them that unless they could reconcile their differences, enemies might move against them.[45] The petty conflicts among these groups, however, were less important than a common policy that ran through all of them, namely a commitment to freedom of religion. After ineffectively blaming Coddington and William Dyer, Williams explained to Vane that the problem was "possibly a sweete cup that rendered many of us wanton and too active. For we have long drunck of the cup of as yet great liberties as any people we can heare of under the whole Heaven." Williams acknowledged that the towns had not only been spared the "iron yokes of wolfish bishops and their Popish ceremonies," but also the war in England and the controlling efforts of "Presbyterian tyrants." In fact, he notes, this colony had not "been consumed with the over-zealous fire of the (so-called) Godly and Christian magistrates."[46]

Within this space of religious liberty, the Hutchinsonians were attracted to a variety of religious systems. John Clarke, a minister who had arrived in Massachusetts in 1637, joined the exiles and established a Baptist congregation in Newport. Nicholas Easton was reported as teaching that "man hath no power or will in himself, but as he is acted by God, and that seeing God filled all things, nothing could be or move but by him, and so he must needs be the author of sin, etc., and that a christian is united to the essence of God," a position that was opposed by the minister John Clarke.[47] William Aspinwall, on the other hand, left Portsmouth and returned to Massachusetts, where he confessed his sin, was accepted by the Boston church, and then submitted a petition to the General Court, which "restored [him] to his former liberty & freedome."[48] Like many others, however, in the early 1650s he returned to England. There he was attracted by the Fifth Monarchists and published several treatises articulating and defending their theology and politics, including his *Brief Description of the Fifth Monarchy, or Kingdome*.[49]

The theology of the inner light as preached by Quakers attracted many of those who had followed Hutchinson out of Massachusetts. William had died in 1641, and Anne, discouraged by the political infighting, had moved to a settlement in New Netherland. Many Quakers saw in Hutchinson's experiences a foreshadowing of their treatment at the hands of the Bay Colony. In his *Glass for the People of New England*, Samuel Groome denounced writings about Hutchinson that "made a notorious Lye on the destroyed Woman" and attacked Mary Dyer and Jane Hawkins, "all of which were known to be Women of honest Lives and Conversations, only protested against their false Church and Worships."[50] In this brief pamphlet, dedicated to denouncing Massachusetts's persecution of individuals who challenged the religious order, Groome cited passages that illustrated the appeal of Hutchinson's preaching. Thomas Leverett, elder of the Boston church, had written a letter to Hutchinson asking, "what was become of the Light she once shined in all their Parts?" Her response: "If it were the True Light, in which you say I did once shine in. I am sure the Author thereof, and the Maintainer of it is God . . . ."[51] Undoubtedly the Quaker Groome found reference to "True Light" irresistible. "*John Wheelwright* preached of a Light in man, and of a Spirit in man . . ." Groome recounted a conversation with Wheelwright during which John Cotton defended Wheelwright's doctrine as "according to God." Yet although the accusers in Massachusetts once had "Good Testimony in their Hearts and Mouthes for God and his Light and spiritual Appearance," Groome found that they had turned from their righteousness. In Wheelwright and Hutchinson he saw a foreshadowing of the Quakers' engagement with the divine as well as the inevitable hostility against it. "Even against God, who is a Spirit, and who is Light in all his Appearances, in either Son or Daughter, before ever a *Quaker* came amongst you: So the God of

Heaven and Earth is clear of all of your Blood, having raised up Testimony after Testimony, even ever since you set up your Inventions, and denied the Light."[52]

Hutchinson's sister Katherine Marbury Scott and husband Richard were among the first Quakers in Rhode Island. Katherine Scott, "a woman of blameless conversation," visited the Quakers imprisoned in Boston after their ears had been cut off, and she was whipped and imprisoned for three weeks, "and great cause had she to witness against their cruelty, for the same spirit had banished her sister *Anne Hutchinson*."[53] Two years before, Williams had presented Katherine, and others, as "Comon Oposers of all Authority."[54] Fox himself also made the connection between the current abuse of the Friends and Hutchinson's experiences a generation earlier. Scott's daughter, Mary, would become wife to Christopher Holder, among the first Quakers, along with John Copeland, William Robinson, and Marmaduke Stephenson, to missionize in New England and be imprisoned in Massachusetts.[55] Several of Hutchinson's followers noted similarities to her claims of connection to the Spirit and may well have been attracted by the sharing of power among all members of the movement, male and female, particularly the power of public speech. Among those who built the twin communities of Portsmouth and Newport the Quaker spirit found followers, including Nicholas Easton, once scorned by Winthrop, Henry Bull, Jeremy Clark, and Philip Sherman. William Coddington, finding in the promise of the inner light a familiar theology and praxis, became an ardent supporter of early efforts to spread the Quaker message and a stalwart member of Newport's Quaker community.[56]

Toward the end of his life, after he had returned to public service as governor of Rhode Island in the 1670s, Coddington wrote a public letter to Richard Bellingham, governor of Massachusetts, to grieve the treatment meted out to himself as well as the Quakers. He began with a statement of his status: "I came over with your Governour, as an Assistant in Commission with him . . . seaven Years in Authority, as a Magistrate and Treasurer of the Country, and equal with you in other respects . . . ."[57] His denunciation of the treatment of the Quakers drew upon his long knowledge of their history. "Now for thee, Friend, that doest not only profess thy self a *Christian*, but one of the highest Forms, and that was against the Bishops in *England*, suffered by them, O! how is that Tenderness lost since the coming into Authority in *New-England* . . ."[58] Many English theologians, authorities, and activists criticized the Bay Colony for rigidity and prosecution of religious nonconformists.

Coddington was among the few who framed his attack within the history of the original colonizers, tracking Massachusetts's policies and actions in light of the persecutors' foundational experience of persecution.

Initially, Coddington wrote as one who has not received the respect his rank deserved; Governor Bellingham destroyed Coddington's letter unread, imprisoning and whipping the messenger carrying the letter because he was accompanied by Quakers Marmaduke Stephenson and William Robinson. Coddington complained that "so many Books that costen ten Pound Sterling" had been sent to him by way of Barbados, but were brought to Boston by mistake and then seized by Bellingham, who responded to Coddington with "scoffing Answer, not becoming that Gravity." He compared Bellingham with the inquisitors of Malaga, Spain, who, having discovered books they considered unsound, merely sealed up the volumes and returned them to the ship on which they had come. The "Papists" put New Englanders to shame.[59] Yes, his essay reflected a rather un-Quakerish sense of his own importance, "a Merchant, and the chiefest" in Massachusetts, yet despite dwelling on insults and financial losses, he did not lose sight of his primary cause: the imprisonment, torture, and execution of Quakers. Recalling his early knowledge of Bellingham, who had spoken against persecution and "stinting or limiting the Spirit of Prophecy in any," Coddington proclaimed that this "is the Day of God's Appearance in his Sons and Daughters, in pouring out his Spirit, so they must prophesie, and who can withhold the Work of the Lord?"[60] Massachusetts's magistrates were portrayed as hypocrites: spiritually lost—perhaps bereft—as well as cruel. The evil first appeared among the leaders when they determined that Hutchinson and Wheelwright must be banished, and "the unclean Spirit like Frogs, came out of the Mouth of the false Prophets, so that Persecution was ushered in . . . ." The ultimate condemnation was not the comparison of Massachusetts's actions not the Spanish Inquisition, but with the Marian courts as recounted in "Fox's Acts and Monuments."[61] Coddington then brought the historical indictment full circle, calling upon them to

> turn to the Light within you, wherewith you are enlightened, that you have contracted and blasphemed as Natural &c, Even Christ in you the Hope of Glory, which was declared to you by the Servant of the Lord *John Cotton* on *Acts.* 4.13 on his Lecture Day, the Ships ready to depart for England . . . it was about *Grace*; he magnified Grace within us, the Priests Grace without or upon them, So all the Difference in the Country was about Grace,

notwithstanding the Difference was as great (saith he) as between Light and Darkness, Heaven and Hell, Life and Death.[62]

The exhortation repeated what Mary Dyer had urged some fifteen years earlier, "search with the light of Christ in you."[63] Coddington wrote in outrage of the death of Dyer in 1660. She was the only Rhode Island resident executed in Massachusetts, her family well connected to Coddington and the Hutchinsons. Her husband William was among those who signed the Portsmouth Compact; he and his family joined Coddington when the early community split and supported Coddington's leadership throughout. Mary, devoted follower of Hutchinson, remained tied to the family through her children: her son Samuel married Ann Hutchinson, daughter of Edward and granddaughter of Anne and William. Coddington asked how Massachusetts justified executing Quakers. Bellingham had reportedly "answered in a fearful Manner, Guilt being upon thee, and wouldst shuffle it off thy self, and saidst, you had a Law by which you put *Jesuites* to Death." Pushed further by questioners, Bellingham granted that he "didst not believe they were *Jesuites*," leading Coddington to conclude that he had committed murder. "And what was *Mary Dyer* a *Jesuite*, whom you murdered, and put to Death, and hanged on your Gallows; and when you had done, your great Major Aderton came into your Court, and boasted to your Court, and to them under the Sentence of Dead and Examination, how *Mary Dyer* hanged like a Flag...."[64]

Coddington followed his accusation with the tale of Aderton, who died soon after and in a violent and public fashion, thrown from his horse on the Boston Common: "Eyes like Sawsers . . . his Blood run through the Floor of your Court-House" in the very place where Aderton had "boasted that *Mary Dyer* hanged like a Flag; but soon the Vengeance of God took hold of him, and made him a Sign to you, and to all other blood-thirsty Persecutors." Coddington presented the sudden, bloody death of an enemy as divine judgment, "a Spectacle for you to gaze at," just as Aderton had boasted of Dyer as a spectacle.[65] He was not the only Quaker writer to interpret Atherton's death this way. George Bishop provided a graphic description of this death, perhaps the first, for it seemed the basis for others. Bishop wrote of "Adderton having been in his pomp"; frightened by a cow, his horse threw him. Bishop offered the images of eyes popping out of the head like saucers, blood from the ears, brains out the nose, and he delineated a larger context. This was the place where Quakers, whipped at the cart tail, were released, and this judgment, an untimely death, was predicted by Wenlock Christison, who had been sentenced to death.[66]

Like William Coddington, Mary Dyer serves the historian as representing a continuity of dissenters' experiences across the first thirty years of colonization.[67] Approximately twenty years younger than the Hutchinsons, the Dyers arrived in Boston in 1635. John Winthrop described Dyer as "a very proper and fair woman, and both [she and husband William] notoriously infected with Mrs. Hutchinson's errors, and very censorious and troublesome (she being of a very proud spirit, and much addicted to revelations)." Winthrop's commentary focused mainly upon the birth of Dyer's stillborn child and his observation that Dyer accompanied Hutchinson when she left the Boston congregation an excommunicate.[68] As already noted, the Dyers joined other Hutchinsonians who settled at Portsmouth, and for the next two decades, Dyer disappears from the record. In 1652 the Dyers visited England; William returned fairly quickly, but Mary stayed there and joined the Quaker movement.

Leaving the heady climate of the Commonwealth, where multiple sectarian preachers were gathering disciples and organizing communities, and where George Fox and Margaret Fell were overseeing the expanding network of Friends, in 1657 Dyer sailed for Rhode Island by way of Boston. Her defenders would claim that she intended to immediately travel on to Newport, but the magistrates hurriedly imprisoned her and would not release her to travel until her husband provided bond that she would not stay for any length of time in Massachusetts, nor would she speak, that is, testify, to any on her way out. Following the example of other Quaker women she had known, she traveled to New Haven, testifying to the inner light and censuring the magistrates: "Woe be unto you for Humphrey Norton's sake! Woe be unto you, because of the Cruelty done to him!"[69] The New Haven government forced her to leave. She then returned to Massachusetts, to work with and comfort Friends, including William Robinson and Marmaduke Stephenson, who were the first to be executed in 1659.[70]

In his *New England Judged*, Bishop echoed John Winthrop, describing Dyer as "a Comely Grave woman, and of goodly Personage, and one of a Good Report, having an Husband of an Estate, fearing the Lord, and a Mother of Children." While the tone was laudatory, Bishop echoed some of Winthrop's critiques. Was she "addicted to revelations"? Well, she attended to the light of Christ within. Moreover, she was certainly censorious, having denounced New England magistrates for their treatment of her colleagues.[71]

From the Quakers' first appearance, the General Court passed laws designed to protect the Bay Colony from the Quaker threat. A ship commander bringing a Quaker to port would be fined one hundred pounds; any inhabitants harboring Quaker books or writings would pay for each text five pounds; anyone holding such opinions, fined forty shillings; and anyone who reviled magistrate or minister would be severely whipped or pay five pounds. For the invading Quakers themselves, the Court prescribed severe measures: "what Quakers soever shall arrive in this country from foraigne pts, or come into this jurisdiction from any parts adjacent, shalbe forthwith committed to the howse of correction, & at their entrance to be severely whipt, & by the master thereof to be kept constantly to worke." These were fairly standard punishments meted out to Quakers in England as well. However, because the magistrates deeply feared the corruption of their own community, they further determined that no one would be permitted "to converse or speake with them dureing the time of their imprisonment, which shalbe no longer than necessity requireth."[72] Clearly, the infliction of pain through imprisonment might not outweigh the opportunity to proselytize, and Quakers had demonstrated their proclivity for speech.

These prohibitions and penalties were again ratified the following year, escalating punishment for sympathizers so that any person entertaining a Quaker would be fined forty shillings for each hour. Further, the Court decided that every male Quaker who returned to the colony following banishment would, for the first offense, have an ear cut off; for the second his other ear, and be kept in prison and put to work until he could cover the costs of his expulsion. A female Quaker would be whipped for each offense and imprisoned pending expulsion. The third time a Quaker defied the order of banishment, he or she would have the tongue bored with a hot iron, an explicit punitive response to unguarded, infectious speaking. Resident offenders would, from this point, suffer the same penalties.[73] The following year, laws against Quakers were reissued, although the tortures were not listed, and punishment for inhabitants hearing or harboring Quakers were clarified. In their condemnation of Quaker sympathizers, the court not only noted the heresy involved but spoke extensively about the disrespect of authority, admonishing "every inhabitant of this jurisdiction . . . stirring up mutiny, sedition, or rebellion against the government, or . . . taking up theire absurd & destructive practices, viz, denying civil respect & reverence to aequalls & superiors . . . ." The disrespect for magistrates' rank and authority apparently outweighed anxieties concerning heresy. The court punished such behaviors with imprisonment and, if there was no retraction, banishment.[74]

Within this atmosphere of fear and fury, Robinson and Stephenson, who had initially traveled to the northern regions to cultivate the embryonic communities there, returned to Boston to face their persecutors. The court imprisoned them for their "rebellion, sedition, & presumptuous obtruding themselves upon us . . . ." Mary Dyer joined their protest, deciding to attend them in prison. All three were sentenced to death, and one week later they were marched to the Boston Commons. Each struggled to speak along the way, but the ritual beating of drums accompanying the walk drowned out their words. The court, in response to the petition of her son, had reprieved Dyer, provided she left the colony within forty-eight hours. Still, the court performed its own cruelty within "their mercy & clemency." They ordered Dyer carried to "the place of execution, & there stand upon the gallows, with a rope about her necke," to witness the execution of her colleagues.[75] Witnesses as well as official and Quaker accounts agreed that Dyer refused to descend, "saying She was there willing to suffer as her Brethren did, unless they would null their wicked Law." She was pulled down and carried by her family out of the colony.[76] The following May, Dyer "rebelliously, after the sentence of death [was] past against her" returned to Boston, came before the court, and was hanged on the first of June.[77]

Although Dyer rarely appears in the records, during the three years of her activism and trials her voice was recorded. In her petition to the General Court, she spoke in the Quaker style, for the creator "having held out his royal scepter unto mee by which I have accesse into his presence and have found such favoure in his sight as to offer up my life freely for his truth and peoples sakes." She called upon the magistrates to search "with the Light of Christ in you." In her case the light had pushed her beyond thought and speech to action. Her presence among them testified against their actions, yet her speech straddled the line between passive conduit and assertive witness. She believed herself a tool in the hand of God. "I have no self and the lord knows for if my life were freely granted by you it would not avail nor be excepted from you soe long as I shal daly hear or see the suffering of my dear brethren." On the other hand, she delivered her prophetic warning so that she would be "clear of your blood." She prophesied the destruction of their government and law, and proclaimed that no matter their actions, God would "send more of his servants coming . . . ."[78]

Her return to Boston in 1660 was accompanied by similar speeches, sometimes witnessed to by Quaker authors, often facilitated by the very people
who wanted to silence her. When condemned a second time, she observed,
"I came in Obedience to the Will of God," urging them to repeal their anti-
Quaker laws and warning that if they failed to do so, "the Lord will send
others of his Servants to Witness against them." When John Endicott asked
her "Whether she was a Prophet—She said, She spake the words that the
Lord spake in her; and now the thing is come to pass."[79] As she was marched
to the scaffold, the court again ordered drums beaten to drown out her voice,
but at the place of execution, there was space for speech. Told she was guilty
because she had returned after banishment, her response included claims
of personal agency, not just spiritual receptivity. "I came to keep Blood-
guiltiness from you . . . for those that do it in the simplicity of their hearts,
I do desire the Lord to forgive them. I came to do the Will of my Father . . ."
She answered questions that were put to her: she did not repent, she recognized no elder among them, she did not want prayers from an elder, but perhaps those of "a child, then a young man, then a strong man, before an Elder
of Christ Jesus."[80]

Mary Dyer stands as an illuminating example of New England's Quaker
women. She was one of a few women arrested during the first moments of
the persecutions, which attested that Quakers were sources of serious disorder and corruption. That the magistrates identified Dyer, as well as several
other women, as Quaker is in itself remarkable. The officials' conduit of information is unknown, but this pointed to an actively informed communications network. Initially imprisoned and banished, she returned to her home
in Newport, traveled to testify in New Haven, only to be banished again,
and then returned home. She next appeared visiting her friends in Boston's
prison, provoking the court to arrest and imprison her again. William Dyer's
petition on her behalf argued that she had only come to visit Robinson and
Stephenson. William asked whether "she came to your meetings to disturb
them as you call itt, or did she come to reprehend the magistrats? [She] only
came to visit her friends in prison." He reminded them that "the worst of
men, the bishops themselves denied not the visitations & Releifs of friends
to their pri[so]ners . . ."[81] The text was filled with the need of the family for
wife and mother, astonishment at the magistrates' treatment of her, and perhaps a bit unconvincing. From the outset, Dyer's speeches challenged the
powerful, echoing those of other Quakers: invocation of the Spirit, the light
of Christ; acknowledgment that she spoke as prophet; prediction of divine

wrath; and never-ceasing commentary on unjust laws. Dyer inspired those who observed her exemplary witness: "my Heart is drawn out unto you in true Love, being sensible of the many Oppositions that you have met . . . and his Righteousness to be your Reward."[82] She was sometimes outraged, sometimes pleading; throughout she demonstrated an unwillingness to compromise. She accepted physical punishment, offering her body as a canvas upon which the righteousness of the Quakers was written in blood drawn by the whip. Mary Dyer differed from her peers in one way only, as the only Quaker woman to be hanged.[83]

Directly following the execution of Robinson and Stephenson, the court detailed the record of Quakers in Massachusetts and proffered six explanations for their judgment. They thought that "the justice of our proceedings . . . perswade us to expect incouragement & commendation from all prudent & pious men, then convince us of any necessity to apologize for the same," but they knew that some individuals "of weaker parts," or out of pity, or lack of information might be "lesse satisfied." Moreover, "men of perverse principles may take occasion hereby to calumniate us, & render us as bloody persecutors . . ." Aware that many in the colony questioned the imprisonment, torture, and execution of the Quakers, the governor and magistrates felt obligated to justify themselves. This speaks to the likelihood that the force used to control the Quakers was not only unsuccessful, it was not widely accepted. The shattering otherness that the ministers and magistrates saw in the Quakers was not so perceived by everyone. Magistrates began with a detailed account of warnings, Quaker appearances, the law of banishment passed patterned English law banning Jesuits, and their own mercy in permitting Mary Dyer to leave. Yet this apparently orderly account of Quaker acts was punctuated by words of notable pugnacity: "insolence," "fanatic fury," "assault," "presumption," "violence," "felon." The court portrayed Quakers as rampantly out of control and themselves as dedicated caretakers of the people who desired Quakers' "life absent rather than theire death present."[84]

Surprisingly, the General Court's observations and complaints about the Quakers actually matched Quakers' own understanding of their work. Christians are required to respect and obey magistrates, but the Quakers were far from reverence and honor, showing instead contempt, with "railing and cursing speeches." Quakers might have challenged this characterization of their speeches, but they certainly expressed their contempt for those who claimed to represent the law but worked against God's commands. The penalty was banishment upon pain of death, and yet Quakers returned. Yes,

Quakers deliberately and articulately flouted this law, explaining their acts as testimony against unjust laws. The court invoked metaphors of householder and father, with the right to protect his holdings against intrusion and his children from infection. Quakers claimed only to be sharing the truth. Quaker Francis Howgill noted that Quakers do indeed acknowledge magistrates who are true magistrates, "as nursing Fathers, who preserve mens Persons and Estates from devourers, as a Father preserves a Child from injury, these are Ordained of God," but in New England they were like wolves.[85]

The court's last justification took up a counterfactual premise. If the magistrates were persecuting the Quakers, which they were not doing but if they were, then those experiencing such persecution should flee. Building their argument upon specific biblical examples of individuals who chose or were instructed to leave difficult situations, the court argued that those who rejected the opportunity to leave the country were "guilty of tempting God, & of incurring their oune hurt." Of course, the court denied persecution, claiming they were merely administering justice.[86] The Quaker texts, on the other hand, were filled with stories of those who suffered afflictions explicitly named as persecution, and in their defiance of banishment, risking imprisonment, torture, and death, Quakers characterized their defiance as testimony. Their goals were no longer limited to spreading the call to listen to the light within, but now included witnessing to the oppression of the people of the Spirit. And they found the court's biblical interpretation politically driven and overly simplistic. "There is a time to suffer persecution, and a time to flee . . . to lay it down as a general rule for Christians to observe that when they are persecuted, they should flee, this is expressly contrary to the Scriptures." Or, as Isaac Penington continued, "They are Christs Souldiers, and their duty is to stand in the battel, and bear all the shots and persecutions of the enemy."[87] The court's defensive tone in its description of the appropriate, Christian response to persecution suggests that Quakers were not the only ones lodging such accusations against the General Court.

Throughout, New England magistrates portrayed themselves as hardworking, sincere fathers defending their colony from disruptive, poisonous invaders. Not trusting oral communication networks, the court published a broadside describing Quakers' appearance and disruption of the countryside, along with the laws passed to control them.[88] In a way, the magistrates and ministers were justified, for many of the inhabitants were drawn to the newcomers. Nicholas Upshall was the first to come before the General Court. He had been among the first wave of colonizers who arrived in 1630 and lived in Dorchester, a man of status and reputation. Outraged by the treatment meted out to Anne Austin and Mary Fisher, Upshall reproached the magistrates and spoke in opposition to the law passed against Quakers. The court imprisoned him until he paid an enormous fine of twenty pounds and gave him thirty days to leave the jurisdiction. Eventually he joined the movement, building the first Quaker meeting house in Massachusetts.[89] Perhaps people simply did not recognize the dangerous heresies brought by the travelers; the court instructed cleric John Norton to examine Quaker theology and provide a clear delineation of the errors promulgated; Norton produced a complex, biblically supported, carefully argued exposé and found Quaker preaching even more dangerous and heretical than imagined.[90] Still, the number of inhabitants who appeared in the record as Quakers shows that many in Massachusetts found the theology attractive and the community pleasing. The old Hutchinsonians in Rhode Island were not the only New Englanders drawn to the new community. While the first Quakers may have arrived from England by way of Barbados, homegrown Quaker congregations soon took root throughout New England.

Predictably, considering the town's history of religious dissent and turmoil, beginning with Roger Williams's successful tenure and ultimate banishment, Salem became a center of Quaker disruption and development.[91] George Bishop argued that initially many Salemites "could no longer partake with you, who mingled blood with your Sacrifices." During these early years, Bishop noted that twenty or more persons gathered at one meeting at the house of Nicholas Phelps, worshiping and hearing from two travelers from England, William Brend and William Leddra. Several residents of Salem were already imprisoned at Ipswich by the Essex County Court. They petitioned the Salem magistrates, complaining that they had been fined and imprisoned although they had broken no law, but were dealt with as "the law pvids for foriane Quakers as you please to call us."[92] From the outbreak of activism and the first fines and whippings, the local practitioners observed and complained that they were viewed and treated as intruders, foreigners. Moreover, the General Court judged them blasphemers and a serious threat to country and brought them before the General Court. In addition to Phelps, who organized meetings at his home, Samuel Shattocke, Joshua Buffam, Laurence and Cassandra Southwicke, and their son Josiah were all sentenced to banishment. Daniel and Provided Southwicke, children of Laurence and Cassandra, were fined for not attending church, and because they were not able to pay their fines, the court empowered the treasurer to sell them to any in Virginia or Barbados (a strategy that was unsuccessful for no ship captain would accept this task).[93]

After the execution of Robinson and Stephenson, the court brought to account eight men who had "entertayned" Quakers. Apparently, the court lacked evidence that these eight were, in fact, Quakers themselves, or perhaps the magistrates chose to ignore that possibility. Whatever the reason, these individuals were prosecuted on lesser charges. James Rawlings, "being more innocent & ingenious then the rest," was merely admonished by the governor. Of the seven punished, the four freemen were disfranchised, and six individuals were fined. The seventh, Edward Wharton, had accompanied the Quakers and guided them from place to place; the court ordered him whipped and imprisoned. He would become a traveling Quaker preacher, and would suffer various penalties until the persecutions were ended by royal decree in 1665.[94] In addition, Salem women continued to disrupt the community. Ann Needham, wife of Anthony, was presented because of her fifteen days' absence from public worship; the magistrates fined her 3*li*. 15*s* (Three pounds, fifteen shillings). "She refused to pay or have it paid for her, and the court, considering her former offensive and provoking speeches, and she desiring to have the punishment inflicted upon her person, order her to be whipped twelve stripes." The following year Nicolas Phelps's wife was presented for stating that the pastor "Higgeson sent abroad his wolves and his bloodhounds amongst the sheep and lambs." She, too, was ordered fined or whipped.[95]

In his catalog of sufferings, Edward Burrough noted eighteen inhabitants, who "being free-born *English*, received **twenty three whippings**, the stripes amounting **to two hundred and fifty**." He further counted sixty-four imprisoned for a total of 519 weeks, and they remained incarcerated during harvest time. He counted eighteen banished, six of them inhabitants, including two aged, "and well known among their Neighbours to be of honest Conversation." He described an "Innocent man" of *Boston*, banished in winter, on threat of imprisonment, and "for returning again, he was put in Prison, and hath been now a Prisoner above a year."[96] Additionally, Burrough complained about fines in Salem "laid upon the Inhabitants for meeting together, and edifying one another as the Saints ever did; and for **refusing to swear**, it being contrary to Christ's Command, **amounting to above a Thousand pound** . . . ."[97]

Inhabitants clearly numbered among the individuals arrested, imprisoned, tortured, and banished. According to George Fox, eleven inhabitants were whipped, forty-five imprisoned, two beaten with pitch ropes, one shut up fifteen days without food, and fines levied totaled £318.[98] Those who attended Quaker meetings were fined ten shillings; for speaking, five pounds. If a person had once been whipped, she or he was taken to the house of correction until the accused organized transit and left the colony or provided bond guaranteeing good behavior. For, as the General Court noted early on, "diverse of our inhabitants have been infected and seduced, notwithstanding all former Laws made upon the experience of [Quakers'] arrogant and bold obtrusions to disseminate their Principles among us, prohibiting their coming into this Jurisdiction, they have not been deterred from their impetuous attempts, to undermine our Peace and hasten our Ruine."[99]

The extraordinary threat felt by the leadership was revealed in the extraordinary language used. The court did not stop with angry accusations of inciting political disorder or contempt for authority. Its members feared the pollution of the social body through the infection and seduction of individuals. From the beginning, ministers and magistrates considered the possibility of witchcraft. In an early account of the attacks, an anonymous Quaker author noted that officials accused "them for Witches: whereupon they took upon them to appoint women to search them, who also took men along with them, which if they had denied or refused, to have bound and constrained them, but such was their innocency that they suffered all whatsoever they attempted to do unto them . . . ."[100] In traditional fashion, accusations of witchcraft were complemented by labels of immorality. The leaders "did openly accuse us of uncleanness . . . in going men and women together, running away from our Parents, wives and children."[101] Gadding about continued to be coded text for promiscuity. In his history of the Quakers, *Hell Broke Loose*, Thomas Underhill asserted that Quakers "deny all Relation, as Brother and Sister, Magistrate, Master, Father, Mother, Son and Daughter, Husband and Wife, and that Husband and Wife should part asunder, and that all Things should be common." And again, linking the depth of natural filth with the specter of the supernatural, "*Quakers* are a carnal and bloody People. That the Quakers are bewitched and possessed by the Devil."[102] A list of a diverse, serendipitous, and exaggerated accusations, including "*Murders, Burning* of *Houses, Blasphemies, Treasons, Rebellions, Witchcrafts, Madness, Enthusiasms,* and what not," included a revealing addition: "Unclean Actions in their Assemblies of Worship."[103] Accusers repeatedly invoked metaphors of filth, pollution of the body. The people of Massachusetts were forced to consume unwholesome ideas and preachers.

The General Court proclaimed one day in October 1658, for example, as a Day of Humiliation. Many families were afflicted "with sickness; unreasonableness of weather and failure of crops; letting loose a scourge upon us those fretting gangrene-like doctrines and persons commonly called Quakers, the spirit of division and dissention in Church and Civil Affairs."[104] These accusations of inflicting poison and disease were even heard across the Atlantic, published in *Mercurius Politicus*, the weekly journal of the Commonwealth. The court endeavored to protect "the souls of simple and ignorant people" from the "cursed generation," with their "hellish Printed Pamphlets" and a "mallicious spirit." The court found itself called to "preserve them by Gods assistance from being bewitched and infected with the spreading Leprosie: their poysonfull and early doctrines . . . ."[105]

Such visceral images of contagion, disfigurement, and corruption suggest leaders struggling against an enemy attacking from multiple directions. The court took action, in escalating stages of pain and constraint, to control the increasingly chaotic environment. After enacting the laws passed in the first two years following the arrival of Quaker itinerants, the General Court failed to follow standard legal processes, a complaint that several Quaker authors noted in petitions to the English government. Cases were tried before magistrates, without juries, even capital cases; magistrates acted as accuser, judge, and special jury. Appeals to higher English courts were denied, and these selective efficiencies enabled magistrates to follow their own path at the expense of individual rights and proper procedures.[106] In some ways, these actions represented the final struggles of the founding generation of leaders to enforce the uniform orthodoxy that they had worked so hard to construct. In the earlier cases of Roger Williams, Anne Hutchinson, and their followers, banishment served to keep order in the Bay Colony. Those who wished to return, like William Aspinwall or even John Wheelwright, petitioned the government, declared their repentance, and accepted the orthodoxy. But now, despite the work of the court, the Quakers successfully converted many inhabitants to their theology and practices, protested the imprisonment, torture, and banishment imposed on missionaries and residents alike, and consequently attracted more colonizers to their cause. Many of the banished returned to their mission work or their homes, despite threats, and while converts constituted a fairly small minority of believers, they were indeed noisy. Ann Needham had delivered "offensive and provoking speeches"; Phelps's wife declared that Salem's pastor had "sent abroad his wolves and his bloodhounds amongst the sheep and lambs." Fines mounted up, jails filled, and despite promises regarding corporal punishments, public whippings continued. In 1661 the General Court, in response to a letter from the king, suspended the laws against the Quakers "so farr as they respect corporall punishment or death . . . ."[107] While the magistrates maintained their efforts to control their cultural world, over the next few years their most egregious practices finally ended.

Although the attention of inhabitants had initially been caught by the oppressive response of the magistrates, some were doubtless attracted to the openness and intense spirituality of the Quakers, to the opportunity to experience God and speak publicly about it. When the *Speedwell* had arrived in Boston in 1656, the eight Quaker passengers were brought before the magistrates. Asked why thy had come to Massachusetts, "they answered, to do the work of God; being asked who sent them, they answered God; being demanded every one of them how they would make it appear that God sent them, they made a great pause and answered nothing." After pondering the query, they finally responded in an echo of Hutchinson twenty years before: "they had the same call Abraham had to come out of his Country."[108] Such mystical sensibilities were not unknown to New Englanders, but the Quakers' performance was inspiring, as was the invitation to speak extended to any person gifted by the Spirit. Quakers gathered themselves together in meetings of silence, seeking the voice of the spirit to be uttered in their hearts and transmitted to others by the spiritually gifted.

The spiritually gifted seemed, however, to subvert the base of order in this society. Among Quakers, women had power that was supposed to be held by men only. Many Quaker women were preachers. Among the most visible public Quakers a majority were women, not because women outnumbered men, but primarily because preaching women attracted much more attention than preaching men. These women's activities, the fact that they were permitted, even encouraged, to leave their husbands and children behind to missionize for the Quaker cause, that they claimed the authority and voice to instruct, even censure, leaders demonstrated to the magistrates that the Quakers had turned away from the sanctity of the family and were set upon destroying society as it had been established in the sacred texts and English tradition. As in the case of Anne Hutchinson, who was admonished by John Cotton that although "I have not herd, nayther do I thinke, you have bine unfaythfull to your Husband in his Marriage Covenant, *yet that will follow upon it*," the General Court, in their denunciations, argued that Quaker beliefs and practices would naturally lead to sexual licentiousness.[109]

So, on the one hand women, empowered by the spirit, behaved like male elders and preachers. This would be problem enough, but, on the other hand, men refused to stop or discipline or even speak out against those women; men supported the women's activities. These men also rejected the necessity or even desirability of study as a mode of understanding God and instead turned to the passive acceptance of the inner light. In other words, men were acting like women. That such passive reception of the spirit empowered these men as well did not alter this gendered dynamic because the men relinquished all power until they were moved by God's spirit. And even more to the point, for Quakers, men could only access power in the same way that women did.

Quaker spirituality was, in the end, a female spirituality, female according to the terms in which gender was constructed in the seventeenth century. I do not mean merely that this religiosity had great appeal for women, although it did; such appeal could be just as easily explained by the fact that Quakers opened power channels to women. But beyond this simple identification of women with Quakerism, Quakers' spirit mysticism demanded of the believer qualities that were considered essentially feminine: submission, passivity, openness, and passion. This religiosity also moved toward a personal, intimate relationship between the believer and God that became gendered because the dominant metaphor for intimacy was sexuality—the male God embraced the believer who must, by definition, be female since the holy sexual paradigm was heterosexual. By their acceptance of the inner light and their willingness to participate in the Quaker meeting, Quaker men proclaimed themselves spiritually feminine. They recognized the potential spiritual power of women, refused to fill their own necessary role in the power dynamics of patriarchy, and established a separate, integrated authority through mystical experience. Quakers themselves may not have fully realized the feminine nature of their mysticism, but the court's attacks indicated such a recognition on the part of the accusers.

In December 1660, Mary Trask and Margaret Smith, Quaker women of Salem, wrote to Governor John Endicott and the other members of the court from the house of correction. They addressed the magistrates as "a cruell & hardhearted people," denounced the "evill of your waies," and promised that "thee shal assuredly feel his judgments who have willfully put forth your hands against his Chosen . . ." However, the women also spoke plaintively of the lost opportunity to "partake of his love to feel his life & power in your owne hearts, if with us, thee might have been brought to be subject to the highest power christ jesus whom you should have been obedient to & hearkened to his judgments while he stood at the dore & Knocked."[110] Really, was this vision so appalling?

Whether fighting a personal battle for their own sense of self or a political battle to enjoy the power that patriarchy gave, magistrates and ministers needed to silence those feminine voices and, by extension, their own feminine side. Part of this process was the transformation of God from lover to father, and the transformation of saint from wife to son or daughter. Out of this construction men were able to identify with the masculinity of God; they became closer to the divinity than women. Another part was rhetoric and practice that emphasized preparation, education, and sanctification and de-emphasized the conversion experience. Now, the devout Puritan man had to develop his mind and educate himself in the deliberately obscure, complicated, technical language used by God. He also had to prepare himself so that he could open his heart and suppress his passions when grace came. Rationality and reason were at a premium, and men reaped the benefits of their superior intellectual abilities and strength of will.

What moved these ideological changes forward in the seventeenth century were the battles fought against identifiable, personal, female foes. Anne Hutchinson was such an enemy, strong in her challenge, dangerous in the appeal she held for others, men and women. But for the second generation, the focus was upon the Quakers, who denied the legitimacy of state power over religion, rejected clerical authority over the soul, and suggested that simply opening one's self to God would bring peace, satisfaction, and authority. The women were strong; the men had relinquished power; they were the upside-down world that Puritanism had promised. Magistrates had done everything in their power, and beyond it, to stop this spiritual force. Yet neither whips and scaffolds nor fines and ridicule could effectively silence the challengers. All that the magistrates and clerics could achieve was a firm, recognized separation between Quakers and New England Congregationalists and the growing alienation of Puritans from the mystical/feminine spirituality of their forebears. In the fight for patriarchal order, Quakers died and suffered, but the Puritans moved themselves one step further away from God. The battle was long and bloody, but casualties fell on both sides.

7

A Froward Woman Beloved of God

"It is said, I will poure my Spirit upon your Daughters, and they shall prophesie," she quoted. "If God give me a gift of Prophecy, I may use it."

The Lord did discover to me all sorts of Ministers, and how they taught, and to know what voyce I heard, which was the voyce of *Moses*, which of *John the Baptist*, and which of Christ; the voyce of my beloved. . . .

Anne Hutchinson, 1637[1]

Like many Christians before them, Puritans longed for God, for a deep, satisfying, personal relationship with the divine. Suffering the scorn, the fines, and, at times, the brutal persecutions of the English religious establishment, these believers found comfort and righteousness in their spiritual search. Puritan leaders also longed to be patriarchs—rulers of an ordered society, their own society, established according to their own vision of the biblical commandments and expectations of God. In the colonies of New England and in the Commonwealth government that overthrew King Charles I, Puritan leaders began to realize their vision for a new social order. At the same time that some Puritans finally achieved earthly power, others had reached the goal of their spiritual journey, experiencing God, hearing God's voice, thrilling to God's presence. And here lay the problem. Divine revelation creates a direct, personal, intimate relationship between God and soul, without the interference or interposition of state, society, or church. Such an experience strengthens the character and power of the individual believer; revelation places the voice of God as heard today from a chosen messenger alongside the knowledge and will of God as understood from biblical injunctions, legitimated through exegesis and theological application, and reinforced by established authorities. For seventeenth-century Puritans, these authorities included English custom, the common law, and a Calvinist theology founded upon biblical precept. Together these ideological authorities constructed and upheld a patriarchal order.

If God were to choose an acceptably powerful messenger, and if the revelation corroborated an orthodox theological and ethical vision, then Puritans might have had no problem. But God did not always act according to human logic. As Paul had written: "O the depnes of the riches, bothe of the wisdome, & knowledge of God! how unsearcheable are his judgements, & his wayes past finding out!"[2] What if the new revelation challenged orthodox doctrine and social prescription? What if the spirit spoke through the ordinary working man, the illiterate, the poor? What if God chose a woman?

Far from hypothetical, these questions challenged and irritated, oppressed and depressed the English Puritan leadership; for the seventeenth century had more than its share of ordinary godly communicators, particularly women. The Puritan perception of God and God's relationship to humanity, as experienced through conversion and acknowledged in the priesthood of all believers, opened the way for a flourishing of the spirit among individuals of every kind. At the same time, the society envisioned by Puritans was one characterized by a communal spirit and a hierarchical order. The Puritan leaders were greatly empowered by their own identity as members of the elect, and they clung to the conversion experience as a marker of their own destiny, their right to lead. These leaders were not willing to share that power with those who, in their minds, had no right to it. Puritan leaders in old and New England confronted the self-proclaimed authority of female prophets and found themselves enmeshed in an irreconcilable conflict between the cultural and political demands of order and control and the spiritual possibilities of conversion and revelation.

Many historians have explored the Hutchinsonian crisis as a conflict disrupting the balance of power among theological and political leaders. The defeat of the Hutchinsonians did not eliminate dissent from the colony: the example of Lady Deborah Moody's and Harvard president Henry Dunster's perseverance in rejecting infant baptism and the growth of the Quaker communities were proof against such a facile conclusion. Still, in the resolution of the Hutchinsonian crisis, the Bay Colony leadership had traversed significant political and spiritual crossings. Mechanisms for identifying and silencing dissent were refined, and clerics developed a language for delineating and justifying those processes. More importantly, clerics addressed directly the egalitarian implications of their own radical religiosity. When women spoke with charismatic authority, it created a strident dissonance. These were spiritually powerful individuals who by gender definition should have no authority. In other words, this controversy was characterized not only by a theological debate concerning salvation and a political discourse about dissent, but also a religio-social discourse concerning gender, religiosity, spiritual charisma, and order.

Of course, within this definition of womanhood, political and religious leaders already had the solution for resolving that dissonance. English society operated within a patriarchal framework buttressed by a cordon of legal, customary, and ideological tools. Puritan New England was patriarchal not only in the broad sense of men dominating women, but also as a carefully designed prescriptive model specific to that community and that century. Patriarchy provided a structure that political leaders and clergymen recognized and claimed with pleasure, envisioning themselves as Old Testament patriarchs. They believed that the Scriptures had ordained a clear, ordered family system that arranged all members of society into dichotomous power relations: master–servant, parent–child, and, especially, husband–wife. Within this domestic system, the father assumed the central role as head of household, a control that was justified not only by law and custom, but by Holy Writ.[3]

Although law, politics, economics, and custom all aligned in support of patriarchy, one ideological force remained outside this network: spiritual experience. Puritan leaders followed John Calvin in the acceptance of a providential, divinely ordained hierarchical order, but their perception of God and God's relationship to the individual soul offered a potential challenge to that order. The conversion experience represented God's struggle with one particular saint, emphasizing the importance of each soul and, perhaps, emphasizing the personhood of woman as well as man. Paradoxically, God was understood to have established a covenanted relationship with the community as a whole, mandating a communal, patriarchal ideology and commitment, even as God had developed a private, personal relationship with each individual. This conversion, translating into election, justified and empowered the New England migration and the creation of a saint-controlled government; it justified and empowered a civil war, the execution of the king, and the pursuant creation of the Commonwealth. But the price for this vision was that everyone had access to it, empowering individual saints within and, potentially, against the community.

Working toward conversion, Puritans believed that God led people to salvation through the Holy Scriptures, preaching, and providence. Literacy,
learning, and Levitical law were valued as tools for understanding and
relating to God. Yet many had recognized something more; they had faith
in the possibility of a divine-human relationship of great personal intimacy,
an experiential conversion that defied rational explanation and, sometimes, deepened into a mystical, ecstatic union with God.[4] Elizabeth Avery
explained it well:

> And so when God, which is our heaven, shall be thus dissolved, and cease
> being covered with a vail, then this vail shall vanish away like smoke, which
> vail is the Ordinance; and heaven being dissolved, the Saints are in a capacity
> to contain this heaven in the flesh; and surely God, who is our heaven, shall
> appear in the flesh of all his Saints shortly, in his glorious manifestations.[5]

These spirit mystics felt that their union with the Holy Spirit was permanent, freeing them from all doubts and failings and empowering them
to move forward, certain in the grace of God. Outside institutional church
structures, their ideology placed such mystics beyond normal controls. In
Massachusetts, Hutchinsonians plagued ministers and magistrates with their
single-minded focus upon free grace and, twenty years later, Quakers and
their inner light wreaked havoc on both sides of the Atlantic. What hope was
there for order in society, when the establishment struggled to disentangle
scripture and providence while radical religionists asserted the simple authority of God's own voice, spoken to them directly?

Although some Puritan men answered the mystical calling, women had
a special affinity for the intensely personal nature of this experience. The
seventeenth-century sectaries, many of them leaning toward the mystical,
often included more women than men, and many individual women stood
out: Eleanor Davies Douglas, incarcerated in Bedlam for predicting, with
frighteningly accurate timing, the destruction of William Laud and Charles
I; penniless Elinor Channel, called from her family to London with a warning
for Oliver Cromwell; Anna Trapnel, Fifth Monarchist, singing doggerel verse
in trances; Elizabeth Poole, challenging Cromwell and the Parliament for
their treatment of the king; Susanna Parr, cofounder, with seven men, of a
sectarian congregation; Margaret Fell, ardent follower of Fox and patron of
the Quaker community. Of course, Anne Hutchinson and Mary Dyer, well
known to historians, belong in these ranks. Hutchinson, convinced that

God had given her a gift of prophecy, asserted her right to use this gift. Dyer instructed the General Court to "search with the light of Christ in you."[6] These female preachers, mystics, and prophets justified their speech with the assurance that the Holy Spirit was working through them.

The conflict between hierarchical leaders and individualistic laypersons became sharpest when those laypersons were women. If women truly heard the voice of the Holy Spirit, then this authority from God must override the constrictions of patriarchy. Some women, including Anne Hutchinson and Eleanor Davies Douglas, saw themselves as individually special; they did not challenge the general systems of social order, but saw themselves as set apart. Other religionists addressed this problem by deciding that earthly hierarchies were false orders subordinating the ways of God to the ways of men. George Fox, Margaret Fell, and the Quakers, the best known of these critics, challenged social rankings created by a variety of artificial factors like wealth, birth, education, and gender; most Quakers witnessed to the authority of God in the voice of Quaker women. The Fifth Monarchists, another sect descended from the Puritans, believed that the time was ripe for Christ to realize his kingship and establish a new order, and they seemed to have no problem hearing and heeding Anna Trapnel and Mary Cary. Many Puritans and their heirs, however, had difficulty accepting women's spiritual authority. In their efforts to undercut, and in some cases deny, that authority, Puritan leaders undermined the radical potential of Puritan spirituality, bolstering and hardening the evolving patriarchal boundaries. To achieve this victory, clerical and political leaders strengthened the society's ideological commitment to rationalism, education, and preparationism—systems that they controlled—at the expense of mystical union with the divine. In so resolving the reason/piety paradox, they transmuted the character of their own personal relationships with God, sacrificing the potential ecstasy and power of charisma for the ordinary authority granted by church, society, and state.

Salvation came through dependence upon God, and knowledge of one's own salvation through conversion. The conversion experience itself came to be defined by the preparatory steps of reading, study, and prayer and sanctified behavior following conversion. This focus upon erudition, preparation, and sanctification appears to be a game attempt to reconfigure an essentially mystical spirituality as a developmental one. A developmental understanding favored men by privileging their intellectual and moral superiority as constructed within science and theology. The fact that a reconstruction was necessary returns to the basic conflict inherent in Puritan religiosity. The very nature of mysticism, a direct, intense irrational relationship with the divine, a relationship available to anyone, depending only upon the arbitrary choice of God, established a basic egalitarian spirituality that empowered the individual in relation to society.

Women, and other disfranchised believers, often refused to accept the limits of that developmental reconstruction and continued to seek direct communion with God. This was certainly a rational decision in terms of personal power since the alternative placed women in a submissive, suppliant relationship to men. However, beyond any political reason, many women found sectarian mysticism a particularly attractive, alluring, perhaps even "natural" spirituality. In the developmental religiosity of education and preparation, God was father and the believer his son or daughter. Men could be seen as more godlike, to have more of the image of God in the same way that sons identified with fathers and daughters with mothers.[7] However, in the mystical language of conversion, God was the bridegroom, the believer was the bride, and rather than strive to uncover the image of God in one's own soul, the believer sought ecstatic communion with God.

Puritan theologians had argued that women required restriction and guidance because they were weak, passionate, sexual. Women were first seduced, and then they seduced others. The construction of the witch who has had carnal relations with Satan, producing imps and familiars that suck nourishment from the witches' teats on her body, represented only the extreme end of a cosmology that conflated sexuality with evil. Despite their scorn of celibacy and praise for marriage, despite their celebration of the nuptial bed, Puritan theologians carried with them the medieval distrust of female beauty and sexuality. The passionate power of a wife was dangerous enough; sexuality unleashed was terrifying.

Yet mystical engagement with God was sexuality unleashed—heterosexual, even marital sexuality—but unarguably sexual. Puritans often invoked the erotic language of the Song of Solomon, the Old Testament love poem that described the

love of Jesus Christ, the true Salomon and King of peace, and the faithful soule or his Church, which he hathe sanctified and appointed to be his spouse, holy, chast and without reprehension. So that here is declared the singular love of the bridegrome toward the bride . . . Also the earnest affection of the Church which is inflamed with the love of Christ desiring to be more and more joined to him in love.[8]

John Cotton had delivered and published a series of sermons upon these canticles, using the sensuous language as a means of enticing his listeners toward God. Thomas Hooker assured believers that they were spouses of Christ, while Thomas Shepard longed to accept Christ as "Lord and Savior and Husband."[9] John Lilburne proclaimed that he "counted my wedding day in which I was married to the Lord Jesus Christ; for now I know he loves me in that he bestowed so rich apparel this day upon me."[10]

Anna Trapnel's oracular performances traversed similar pathways. Addressing Jesus, she expressed anxieties: "it was a time of darkness then, I could not discern thee; but I took Graces for thee, and thee for them: I had not a distinct apprehension of thee but at length thou brakest forth with a spirit of life and power, and didst say, *I am thine, and thou art mine.*" Yet at another moment "the Lord greatly ravished my soul with his smiling looks on me, and he filled me that day with prayer, and singing," and again, while she was in prison, "The Lord indeed counselled me, and took me into the mount of heavenly rapture that day, so that all my friends were fain to take me off my knees and lay me upon my bed, where I lay praying and singing."[11]

Anne Hutchinson heard the "voice of my beloved," while Susanna Parr took "delight in the Image of God," and Anne Wentworth proclaimed that "his Spirit . . . has stirred me up. My heavenly bridegroom is come . . . ."[12] Anne Bradstreet once spoke of God, "who will not be tied to time nor place, nor yet to persons, but takes and chooses, when and where and whom He pleases." And in the very last poem she composed, Bradstreet looked toward decline and death as the "bed Christ did perfume," and awaited with trembling to welcome the joys of death:

> Then the soul and body shall unite
>   And of their Maker have the sight;
> Such lasting joys shall there behold
>   As ear ne'er heard nor tongue e'er told;
> Lord make me ready for that day,
>   Then come, dear Bridegroom, come away.[13]

The most graphic, illustrious example of such emotional outpourings remains the poetry of Edward Taylor, who, in his meditations upon the Canticles, compared his experience of the excitement and joys of spirituality to the thrills and pleasures of marital sexuality.

Thy Saving Grace my Wedden Garment make:
Thy Spouses Frame into my Soul Convay.
I then shall be thy Bride Espousd by thee
And thou my Bridesgroom Deare Espousde shalt bee.[14]

In using sexual language to describe spiritual realities, both glorious and terrible, Puritans could speak either analogically or literally. The problem was that they claimed to do both. Marital love was a metaphor for one's relationship with God; witches actually had carnal relations with the Devil. The saint was swept up in the love of God like a bride awaiting her lover; female heretics were mothers of actual monsters. In other words, in their efforts to portray human engagement with the supernatural, Puritans gave voice to grammatically parallel statements that were meant to be understood in radically different ways, sometimes as metaphor and sometimes as literal fact. The inconsistency is intellectually suspect yet politically predictable, and perhaps it does make a kind of sense in a transitional society turning from a magical toward a scientific view of the universe.

Rather than accept that the manifest meaning of these statements is either metaphorical or literal, and that Puritans always knew which was meant, I would like to explore the possibility that alternative, parallel meanings were heard, and that these plural readings had a significant impact upon flowering Puritan spirituality. Seventeenth-century English Christians believed they had the physical evidence of monstrous births, witches' teats, and familiars roaming about the landscape, yet few were so simple-minded as to interpret every black cat, pimple, or childbirth tragedy as evidence of supernatural evil. Witch trial examinations indicate that it was a signed, Faustian contract that mattered, suggesting that carnality had become a figurative expression of the depth of evil associated with witchcraft. Even here, however, the legal image works in tandem with the sexual construction, conveying a fluid exchange of woman's blood signature for the Devil's semen. Moreover, the movement between the figurative and the literal meaning was reflected in the frequent sexual accusations leveled at women who had been or would be accused of witchcraft.

If the sexual signification of evil could not always be read literally, the rapturous language of mysticism was not entirely metaphorical. Decoding mystical texts has long been recognized as a difficult task, in part because the nonlinear or, as many would have it, impenetrable quality of the texts renders the language inaccessible to rationalist reading. In her perceptive writing on

medieval religious women, Caroline Bynum has crafted illuminating analyses, in part because she takes the narrative and the language seriously and
considers the range of possible meanings of the texts. New England Puritans
were not medieval mystics, but Bynum's examination of the relationship between spirituality, the body, and sexuality and her emphasis upon the connection between body and spirit in the minds of her religious, men and
women, produces interpretations beyond a rationalist reading of metaphor
and enables an exploration of spirituality in the seventeenth-century saint's
own terms.[15]

Like their Catholic forebears, the Puritans did not believe the converted
saint had enjoyed a physical, sexual connection with God, but the emotional
tension and exuberance experienced during mystical communion in some
ways mirrored the individual's personal knowledge of the physical pleasure
and psychic excitement of sexual relations. The sexual nature of mystical
communion was experienced as an intimate, electrifying, and breathtaking
reality for the saint. I find it plausible that this spiritual experience stimulated
not only the same emotions and passions but also the physical sensations
usually aroused during pleasurable sexual relations.

The sexuality of Puritan religiosity becomes profoundly important in
light of their constructions of masculinity and femininity through sexuality.
Within the narrow boundaries of acceptable, heterosexual relations, man
was active but reasonable, woman passive but passionate. When Puritans
imagined (or actually experienced) their relationship with God as a sexual
one, they brought understandings of divine/male activity in opposition
to human/female passivity. The sexual language used not only incorporated an extensive vocabulary of marital bliss—bridal bowers and comely
bridegrooms—and terms of deep affection—the beloved—but also the language of sexual violence. "Ravish," a seventeenth-century synonym for rape,
appeared again and again in the confessions of believers, frequently men, as
if to emphasize, in opposition to their active maleness, their passivity in the
face of God's aggressive pursuit, capture, and embracing love for the saint.[16]

In a society that recognized only marital (or in a pinch, betrothed) sexuality as a legitimate outlet for sexual desires and passions, the Puritans' political and social essentialization of gender might well have interfered with
men's ability to experience a mystical, sexualized communion with a male
God, even as it may have promoted women's spirituality. True, many male
Puritans answered the mystical calling and claimed to have taken on the female role in relation to God, assuming a spiritual identity that could cross

gender sex lines. Nonetheless, women seemed to have a special affinity for the intimate, personal nature of this experience.[17] Anne Hutchinson and Mary Dyer are merely the better-known New England representatives of a large number of female English religionists empowered by the Holy Spirit to preach, prophesy, and proclaim God's truth.[18]

This conflation of sexuality and spirituality and the narrow boundary between the glorious and the despicable become clearest in writings produced by sectarians and in opposition to sectaries. The late sixteenth-century followers of Henrik Niclaes, in communion, or godded, with God, had rejected learning in favor of opening themselves to the spirit of divine love. Niclaes himself once described the spiritual children of God as "not covered with any foreskin of the sinful flesh, nor yet with fleshly or earthly mindes, therefore do they likewise (with their spiritual members) walk naked and uncovered, both before God, and before one another."[19] He and his revitalized community of followers called for the creation of a grand family of love, provoking several commentators into scurrilous attacks, including, predictably, accusations of sexual misbehavior if not down-right perversion. "Here's a loving sect presented to you they thinke that a man may gaine salvation by shewing himselfe loving, especially to his neighbours wife . . . ."[20]

While the sensationalist popular press was unrestrained in its attacks upon sectaries, radical leaders preached and celebrated the plainness of the gospel, the purity of the spirit, and the free love of God. One spokesman for the radicals claimed astonishment that anyone would want to silence believers "from declaring the sweet injoyments of their transcendant excellencies of their beloved, of their God, of their King, and of their Jesus, communicated to them, rayling against them, with reviling, vilifying speeches, calling them disgracefully *illiterate mechanicks, Taylors, Pedlers, Tinkers, Coblers, and the like*." He further attacked his critics as "carnally supposing (so far as I am able to spell their meaning) the gifts of the spirit to be centred in, and confined to the members of an University . . ."[21] Another echoed this attack upon the erudition and developmental spirituality of his opponents as, of course, dead religion, glorying instead in the divine love enjoyed by himself and his community.

> And the more this faith of free justification, and of having on this wedding garment, increaseth: the more this peace and joy in the Holy Ghost increaseth. . . . And the more this peace and joy increaseth, the more the

foresaid love increaseth, and inflameth the heart to walk freely, cheerfully, and zealously in all Gods will . . . .[22]

Stories were published of Adamites who prayed together naked in the woods, Ranters whose meetings were spent "in drunkenness, uncleanness, blasphemous words, filthy songs, mixt dances of men and women stark naked," and an unnamed sectary where, following upon the satisfaction of their carnal lusts, they fell into a sport called "whipping of the Whore."[23] Anabaptists and Familists were said to believe in the "Lawfullness of the common use of all Weomen and soe more dayngerous Evells and filthie Unclenes and other sines . . . ."[24] Separatists were attacked as conventiclers who met in "secret and obscure places, in which voluptuous wantonnesse has her meeting, where the Spirit enlightens the understanding to see a sister in the darke," as communities where "many chast virgins becom harlots, and the mothers of bastards."[25] Hutchinson herself came under such an attack from no other than John Cotton, who warned her of "that filthie Sinne of the Communitie of Woemen and all promiscuus and filthie cominge togeather of men and Woemen without Distinction or Relation of Marriage. . . . And though I have not herd, nayther do I thinke, you have bine unfaythfull to your Husband in his Marriage Covenant, *yet that will follow upon it . . .*"[26]

These theologians saw a clear relationship between heresy, gender, and deviant sexuality. Their vision did not, generally, include the mirror image of that picture, that is, the relationship between mystical communion, celebrated sexuality, and gender. Yet the connection appears strong and demonstrable both in the large number of female adherents and leaders and in the language used by these dissenters to describe their religiosity. In their rejection of erudition and other artificial hierarchies and their emphasis upon the equal ability of all believers to approach God, radical Puritan men opened doors to spiritual power that were happily entered not only by themselves but also by women and members of the lower classes.[27] Certainly these egalitarian promises were important, but I do not believe that this was the sole attraction. Opponents accused radical sectaries of ideological, behavioral, and sexual excess, an excess they equated with essential femaleness. With an impressive circularity, commentators argued that sectaries were obviously ignorant and oversexed because they were dominated by women and that women were attracted to sectaries because of the convoluted theology and sexual extravagances. In this effort to deprecate ecstatic spirituality, particularly if enjoyed without the guidance and blessing of a learned, institutionalized clergy, Puritan leaders successfully undermined its credibility among and attraction for male believers. Yet in their disparagement of mystical sectaries as feminine religions, commentators may have inadvertently revealed a deep truth: namely that Puritan mysticism was sexual in nature, and that this culture's construction of gender along with its gendering of God as male naturally promoted a sexualized piety more accessible to women than men. Perhaps those weaknesses that rendered women easy prey for the Devil also made them easy marks for God.

8

Epilogue

Everybody Knows Her Name

In September 1930, Boston celebrated its tercentenary. The parade covered three and a half miles and included forty thousand marchers, two hundred floats, and one hundred bands. More than one million people enjoyed the festival.[1] The anniversary was also commemorated with the publication of three biographies. As premier historian Samuel Eliot Morison remarked, it was "typical of New England celebrations that in the tercentennial year there should be not a single new life of sainted founders like Winthrop, Dudley, Endecott, Wilson, Cotton, Eliot, and Shepard . . . and three of the lady whom all the sainted founders, excepting Cotton, regarded as an unmitigated nuisance . . ."[2] Anne Hutchinson, Morison's "pythoness," continued to live in the hearts and minds of Bostonians. Remarkable.

How did this happen?

Almost nothing is known of this woman; she left no letters, no journal, no comments upon her sufferings as one of many English immigrants who traveled to New England to join the godly effort to create a new world. Magistrates, clergymen (and their wives), merchants, and farmers (and their wives) gathered and built a society of political strength, economic prosperity, and religious stability. They appeased the English Crown, negotiated environmental safety, patched over conflicting goals, and resolved disagreements. An opinionated people with views upon everything, from salvation to survival, they formed alliances and factions.

Amid the struggles of the first decade, Hutchinson was able to inspire a community of Bostonians. She spoke to them of God, led them in study and devotions, and gathered them around her in admiration and wonder. As social divisions increased, she sat at the vortex of the turmoil and called her disciples to heed the voice of God, in opposition to those she believed were working against the divine plan. Henry Vane, the aristocratic one-time governor, and William Coddington, the top-ranked treasurer of the colony, followed her guidance and celebrated her leadership and inspiration.

Winthrop and his coalition met the challenge, disarmed and disfranchised her followers, and tried, excommunicated, and banished her.

Defeated and banished from the colony, she ought to have disappeared from the record. After all, history is written by the winners, months of turmoil had ended, and the rulers undoubtedly hoped that this incident would be relegated to a few lines in the General Court record. Yet the winners inadvertently etched Hutchinson's story into the record. John Winthrop spun his tale, and Thomas Weld, running second, echoed him in a prefatory commentary. The *Short Story* detailed the questions and responses of theologians who talked, disagreed, and navigated their way to a tolerance. The reader was plunged deeply into the theological esoterica and wrangling, ending with a clear, uncomplicated summary attack on Anne Hutchinson. John Cotton provided his own similar defensive account.[3]

New England Puritans had envisioned themselves as the chosen people of the New Testament. They were so certain of their importance and so impressed by their own efforts and success that they began to chronicle and publish their history almost immediately—such hubris, crafting a history while most of the founders were still alive. Notably, in this march of triumph Anne Hutchinson always appears. Edward Johnson, in his 1652 history, devoted about ten pages to the theological controversy, with pointed paragraphs about an unnamed woman who spoke "from the mere motion of the spirit, without any study at all . . . ." He described her attraction:

> . . . the weaker Sex prevailed so farre, that they set up a Priest of their own Profession and Sex, who was much thronged after, abominable wresting the Scriptures to their own destruction: this Master-piece of Womens wit, drew many Disciples after her, and to that end boldly insinuated herself into the favor of none of the meanest, being also backed with the Sorcery of a second, who had much converse with the Devill by her own confession.[4]

Johnson called her a "priest" (a grave calumny in Protestant New England), and the scriptural study "abominable," wrapping up by crediting her success to friendship with a witch. Cotton Mather, John Cotton's grandson, did not go quite this far, though he, too, refused to name her. He explained that "her *faith* was not *produced*, and scarce ever *strengthened*, according to her own relation, by the public ministry of the word, but by her own private meditations and revelations." Considering that the controversy revolved to a certain extent around the preaching of John Cotton, this observation appears ignorant, at best. Mather reminded his readers that "this gentlewoman was not the Priscilla pretended," recalling Hutchinson's allusion to Aquila and Priscilla, "but rather deserving the name of the prophetess in the Church of Thyatira."[5] Here, the godly Pauline exhorter Priscilla is replaced by Jezebel, who "calleth her self a Prophetesse, to teach and to deceive my servants to make them commit fornication, & to eat meats sacrificed unto idoles."[6] The violence of these denunciations astonishes.

In his history of Massachusetts, Hutchinson's great-great-grandson Thomas Hutchinson picked up the narrative. He is among the earliest to argue that the ideas his ancestor advanced could have produced "ruin both to church and state. The vigilance of some, of whom Mr. Winthrop was the chief, prevented, and turned the ruin from the country upon herself and many of her family and particular friends."[7] These histories exhibit a triumphalist attitude, celebrating the patriarchs' successful rout of deviants and heretics, maintaining the strength and prosperity of New England.

The nineteenth century changed attitudes and conclusions about the early New Englanders. Nathaniel Hawthorne was an early voice who moved from lauding Puritan efforts and heroics to decrying their rigidity and intolerance. Among the first to express sympathy and praise for Hutchinson, Hawthorne celebrated her as "a woman of extraordinary talent and strong imagination, whom the latter quality, following the general direction taken by the enthusiasm of the times, prompted to stand forth as a reformer in religion."[8] Such sentiments were echoed by Charles Francis Adams in his history. He described Hutchinson's "premature revolt against an organized and firmly-rooted oligarchy of theocrats." The rigidity and intolerance of the society are contrasted with her "deep spiritual enthusiasm" and her claims of "direct divine revelations." Like many others, Adams placed Hutchinson squarely within his own world and day, an exemplary New England woman, "essentially transcendental."[9] With terms like "religious reformer" and "transcendental," the mistaken role assignments of Hutchinson had begun. George Bancroft produced the century's definitive account of US history. He, too, devoted pages to Hutchinson, "a woman of such admirable understanding 'and profitable and sober Carriage,' that she won over a powerful party in her country, and her enemies could never speak of her without acknowledging her eloquence and her ability." He compared her to Descartes, saying that "both asserted that the conscious judgment of the mind is the highest authority to itself."[10] In what better company could Hutchinson find herself?

The admiration, even adulation, is palpable and seems matched by the outrage, however politely masked, in Morison's remark about the three Hutchinson biographies. In response, historians began immediately to produce studies defending John Winthrop as well as the Puritan clergy and magistrates. Early histories had been filled with the fear of societal destruction and the triumph of resolution. Nineteenth-century histories were characterized by embarrassed condemnation of Puritan leaders and the offer of apologies, grace, and praise. Twentieth-century historians would redeem John Winthrop and the clerical community by justifying their actions and, ironically, demonstrating that Hutchinson did not matter at all.

Anne Hutchinson was not a proto-feminist, a political dissident, colonial reformer, certainly not a suffragette. She received divine revelations, prophesied to Bostonians, and gathered disciples around her. She must have had extraordinary charisma to inspire so many followers and to receive praise from someone of the rank and status of Coddington almost forty years after her death. She must have had extraordinary, self-realized power and authority to bring so many enemies to congratulate themselves upon defeating her. They had feared, apparently, that she would destroy their world. In fact, the Puritan patriarchs destroyed their own world when they destroyed her. The attraction of Anne Hutchinson, the lure, is the strength of her charismatic promise; the hope that women and men can recover what has been lost.

Notes

Introduction

1. Perry Miller, *The New England Mind: From Colony to Province* (Cambridge, MA: Harvard University Press, 1953); Bryce Traister, *Female Piety and the Invention of American Puritanism* (Columbus: Ohio State University Press, 2016).
2. John Winthrop, *A Short Story of the Rise, Reign, and Ruine of the Antinomians, Familists, & Libertines,* with a preface by Thomas Weld (London, 1644). References come from the excellent collection, David D. Hall, ed., *The Antinomian Controversy, 1636–1638: A Documentary History* (1968; Durham, NC: Duke University Press, 1990), 201–310.
3. Edmund S. Morgan, *The Puritan Dilemma: The Story of John Winthrop* (Boston: Little, Brown, 1958), 134–154; Darrett Rutman, *Winthrop's Boston: Portrait of a Puritan, 1630–1649* (New York: Norton, 1965), 135–163; Norman Pettit, *The Heart Prepared: Grace and Conversion in Puritan Spiritual Life* (New Haven, CT: Yale University Press, 1966), 125–157; Kai T. Erikson, *Wayward Puritans: A Study in the Sociology of Deviance* (New York: Allyn and Bacon, 1966), 33–107. Hutchinson has also earned a full historiography of her own, including Charles Francis Adams, ed., *Antinomianism in the Colony of Massachusetts Bay, 1636–1638* (Boston: Prince Society, 1894); Winifred King Rugg, *Unafraid: A Life of Anne Hutchinson* (New York: Houghton Mifflin, 1930); Edith Curtis, *Anne Hutchinson: A Biography* (Cambridge, MA: Washburn & Thomas, 1930); Helen Augur, *An American Jezebel: The Life of Anne Hutchinson* (New York: Brentano's, 1930); Emery Battis, *Saints and Sectaries: Anne Hutchinson and the Antinomian Controversy in the Massachusetts Bay Colony* (Chapel Hill: University of North Carolina Press, 1962); Richard B. Morris, "Jezebel before the Judges: Anne Hutchinson Tried for Sedition," in his *Fair Trial* (New York: Harper and Row, 1967), 3–32; Lyle Koehler, "The Case of the American Jezebels: Anne Hutchinson and Female Agitation during the Years of the Antinomian Turmoil, 1636–1640," *William and Mary Quarterly* 31 (1974), 55–78; Amy Shrager Lang, *Prophetic Woman: Anne Hutchinson and the Problem of Dissent in the Literature of New England* (Berkeley: University of California Press, 1987); Selma R. Williams, *Divine Rebel: The Life of Anne Marbury Hutchinson* (New York: Henry and Holt, 1981); Michael P. Winship, *Making Heretics: Militant Protestantism and Free Grace in Massachusetts* (Princeton, NJ: Princeton University Press, 2002); Winship, *The Times and Trials of Anne Hutchinson: Puritans Divided* (Lawrence: University of Kansas Press, 2005). Several key articles have been collected by Francis J. Bremer in *Troubler of the Puritan Zion* (New York: Krieger, 1981). For a different approach, see Michael W. Kaufmann, "Post Secular Puritans: Recent Trials of Anne Hutchinson," *Early American Literature* 45 (2010), 331–359.
4. Winthrop, *Short Story*, 308–310; quotation 310.

5. See, for example, Williams, *Divine Rebel*; Eve LaPlante, *American Jezebel: The Uncommon Life of Anne Hutchinson, the Woman Who Defied the Puritans* (New York: HarperCollins, 2004).

6. Ann Kibbey, *The Interpretation of Material Shapes in Puritanism: A Study of Rhetoric, Prejudice, and Violence* (Cambridge: Cambridge University Press, 1986); Carol Karlsen, *The Devil in the Shape of a Woman: Witchcraft in Colonial New England* (New York: Norton, 1987); Mary Beth Norton, *Founding Mothers and Fathers: Gendered Power and the Forming of American Society* (New York: Vintage Press, 1997); Jane Kamensky, *Governing the Tongue: The Politics of Speech in Early New England* (New York: Oxford University Press, 1997); Lyle Koehler, *A Search for Power: The "Weaker Sex" in Seventeenth-Century New England* (Urbana: University of Illinois Press, 1980). Bryce Traister has incorporated his reading of this episode, one of four, in his own reconstruction of Puritan historiography and the progress toward secular modernity in his *Female Piety*, 29–68.

7. "The Examination of Mrs. Anne Hutchinson at the Court at Newtown," in Hall, *Antinomian Controversy*, 337.

8. Winthrop, *Short Story*, 273–274.

9. Winthrop, *Short Story*; "Examination of Hutchinson," in Hall, *Antinomian Controversy*, 311–348; "A Report of the Trial of Mrs. Anne Hutchinson before the Church in Boston," in Hall, *Antinomian Controversy*, 350–388; "Proceedings of the Boston Church Against the Exiles," in Hall, *Antinomian Controversy*, 390–395; S[amuel] G[roome], *A Glass for the People of New England* (London, 1676), 9–10.

10. "Puritan" is the label frequently used to identify the English who colonized Massachusetts Bay in the seventeenth century. However, it has also been applied to a vast collection of English dissenters in the sixteenth and seventeenth centuries. "Puritan" was initially a pejorative label used by the enemies of these dissenters; they never used the term themselves. The name signified their desire to "purify" the Church of England from all Roman Catholic aspects and influences. Historians have long utilized this term, I among them, knowing full well that our subjects would probably not approve.

11. An excellent introduction to the Puritan movement can be found in the works of Patrick Collinson, specifically *The Elizabethan Puritan Movement* (Berkeley: University of California Press, 1967) and *Godly People: Essays on English Protestantism and Puritanism* (London: Hambledon Press, 1983). On Puritanism and the English Civil War, see Christopher Hill, *Society and Puritanism in Pre-revolutionary England* (1958; New York: Schocken Books, 1965) as well as his popular *The World Turned Upside-Down: Radicalism and Religion during the English Revolution* (New York: Viking, 1972).

12. Richard Hooker, *The Laws of Ecclesiastical Polity* as quoted in Collinson, *Godly People*, 274.

13. This spirituality is justifiably labeled feminine by Amanda Porterfield, *Female Piety in Puritan New England: The Emergence of Religious Humanism* (New York: Oxford University Press, 1992). See also Elizabeth Reis, *Damned Women: Sinners and Witches in Puritan New England* (Ithaca, NY: Cornell University Press, 1997). For an engaging exploration of the hypermasculinity of Puritan culture, see Roger Thompson, *Women*

in Stuart England and America: A Comparative Study (London: Routledge & Kegan Paul), 1974.

14. See Kathleen M. Brown, *Good Wives, Nasty Wenches, and Anxious Patriarchs: Gender, Race, and Power in Colonial Virginia* (Chapel Hill: University of North Carolina Press, 1996), for an exceptional, coherent consideration of actual, established gender hierarchies and the use of such gender categories to rhetorically construct and explain patterns of inequality.

15. Philip Gura, *A Glimpse of Sion's Glory: Puritan Radicalism in New England, 1620–1660* (Middleton, CT: Wesleyan University Press, 1984); Stephen Foster, *The Long Argument: English Puritanism and the Shaping of New England Culture, 1570–1700* (Chapel Hill: University of North Carolina Press, 1991); Janice Knight, *Orthodoxies in Massachusetts: Rereading American Puritanism* (Cambridge, MA: Harvard University Press, 1997); Theodore Dwight Bozeman, *The Precisianist Strain: Disciplinary Religion and Antinomian Backlash in Puritanism to 1638* (Chapel Hill: University North Carolina Press, 1996).

16. Perry Miller, *The New England Mind: The Seventeenth Century* (Cambridge, MA: Harvard University Press, 1939), 3–63.

Chapter 1

1. Edward Johnson, *Wonder-Working Providence of Sions Saviour in New England* (1654; Andover, MA: W.F. Draper, 1867); Cotton Mather, *Magnalia Christi Americana; or, The Ecclesiastical History of New England* (1702; New York: F. Ungar, 1970); Thomas Hutchinson, *History of the Colony and Province of Massachusetts Bay* (Boston, 1767); Nathaniel Hawthorne, "Mrs. Hutchinson," *Salem Gazette* (1830), at http://people. ucls.uchicago.edu/~pdoyle/bustlesandbeaux.wordpress.com-Mrs_Hutchinson_by_Nathaniel_Hawthorne1830.pdf; Adams, *Antinomianism in the Colony*; Rugg, *Unafraid*; Curtis, *Anne Hutchinson*; Augur, *American Jezebel*. The publication of Edmund S. Morgan, "The Case against Anne Hutchinson," *New England Quarterly* 10 (1937), 633–649, initiated the modern struggle to understand the crisis, while Jonathan Beecher Field, "The Antinomian Controversy Did Not Take Place," *Early American Studies* 6 (2008), 448–463, challenges the standard interpretation in terms of historians' failure to problematize their sources. Recently, Bryce Traister has incorporated his reading of this episode, one of four, in his own reconstruction of Puritan historiography and the progress toward secular modernity in his *Female Piety*, 29–68. Along similar lines, see Kaufmann, "Post Secular Puritans," 3.

2. From Winthrop, *Short Story*. The text cited throughout is found in Hall, *Antinomian Controversy*.

3. Battis, *Saints and Sectaries*, provides an excellent genealogy. For the names of the servants, see *The Records of the First Church in Boston, 1630–1868*, ed. Richard D. Pierce (Boston: Colonial Society of Massachusetts, 1961), 16–22.

4. Rutman, *Winthrop's Boston*, remains the best discussion of early Boston. See especially his discussion of the early Boston gentry (71–77).

5. Pierce, *Records of First Church*, 16–22.

6. "Examination of Hutchinson," in Hall, *Antinomian Controversy*, 322–323; "Report of the Trial," in Hall, *Antinomian Controversy*, 371–372; Pierce, *Records of First Church*, 19. The scriptural quotation is John 16:12.

7. Thomas Weld, "Preface" to Winthrop, *Short Story*, 207; John Winthrop, *The Journal of John Winthrop, 1630–1649*, ed. Richard S. Dunn, James Savage, and Laetitia Yeandle (Cambridge, MA: Belknap Press, 1996), September 1637, 234.

8. "Report of the Trial," in Hall, *Antinomian Controversy*, 370.

9. On the centrality of Thomas Shepard and his challenge to John Cotton, see Winship, *Making Heretics*, 2002.

10. Two excellent discussions of preparationism can be found in Pettit, *Heart Prepared*; Charles E. Hambrick-Stowe, *The Practice of Piety: Puritan Devotional Disciplines in Seventeenth-Century New England* (Chapel Hill: University of North Carolina Press, 1982). While Pettit accepts the Hutchinsonian vision of preparationism as legalistic, with individuals encouraged to actively prepare themselves for God, Hambrick-Stowe argues that preparationists were merely chronicling in greater detail the process by which the Spirit prepares the believer for grace. See chapter 4 for my own construction of the debate in light of the Hutchinsonian crisis.

11. John Cotton, *Sixteene Questions of Serious and Necessary Consequence, Propounded unto Mr. John Cotton of Boston in New-England, Together with His Answers to Each Question* (London, 1644) in Hall, *Antinomian Controversy*, 46–59. See the preface (46) for Cotton's personal commentary. Hall's collection includes a responsive statement by the ministers (61–77) and Cotton's fairly detailed rejoinder to the ministers (79–151). Although the queries and nuances involved did, by August, reproduce themselves into eighty-two errors, the dispute continued to revolve on this primary axis of sanctification. A further discussion of the intricacies of the theological dissection can be found in chapter 4.

12. John Wheelwright, *Fast-Day Sermon*, 1637, in Hall, *Antinomian Controversy*, 153–172, citations 161, 156.

13. Winthrop, *Short Story*, 248.

14. *Records of the Governor and Company of the Massachusetts Bay*, ed. Nathaniel B. Shurtleff (Boston: W. White, 1853–54), May 17, 1637, 1:194–195.

15. Winthrop, *Journal*, September 1637, 234.

16. Winthrop, *Short Story*, 262–263.

17. Winthrop, *Short Story*, 256, 262.

18. There are two, independent, near-verbatim accounts of this trial, both of which have been printed in Hall, *Antinomian Controversy*: Winthrop, *Short Story*, 262–280; and "The Examination of Mrs. Anne Hutchinson at the Court at Newtown," a less hostile record, now lost, but appended by Hutchinson to his *History of the Colony and Province of Massachusetts Bay*. At many points, the same statements are found in both texts.

19. Actually, as will be seen in chapter 3, women did sometimes initiate and sign petitions, but those generally involved questions or problems that impacted them directly. Generally, women were not involved in political maneuvers, and in this particular case Hutchinson had not joined the effort.

20. "Examination of Hutchinson," in Hall, *Antinomian Controversy*, 314.

21. Winthrop, *Short Story*, 269; "Examination of Hutchinson," in Hall, *Antinomian Controversy*, 316.

22. "Examination of Hutchinson," in Hall, *Antinomian Controversy*, 316.

23. "Examination of Hutchinson," in Hall, *Antinomian Controversy*, 316–319.

24. Shurtleff, *Records of Massachusetts Bay*, March 9, 1636/7, 1:189.

25. "Examination of Hutchinson," in Hall, *Antinomian Controversy*, 319–326, citations 319, 320; Winthrop, *Short Story*, 269–270.

26. "Examination of Hutchinson," in Hall, *Antinomian Controversy*, 326–333, citation 327; Winthrop, *Short Story*, 270.

27. "Examination of Hutchinson," in Hall, *Antinomian Controversy*, 332–337, citations 333, 334.

28. For an excellent discussion of the legal structure and manipulations during the trial, see Ann Fairfax Withington and Jack Schwartz, "The Political Trial of Anne Hutchinson," *New England Quarterly* 51 (1978), 226–240. See also Winship, *Times and Trials* for an alternative perspective.

29. "Examination of Hutchinson," in Hall, *Antinomian Controversy*, 336–337. This exchange is also summarized in Winthrop, *Short Story*, 273–274.

30. "Examination of Hutchinson," in Hall, *Antinomian Controversy*, 345.

31. See, for example, Morgan, "Case against Anne Hutchinson," 647; Morris, "Jezebel before the Judges," 24; Battis, *Saints and Sectaries*, 346; Hall, "Introduction," *Antinomian Controversy*, 10.

32. "Examination of Hutchinson," in Hall, *Antinomian Controversy*, 338–348, citation 348. The official records of the court are more precise, noting that Hutchinson was convicted for "traduceing the mi^{rs} & their ministery in this country, shee declared volentailyry her revelations for her ground, & that shee should bee delivred & the Court ruined." Shurtleff, *Records of Massachusetts Bay*, November 2, 1637, 1:207.

33. "Examination of Hutchinson," in Hall, *Antinomian Controversy*, 337.

34. Winthrop, *Short Story*, 274; emphasis mine. Michael G. Ditmore, "A Prophetess in Her Own Country: An Exegesis of Anne Hutchinson's Immediate Revelation," *William and Mary Quarterly* 57 (2000), 349–392, agrees that Hutchinson's claim to revelation was the primary reason for her banishment, although he leaves open the question as to whether she believed she had received immediate revelation. Ditmore finds the key problem to be her use of "revelation" to criticize the established order.

35. The challenge posed by Williams and the resulting exile is discussed in chapter 2.

36. "Report of the Trial," in Hall, *Antinomian Controversy*, 349–374, citation 368.

37. Patricia Caldwell, "The Antinomian Language Controversy," *Harvard Theological Review* 69 (1976), 345–367, provides an excellent analysis of Hutchinson's differentiation between speech/expression and thought/belief along with a consideration of the hostility that this response provoked.

38. "Report of the Trial," in Hall, *Antinomian Controversy*, 374–388, citations 379, 388.

39. The witness of Mary Dyer will be taken up in chapter 6.

40. Weld, "Preface" to Winthrop's *Short Story*, 218.

41. Winthrop, *Short Story*, and John Cotton, *The Way of Congregational Churches Cleared: In Two Treatises* (London, 1648), are the best-known texts published in response to such queries. Winthrop's text is entirely focused upon the Hutchinsonian crisis; Cotton's discourse, though broad in scope, devoted at least a fourth of its long text to the resolution of the crisis.

Chapter 2

1. "Examination of Hutchinson," in Hall, *Antinomian Controversy*, 317–318, 343.
2. Miller, *New England Mind: From Colony to Province*, 53–68; Pettit, *Heart Prepared*, 125–157; Gura, *Glimpse of Sion's Glory*, 237–275; Winship, *Making Heretics*. Winship provides one of the best explorations of the theological disputes among the clergy. He brings Thomas Shepard, a generally overlooked participant, into his analysis of the clerical conversations and persuasively argues for the central importance of Shepard's role. See also Hall, "Introduction," *Antinomian Controversy*, 3–23; James Fulton Maclear, "New England and the Fifth Monarchy: The Quest for the Millennium in Early American Puritanism," *William and Mary Quarterly* 32 (1975), 223–260; Jesper Rosenmeier, "New England's Perfection: The Image of Adam and the Image of Christ in the Antinomian Crisis, 1634–1638," *William and Mary Quarterly* 27 (1970), 435–459; William K. Stoever, "Nature, Grace and John Cotton: The Theological Dimension in the New England Antinomian Controversy," *Church History* 44 (1975), 22–33; George Selement, "John Cotton's Hidden Antinomianism: His Sermon on Revelation 4:1–2," *New England Historical and Genealogical Register* 129 (1975), 278–294.
3. Historians from Miller onward have assumed a religious uniformity at least among colonizers, but as Gura, *Glimpse of Sion's Glory*, among others, has demonstrated, homogeneity was an illusion. See also Foster, *The Long Argument*.
4. Winthrop, *Journal*, March 4, 1635, 142; May 6, 1635, 144–145; Shurtleff, *Records of Massachusetts Bay*, March 4, 1634/5, 1:137; May 6, 1635, 1:146.
5. Virginia DeJohn Anderson, "Migrants and Motives: Religion and the Settlement of New England, 1630–1640," *New England Quarterly* 58 (1985), 339–383. See also her *New England's Generation: The Great Migration and the Formation of Society and Culture in the Seventeenth Century* (Cambridge: Cambridge University Press, 1991), especially 12–46, 89–130. The extensive scholarship on town formation also includes efforts to organize congregations. See, for example, Rutman, *Winthrop's Boston*; Kenneth A. Lockridge, *A New England Town: The First Hundred Years* (New York: Norton, 1970); Philip J. Greven, *Four Generations: Population, Land, and Family in Colonial Andover, Massachusetts* (Ithaca, NY: Cornell University Press, 1972.
6. John Winthrop, *A Modell of Christian Charity* (1630), as printed in *The Puritans: Sourcebook of Their Writings*, ed. Perry Miller and Thomas H. Johnson (1938; New York: Harper and Row, 1963), 198.
7. Miller, *New England Mind: From Colony to Province*, 21–26, was the first among historians to reconstruct and describe this contractual relationship, or the federal covenant, as understood by New England Puritans.

8. On English Puritanism, see Collinson, *The Elizabethan Puritan Movement*; Collinson, *Godly People*; Collinson, *From Cranmer to Sancroft: Essays on English Religion in the Sixteenth and Seventeenth Centuries* (London: Bloomsbury Academic, 2006); Peter Lake, *Moderate Puritans and the Elizabethan Church* (Cambridge: Cambridge University Press, 1982); Lake, *The Boxmaker's Revenge: "Orthodoxy," "Heterodoxy" and the Politics of the Parish in Early Stuart London* (Stanford, CA: Stanford University Press, 2001), especially 11–83; Foster, *The Long Argument*; Francis Bremer, *Puritanism: Transatlantic Perspectives on a Seventeenth-Century Anglo-American Faith* (Boston: Massachusetts Historical Society, 1993).

9. See, for example, Collinson, *Godly People*, 1–18.

10. The exception represented by Henry Vane, son of a courtier, is perhaps proof enough of the scarcity of the nobility in New England. It was so unusual to have one of Vane's rank in Massachusetts that although he was extraordinarily young, twenty-two years old, he was elected governor in 1635.

11. On the group of Puritan colonists who arrived with a more cosmopolitan, internationalist attitude, see Louise A. Breen, *Transgressing the Bounds: Subversive Enterprises among the Puritan Elite in Massachusetts, 1630–1692* (New York: Oxford University Press, 2001). Her arguments emphasizing the importance of this group during the Antinomian Controversy (17–56) are addressed later in this chapter.

12. See her autobiographical statement in "Examination of Hutchinson," in Hall, *Antinomian Controversy*, 337.

13. On Francis Marbury, see Frederick Gay, "Rev. Francis Marbury," *Proceedings of the Massachusetts Historical Society* 48 (1915), 281ff., and the documents that have been reprinted in the same volume, 287–290. See also J. Venn and J. A. Venn, *Alumni Cantabrigiensis*, Part I (Cambridge: Cambridge University Press, 1922), 3:139; Meredith B. Colket, *The English Ancestry of Anne Marbury Hutchinson and Katherine Marbury Scott* (Philadelphia: Magee Press, 1936).

14. Battis, *Saints and Sectaries*, 9–10, argues that the bishops found Marbury "at least clear of the Puritan taint," drawing this conclusion from Marbury's appointment to three livings after the dismissal of more than three hundred clerics.

15. Collinson, *The Elizabethan Puritan*, 433–434, notes that during Elizabeth's reign, Marbury's Puritan outspokenness was such that he was suspected of being Martin Marprelate, the scathing Puritan satirist of the late 1580s.

16. Francis Marbury, "Preface" to Robert Rollock, *A Treatise of Gods Effectual Calling*, trans. Henry Holland (London, 1603), 114.

17. Francis Marbury, *A Sermon Preached at Paules Cross* (London, 1602), 38.

18. Francis Marbury, *Notes on the Doctrine of Repentance* (London, 1602), 57–68, citation 65.

19. Marbury, *Sermon at Paules Cross*, 23.

20. Marbury, *Sermon at Paules Cross*, 17–20, 42–59, 84–95; Francis Marbury, *A Fruitful Sermon Necessary for the Time* (London, 1602), 48–50.

21. Marbury, *Fruitful Sermon*, 51, 62–63.

22. In his preface to Rollock's *God's Effectual Calling*, 2, Marbury even takes the time to deliver many laudatory remarks celebrating the union of Scotland and England under the new king, James I.

23. Marbury, *Fruitful Sermon*, 52–55, citation 53. For Bradstreet, see "In Honour of That High and Mighty Princess Queen Elizabeth of Happy Memory," in *The Works of Anne Bradstreet*, ed. Jeannine Hensley (Cambridge, MA: Harvard University Press, 1967), 195–198, including "Was ever people better ruled than hers? / Was ever land more happy freed from stirs?" (196) as well as more general affirmations:

> Now say, have women worth? or have they none?
> Or had they some, but with our Queen is't gone?
> Nay masculines, you have thus taxed us long,
> But she, though dead, will vindicate our wrong.
> Let such as say our sex is void of reason,
> Know 'tis slander now but once was treason. (197–198)

24. Marbury, *Doctrine of Repentance*, 7, 66, 78, 82.

25. Marbury, *Sermon at Paules Cross*, 26.

26. Marbury, *Doctrine of Repentance*, 54.

27. Marbury, *Sermon at Paules Cross*, 31.

28. Marbury, *Sermon at Paules Cross*, 70–71.

29. One of the best discussions on preparationism and regeneration in Puritan theology remains Pettit, *Heart Prepared*; see especially "The English Preparationists," 48–85. Michael McGiffert also considered this question, "Grace and Works: The Rise and Division of Covenant Divinity in Elizabethan Puritanism," *Harvard Theological Review* 75 (1982), 463–502. See also Hambrick-Stowe, *Practice of Piety*, especially 54–90. In his portrayal of New England Puritanism, Hambrick-Stowe must, of necessity, devote extensive analysis to New England's first generation, all of whom came to maturity in England. Winship, *Making Heretics*, also tracks back into English origins, while Bozeman, *Precisionist Strain*, has provided an illuminating introduction to the troubling questions of behavior in early Puritanism.

30. Marbury, *Doctrine of Repentance*, especially 15–78.

31. Marbury, *Doctrine of Repentance*, 78, citing 2 Corinthians 3:18.

32. See, for example, John Winthrop, "Common Grevances Groaninge for Reformation," in *The Winthrop Papers*, 5 vols. (Boston: Massachusetts Historical Society, 1929–47), February–March 1623/4, 2:295–310, for one Puritan's detailed list of complaints against English government and society, both religious and secular. In her *New England's Generation*, Virginia DeJohn Anderson provides an illuminating discussion of motivations of Englishmen and women who pursued the colonial enterprise.

33. Anderson, *New England's Generation*. Her figures indicate that women constituted 43 percent of the migrants; children fourteen years and younger 32 percent. Her occupational distribution of 139 adult men noted that 58 percent were artisans, 25 percent in the cloth trades, while 34 percent had worked in agriculture, and 8 percent in trade, maritime, or professional occupations (appendices, 222–226). For additional discussion of the population, particularly in reference to Boston, see Rutman, *Winthrop's Boston*, 164–201.

34. Rutman, *Winthrop's Boston*, 178–183, provides an excellent account of the development of Boston as the economic center of the colony during its formative, initially prosperous years.

35. Battis, *Saints and Sectaries*, Appendix V, 329–344, provides a list of Boston's male inhabitants ca. 1637. Of the almost 200 (out of 359) men whose occupation he can identify, Battis found 110 artisans or servants of artisans; thirty-one shopkeepers, merchants, or servants of merchants; twelve laborers or seamen; and three tavern keepers. Additional occupants included thirteen more servants, nine husbandmen or farmers, seven clergymen, two physicians, a soldier, and one gentleman (Henry Vane). The best treatment of the rising merchant class remains Bernard Bailyn, *The New England Merchants in the Seventeenth Century* (New York: Harper, 1955).

36. For a basic overview of early Massachusetts government, see Morgan, *Puritan Dilemma*, 84–114, and Rutman, *Winthrop's Boston*, 41–67, 164–202.

37. Dudley's criticism came early in Winthrop's career, 1632, but the conference (with the requisite day of fasting and humiliation) held to engage these problems and achieve peace among the leadership was held four years later, in 1636. See Winthrop, *Journal*, January 18, 1635/36, 165–168.

38. Winthrop, *Journal*, September 4, 1634, 125–128, gives some indication of the dissatisfactions felt in 1634, though it was in fact two years later that the departure finally took place. Perhaps more interesting is the fact that when the accusations of leniency against Winthrop were revived in January 1636, they included criticisms from Thomas Hooker and then-governor John Haynes who would accompany Hooker to Connecticut.

39. This is, of course, the case of Goody Sherman who, in 1636, accused the rich, unpopular merchant Robert Keayne with secretly killing and eating her sow. Initially Sherman brought her complaint before the church elders, who decided that Keayne was innocent. The case was then appealed to the local court, the Assistants' or Magistrates' Court, and the General Court, all of whom decided in favor of Keayne. It should also be noted that while all the evidence favored Keayne, he made himself even more unpopular by suing Sherman for slander (and winning). This long, convoluted case, which did end with the establishment of a bicameral legislature in Massachusetts, is chronicled fairly lucidly in Winthrop, *Journal*, June 22, 1642, 395–398; June–September 1643, 451–458.

40. For an excellent description and analysis of the process by which church membership and visible sainthood became entwined, see Edmund S. Morgan, *Visible Saints: The History of a Puritan Idea* (New York: New York University Press, 1963).

41. Carla Gardina Pestana, *Quakers and Baptists in Colonial Massachusetts* (New York: Cambridge University Press, 1991), 4–6.

42. Although Williams left voluminous writings, most were produced and published long after he had been banished from Massachusetts. As with Anne Hutchinson, the best knowledge that we have of Williams's early views comes from the account of his opponent, John Winthrop. See Winthrop, *Journal*, April 12, 1631, 50.

43. William Bradford, *History of Plimoth Plantation* (Boston: Wright & Potter, 1896), 2:161–164.

44. Winthrop, *Journal*, December 27, 1633, 107; November 27, 1634, 137; April 30, 1635, 144; July 8, 1635, 149–150.
45. Winthrop, *Journal*, July 12, 1635, 151; November 1, 1635, 158; January 1635/36, 163–164.
46. Winthrop, *Journal*, July 12, 1635, 151; Morgan, *Puritan Dilemma*, 126.
47. Battis has identified 187 men as explicitly connected to the Hutchinsonian movement. Of the thirty-eight "core supporters" who would leave the colony, either by force or choice, in the wake of Hutchinson's and Wheelwright's banishments, twenty-six had been residents of Boston; of the fifty-nine who had been active supporters but generally chose to remain in Massachusetts, thirty-nine had been Bostonians. In other words, of the ninety-seven men who can be identified as active supporters of Hutchinson, two-thirds lived in Boston, while of the ninety additional individuals named as peripheral supporters, one-third were residents of Boston. Of thirty-three wealthy officeholders, twenty-four were Hutchinsonians, while only half of the twenty-one middling officeholders could be so counted. The wealthiest merchants and craftsmen include twenty-two of twenty-seven. See Battis, *Saints and Sectaries*, 257–280, 300–344.
48. Battis, *Saints and Sectaries*, 265–268.
49. Bailyn, *New England Merchants*, 40–41, The predominance of merchants and city leaders among the Hutchinsonians was also echoed in Rutman, *Winthrop's Boston*, 135–163.
50. Battis, *Saints and Sectaries*, 273.
51. Breen, *Transgressing the Bounds*, 17–56. Her discussion of Stoughton as an unlikely Hutchinson ally (17–28) is particularly enlightening.
52. The future careers of notable Hutchinsonians are discussed in chapter 6.
53. Historians have long argued about the level of theological disagreement, in reality an argument about Cotton's own positions. The basic theological conflict, outlined in chapter 1, is elaborated upon in the fourth chapter, and there I will provide my own case in support of those who believe that Cotton's theology directly challenged that of his colleagues.
54. John Cotton to John Wheelwright, April 18, 1646, Cotton Family Papers.
55. "Examination of Hutchinson," in Hall, *Antinomian Controversy*, 335–336, 342, 343.
56. Cotton, *Way of Congregational Churches*, as found in Hall, *Antinomian Controversy*, 414, 415.
57. See the recorded examination and censures in "A Report of the Trial of Mrs. Anne Hutchinson before the Church in Boston," a manuscript copy of a missing original made by Ezra Stiles, Stiles Papers, Yale University Library, in Hall, *Antinomian Controversy*, 349–388.
58. It is in part the church trial that has led to the extraordinary outpouring of scholarship on the complex associated theological issues raised by the Antinomian Controversy. See, for example, Rosenmeier, "New England's Perfection"; Caldwell, "Antinomian Language Controversy"; James Fulton Maclear, "Anne Hutchinson and the Mortalist Heresy," *New England Quarterly* 54 (1981), 74–103. While I cannot deny that the clergy were deeply concerned about these errors and that their own cosmology may even have predicted such heretical opinions as connected to previous errors that had

been identified, I agree with Winship, *Making Heretics*, that the primary theological/ spiritual issues were the questions of free grace, revelation, and the nature of rebirth that had been raised at the outset. These new issues allowed the clergy to focus general attention upon the risks of laypersons delving into obscure theology, in the process reaffirming their own professional status, and to focus Cotton upon the enormous errors latent in Hutchinson's ideas if they were to be taken to their conclusion.

59. "Report of the Trial," in Hall, *Antinomian Controversy*, 372.

60. "Report of the Trial," in Hall, *Antinomian Controversy*, 379, 381.

61. In research pursued in other regions and periods, I have found that the clergy, whose primary networks are other clergy, are better able to adapt to and tolerate difference. See, for example, Westerkamp, *Triumph of the Laity: Scots Irish Piety and the Great Awakening* (New York: Oxford University Press, 1988), especially 74–104.

62. The predestined finale of her trials has been a matter of some dispute, with many historians, beginning with Morgan, "Case against Anne Hutchinson," arguing that Hutchinson's own testimony led to a condemnation that might not have occurred without it. On the inevitability of conviction and banishment, see Morris, "Jezebel before the Judges"; and Withington and Schwartz, "Political Trial of Hutchinson."

63. Winthrop, *Journal*, October 1644, 505–507.

64. Report of the commissioners who visited Rhode Island, as noted by Robert Keayne, in Hall, *Antinomian Controversy*, 390–395, citation 392.

65. Winthrop, *Short Story*, 263, 275.

66. "Report of the Trial," in Hall, *Antinomian Controversy*, 383. Hugh Peters's rejection of Hutchinson indicates the incompleteness of Breen's explanation of Hutchinson's cadre. To be fair, she does not claim to have provided an argument for every single supporter. But it remains interesting that in every way Breen finds that Peters's career models the cosmopolitan, outward-looking Puritan, but then Peters was a clergyman and his status and authority was explicitly challenged. His failure to support Hutchinson, and his focus upon her gender and her presumed authority, demonstrate the limits of his open-mindedness.

67. During the sixteenth and seventeenth centuries, children born with physical deformities, no matter the severity, were described as monsters, and the possible explanations of such births included the disorder of the mother's mind in terms of religious errors she espoused. See, for example, Katharine Park and Lorraine Daston, "Unnatural Conceptions: The Study of Monsters in Sixteenth- and Seventeenth-Century France and England," *Past and Present* 92 (1981), 20–54; Daston and Park, "Monsters: A Case Study," in their *Wonders and the Order of Nature* (New York: Zone Books, 2001), 173–214, 408–417. More specifically, see Anne Jacobson Schutte, "'Such Monstrous Births': A Neglected Aspect of the Antinomian Controversy," *Renaissance Quarterly* 38 (1985), 85–106; Johan Winsser, "Mary Dyer and the 'Monster' Story," *Quaker History* (1990), 20–34; Lindal Buchanan, "A Study of Maternal Rhetoric: Anne Hutchinson, Monsters, and the Antinomian Controversy," *Rhetoric Review* 3 (2006), 239–259; Karyn Valerius, "So Manifest a Sign from Heaven: Monstrosity and Heresy in the Antinomian Controversy," *New England Quarterly* 83 (2010), 179–199.

68. "Report of the Trial," in Hall, *Antinomian Controversy*, 365, 384.

Chapter 3

1. Edmund S. Morgan, *The Puritan Family: Religion and Domestic Relations in Seventeenth-Century New England* (1956; New York: Harper & Row, 1966), was the earliest exploration of this system.

2. Of course, it's not quite so monolithic. Among the interesting, transitional developments of this century was the rise of male midwives and the beginning of the male challenge to female reproductive health.

3. Mary Ryan, *Womanhood in America: From Colonial Times to the Present*, 3rd ed. (New York: Franklin Watts, 1983); Gerda Lerner, *The Majority Finds Its Past: Placing Women in History* (New York: Oxford University Press, 1979), 15–30. Both begin with the seventeenth century in order to document a decline in status following the growth of industrial capitalism in the nineteenth century. For a similar argument focused on the colonial period, see Thompson, *Women in Stuart England*. Mary Beth Norton, *Liberty's Daughters: The Revolutionary Experience of American Women* (New York: Little, Brown, 1980), has provided an excellent critique of this colonial period as a "golden age of womanhood," while her *Founding Mothers and Fathers* persuasively reconstructs the multiple dynamics of gendered power.

4. Karlsen, *Devil in the Shape of Woman*. Mary Beth Norton, "The Evolution of White Women's Experience in Early America," *American Historical Review* 89 (1984), 593–619, provides a good introduction to the historiography as well as an overview of women in colonial society, while Laurel Thatcher Ulrich, *Good Wives: Image and Reality in the Lives of Women in Northern New England, 1650–1750* (New York: Knopf, 1982), offers a balanced overview of the status of women that takes into account women's work and status within a frontier environment. On colonial law, see Marylynn Salmon, *Women and the Law of Property in Early America* (Chapel Hill: University of North Carolina Press, 1986); Cornelia Dayton, *Women before the Bar: Gender, Law, and Society in Connecticut, 1639–1789* (Chapel Hill: University of North Carolina Press, 1995), pursues legal status and women as agents further still in terms of the law and the courts.

5. Thomas Gataker, *A Good Wife Gods Gift; and, A Wife Indeed* (London, 1623), 13; William Gouge, *Of Domesticall Duties, Eight Treatises* (London, 1622), 183.

6. *The Geneva Bible: A Facsimile of the 1560 Edition*, introduction by Lloyd E. Berry (Madison: University of Wisconsin Press, 1969), Matthew 19:10–12, with commentary, NT leaf 11. The Geneva Bible was the version preferred among English Calvinists throughout the late sixteenth and well into the seventeenth century, despite the printing of other "official" English Bibles, possibly because the King James Version was originally printed in folio only, while the Geneva Bible was easily available in quarto and octavo editions. Although the translation itself is sometimes quite intriguing, I find the marginalia designed to assist the lay reader most revealing. Produced under the guidance of Calvin, these annotations provide a set of interpretations Calvinist scholars applied to passages. Pagination is by leaf, obverse and reverse, rather than by page, with separate numeration in Old and New Testaments.

7. *Geneva Bible*, 1 Corinthians 7:1; commentary to 1 Corinthians 7:1, 7:28, NT leaves 78–79. In several margin notes to this chapter, the commentator reiterates the conclusion that celibacy is preferred only because marriage brings worldly cares.

8. Porterfield, *Female Piety*, has also noted in the plethora of domestic manuals evidence of the rapidly increasing importance of the family in Puritan ideology. However, while she sees this cultural change as one that improved the status of women, I argue that such improvement was superficial and short-lived.

9. Henrich Bullinger, *The Christian State of Matrimonye*, trans. Miles Coverdale (London, 1541).

10. Robert Cleaver, *A Godly Forme of Household Government: For the Ordering of Private Families According to the Direction of Gods Word* (London: 1598); John Dod and William Hinde, *Bathshebaes Instructions to Her Sonne Lemuel* (London, 1614. John Dod also produced, with Robert Cleaver, *A Plaine and Familiar Exposition of the Ten Commandements* (London, 1615), which includes a mini-manual, the essay upon the fifth commandment (185–256).

11. Daniel Rogers, *Matrimonial Honour: Or the Mutuall Crowne and Comfort of Godly, Loyall, and Chaste Marriage* (London, 1642); Gouge, *Of Domesticall Duties*. In New England, books on family life don't appear until the end of the seventeenth century, so that prescriptions must have been provided by delivered sermons, private guidance, and English publications. When they are published, New England books echoed these same themes. See, for example, Cotton Mather, *A Family Well Ordered* (Boston, 1699) and Benjamin Wadsworth, *The Well-Ordered Family* (Boston, 1721).

12. In addition to his two sermons *A Good Wife Gods Gift; and, A Wife Indeed*, cited earlier, Thomas Gataker published *Marriage Duties Briefely Couched* (London, 1620) and *A Mariage Praier* (London, 1624).

13. Gouge, *Of Domesticall Duties*, 11; Thomas Taylor, *The Works of That Faithful Servant of Jesus Christ, Dr. Thomas Taylor* (London, 1653), 190; Francis Cheynell, *A Plot for the Good of Posterity* (London, 1646), 17.

14. Rogers, *Matrimonial Honour*, 2–3; Alex[ander] Niccholes, *A Discourse of Marriage and Wyving* (London, 1615), 6.

15. Cheynell, *Good of Posterity*, 11.

16. On the strength and power of the convent as a female institution see, for example, Caroline Walker Bynum, *Holy Feasts Holy Fasts* (Berkeley: University of California Press, 1987); Jeffrey F. Hamburger and Susan Marti, eds., *Crown and Veil: Female Monasticism from the Fifth to the Fifteenth Centuries*, trans. Dietlinde Hamburger (New York: Columbia University Press, 2008); Penelope D. Johnson, *Equal in Monastic Profession: Religious Women in Medieval France* (Chicago: University of Chicago Press, 1991). There has also developed a massive literature on Julian of Norwich, but I have found most helpful Eleanor McLaughlin's "Women, Power and the Pursuit of Holiness in Medieval Christianity," in *Women of Spirit*, ed. Eleanor McLaughlin and Rosemary Ruether (New York: Simon and Schuster, 1979), 99–130, particularly in terms of her discussion of the power that holiness gave to individual, unmarried women.

17. Proverbs 31:10–12, OT leaf 277.

18. Gataker, *A Wife Indeed*, 16; Dod and Hinde, *Bathshebaes Instructions*, 23; Elizabeth Jocelin, *The Mothers Legacie, To Her Unborne Childe* (London: John Haviland for William Barret, 1624), 8. Convinced that she would die in childbirth (she did), Jocelin wrote this "letter" to her child.

19. [R. Aylett], *Susanna, or the Arraignment of the Two Unjust Elders* (London 1654), 12–15, citation 3.

20. Taylor, *Works*, 153.

21. Dod and Hinde, *Bathshebaes Instructions*, 32–38, citations 37, 36. Proverbs 31:15 notes that "she riseth, while it is yet night: and giveth the porcion to her hous holde, and the ordinarie to her maids." Bathesheba, Solomon's mother, was thought to be the subject of Proverbs 31.

22. Gataker, *A Mariage Praier*, 18–19. See also his *Marriage Duties Briefely Couched*, 20–24, for a brief outline of a housewife's practical duties.

23. See, for example, *Martha Washington's Booke of Cookery*, ed. Karen Hess (New York: Columbia University Press, 1981). As the title indicates, this was "a Family Manuscript, curiously copied by an unknown Hand sometime in the seventeenth century, which was in her Keeping from 1749, the time of her Marriage to Daniel Custis." Hess argues that this generally seventeenth-century collection was regarded more as a family heirloom than a cookbook, and that many of the recipes date from the sixteenth century. In my research of housewifery texts, I am indebted to Karen Hess's bibliography for the identification of several texts that were hitherto unknown to me.

24. Richard Gardiner, *Profitable Instructions for the Manuring, Sowing and Planting of Kitchin Gardens* (London, 1603; facsimile Norwood, NJ: Walter J. Johnson, 1973). See also *The Country House-wives Garden, Containing Rules for Hearbs and Seeds of Common Use . . . Together, with the Husbandry of Bees, Published with Secrets Very Necessary for Every House-wife* (1637); Milford, CT: Rosetta E. Clarkson, 1940).

25. Wylliam Turner, *The Names of Herbes in Greke, Latin, Englishe, Duche, Frenche with the Commone Names Herbaries and Apothecaries Use* (London, 1548); Thomas Cogan, *The Haven of Health: Chiefly Gathered for the Comfort of Students, and Consequently of All Those That Have a Care of Their Health* (London, 1584); [Elizabeth Grey], *A Choice Manuall, of Rare and Select Secrets in Physick and Chirugery: Collected, and Practised by the Right Honourable, the Countesse of Kent, Late Deceased* (London, 1653); Nicholas Culpeper, *A Physical Directory* (London, 1651).

26. G[ervase] M[arkham], *The English Hus-wife* (London, 1615; facsimile, Norwood, NJ: Walter Johnson, 1973). For other general housewifery books, see Thomas Dawson, *The Good Huswifes Jewell* and *The Second Part of the Good Hus-wives Jewell* (London, 1596/97 bound together; facsimile, Norwood, NJ: Walter J. Johnson, 1977); A. W., *A Booke of Cookrye, Very Necessary for All Such as Delight Therein* (London, 1591; facsimile, Norwood, NJ: Walter J. Johnson, 1976).

27. Ulrich, *Good Wives*, 15–34. See especially her discussion (18–24) of the will and inventory of Francis Plummer, 1672. See also Carole Shammas, *The Pre-industrial Consumer in England and America* (Oxford: Clarendon Press, 1990), for an excellent discussion of household labor and consumption.

28. A recipe from *The Compleat Housewife* (1730) as cited in Sally Smith Booth, *Hung, Strung and Potted* (New York: Clarkson Potter, 1971), 90.

29. R. Aylett, *A Wife, Not Ready Made but Bespoken* (London, 1653), 5. Aylett continues upon this theme for the next seven pages.

30. Ulrich, *Good Wives*, 26–27, discusses this briefly in an analysis of a shopkeeper's inventory.

31. Rogers, *Matrimonial Honour*, 270–272.

32. Ulrich, *Good Wives*, 35–50, develops this concept of "deputy husband" in some detail.

33. See Porterfield, *Female Piety*, especially chapter 3, 80–114, for her argument on the relationship between the rising importance of the domus and the influence of women.

34. This, of course, implies that female sexuality is exclusively heterosexual and that sexuality is meaningful only in terms of relationships among human persons. Such assumptions are not historically valid in an early modern European society that feared and punished sodomy and bestiality and believed that witches enjoyed sexual relations with Satan. Moreover, scholars should, by this time, be beyond such a limited interpretation. Aside from the obvious, that is, discoveries of homosexual inclinations and behaviors within monasteries and convents, one can also see in the writings and actions of such holy women (and men) as described spiritual/sexual relationships with God. This last question will be dealt with in some detail in chapter 7.

35. Anne Bradstreet, "An Epitaph on My Dear and Ever-Honoured Mother, Mrs. Dorothy Dudley, Who Deceased December 27, 1643, and of Her Age, 61" (1678), in *Works of Anne Bradstreet*, 204.

36. See McLaughlin, "Women and Pursuit of Holiness"; Caroline Walker Bynum, *Fragmentation and Redemption: Essays on Gender and the Human Body in Medieval Religion* (New York: Zone Books, 1991); Bynum, *Jesus as Mother: Studies in the Spirituality of the High Middle Ages* (Berkeley: University of California Press, 1982).

37. Margaret Cavendish Newcastle, *Orations of Divers Sorts, Accommodated to Diverse Places* (London, 1662), 226–227.

38. Gouge, *Of Domesticall Duties*, 271–348, citations 317, 282. He also provided appropriate instructions for husbands. A man might call his spouse Wife, or perhaps Love, or Dove, but certainly not Lady, Mistress, Dame, or Mother, all of which gave too much respect (371–372). Additionally, neither husband nor wife should use demeaning or insulting titles such as "ducks" or "wench," "man" or "woman," "rogue" or "slut." "Vashtie-like stoutness" refers to the first wife of Ahasuerus. Vashti refused to come when she was called and was then put aside in favor of the new wife Esther.

39. Gataker, *A Wife Indeed*, 14; Rogers, *Matrimonial Honour*, 260. See also Dod and Cleaver, *Exposition on Commandments*, 227–232; Taylor, *Works*, 150–155.

40. Rogers, *Matrimonial Honour*, 160, 275–278.

41. Rogers, *Matrimonial Honour*, 270–274; Gouge, *Of Domesticall Duties*, 302–306; Cleaver, *Godly Forme*, 168–170.

42. "Report of the Trial," in Hall, *Antinomian Controversy*, 371.

43. See "Examination of Hutchinson," in Hall, *Antinomian Controversy*, 317–319; Rogers, *Matrimonial Honour*, 266, 207; Gouge, *Of Domesticall Duties*, 30. See also Rogers, 260–269; Dod and Hinde, *Batheshebas Instructions*, 61–70; Gataker, *Marriage*

Duties Briefely Couched, 47–48. These manuals reinforce the conclusions of Ben Barker-Benfield, who argued in his "Anne Hutchinson and the Puritan Attitude toward Women," *Feminist Studies* 1 (1972), 65–96 that the Puritan male leadership in England and Massachusetts Bay restricted the priesthood of all believers to men, thus becoming, themselves, "priests" for women.

44. Gataker, *Marriage Duties Briefely Couched*, 29–30; Gouge, *Of Domesticall Duties*, 274–276, 326–327; Rogers, *Matrimoniall Honour*, 262–264.

45. Gataker, *Marriage Duties Briefely Couched*, 13, also 10, 34; Gouge, *Of Domesticall Duties*, 273, also 278.

46. Gouge, *Of Domesticall Duties*, 26.

47. Rogers, *Matrimonial Honour*, 255.

48. Taylor, *Works*, 151. See also Gataker, *Marriage Duties Briefely Couched*, 8; Rogers, *Matrimonial Honour*, 253–255.

49. Taylor, *Works*, 153; Gataker, *Marriage Duties Briefely Couched*, 14; Rogers, *Matrimonial Honour*, 162, 128. See also Gataker, *Marriage Duties Briefely Couched*, 9, 12, 33–34; Gouge, *Of Domesticall Duties*, 44–46, 346–348.

50. *The Lawes Resolutions of Women's Rights* (London, 1632), as cited in Thompson, *Women in Stuart England*, 162. Thompson provides a sound summary of the common law in terms of seventeenth-century Englishwomen in his chapter "Women's Legal Position and Rights," 161–186. Salmon's *Women and Law of Property* is the best, most comprehensive study of this subject for the colonies. Although most of her evidence is drawn from the eighteenth century, she does address the development of the law from the earlier decades, and her understanding of the intricacies of the law combined with her clarity of exposition is unparalleled. See also, Norton, *Founding Mothers and Fathers*, especially 27–180.

51. Gouge, *Of Domesticall Duties*, 253.

52. Salmon, *Women and Law of Property*, 14–40. There was an exception to coverture in the concept of a femme sole trader, a concept that allowed a wife who had a business completely separate from her husband to engage in contracts, suits, etc., involving that business.

53. A sample of ninety-nine wills was selected from George Francis Dow, ed., *Records and Files of the Quarterly Courts of Essex County, Massachusetts*, 8 vols., 1636–1683 (Salem, MA: Essex Institute, 1911–1921). Inventories accompanied most wills, and estate values ranged from twenty to five thousand pounds. The wills were selected because there was both a widow and children or grandchildren to be considered, and the bequests were a measurable fraction of the estate.

54. Will of John Balch, 1648, in Dow, *Records of Essex County*, 1:143–144; Will of Joseph Parker, 1678, in Dow, *Records of Essex County*, 7:142.

55. Will of John Legg, 1672, in Dow, *Records of Essex County*, 5:368–369. For examples of mandated house sharing, see the wills of Richard Dodge, 1670, 4:404–406, and Thomas Wells, 1666, 3:358–359. This last is especially interesting for the detailed list of property that the widow was to inherit.

56. Samuel Sewall, *Diary of Samuel Sewall*, ed. M. Halsey Thomas (New York: Farrar, Straus and Giroux, 1973), entries for 1722, 2:987–1002; John Wilson to John

Winthrop, 1642, *Winthrop Papers* (New York: Russell & Russell, 1968), 4:346–437; Dorothy Symonds to John Winthrop Jr., March 19, 1645/6, *Winthrop Papers*, 5:69.

57. Dorothy Leigh, *A Mothers Blessing* (London, 1616), 16; Jocelin, *The Mothers Legacie*, 8–10.

58. Notes on the church trial of Ann Hibbens, 1640, were recorded by Robert Keayne. Two edited transcriptions of her examination and conviction can be found in Nancy F. Cott, ed., *Roots of Bitterness: Documents of the Social History of American Women* (New York: Dutton, 1972), 47–58; and John Demos, ed., *Remarkable Providences* (New York: G. Braziller, 1972), 222–239. "Report of the Trial," in Hall, *Antinomian Controversy*, 369, 386.

59. Karlsen, *Devil in the Shape of Woman*, 84–89. In her third (77–116) and sixth (182–221) chapters, Karlsen provides several examples as well as a detailed analysis of the problem posed to the society by women exercising their "rights."

60. Newcastle, *Orations*, 92–93.

61. Salmon, *Women and Law of Property*, 58–80; Thompson, *Women in Stuart England*, 169–178. Poet John Milton, author of *The Doctrine and Discipline of Divorce* (1645) and three other treatises, is the best known of Puritan writers on divorce, though he was neither the only one nor the first. See, for example, William Perkins, *Christian Oeconomie* (London, 1609).

62. Rogers, *Matrimoniall Honour*, 271.

63. Cleaver, *Godly Forme*, 168–169.

64. Cleaver, *Godly Forme*, 154, 176; Gataker, *A Wife Indeed*, 36; Niccholes, *Marriage and Wyving*, 10, 35–end. See also Gouge, *Of Domesticall Duties*, 182.

65. Gataker, *A Wife Indeed*, 36.

66. Gouge, *Of Domesticall Duties*, 506.

67. Keith Thomas, *Religion and the Decline of Magic* (New York: Scribner's Sons, 1970), 42–43, 68–69, provides an excellent discussion of the structure, significance, and decline of this ritual, though it is unclear whether he would agree with the analysis in the remainder of this paragraph. For parallel, but differently situated, discussions of female purification rituals see Mary Douglas, *Purity and Danger: An Analysis of Concepts of Pollution and Taboo* (1965; London: Routledge, 2002).

68. Nicholas Culpeper, *Culpeper's Directory for Midwives*, First and Second Parts (1651; London, 1675–76). Other midwifery guides included J. Rueff, *The Expert Midwife* (London, 1637); J. Pechey, *The Compleat Midwifes Practice Enlarged* (London, 1698); and R. Barrett, *A Companion for Midwives* (London, 1699). For examples of medical texts, see Thomas Willis, *The London Practice of Physick* (London, 1685); Thomas Sydenham, *The Whole Works of That Excellent Practical Physician*, trans. John Pechy (London, 1696).

69. Actually, students of the body now know better and question the absolute authority of medical science, seeing medicine partly driven by social, ideological, and medical politics. See, for example, the extensive work of Margaret Lock, especially "Cultivating the Body: Anthropology and Epistemologies of Bodily Practice and Knowledge," *Annual Review of Anthropology* 22 (1993), 133–155, and Londa Schiebinger, especially *Nature's Body: Gender in the Making of Modern Science* (Boston: Beacon Press, 1993).

70. Judith Coffin's epitaph as cited in Ulrich, *Good Wives*, 146. In her chapter "Mother of All Living," 146–163, Ulrich provides an excellent consideration of the honorable duties of motherhood, including the high regard that fecundity earned in New England society.

71. Cotton Mather, *Elizabeth in Her Holy Retirement* (Boston, 1710), 4.

72. Rogers, *Matrimoniall Honour*, 279; Mather, *Elizabeth*, 35.

73. Dod and Cleaver, *Exposition on Commandments*, 201; Cotton Mather, *Ornaments for the Daughters of Zion* (Boston, 1692), 93. See also Gouge, *Of Domesticall Duties*, 507–518; Cleaver, *Godly Forme*, 231.

74. Elizabeth Clinton, *The Countesse of Lincolnes Nurserie* (Oxford, 1622), citation 19.

75. See Ulrich, *Good Wives*, 126–145, for a good discussion of pregnancy, labor, and women's rituals surrounding birthing during the late seventeenth and early eighteenth centuries.

76. Newcastle, *Orations*, 182, 183.

77. Anne Bradstreet, "Of the Four Ages of Man," in *Works of Anne Bradstreet*, 53.

78. In exploring the specter of infant mortality in New England, one might note Samuel Sewall's wife Hannah, who bore fourteen children and lost seven in infancy, and Cotton Mather's wife, who bore thirteen children and lost seven as well.

79. John Demos, *A Little Commonwealth* (New York: Oxford University Press, 1970), 66, and Greven, *Four Generations*, 27, 110, both suggest that the number of women who died in childbirth in Plymouth and Andover, respectively, was as high as 20 percent. Roger Schofield, "Did the Mothers Really Die? Three Centuries of Maternal Mortality in 'The World We Have Lost,'" in *The World We Have Gained: Histories of Population and Social Structures*, ed. Lloyd Bonfield, Richard M. Smith, and Keith Wrightson (Oxford: Basil Blackwell, 1986), 230–260 has considered this problem for the English countryside and argued for a sharply lower rate: approximately 7 percent, estimating that London figures would be approximately 50 percent higher.

80. Schofield, "Did the Mothers Really Die," 259–260. R. A. Houston, *The Population History of Britain and Ireland, 1500–1750* (London: Macmillan Education, 1992), based upon Schofield's figures, concluded that "women must have been aware of the risks but may have seen them as distant" (56).

81. Anne Bradstreet, "Before the Birth of One of Her Children," in *Works of Anne Bradstreet*, 224.

82. Cotton Mather, *Memorials of Early Piety: The Memoirs of Jerusha Oliver* (Boston, 1711), 28.

83. Jocelin, *The Mothers Legacie*, Approbation 13; Sarah Goodhue, *A Valedictory and Monitory Writing*, cited in Ulrich, *Good Wives*, 154–155.

84. For an informative and illuminating analysis of women as healers, including midwifery, see Rebecca J. Tannenbaum, *The Healer's Calling: Women and Medicine in Early New England* (Ithaca, NY: Cornell University Press, 2009). Norton, *Founding Mothers and Fathers*, 183–239, also includes extensive discussion of the birthing chamber as a women's space.

85. Willis, *London Practice of Physick*, 625–648; Sydenham, *Whole Works*, 470–475, citation 471. Reflecting the twentieth-century bias that ranks "scientific" knowledge above experience and privileges the words of scientific men above that of ordinary men and women is Lawrence Stone's summary dismissal of English midwifery: "For

women, childbirth was a very dangerous experience, for midwives were ignorant and ill trained, and often horribly botched the job, while the lack of hygienic precautions meant that puerperal fever was a frequent sequel." *The Family, Sex and Marriage in England, 1500–1800* (New York: Harper and Row, 1977), 79. Stone might well have added that all medical practitioners failed to take hygienic precautions, and the more interference in a birth, even the skilled efforts of a man-midwife, the more likely the development of infection. Audrey Eccles, *Obstetrics and Gynaecology in Tudor and Stuart England* (London: Croom Helm, 1982), remains the most comprehensive technical history of midwifery and obstetrical care. She demonstrates that by the middle of the eighteenth century, obstetrics had made great strides in its ability to deliver women experiencing complications. Such advances were technical and came from man-midwives and surgeons, not female midwives, who were generally excluded from knowledge acquisition, and not physicians. "Although faith in humoral medicine was declining in other areas of practice also, in obstetrics the process was particularly marked. It was a field in which the failure of humoral medicine was early and clearly demonstrated, and where manual and surgical expertise was plainly seen to have more therapeutic value than the prescriptions of the learned physician" (122). She, too, points out the risk of sepsis rising from manual interference, and notes that while in the seventeenth century, man-midwives might be inclined to show off their skills and instruments, thus increasing women's risk, by the eighteenth century, opinion was against unnecessary intervention.

86. Willis, *London Practice of Physick*, 626–627. Eccles is not alone when she notes that many poor women and rural women undergoing normal childbirths benefited by their inability to purchase top-of-the-line obstetric care, a benefit that early colonial women undoubtedly shared. While I have not come across any seventeenth-century midwife's opinion of physicians, the journal of Martha Ballard, 1791–1810, the subject of Laurel Thatcher Ulrich, *A Midwife's Tale* (New York: Vintage, 1990), reveals not only Ballard's consciousness of her medical superiority in reproductive matters, but a rather grim complacency in her skills.

87. Louise Bourgeois, *Observations diverses . . . sur les accouchments, maladies des femmes, et des nouveaux naiz* (Paris, 1609). Other texts included Jacques Guillemeau, *Child-birth, or The Happy Deliverie of Women* (trans. from French; London, 1612); Rueff, *The Expert Midwife*; Pechey, *Compleat Midwife's Practice Enlarged*; Barrett, *A Companion for Midwives*; Culpeper, *Directory for Midwives*; Jane Sharp, *Compleat Midwife's Companion* (4th ed., London, 1725).

88. Charles Thornton Libby, Neal W. Allen, and Robert E. Moody, eds., *Province and Court Records of Maine* (Portland: Maine Historical Society, 1928–64), 2:308, as cited in Koehler, *Search for Power*, 117. In addition to Eccles, *Obstetrics and Gynaecology*, and Tannenbaum, *Healer's Calling*, see Jean Donnison, *Midwives and Medical Men: A History of the Struggle for the Control of Childbirth* (London: Historical Publications, 1988). Although a male midwife or physician might be called in to a difficult case, female midwives held almost absolute control over the birthing chamber until at least 1750. In fact, in a difficult case it was far more likely, especially in New England, to see a second, more experienced female midwife called.

89. *Records of Suffolk County Court* (Boston: Colonial Society of Massachusetts, 1933), September 1675, no. 1412.

90. Records of the General Court (*Records of the Governor and Company of the Massachusetts Bay in New England*), ed. Nathaniel B. Shurtleff (Boston: W. White, 1853–54), May 12, 1657.

91. Karlsen, *Devil in the Shape of Woman*, 142–144.

92. Karlsen, *Devil in the Shape of Woman*, 143.

93. Winthrop, *Short Story*, 263.

94. Winthrop, *Journal*, March 27, 1638, 255. The editors' note indicates that the use of mandrake oil might be seen as less sorcery than biblical, since in Genesis 30:14–17, Leah's son Reuben brings mandrakes to her to assist her fertility.

95. This story has been reconstructed from a sequence of eight petitions presented to the General Court along with the records of the court itself. These petitions are in Miscellaneous Papers, Massachusetts State Archives, photostats at Massachusetts Historical Society. The General Court's response is recorded in Shurtleff, *Records of Massachusetts Bay*, May 23, 1650, 3:197; June 21, 1650, 3:209; June 22, 1650, 4.1:24– 25. For a fuller discussion of this crisis, see Mary Beth Norton, "'The Ablest Midwife That Wee Know in the Land': Mistress Alice Tilly and the Women of Boston and Dorchester, 1649–1650," *William and Mary Quarterly* 55 (1998), 105–134.

96. Petition of Liddea Williams to the General Court, March 8, 1648/9.

97. A petition of "divers Women in Boston" to the General Court, May? 1650?, signed by 130 women. All the citations in this paragraph are taken from these petitions thought to have been presented in May 1650.

98. Shurtleff, *Records of Massachusetts Bay*, June 22, 1650, 4.1:24.

99. William Hill, *A New-Years Gift for Women Being a True Looking-Glass* (London, 1660), 2. Ulrich, *Good Wives*, uses these two characters (along with Jael) in her portrayal of Puritan women's lives. It is notable that just as Eve is considered an active temptress of Adam rather than the dupe of the serpent, Bathsheba is seen as a seductress rather than a victim to David's lust.

100. [J.] S., *A Brief Anatomie of Women* (London, 1653), 5.

101. See, for example, Hill, *New-Years Gift*, 22–31; [J.] S., *Brief Anatomie of Women*, 5; Aylett, *Susanna*; Jocelin, *The Mothers Legacie*, 38–50.

102. Charles Gerbier, *Elogium Heroinum: or, the Praise of Worthy Women* (London, 1651), 82–114; Hill, *New-Years Gift*, 31–32; Joseph Swetnam, *The Arraignment of Lewd, Idle, Froward, and Unconstant Women* (1615; London, 1637), 45. Even he reflected upon good biblical women, with Mary honored for her humble mind, Sara for her conjugal love as demonstrated by her calling her husband "Lord," and Susanna "for her chastitie, and for creeping on her knees to please her husband" (46). His pamphlet attacking women angered a generation who challenged his position fully and enthusiastically in a series of pamphlets: Constantia Munda (pseud.), *The Worming of a Mad Dogge* (London, 1617); Ester Sowerman (pseud.), *Ester Hath Hang'd Haman* (London, 1617); Rachel Speght, *A Mouzell for Melastomus* (London, 1617); Mary Tattle-well and Joane Hit-him-home (pseud.), *The Womens Sharpe Revenge* (London, 1640).

103. Cotton Mather, as Ulrich notes in *Good Wives*, 168–169, found in Jael a model of Puritan women. He invoked this image, however, in his praise of a woman who had already avenged herself against an Indian raid. In other words, in this case Jael was less a prescription than an analogy.

104. See, for example, Gouge, *Of Domestical Duties*, 317–319; Gataker, *A Wife Indeed*, 61; Gataker, *A Mariage Praier*, 14; Hill, *New-Years Gift*, 39; [J.] S., *Anatomie of Women*, 1–2. See also *Geneva Bible* commentary on Jezebel, 1 Kings 16:31, OT leaf 160; 1 Kings 19:1–2, OT leaf 161; 1 Kings 21, OT leaf 163; 2 Kings 9:30–37, OT leaf 169.

105. [I.] H., *A Strange Wonder or A Wonder in a Woman* (London, 1642), 2.

106. Swetnam, *Arraignment of Women*, preface 2; [J.] S., *Anatomie of Women*, 2. Karlsen, *Devil in the Shape of Woman*, has noted that "scold," the label for an angry women, has particularly negative connotations, in some cases synonymous with "witch." She further comments that there is no comparable accusatory label for an angry man (130). For an excellent, multilayered analyses of speech and the gendering of transgressions, see Kamensky, *Governing the Tongue*, especially 43–98, Dayton, *Women before the Bar*, especially 285–327.

107. Swetnam, *Arraignment of Women*, 1, 2, 7, 8, 10; [J.] S., *Anatomie of Women*, 3; Gouge, *Of Domestical Duties*, 26, 269.

108. Gerbier, *Elogium Heroinum*, 7–8.

109. Taylor, *Works*, 152–153.

110. Cleaver, *Godly Forme*, 157, 160–161.

111. Rogers, *Matrimonial Honour*, 248; Gataker, *Marriage Duties Briefely Couched*, 41; I. H., *Strange Wonder*, 3.

112. Jocelin, *The Mothers Legacie*, 33; Leigh, *A Mothers Blessing*, 56. Even the budding feminist Margaret Newcastle, *Orations*, granted the inferiority of women, but she argued that the cause was lack of education, conversation, and activity (225–232).

113. Rogers, *Matrimonial Honour*, 153; Gataker, *Marriage Duties Briefely Couched*, 10.

114. Winthrop, *Journal*, March 11, 1639, 290. Porterfield, *Female Piety*, has argued that gender definitions were somewhat permeable, and that men, in particular, were encouraged to develop the feminine side of their spirituality. While I would agree that expressions and experiences of piety were often feminine, I think that the feminine side of this piety was sometimes quite disturbing to Puritan men since gender definitions were not, in the mind of the Puritan cleric, at all flexible. Puritans saw humanity as dichotomized by sex, and when individuals stepped outside of their rigidly defined positions, they created great confusion for the society and, often, for themselves. This argument is developed in greater detail in chapter 4, on piety, and in chapter 7, on the patriarchal response to female power.

115. Gouge, *Of Domesticall Duties*, 188–189.

116. Willis, *London Practice of Physick*, 297–298.

117. Sydenham, *Whole Works*, 441, 450, 447, 440. Pages 440–452 provide an excellent outline of the contemporary vision of hysteria, its symptoms and its causes.

118. Culpeper, *Directory for Midwives*, 100; Willis, *London Practice of Physick*, 614, 633.

119. Phyllis Mack, *Visionary Women: Ecstatic Prophecy in Seventeenth-Century England* (Berkeley: University of California Press, 1992), 24–27, discusses the

seventeenth-century meaning of female wetness in some detail, not merely in terms of physiology but also in terms of personality and moral character. For more detailed descriptions and analyses of scientific and culture constructions of gender and biology, see Thomas Laqueur, *Making Sex: Body and Gender from the Greeks to Freud* (Cambridge, MA: Harvard University Press, 1990), especially 63–148.

120. Gerbier, *Elogium Heroinum*, 72; Niccholes, *Marriage and Wyving*, 7–10; [J.] S., *Anatomie of Women*, 2–3.

121. Culpeper, *Directory for Midwives*, 25. Needless to say, men's reproductive anatomy was not described in the same light.

122. I. H., *Strange Wonder*, 3; Swetnam, *Arraignment of Women*, 15; Dod and Hinde, *Bathshebaes Instructions*, 26.

123. Title pages of *The Virgins Complaint* (London, 1642/43) and *The Widows Lamentation for the Absence of Their Deare Children* (London, 1643).

124. *The Virgins Complaint*, 6.

125. *The Wandering Whore* (London, 1660); *The Wandering Whore Continued*, second installment (London, 1660); *The Wandering Whore Continued*, third installment (London, 1660). Citations from second installment, 12; third installment, 10; second installment, 9. The man described offered increasing amounts of money to solicit sex from a virgin. The author acknowledges the economic issues, and yet turns the story around to blame the woman as seeking after sex.

126. Sowerman, *Ester Hath Hanged Haman*, 24–25, 44–47, citations 46–47, 44.

127. Tattle-well and Hit-him-home, *The Womans Sharpe Revenge*, 99, 134–135.

128. Leigh, *A Mothers Blessing*, 32–33.

129. The records of the Suffolk and Essex County Courts both reflect this development. For an excellent discussion of the increasing blame attributed to women during the seventeenth century, see Karlsen, *Devil in the Shape of Woman*, 194–202. She also comments upon the connection between sexual culpability and class status in that poor men could easily be found guilty, but not so middling or upper-class men. See also Dayton, *Women before the Bar*, 231–284.

130. Culpeper, *Directory for Midwives*, 70. See Laqueur, *Making Sex*, 161–162.

131. These and other stories are explored in detail in Ulrich, *Good Wives*, 89–105. For a developed analysis of rape in early America, see Sharon Block, *Rape and Sexual Power in Early America* (Chapel Hill: University of North Carolina Press, 2006). The Greenland-Rolfe case is recorded in Dow, *Records of Essex County*, 1663; the Collins-Bond case in Libby, Allen, and Moody, *Province and Court Records of Maine*, 1650.

Chapter 4

1. These numbers come from Battis's list of Hutchinson's male supporters, previously discussed in chapter 2, who lived in Boston and were therefore better able to attend. See the appendices in Battis, *Saints and Sectaries*, 301–328.

2. Winthrop, *Short Story*, 264.

3. "Report of the Trial," in Hall, *Antinomian Controversy*, 370.

4. Weld, "Preface" to Winthrop, *Short Story*, 208.

5. Ulrich, *Good Wives*, 165–183. Thomas Edwards, English Presbyterian and polemicist, used "Jael" as a negative allusion in his description of a female religious leader whom he despised. See his *The Third Part of Gangraena* (London, 1646), 170–171. Edwards's three-volume *Gangraena* is further discussed in the next chapter.

6. Romans 16:11. Spellings and citation from *Geneva Bible*, NT leaf 76.

7. Winthrop, *Short Story*, 268–269; "Examination of Hutchinson," in Hall, *Antinomian Controversy*, 315–316. Texts referred to are Titus 2:3–5; Acts 18:24–27.

8. Winthrop, *Short Story*, 268.

9. The concept of "spirit mystic" is first articulated by Jerald Brauer, "Types of Puritan Piety," *Church History* 56 (1987), 51–58. Brauer argues that spirit mystics find the union with the Holy Spirit to be not fleeting but permanent.

10. Admittedly, this also added to the grievances of the rising gentry and commercial classes already dissatisfied with the unfair distribution of wealth. They were especially unhappy with their own inability, despite their wealth, to purchase land (since land was unavailable) and move into a gentry class characterized explicitly by landholding.

11. Even Perry Miller who, fascinated by Puritan cosmology, convinced generations of scholars that they must understand the Puritans' focus upon learning and the map of their knowledge, began his definitive *The New England Mind: The Seventeenth Century* with two chapters upon Augustinian piety. This piety, he emphasized throughout his analytical description of Puritan theories of knowing, was the foundation of Puritan culture.

12. Anne Bradstreet, "Meditations Moral and Divine," in *Works of Anne Bradstreet*, 288.

13. Cotton, *Sixteene Questions*, in Hall, *Antinomian Controversy*, 51. Cotton continued his definition thus: "Our Sanctification in Christ hath in it this more; Faith in the Righteousnesse of Christ, and Repentance from dead Works, (and that which is the Root of [both]) the indwelling Power of the Spirit, to act and keep Holinesse in us all, which Adam wanted," but the clergy in Massachusetts argued that such was not appropriately called sanctification. See Elders Reply, manuscript in the Massachusetts Historical Society, in Hall, *Antinomian Controversy*, 67.

14. John Cotton, Rejoynder to the Elders, manuscript in the Massachusetts Historical Society, in Hall, *Antinomian Controversy*, 101.

15. Elders Reply, in Hall, *Antinomian Controversy*, 68, 69.

16. Cotton, *Sixteene Questions*, in Hall, *Antinomian Controversy*, 52–56, citation 52.

17. Peter Bulkeley to John Cotton, [March 25, 1637], Cotton Family Papers, Prince Collection, Boston Public Library.

18. Cotton, *Sixteene Questions*, in Hall, *Antinomian Controversy*, 49; Peter Bulkeley, *The Gospel Covenant; or the Covenant of Grace Opened* (London, 1651), 60; Elders Reply, in Hall, *Antinomian Controversy*, 68.

19. Cotton, *Sixteene Questions*, in Hall, *Antinomian Controversy*, 51. See also Cotton, Rejoynder to the Elders, in Hall, *Antinomian Controversy*, 104–107.

20. Miller, *The New England Mind: The Seventeenth Century*, 3–63; Morgan, *Visible Saints*, 66–73; Hambrick-Stowe, *Practice of Piety*, 76–90; Charles Lloyd Cohen, *God's Caress: The Psychology of Puritan Religious Conversion* (New York: Oxford University Press, 1986), 5–11; Winship, *Making Heretics*, 69–77.

21. George Selement and Bruce C. Woolley, eds., *Thomas Shepard's Confessions* (Boston: Colonial Society of Massachusetts, 1981), 61, 65–69, citations 68, 69.

22. An illuminating consideration of the conversion narrative as an expressive genre is Patricia Caldwell, *The Puritan Conversion Narrative: The Beginnings of American Expression* (Cambridge: Cambridge University Press, 1983). Although Caldwell does not use the term "performance," her excellent analysis displays the movement of the New England narratives toward formulaic consistency, the means by which this was accomplished, and the insights revealed despite the paradigmatic restrictions.

23. Cotton, *Sixteene Questions*, in Hall, *Antinomian Controversy*, 58. See also Cotton's response to Peter Bulkeley, undated manuscript, Cotton Family Papers, in Hall, *Antinomian Controversy*, 37–42, for a detailed discussion of Cotton's views on humanity's inability to achieve anything beyond passivity in its engagement with divine grace.

24. Thomas Hooker, *The Soules Humiliation* (London, 1640), 145, 55–56. His other publications on preparationism include *The Soules Preparation for Christ* (London, 1632); *The Unbelievers Preparing for Christ* (London, 1638); *The Soules Implantation into the Naturall Olive* (London, 1640); *The Covenant of Grace Opened* (London, 1649); *The Application of Redemption* (London, 1659).

25. Thomas Shepard, *The Parable of the Ten Virgins* (1660; Falkirk, 1997), 262, 286.

26. Hooker, *Soules Preparation for Christ*, 52.

27. Hooker, *The Soules Humiliation*, 18, 134; Hooker, *Soules Preparation for Christ*, 108; Elders Reply, in Hall, *Antinomian Controversy*, 73.

28. Hooker, *The Soules Humiliation*, 131–132; Hooker, *Soules Preparation for Christ*, 117.

29. Bulkeley, *Gospel Covenant*, 48–49.

30. Hooker, *The Soules Humiliation*, 59; see also 8–12.

31. Hooker, *Soules Preparation for Christ*, 90, 36.

32. Edward Collins testimony, in Selement and Woolley, *Thomas Shepard's Confessions*, 84; John Trumbull's testimony, in Selement and Woolley, *Thomas Shepard's Confessions*, 107.

33. Hooker, *Soules Preparation for Christ*, 1.

34. Thomas Shepard to John Cotton, 1636, in Hall, *Antinomian Controversy*, 25–29. In his excellent description of preparationism, Pettit, *Heart Prepared*, argues that these theologians were speaking of human endeavor and therefore compromising Calvin's concept of complete human dependence upon divine grace. Hambrick-Stowe, *Practice of Piety*, challenges Pettit's argument and claims, following Hooker, that these theologians were describing divine preparation of the passive believer (see 80 n. 32). In navigating this controversy, Winship, *Making Heretics*, provides the most sophisticated deconstruction of this theological debate. His focus upon Thomas Shepard, who also judged God as the primary force and yet challenged Cotton's emphasis upon passivity, facilitates Winship's profound discussion of the issues.

35. Galatians 3:28, citation from *Geneva Bible*, NT leaf 88.

36. Arthur Lake, *Sermons with Some Religious and Divine Meditations* (London, 1629), 70.

37. See, for example, Dod and Hinde, *Bathshebas Instructions*, 62–63.

38. Shurtleff, *Records of Massachusetts Bay*, June 14, 1642, 2:6.

39. David D. Hall, *Worlds of Wonder, Days of Judgment: Popular Religious Belief in Early New England* (Cambridge, MA: Harvard University Press, 1990), 21–70.

40. See, for example, Thomas Shepard, "Autobiography," in *God's Plot: The Paradoxes of Puritan Piety, Being the Autobiography & Journal of Thomas Shepard*, ed. Michael McGiffert (Amherst: University of Massachusetts Press, 1972), 40–46.

41. Like Anne Hutchinson, Anne Bradstreet stands as an accomplished woman among the first generation of immigrants to New England. A generation younger than Hutchinson but of equally high rank, Bradstreet was the daughter of Thomas and Dorothy Dudley, and wife of sometime governor Simon Bradstreet. Unlike Hutchinson, however, Bradstreet has become known for her own accomplishments as a poet. A volume of her poems was published during her life in the 1661; however, most literary critics agree that the superior poems are those verses growing out of her personal experiences and written for private consumption. Some were published right after her death, others only appeared in an 1867 edition. For an excellent edition of her collected poems, see Hensley, *Works of Anne Bradstreet.*

42. For a basic measure of literacy, see Kenneth A. Lockridge, *Literacy in Colonial New England* (New York: Norton, 1974). Beginning with the basic evidence of will signatures, Lockridge (38–42) estimates that the rate of literacy among women was half that of men. Many scholars now examining literacy, however, find that signatures provide a conservative estimate of literacy, arguing that many more people could read than write. See Hall, *Worlds of Wonder*, 21–70. Some brief discussion of girls' schooling can be found in Thompson, *Women in Stuart England*, 195–210, and in Koehler, *Search for Power*, 41–42.

43. Shurtleff, *Records of Massachusetts Bay*, 2:203.

44. Gouge, *Of Domesticall Duties*, 30; Gerbier, *Elogium Heroinum*, 7. This, in fact, is the question asked by Barker-Benfield, "Anne Hutchinson." He argues that, ultimately, in Puritan theology the Protestant precept "priesthood of all believers" became "priesthood of all male believers."

45. Thomas Welde, *An Answer to W.R.* (London, 1644), 19.

46. Gouge, *Of Domesticall Duties*, 271.

47. Culpeper, *Directory for Midwives.*

48. John Brinsley, *A Looking-Glasse for Good Women* (London, 1645), 7, 4.

49. Rodgers, *Matrimonial Honour*, 34.

50. *A Spirit Moving in the Women-Preachers* (London, 1645), 4.

51. Winthrop, *Journal*, April 13, 1645, 570.

52. John Elborow, *Euodias and Syntyche: or, The Female Zelots of the Church of Philippi* (London, 1637), 4.

53. Lake, *Sermons*, 68.

54. Elborow, *Euodias and Syntyche*, 4, 6–7.

55. Hill, *New-Years Gift*, 41; Lake, *Sermons*, 72.

56. Rodgers, *Matrimonial Honour*, 34; Brinsley, *Looking-Glasse for Women*, 4; Elborow, *Euodias and Syntyche*, 6; *Spirit Moving in Women-Preachers*, 2.

57. [J.] S., *Brief Anatomie of Women*, 1.

58. Culpeper, *Directory for Midwives*, 100; Bulkeley, *Gospel Covenant*, 79.

59. Park and Daston, "Unnatural Conceptions"; Daston and Park, *Wonders*, 173–214; Thomas, *Decline of Magic*, 90–132; Hall, *Worlds of Wonder*, 71–116; Schutte, "Such Monstrous Births."

60. Culpeper, *Directory for Midwives*, 1.

61. *Strange Newes from Scotland* (London, 1647); *Mrs RUMP Brought to Bed of a Monster* (n.p., n.d.). Tessa Watt, *Cheap Print and Popular Piety, 1550–1640* (New York: Cambridge University Press, 1991), 124, 143, 165, 288, notes the popularity of this subject in the popular press. She found that such publications, whether broadsides or penny godlies, generally included a picture and always a vivid, detailed description.

62. For a detailed medical discussion of the Dyer and Hutchinson births, see Schutte, "Such Monstrous Births," 90–91 nn. 13, 14; Buchanan, "Study of Maternal Rhetoric"; Valerius, "So Manifest a Sign." Dyer's child has been judged anencephalic with severe spina bifida, while Hutchinson is thought to have expelled a hydatidiform mole.

63. Winthrop, *Journal*, 254; Winthrop, *Short Story*, 281.

64. Weld, "Preface" to Winthrop, *Short Story*, 214.

65. Weld, "Preface" to Winthrop, *Short Story*, 214–215.

66. Christina Larner, *Witchcraft and Religion: The Politics of Popular Belief* (Oxford: Blackwell, 1984), 84–91, 85; Thomas, *Decline of Magic*, 620–621; John Putnam Demos, *Entertaining Satan: Witchcraft and the Culture of Early New England* (New York: Oxford University Press, 1982), 60–64; Karlsen, *Devil in the Shape of Woman*, 47–52. For New England, both Demos and Karlsen estimate that about half of the men accused were connected to accused women. See Robin Briggs, *Witches and Neighbors: The Social and Cultural Context of European Witchcraft* (New York: Viking Press, 1996), especially 257–286, for a complicating argument about the gendering of witchcraft.

67. The best discussion of the conception of witchcraft in England within the larger ideological and religious frameworks is Thomas, *Decline of Magic*, 517–680. These two paragraphs on the competing definitions of witchcraft are based upon Thomas's work.

68. According to Thomas, English witch trials always rose out of popular concerns and fears, while on the continent witch hunts began with the efforts of the leaders. Briggs, on the other hand, sees on the continent similar patterns of popular fears and, frequently, anger. One exception to this pattern in England involved professional witch hunter Matthew Hopkins, but, for the most part, English trials were responses to concrete problems perceived to be caused by sorcery.

69. On the statutes, see Thomas, *Decline of Magic*, 525–527.

70. Among Puritan writings on witchcraft, one of the clearest and most detailed is William Perkins, *A Discourse of the Damned Art of Witchcraft* (Cambridge, 1608). Most of what New England theologians wrote about witchcraft was informed by Perkins's work.

71. Winthrop, *Journal*, June 4, 1648, 711.

72. Brinsley, *Looking-Glasse for Women*, 9.

73. Winthrop, *Journal*, June 4, 1648, 712.

74. Brinsley, *Looking-Glasse for Women*, 9.

75. Montague Summers, trans. and ed., *The "Malleus Maleficarum" of Heinrich Kramer and Jacob Sprenger* (New York: Dover, 1971).

76. William of Malmsbury, "The Sorceress of Berkeley" (ca. 1140), in *Witchcraft in Europe, 400–1700: A Documentary History*, ed. Alan Charles Kors and Edward Peters, 2nd ed. (Philadelphia: University of Pennsylvania Press, 2001), 70–72, citation 71. Jeffrey Richards, *Sex, Dissidence and Damnation: Minority Groups in the Middle Ages* (London: Routledge, 1990), 74–87, provides an excellent summary of the medieval perception of witchcraft.

77. Winthrop, *Journal*, June 1648, 712.

78. On New England, see Karlsen, *Devil in the Shape of Woman*, 134–141.

79. For a persuasive analysis of the gendering of good and evil, see Reis, *Damned Women*.

80. John Cotton, *A Conference Mr. John Cotton Held at Boston with the Elders of New-England* (1646) in Hall, *Antinomian Controversy*, 177.

81. John Brinsley, *Mystical Implantation: or, The Great Gospel Mystery of the Christian's Union and Communion with and Conformity to Jesus Christ* (London, 1652), 226, 21, 28.

82. Selement and Woolley, *Thomas Shepard's Confessions*, 102, 195, 91. In Shepard's church, women frequently testified before the congregation.

83. Winthrop, *Short Story*, 272.

84. Selement and Woolley, *Thomas Shepard's Confessions*, 102.

85. Selement and Woolley, *Thomas Shepard's Confessions*, 104, 59, 140, 51, 40, 71, Trumbull's Testimony, 108, 84.

86. Thomas Hooker, *The Soules Vocation or Effective Calling to Christ* (1638), 257, as cited in Cohen, *God's Caress*, 126.

87. Selement and Woolley, *Thomas Shepard's Confessions*, 41, 143, 63, 135.

88. Brother Jackson's Maid, Testimony, in Selement and Woolley, *Thomas Shepard's Confessions*, 120, 177, 41.

89. Edward Taylor, "Meditation. I Cor. 3.22. Things Present," in *The Poems of Edward Taylor*, ed. Donald E. Stanford (New Haven, CT: Yale University Press, 1960), 56.

90. "Examination of Hutchinson," in Hall, *Antinomian Controversy*, 337.

91. Brinsley, *Mystical Implantation*, 32. On the mystical nature of the conversion experience, see Miller, *The Seventeenth Century*, 3–63. See also McGiffert, "Introduction" to *God's Plot*, 3–29; Cohen, *God's Caress*, 11–133.

92. For explorations of the relationship between Puritan spirituality and political and social identity, see Miller, *New England Mind: The Seventeenth Century*, 398–431, 463–484; Miller, *New England Mind: From Colony to Province*, 21–26; Edmund S. Morgan, "Introduction" to *Puritan Political Ideas* (New York: Bobbs-Merrill, 1965), xiii–xlvii; Christopher Hill, *God's Englishman: Oliver Cromwell and the English Revolution* (New York: Penguin, 1970), 201–216.

93. John Russell Bartlett, ed., *Records of the Colony of Rhode Island and Providence Plantations, in New England* (Providence, RI: A. Crawford Greene and Brother, 1857), noted 1637, 1:16.

94. Elizabeth Olbon and Jane Holmes, for example, both credited women with having a transformative influence over their spiritual journeys. See Woolley and Selement, *Thomas Shepard's Confessions*, 39, 77.

95. "Examination of Hutchinson," in Hall, *Antinomian Controversy*, 317.

96. The paradigm of separate spheres, perhaps more appropriate to the analysis of urban, industrial cultures, might be said to be entirely inapplicable to the organic, agricultural communities of the seventeenth century. Yet the interpretive model provides a useful insight into the sociopolitical dynamics operating in the church. Puritan leaders placed a premium upon status, deference, and order, but within their society role assignments, spheres of labor, and fields of authority were haphazardly defined with vague, fluid boundaries. Within such a transitional culture moving toward more strictly guarded dichotomous constructions, such middle grounds as the church served as arenas of conflict resolution.

97. "Examination of Hutchinson," in Hall, *Antinomian Controversy*, 328. This was said following Winthrop's assertion that the testifying ministers would be asked to swear an oath in the court. He does not indicate who made the private speech public.

98. "Examination of Hutchinson," in Hall, *Antinomian Controversy*, 346.

99. "Examination of Hutchinson," in Hall, *Antinomian Controversy*, 319.

100. Winthrop, *Short Story*, 268. Note, as well, that Hutchinson's exposition is recast as public criticism.

101. Winthrop, *Short Story*, 308.

Chapter 5

1. Two versions of her self-revelation can be found in Winthrop, *Short Story*, 268–273, and "Examination of Hutchinson," in Hall, *Antinomian Controversy*, 336–338. For quotations see 268, 272, 338, 269. The verse referenced is Joel 2:28–29, "And afterwarde wil I powre out my Spirit upon all flesh: and your sonnes and your daughters shal prophecie: your olde men shal dreame dreames, & you yong men shal se visions, And also upon the servants, and upon the maides, in those daies will I powre my Spirit." This text that is repeated so often in women's texts it takes on the character of a battle cry.

2. Pierce, *Records of First Church*, November 22, 1646, 46; November 29, 1655, 56. Sarah Keayne was later excommunicated, possibly for continuing in her prophesying, but the records, acknowledging the sin of "irregular prophesying," noted an additional sin: "odious, lewd, and scandalous uncleane behaviours with one Nicholas Hart an Excommunicate person" (October 24, 1647, 49). It is difficult to consider the sexual sins separate from the "irregular prophesying," since outspoken women were so often automatically tied to sexual deviance (see chapter 7).

3. Winthrop, *Journal*, June 22, 1643, 462–463.

4. Winthrop, *Journal*, December 13, 1638, 275–276, citation 275. It is difficult to know just how able or zealous Oliver was, since Winthrop generally embraced opportunities to critique Hutchinson's piety and disparage her abilities.

5. Winthrop, *Short Story*, 253–254.

6. Historians who have argued the appeal of Hutchinsonianism to the merchants include Bailyn, *New England Merchants*; Battis, *Saints and Sectaries*; Rutman, *Winthrop's Boston*, 98–134; and Breen, *Transgressing the Bounds*, 17–56, as was discussed in chapter 2.

7. Robert Keayne, *The Apologia of Robert Keayne*, ed. Bernard Bailyn (New York: Harper, 1965). An extremely successful, and rather unpopular, merchant, Keayne was frequently before the courts defending himself for his high profits. He was also committed to his spiritual search, taking copious notes at sermons and church trials, and producing an impassioned will in which he strove to justify himself to man as well as God.

8. On the importance of conventicle-type meetings, see Collinson, *The Elizabethan Puritan Movement*, 356–382 and especially Collinson, "Towards a Broader Understanding of the Early Dissenting Tradition," in *Godly People*, 527–562.

9. Winthrop, *Journal*, March 29, 1631, 48–49; December 5, 1633, 106.

10. Weld, *An Answer to W.R.*, 37–38, 61.

11. Stephen Foster, "New England and the Challenge of Heresy, 1630–1660: The Puritan Crisis in Trans-Atlantic Perspective," *William and Mary Quarterly* 38 (1981), 624–660, argues that Hutchinson's popularity owed far more to her willingness to host spiritual meetings than to any particularly appealing theology.

12. *The Acts and Monuments of John Foxe*, ed. Josiah Pratt (London: George Seeley, 1870), 5:551, 550. Askew's own record of the examinations can be found in Anne Askew, *The First Examinacyon of Anne Askew, Lately Martyred in Smythfelde, by the Romysh Popes Upholders, with Elucydacyon of Johan Bale* (Wesel, 1546) and Anne Askew, *The Lattre Examinacion of the Worthye Servaunt of God Mastres Anne Askewe* (Wesel, 1547), both of which were reprinted several times, including in *Acts and Monuments*, 538–549. On Anne Askew's writings, see Elaine V. Beilin, "Anne Askew's Self-Portrait in the *Examinations*," in *Silent but for the Word: Tudor Women as Patrons, Translators, and Writers of Religious Works*, ed. Margaret Patterson Hannay (Kent, OH: Kent State University Press, 1985), 77–91.

13. Foxe, *Acts and Monuments*, vols. 7 and 8. Not all of the individuals that Foxe discusses were executed. Historians of the persecutions have found that fifty-five, or 20 percent, of the Marian martyrs were female. A. G. Dickens, *The English Reformation* (New York: Schocken Press, 1964), 364–365; Retha Warnicke, *Women of the English Renaissance and Reformation* (Westport, CT: Greenwood Press, 1983), 74.

14. Foxe, *Acts and Monuments*, 8:385, 538–548, 327.

15. John Bale, "Preface" to Askew, *Lattre Examinacion*.

16. Foxe, *Acts and Monuments*, 8:247–250.

17. Thomas Freeman, "'The Good Ministrye of Godlye and Vertuouse Women': The Elizabethan Martyrologists and the Female Supporters of the Marian Martyrs," *Journal of British Studies* 39 (2000), 8–33.

18. On English Protestant women during the Marian and Elizabethan eras, see Diane Willen, "Godly Women in Early Modern England: Puritanism and Gender," *Journal of Ecclesiastical History* 43 (1992), 561–580; Collinson, "Early Dissenting Tradition"; Mary Prior, "Reviled and Crucified Marriages: The Position of Tudor Bishops' Wives," in *Women in English Society, 1500–1800*, ed. Prior (London: Methuen, 1985), 118–148; Warnicke, *Women of the English Renaissance*.

19. Thomas Hall, *A Practical and Polemical Commentary* (London, 1658), 469–470, as quoted in Patricia Crawford, *Women and Religion in England, 1500–1720* (London: Routledge, 1993), 67–68.

20. Collinson, *The Elizabethan Puritan Movement*, 93; Calendar of State Papers Domestic, 1547–1580, as cited in Collinson, *The Elizabethan Puritan Movement*, 82.

21. Patrick Collinson, "The Role of Women in the English Reformation Illustrated by the Life and Friendships of Anne Locke," in Collinson, ed., *Godly People*, 273–287. See also Prior, "Reviled and Crucified Marriages."

22. Mary Ellen Lamb, "The Cooke Sisters: Attitudes toward Learned Women in the Renaissance," in Hannay, *Silent but for the Word*, 107–125.

23. Richard Hooker, *Works*, ed. J. Keble, 1:152–153 as quoted in Collinson, "Role of Women," 274. This dynamic was observed of nineteenth-century upstate New York and skillfully analyzed in Mary P. Ryan, *Cradle of the Middle Class: The Family in Oneida County, New York, 1790–1865* (New York: Cambridge University Press, 1981).

24. Askew, *First Examinacyon*; Askew, *Lattre Examinacion*; Foxe, *Acts and Monuments*, 8:538–549. My own interpretation of Askew's writings reflects the arguments of Beilin, "Anne Askew's Self-Portrait," who provides an extraordinarily astute reading of Askew's publications.

25. Many anthropologists, historians, and feminist theorists, including Max Weber, *The Sociology of Religion*, trans. Ephraim Fischoff (Boston: Beacon Press, 1963); I. M. Lewis, *Ecstatic Religion: An Anthropological Study of Spirit Possession and Shamanism* (New York: Penguin, 1971); Mary Douglas, *Natural Symbols: Explorations in Cosmology* (New York: Vintage, 1973); Thomas, *Decline of Magic*; Bynum, *Fragmentation and Redemption*; Mack, *Visionary Women*; and Julia Kristeva, *In the Beginning Was Love: Psychoanalysis and Faith*, trans. Arthur Goldhammer (New York: Columbia University Press, 1988), have argued for the connection between mysticism and women. Here I am concerned with documenting this attraction among Englishwomen during the century between 1580 and 1680.

26. On Niclaes himself, see Jean Dietz Moss, *"Godded with God": Hendrik Niclaes and His Family of Love* (Philadelphia: American Philosophical Society, 1981). It is worth noting that for the overwhelming majority of Protestants throughout England, to come from Munster was damning in and of itself. The notorious Munster, said to be the site of chaotic, unbridled behavior posing as reform, was, until the 1670s, evoked as a warning against sectarian abuses.

27. Nigel Smith, "The Writings of Hendrik Niclaes and the Family Love in the Interregnum, in his *Perfection Proclaimed: Language and Literature in English Radical Religion, 1640–1660* (Oxford: Clarendon Press, 1989), 144–184.

28. See the prefaces and introductory pages of the following: Henrik Niclaes, *Revelatio Dei. The Revelation of God* (1575; London, 1649); Niclaes, *Terra Pacis. A True Testification of the Spiritual Land of Peace* (1575; London, 1649); Niclaes, *The Prophecy of the Spirit of Love* (1574; London, 1649); Niclaes, *An Introduction to the Holy Understanding of the Glasse of Righteousnesse* (1575; London, 1649); *Evangelkium Regni. A Joyful Message of the Kingdom* (ca. 1575; London, 1652).

29. Niclaes, *Revelatio Dei*, 51–55.

30. Niclaes, *Glasse of Righteousnesse*, 118.

31. Niclaes, *Revelatio Dei*, 63–112, citation, 80. See also Niclaes, *Prophecy of the Spirit*, 49ff. On falsely grounded knowledge as a source of schism, see Niclaes, *Terra Pacis*, 26–28.

32. Niclaes, *Terra Pacis*, 29–35, citations 31, 32.

33. Niclaes, *Terra Pacis*, 127–131; citation, Niclaes, *Glasse of Righteousnesse*, 194.

34. From the articles against Brearly, 1617, as cited in Foster, "New England," 632.

35. See John Eaton, *The Honey-combe of Free Justification by Christ Alone* (London, 1642); John Eaton, *The Discovery of the Most Dangerous Dead Faith* (London, 1641). Although Eaton died before 1630, his writings, like those of Niclaes, Eaton's were reprinted during the Civil War.

36. On the sectaries see, in addition to Foster, "New England," Geoffrey F. Nuttall, *The Holy Spirit in Puritan Faith and Experience* (New York: Oxford University Press, 1946); Rufus M. Jones, *Mysticism and Democracy in the English Commonwealth* (Cambridge, MA: Harvard University Press, 1932), lectures 3, 4.

37. Crawford, *Women and Religion*, 54, 121–124; Richard L. Greaves, "Foundation Builders: The Role of Women in Early English Nonconformity," in *Triumph over Silence: Women in Protestant History*, ed. Richard L. Greaves (Westport, CT: Greenwood Press, 1985), 76.

38. Lake, *Sermons*, 70. Lake was bishop between 1616 and 1625, so the sermon must have been delivered during those years.

39. Shepard, *God's Plot*, 56. On Anne Fenwick, see David R. Como, "Women, Prophecy, and Authority in Early Stuart Puritanism," *Huntington Library Quarterly* 61 (1999), 203–222. Como's interest in Fenwick lies less in her gender than in her activities as a radical avidly opposed to ceremonies of all kinds.

40. Ephraim Pagitt, *Heresiography* (London, 1654).

41. Foster, "New England," 642.

42. Samuel Gorton, *Simplicities Defence against Seven-headed Policy* (London, 1646); Harvard M. Chapin, *The Documentary History of Rhode Island* (Providence, RI: Preston and Rounds, 1916), 128–197; Shurtleff, *Records of Massachusetts Bay*, November 4, 1646, 3:92–98. For a detailed analysis of Samuel Gorton and his followers, see Gura, *Glimpse of Sion's Glory*, 276–303.

43. Gura, *Glimpse of Sion's Glory*, 4, 44–45.

44. John Clark, *Ill Newes from New-England: or A Narative of New-Englands Persecution* (London, 1652), printed in *Collections of the Massachusetts Historical Society*, 4th series (Boston: Massachusetts Historical Society, 1854), 2:1–113; Gura, *Glimpse of Sion's Glory*, 49–125; Pestana, *Quakers and Baptists*.

45. The Quakers are further discussed in chapter 6.

46. Shurtleff, *Records of Massachusetts Bay*, May 9, 1649, 3:158–159; June 21, 1650, 4.1:21; May 7, 1651, 4.1:42–43; October 24, 1651, 4.1:71; May 26, 1652, 4.1:90, citation 4.1:42. Marmaduke Matthews's response to accusations, May 26, 1652, 4.1:90; Letter from Matthews to General Court, June 13, 1651 and Petition from the women of Malden to the General Court, October 28, 1651, all in the Massachusetts State Archives.

47. The comparability of the two situations has frequently been observed among historians of England, who have treated New England during the 1630s and 1640s as a subcommunity of England. See, for example, Jones, *Mysticism and Democracy*, 130–133, 146–149; Collinson, "Early Dissenting Tradition"; Crawford, *Women and Religion*, 123–124; Mack, *Visionary Women*, 24–44, 256–260. These historians all use

examples from New England to elucidate English Puritanism. From the New England side, see Foster, *The Long Argument*; and Gura, *Glimpse of Sion's Glory*.

48. The long-term as well as immediate causes of the English Civil War have been thoroughly described and debated; entering that debate is clearly beyond the scope of this study. On the economic, social, constitutional, as well as religious causes, see Hill, *Society and Puritanism*; Hill, *The Intellectual Origins of the English Revolution*, rev. ed. (1965; New York: Oxford University Press, 2001); Lawrence Stone, *The Crisis of the Aristocracy, 1558–1641* (New York: Oxford University Press, 1965); Stone, *The Causes of the English Revolution, 1529–1642* (New York: Harper, 1972); Anthony Fletcher, *The Outbreak of the English Civil War* (New York: New York University Press, 1981); Conrad Russell, *The Causes of the English Civil War* (New York: Oxford University Press, 1990); Robert Ashton, *Conservatism and Revolution, 1603–1649* (New York: Norton, 1978); Ashton, *Counter-revolution: The Second Civil War and Its Origins, 1646–48* (New Haven, CT: Yale University Press, 1994).

49. "Ranter" was a generic term used to attack lay preachers and their followers who belonged to no organized religious group. Levellers were a political movement focused upon equality before the law, including the franchise. Seekers represent the original communities that would become the Society of Friends, or Quakers. Fifth Monarchists were an organized group of lay preachers and followers. They were millennialists who grounded their beliefs on the prophecies of Daniel, looked toward the Fifth Monarchy, following the first four (Babylonian, Persian, Macedonian, Roman), when Jesus Christ would become king and the millennium would begin. They were among the very few groups not tolerated by the Commonwealth government since they challenged the legitimacy of Cromwell as Protectorate.

50. On radical religion during the English Civil War, see Hill, *World Turned Upside Down*; Thomas, *Decline of Magic*; Arthur L. Morton, *The World of the Ranters: Religious Radicalism in the English Revolution* (London: Lawrence and Wishart, 1970); Bernard Capp, *The Fifth Monarchy Men: A Study in Seventeenth-Century English Millenarianism* (London: Faber and Faber, 1972); J. F. McGregor and Barry Reay, eds., *Radical Religion in the English Revolution* (New York: Oxford University Press, 1984); Christopher Hill, Barry Reay, and William Lamont, *The World of the Muggletonians* (London: T. Smith, 1983); F. D. Dow, *Radicalism in the English Revolution, 1640–1660* (London: Basil Blackwell, 1985).

51. Thomas Edwards, *The First and Second Part of Gangraena: Or a Catalogue and Discovery of Many of the Errors, Heresies, Blasphemies, and Pernicious Practices of the Sectaries*, 3rd ed. (London, 1646); Edwards, *Third Part of Gangraena*. Edwards's first publication in this war was *Antapologia: Or, A Full Answer to the Apologeticall Narration* (London, 1646), itself a reply to Thomas Goodwin, Philip Nye, Sedrach Simpson, Jeremiah Burroughs, and William Bridge, *An Apologeticall Narration* (London, 1643). *Gangraena* mobilized the publishing industry as nothing else had, setting off a slew of respondents, many of whom were defending themselves against Edwards's personal attacks in his writings. See, for example, Edward Draper, *A Plain and Faithfull Discovery of a Beame in Master Edwards His Eye* (London, 1646); John Goodwin, *An Apologesiates Antapologias* (London, 1646); Goodwin, *Cretensis* (London, 1646); John Maddocks and Henry Pinnell, *Gangraenachrestum,*

or, A Plaister to Alay the Tumor (Oxford, 1646); John Saltmarsh, *Groanes for Liberty* (London, 1646); William Walwyn, *A Whisper in the Eare of Mr. Thomas Edwards Minster* (n.p., 1646); Walwyn, *An Antidote against Master Edwards His Old and New Poyson* (London: Thomas Paine, 1646); Walwyn, *A Word More to Mr. Thomas Edwards* (London, 1646). In defense of Edwards, see John Bastwick, *The Utter Routing of the Whole Army of All the Independents & Sectaries* (London, 1646); John Vicars, *The Schismatick Sifted* (London, 1646). On Edwards's *Gangraena* see Ann Hughes, *"Gangraena" and the Struggle for the English Revolution* (New York: Oxford University Press, 2004), especially 55–129.

52. Edwards was not alone in this conceit; some even placed Roman Catholics, or "papists," in the same category as the others. See, for example, *A Discovery of 29 Sects Here in London* (London, 1641).

53. Edwards, *Gangraena*, 1:58.

54. Edwards, *Gangraena*, 1:26. For a discussion of the problems using heresiography as evidentiary source material, see Hughes, "Introduction," *Gangraena*, 1–54.

55. Lake, *Sermons*, 70.

56. Elborow, *Euodias and Syntyche*, 12. Euodias and Syntyche were two women chided by Paul for leading opposing factions in the church; see Philippians 4. Bernice was a daughter of King Herod Agrippa, present during Paul's examination by Agrippa in Acts 25–26.

57. *Spirit Moving in Women-Preachers*, title page, 3, 1. The language of the Beast is a reference to Revelation 13. The Revelation of John, the final book of the Bible, was prime fodder for writers of these decades.

58. John Taylor, *The Brownists Conventicle* (n.p., 1641), 6, 2–3; Vicars, *The Schismatick Sifted*, 34. "Mechanick preachers" became a byword for male preachers of the lower classes. In this kind of grouping, the construction of manhood becomes a status differentiated not only from womanhood but also from boys and the lower classes. This ideological complex, particularly in terms of the feminization of the lower classes, will be taken up in greater detail in chapter 7.

59. *A Discoverie of Six Women Preachers* ([London], 1641), 2, 3, 5; Humphry Ellis, *Pseudochristus* (London, 1650), title page.

60. Edwards, *Gangraena*, 1:29. The woman of Ely could be Elizabeth Bancroft, named in *Six Women Preachers*. Emery Battis has argued that the woman of Ely is the "woman of Elis" to whom Hugh Peter referred during Hutchinson's church trial. See Battis, *Saints and Sectaries*, 43n; "Report of the Trial," in Hall, *Antinomian Controversy*, 380. Battis's only reference to this person is *Gangraena*. For notes on women who heckled ministers, see *Gangraena*, 2:6, 3:34, 3:253.

61. Edwards, *Gangraena*, 1:32; there is also a reference to a woman in Kent on 2:87. John Saltmarsh, in his *Groanes for Liberty*, 26, denied the existence of a woman preacher in Kent, yet Edwards cites seven witnesses in *Gangraena*, 2:19–20.

62. Edwards, *Gangraena*, 3:22.

63. Edwards, *Gangraena*, 1:25, 1:29–30, citation 31, 32. The texts she cited include 1 Peter 4:10, 11; Hebrews 10; Malachi 3:16; and Titus on the gifts of the spirit (no chapter/verse identified.) On her marital crimes, see 1:113–115, 2:9. The association of marital sins with female preachers is further discussed in chapter 7.

64. Edwards, *Gangraena*, 1:25, 3:170–171. See the following publications of Katherine Chidley: *The Justification of the Independent Churches of Christ. Being an Answer to Mr. Edwards His Booke, Which Hee Hath Written against the Government of Christ's Church, and Toleration of Christs Publike Worship* (London, 1641) and *A New-Yeares Gift, or a Brief Exhortation to Mr. Thomas Edwards* (n.p., 1645). She also authored an early broadside *Good Counsell, to the Petitioners for Presbyterian Government That They May Declare Their Faith before They Build Their Church* (London, 1645). On Jael, see chapter 3. Puritan prescribers of female behavior generally avoided references to such strong women. For a discussion of Katherine Chidley as an effective polemicist, see Marcus Nevitt, *Women and the Pamphlet Culture of Revolutionary England, 1640–1660* (Aldershot, UK: Ashgate, 2006), 21–48.

65. Hughes, "Introduction," *Gangraena*, esp. 3–8; "Gangraena as Heresiography," *Gangraena*, esp. 73–78.

66. All recent historians of women leaders in this period are indebted to the research of Dorothy Paula Ludlow, whose "'Arise and Be Doing': English 'Preaching' Women, 1640–1660" (PhD diss., Indiana University, 1978), is a masterful treatment of the material. Of equal importance to my work has been Mack, *Visionary Women*, which includes appendices (413–424) identifying 280 religious activist women, of whom 243 were Quakers. See also Stevie Davies, *Unbridled Spirits: Women of the English Revolution, 1640–1660* (London: Women's Press, 1998); Hilary Hinds, *God's Englishwomen: Seventeenth-Century Radical Sectarian Writing and Feminist Criticism* (Manchester, UK: Manchester University Press, 1996). Earlier treatments include Keith Thomas, "Women and the Civil War Sects," *Past and Present* 13 (1958), 42–62, and Phyllis Mack, "Women as Prophets during the English Civil War," *Feminist Studies* 8 (1982), 19–45.

67. Elizabeth Warren, *The Old and Good Way Vindicated* (London, 1646); *Spiritual Thrift, or Meditations* (London, 1647); *A Warning-Peece from Heaven* (London, 1649).

68. See, for example, Eleanor Douglas, *The Blasphemous Charge against Her* (n.p., 1636); *The Lady Eleanor, Her Appeale to the High Court of Parliament* (n.p., 1641); *The Gatehouse Salutation from the Lady Eleanor* (n.p., 1646); *The New Jerusalem at Hand* (n.p., 1649); and *The Restitution of Prophecy; That Buried Talent to Be Revived* (n.p., 1651). On women's use of print as a means of communication, see Margaret J. M. Ezell, "Performance Texts: Arise Evans, Grace Carrie, and the Interplay of Oral and Handwritten Traditions during the Print Revolution," *English Literary History* 76 (2009), 49–73.

69. See Anna Trapnel, *The Cry of a Stone, or a Relation of Something Spoken in Whitehall* (London, 1654), and *Anna Trapnel's Report and Plea, or, A Narrative of Her Journey from London into Cornwal* (London, 1654).

70. Susanna Parr, *Susanna's Apology against the Elders* (n.p., 1659).

71. Elinor Channel, *A Message from God, by a Dumb Woman to His Highness* (n.p., 1654), citation 2. Arise Evans also took this opportunity to publish his own visions. Perhaps the utterances of women were more likely to sell than those of men.

72. Douglas, *Appeale to High Court.*

73. Mary Pope, *A Treatise of Magistry* ([London], 1647); Elizabeth Poole, *A Vision, Wherein Is Manifested the Disease and Cure of the Kingdome* (London, 1648); Poole, *An Alarum of War Given to the Army* (London, 1649); Poole, *Another Alarum of War*

Given to the Army (London, 1649). See Manfred Brod, "Politics and Prophecy in Seventeenth-Century England: The Case of Elizabeth Poole," *Albion* 31 (1999), 395–412. Ludlow, "Arise and Be Doing," 196–200, provides an account of the relationship of Pope and Poole with Parliament.

74. Channel, *Message from God*.

75. Chidley, *Justification of Independent Churches*. Ludlow, "Arise and Be Doing," devotes an entire chapter to Chidley; see 119–126 on Chidley as Leveller and author of the anonymous *The Humble Petition of Divers Wel-affected Women* (London, 1649), dated April 23, 1649.

76. Mary Overton, *To the Right Honourable, the Knights, Citizens, and Burgesses of the Parliament of England . . . Petition of Mary Overton, Prisoner in Bridewell* (London, 1647). Many historians have suggested, with some justification, that the vast support of women for the Leveller movement was in part a personal devotion to the attractive personality of John Lilburne, Leveller leader, and partly due to family loyalties. While such ties were obviously present in the literature, the egalitarian principles of the Levellers might well have appealed to women. The question of preaching women and egalitarian politics is discussed later.

77. Mary Cary, *The Little Horns Doom and Downfall: Or a Scripture-Prophesie of King James, and King Charles, and of the Present Parliament Unfolded* (London, 1651), 39.

78. Trapnel, *Cry of a Stone*, 52.

79. See, for example, Eleanor [Douglas], *The Mystery of General Redemption* (n.p., 1647); [Douglas], *The Writ of Restitution* (n.p., 1648).

80. Capp, *Fifth Monarchy Men*, 82.

81. Clarendon State Papers II, 383, as cited in Thomas, "Women and the Civil War Sects," 47.

82. Mack, *Visionary Women*, 415–424.

83. Chidley, *Good Counsell*.

84. Chidley, *Justification of Independent Churches*; this particular discussion is found on p. 5. See also Chidley, *A New-Yeares Gift* and Ludlow, "Arise and Be Doing," 90–115, on Chidley's direct critique of Edwards on Independency.

85. Warren, *Spiritual Thrift*, 13, Warren, *Good Way Vindicated*, 15, 16.

86. Warren, *Warning-Peece from Heaven*.

87. See Winthrop, *Short Story*, 267, 268–269 (Titus 2:3–5 and Acts 19:26), 272–273 (Isaiah 30:20, 46:12–13; Jeremiah 46:28); "Examination of Hutchinson," 315, 330, 336–337.

88. Winthrop, *Short Story*, 301–302; "Report of the Trial," in Hall, *Antinomian Controversy*, 351–363. Texts cited here include Ecclesiastes 3:18–21; 1 Corinthians 6:19, 15:4; Hebrews 4; Luke 19:10; 1 Corinthians 6; Matthew 10:28; 1 Thessalonians 5:23; 1 Peter 3:19; Isaiah 53:10–11; John 12; 1 Corinthians 4:16, 15:37–44; Romans 6:1, 2–7.

89. Douglas, *Blasphemous Charge against Her*, 9, 10. For similar references, see the following Douglas publications: *Appeale to High Court* and, especially, *Apocalypse Ch. 11 Yt Accomplishment Shewed from the Lady Eleanor* (n.p., 1641) and *The Everlasting Gospel* (n.p., 1649), in which Douglas explicitly deconstructs the prophecies of Daniel and Revelation.

90. Elizabeth Avery, *Scripture Prophecies Opened* (London, 1647).

91. Poole, *Vision*; Warren, *Warning Peece from Heaven*, 40.

92. Parr, *Susanna's Apology*, 11, 23, "To the Reader," 3, 27, 51, 68, 92, 79, 83, 106, 104, 107, 112.

93. Margaret Fell, *Womens Speaking Justified, Proved and Allowed of by the Scriptures* (London, 1667), 5–9, 14, 15. The text is 1 Corinthians 3:5.

94. Margaret Fell, *The Standard of the Lord Revealed* (n.p., 1667). The section on 2 Kings is 68–85.

95. Hilary Hinds makes this argument in her edition of *The Cry of a Stone* (Tempe: Arizona Center for Medieval and Renaissance Studies, 2000), 85, n. 16.

96. Hinds, *Cry of a Stone*, 11, 14, 16–17, 47, 49, 58. The identification of specific citations is Hinds's. A huge volume of Trapnel's prophecies, a folio of more than a thousand pages (n.p., 1659), incorporates similar levels of scriptural citation, although no editor has taken on the gargantuan task of editing this tome. This volume is held at the Bodleian Library, Oxford University, and will hereafter be referred to as "Poetical Addresses."

97. Hutchinson as quoted by John Winthrop, *Short Story*, 273. This discussion is also reported in "Examination of Hutchinson," in Hall, *Antinomian Controversy*, 337.

98. Spoken by William Bartholomew, deputy of Ipswich, at her state trial, "Examination of Hutchinson," in Hall, *Antinomian Controversy*, 338.

99. Como, "Women, Prophecy, and Authority," 215–216.

100. See especially, Eleanor Davies Douglas, *The Excommunication out of Paradise* ([London]: John Feild, 1647); Douglas, *The Everlasting Gospel* (n.p., 1649); Douglas, *The Serpents Excommunication* (n.p., 1651); Douglas, *Blasphemous Charge against Her*; Douglas, *Appeale to High Court*; Douglas, *Day of Judgements Modell* (n.p., 1646); Douglas, *New Jerusalem at Hand*; Douglas, *Apocalypse*, Ch. 11.

101. This stands as a revealing and, I believe, surprising ethnocentric premise. It is strange enough that despite British merchant networks and colonizing efforts, Asia, Africa, and America were fairly peripheral to English cosmology. However, Europe had been enmeshed in a devastating war since 1618, and many Europeans saw and wrote about the Thirty Years War in apocalyptic terms. Despite connections to world networks, the English, like other Europeans, were still inwardly focused.

102. Anne Gargill, *A Warning to All the World* (London, 1656), 1–2.

103. Mary Cary, *The Resurrection of the Witness* (London, 1649), 1–3, "To the Reader," 12, 87–88. On Mary Cary and her extensive, intelligent use of biblical texts, see David Loewenstein, "Scriptural Exegesis, Female Prophecy, and the Radical Politics in Mary Cary," *Studies in English Literature, 1500–1900* 46 (2006), 133–153.

104. Avery, *Scripture Prophecies Opened*, 3, 4.

105. Trapnel, *Cry of a Stone*, 5. Absalom, one of the sons of David, king of Israel, sought to build a following, through deceit, to take the kingship from his father. 2 Samuel 15.

106. Trapnel, *Report and Plea*, 20ff.

107. Ludlow, "Arise and Be Doing," 115–119. Ludlow also mentions Dorothy Hazzard (115), whose work is discussed in greater detail in Clare Cross, "'He-Goats before the Flocks': A Note on the Part Played by Some Women in the Founding of Some Civil War Churches," *Studies in Church History* 8 (1972), 195–202.

108. Warren, *Spiritual Thrift*, 2.

109. "Report of the Trial," in Hall, *Antinomian Controversy*, 370; Winthrop, *Short Story*, 308.

110. Parr, *Susanna's Apology*, 6.

111. Parr, *Susanna's Apology*, 4; Lewis Stucley, *Manifest Truth: Or an Inversion of Truth's Manifest* (London, 1658), 43. *Susanna's Apology* also repeats these charges on p. 75–76.

112. Parr, *Susanna's Apology*, 8–11, 81–82. According to Parr's account, her vote against accepting specific individuals was fully justified by later events—one became a "papist," another a Quaker.

113. Parr, *Susanna's Apology*, 15–17, 29, 36, 38, 39–40.

114. Toby Allein, *Truths Manifest* (London, 1658); Stucley, *Manifest Truth*; Thomas Mall, *A True Account of What Was Done by a Church of Christ in Exon* (London, 1658); Toby Allein, *Truths Manifest Revived* (London, 1659).

115. Poole, *Another Alarum of War*.

116. Thomas Parker, *The Copy of a Letter . . . to . . . Elizabeth Avery* (London, 1650), 5.

117. Chidley, *Justification of Independent Churches*, 26.

118. Mack, "Women as Prophets"; Trapnel, "Poetical Addresses," 211.

119. Winthrop, *Short Story*, 269.

120. Fell, *Womens Speaking Justified*, 8.

121. Trapnel, "Poetical Addresses," 424, 425.

122. As noted earlier, the verses are Hebrews 10, Titus, possibly chapter 3, Malachi 3:16, and 1 Peter 4:10.

123. E. T., *Diotrephes Detected, Corrected, and Rejected* (London, 1658), 6–7.

124. Trapnel, *Cry of a Stone*, 25; Avery, *Scripture Prophecies Opened*, "To the Reader," 1.

125. Preface to Trapnel, *Report and Plea*, 2. On Anna Trapnel's sense of self and her centrality as speaker, see Susannah B. Mintz, "The Specular Self of 'Anna Trapnel's Report and Plea,'" *Pacific Coast Philology* 35 (2000), 1–16.

126. Letter from T. P. in Poole, *An Alarum of War*, 9.

127. Channel, *Message from God*, 2; Avery, *Scripture Prophecies Opened*, "To the Reader," 1; Trapnel, *Cry of a Stone*, 16.

128. Cary, *Resurrection of the Witness*, 135–136, 134.

129. Fell, *Womens Speaking Justified*, 12.

Chapter 6

1. The variety of these colonizers' cosmologies and intentions was laid out by Breen, *Transgressing the Bounds*. These differences were discussed in greater detail in chapter 2.

2. In fact, the unity of Scottish clerics was less about polity and theology than a general agreement to reject the authority of the Church of England over Scotland. For Scottish Presbyterians, the Westminster Assembly was far more significant than for the English. The Westminster Confession and Catechism became foundational to the Presbyterian Church of Scotland, but far less significant to English dissenters.

3. Winthrop, *Short Story*, and Cotton, *Way of Congregational Churches*, were both written in defense of Massachusetts's congregational system.

4. These groups were discussed in detail in chapter 5. Fifth Monarchists were condemned because they challenged the rightful authority of the Commonwealth government, calling for the recognition of a monarchy of Jesus Christ.

5. Details of the harsh treatment of Quakers in New England are recorded in George Fox, *To the Parliament of the Commonwealth of England* (n.p., ca. 1659). On Austin, Fisher, and Burden, see George Bishop, *New England Judged, by the Spirit of the Lord. In Two Parts* (1661; 1667; reprint, London, 1703), 3–13, 47–50, citation 48.

6. Initially, Miller, *New England Mind: From Colony to Province*, articulated an argument for magistrates struggling to maintain orthodoxy and order, though he lays this out for the Hutchinsonian controversy and provides almost no discussion of the Quaker threat; the theme was picked up in relation to Quakers by Jonathan Chu, *Neighbors, Friends, or Madmen: The Puritan Adjustment to Quakerism in Seventeenth-Century Massachusetts* (Westport, CT: Greenwood Press, 1985). Carla Gardina Pestana, "The City upon a Hill under Siege: The Puritan Perception of the Quaker Threat to Massachusetts Bay, 1656–1661," *New England Quarterly* 56 (1983), 323–353, although sympathetic to the Quakers, provides convincing evidence that far from docile, quiet, and minding their own business, early Quaker practices were generally disruptive of peace and order.

7. On the legal circumstances surrounding the penalties and enforcement of Quakers' banishment, see Nan Goodman, *Banished: Common Law and the Rhetoric of Social Exclusion in Early New England* (Philadelphia: University of Pennsylvania Press, 2012), especially 86–114.

8. Leaving aside the validity of the charges, as discussed in the earlier chapters, the magistrates were responding to specific disruptions within the colony.

9. Fox, *To the Parliament*; Bishop, *New England Judged*; John Norton, *The Heart of New England Rent at the Blasphemies of the Present Generation* (London, 1660).

10. The escalating brutality of acts passed against Quakers can be found in Shurtleff, *Records of Massachusetts Bay*, 3:415–416, 4.1:277–278, 308–309, 321, 345–347. These acts were also published in a series of broadsides. See, for example, *A Declaration of the General Court of Massachusetts* (Boston, 1659).

11. Nuttall, *Holy Spirit*; Rufus M. Jones, *Spiritual Reformers in the Sixteenth and Seventeenth Centuries* (Boston: Beacon Press, 1914), and *Mysticism and Democracy*. So, too, Winship, *Making Heretics*, 240–242, notes that aspects of Quaker spirituality worked in tandem with New England spiritual sensibilities, though he underscores the differences, while I see the similarities as primary.

12. Francis Howgill, "The Glory of the True Church Discovered, as It Was in Its Purity in the Primitive Times" (1661), reprinted in *The Dawnings of the Gospel-Day, and Its Light and Glory Discovered* (London, 1676), 401–496, citation 433.

13. Margaret Fell, *A Touch-Stone, or, A Perfect Tryal by the Scriptures* (London 1667), 30.

14. George Fox, *A Warning to the World* (London, 1655), 8.

15. Priscilla Cotton and Mary Cole, *To the Priests and People of England* (London, 1655), 4, 3.

16. Fell, *Touch-Stone*, 15–16.

17. "Examination of Hutchinson," in Hall, *Antinomian Controversy*, 336. The passage cited is Hebrews 9:16: "For where a testament is, there must be the death of him that made the testament." *Geneva Bible*, NT leaf 104. The meaning Hutchinson is pulling from the text is clear from the preceding verse, Hebrews 9:15: "And for this cause is he the Mediatour of the new Testament, that through death which was for the redemption of the transgressions that were in the former Testament, they were called, might receive the promes of eternal inheritance."

18. Esther Biddle, *The Trumpet of the Lord Sounded Forth unto These Three Nations* (London, 1662), 15.

19. Sarah Blackborow, *A Visit to the Spirit in Prison* (London, 1658), 7; Mary Dyer, Petition to the General Court of Massachusetts Bay, October 26, 1659, Massachusetts State Archives.

20. Margaret Fell, *A True Testimony from the People of God* (London, 1660), 6.

21. George Fox, *Primitive Ordination and Succession of Bishops, Deacons, Pastors, and Teachers in the Church of Christ* (n.p., 1675), 31.

22. Blackborow, *Visit to the Spirit*, 5.

23. October 14, 1656, in Shurtleff, *Records of Massachusetts Bay*, 4.1:277.

24. Francis Howgill, "The Heart of New-England Hardened through Wickedness" (1659), as reprinted in *Dawnings of Gospel-Day*, 304.

25. George Fox, *Possession above Profession* (n.p., 1675), 4.

26. Francis Howgill, *The Popish Inquisition New Erected in New England whereby Their Church Is Manifested to Be a Daughter of Mysterie-Babylon* (London, 1659), 46–47.

27. George Fox, *New-England-Fire-Brand Quenched* (London, 1678), 23.

28. "Examination of Hutchinson," in Hall, *Antinomian Controversy*, 337.

29. Mary Stout, "Reply to William Haworth's Answer," published after *The Testimony of the Hartford Quakers* (n.p., 1676), 41.

30. Fell, *True Testimony*, 7.

31. Blackborow, *Visit to the Spirit*, 6.

32. Fell, *Standard of the Lord*, 105.

33. George Fox, Epistle 79, 1654, in *A Collection of Many Select and Christian Epistles* (London, 1698), 2:71.

34. Blackborow, *Visit to the Spirit*, 5, 10–11.

35. Fox, Epistle 35, 1653, in *Collection of Christian Epistles*, 2:31.

36. Margaret Vivers et al., *The Saints Testimony Finishing through Sufferings* (London, 1655), 8, 3–4, 10. See Catie Gill, "Evans and Cheever's *A Short Relation* in Context: Flesh, Spirit, and Authority in Quaker Prison Writings, 1650–1662," *Huntington Library Quarterly* 72 (2009), 265–269.

37. Hutchinson's speech as recorded in Winthrop, *Short Story*, 268, 267; Margret Killin and Barbara Patison, *A Warning from the Lord to the Teachers and People of Plimoth* (London, 1656), 1; Vivers et al., *Saints Testimony*, 15. Although not explicitly identified, internal evidence points to Margaret Vivers as the speaker.

38. George Fox, *Concerning Revelation, Prophecy, Measure, and Rule* (n.p., 1676), 24–25; Margaret Fell, *The Daughter of Sion Awakened* (n.p., 1677), 16. See also George Fox, *The Woman Learning in Silence* (London, 1656).

39. Fell, *Womens Speaking Justified*.

40. Fell, *Womens Speaking Justified*, 3. See Foxe, *Acts and Monuments*, 5:550–551; John Bale, "Preface" to Askew, *Lattre Examinacion*.

41. Fell, *Womens Speaking Justified*, 5–7. She picks up this discussion again on p. 11.

42. Fell, *Womens Speaking Justified*, 7–8, citation 8.

43. Fell, *Womens Speaking Justified*, 11–12, citation 12. On the contradictions found in 1 Corinthians, also see, Fox, Epistle 199, 1661, in *A Collection of Epistles*, 2:155–156.

44. "Portsmouth Compact," March 7, 1637/38, in Chapin, *Documentary History of Rhode Island*, 2:19.

45. Henry Vane to Inhabitants of Providence, February 8, 1653/54, in Bartlett, *Records of the Colony*, 1:285.

46. Roger Williams to Henry Vane, August 27, 1654, in *Records of the Colony of Rhode Island*, 1:287–288.

47. Winthrop, *Journal*, 363–364. This is the only record of Easton's "theology"; Winthrop's distance from Newport, and his scorn for Easton as a tanner, what some might call a "mechanick preacher," renders this report on the theology suspect, particularly since Easton might be better thought of as a master craftsman. He rose in prominence in Rhode Island quite early, serving as assistant to Coddington and later as president (1650, 1651, and 1654) and governor (1672–74) of the colony. The note did, in fact, follow Winthrop's report that "Mrs. Hutchinson and those of Aquiday island broached new heresies every year" (362–363).

48. Shurtleff, *Records of Massachusetts Bay*, 1642, 2:3. See also Winthrop, *Journal*, January 27, 1642, 386–387.

49. William Aspinwall, *A Brief Description of the Fifth Monarchy, or Kingdome, That Shortly Is to Come into the World* (London, 1653). See also his *Thunder from Heaven against Back-Sliders, and Apostates of the Times. In Some Meditations on the 24 Chapter of Isaiah* (London, 1655) and *The Legislative Power Is Christ's Peculiar Prerogative—Proved from the 9th of Isaiah, Vers. 6.7* (London, 1656).

50. Groome, *Glass for the People*.

51. Exchange between Thomas Leverett and Anne Hutchinson, March 1643, as printed in Groome, *Glass for the People*, 9–10.

52. Groome, *Glass for New England*, 3–8, citations 4, 7, 8.

53. Fox, *To the Parliament*, 10.

54. *Rhode Island Court Records: Records of the Court of Trials of the Colony of Providence Plantations, 1647–1662* (Providence, 1920), March 131656/57, 26. The group included husband Richard Scott, Robert West, Ann Williams, and Rebecca Throckmorton. No one came to "make good the charge against them," and they were acquitted.

55. See Christopher Holder, "A Warning from the Spirit of the Lord. To the Governor & Magistrates: & People of the Massachusetts Bay," September 1, 1650, printed in *Transactions of the Colonial Society of Massachusetts* 8:72. He and John Copeland returned to England and successfully argued the case of the Quakers before King Charles II.

56. Sarah Birckhead, in her sketch "Governor William Coddington," *Bulletin of Newport Historical Society* 5 (1913), 19, noted Coddington had "discovered in the doctrine of

Interior Light an affinity with the doctrine of Grace which he had long entertained, and traced in his own mind to the early teaching of John Cotton. "

57. William Coddington, *The Demonstration of True Love unto You the Ruleres of the Colony of the Massachusetts in New England* (London, 1674), 5–6, citation 6.

58. Coddington, *Demonstration of True Love*, 5.

59. Coddington, *Demonstration of True Love*, 7; reference to inquisition at Malaga, 11.

60. Coddington, *Demonstration of True Love*, 13, 10.

61. Coddington, *Demonstration of True Love*, 12, 16.

62. Coddington, *Demonstration of True Love*, 17.

63. Dyer, Petition to the General Court, 1659.

64. Coddington, *Demonstration of True Love*, 8. The boasting officer is Major Humphrey Atherton, at this point assistant governor of Massachusetts.

65. Coddington, *Demonstration of True Love*, 9.

66. See Bishop, *New England Judged*, 305–306. Some historians have seen Bishop as the first to chronicle the sufferings of the Quakers in New England; many accounts, published after, appear to have significant chunks of text— whole paragraphs— recounting incidents taken from Bishop. The similarities in the details of Atherton's death might argue for Coddington borrowing from Bishop, or it might reflect a memorable story told and repeated among Quakers.

67. Mary Dyer, as a representative woman dissenter, or heretic, is rarely discussed. Most often she appears as an example of Massachusetts's persecution of Quakers or in essays concerning monstrous births, such as Valerius, "So Manifest a Sign." Anne G. Myles takes exception to this, framing Mary Dyer as an important woman in early New England history. See her "From Monster to Martyr: Re-presenting Mary Dyer," *Early American Literature* 36 (2001), 1–30.

68. Winthrop, *Journal*, March 27, 1638, 253. See also Winthrop, *Short Story*, 280–282.

69. Bishop, *New England Judged*, 205.

70. See William Robinson and William Leddra, *Several Epistles Given Forth by Two of the Lords Faithful Servants* (London, 1669); Marmaduke Stephenson, *A Call from Death to Life* (1669).

71. Bishop, *New England Judged*, 157.

72. Shurtleff, *Records of Massachusetts Bay*, October 14, 1656, 3:415–416, citation 416.

73. Shurtleff, *Records of Massachusetts Bay*, October 14, 1657, 4.1:308–309. As noted earlier, these acts were also published in a series of broadsides between 1656 and 1662. Despite the threat, I have not come across any evidence that the last penalty was performed in Massachusetts. As frustrations increased, the court chose to take the final step of execution.

74. Shurtleff, *Records of Massachusetts Bay*, October 19, 1658, 4.1:345–346.

75. Shurtleff, *Records of Massachusetts Bay*, October 18, 1659, 4.1:385, 384.

76. [Edward Burrough], *A Declaration of the Sad and Great Persecution and Martyrdom of the People of God, Called Quakers, in New England* (London, [1660]), 25.

77. Burrough, *Declaration of the Persecution*, 28–29; Shurtleff, *Records of Massachusetts Bay*, May 30, 1660, 4.1:419.

78. Dyer, Petition to the Court, 1659.

79. Burrough, *Declaration of the Persecution*, 28. See also Bishop, *New England Judged*, 310–312.

80. Burrough, "The Words of Mary Dyar upon the Ladder," in his *Declaration of the Persecution*, 29–30.

81. William Dyer, Petition, September 6, 1659, in *Two Letters of William Dyer of Rhode Island, 1659–1660*, facsimile of transcript (Cambridge, MA, n.d.).

82. Francis Howgill, "To All Friends and Brethren Who Have Been Called of the Lord into That Place of New-England" (1660), reprinted in *Dawnings of Gospel-Day*, 369.

83. See Michele Lise Tarter, "Quaking in the Light: The Politics of Quaker Women's Corporeal Prophecy in the Seventeenth Century Transatlantic World," in *A Centre of Wonders: The Body in Early America*, ed. Janet Moore Lindman and Michele Lise Tarter (Ithaca, NY: Cornell University Press, 2001), 145–162, for an excellent discussion of torture as text within the brutality of Quaker experience.

84. Shurtleff, *Records of Massachusetts Bay*, October 18, 1659, 4.1:384–386, citations 384–385, 386.

85. Shurtleff, *Records of Massachusetts Bay*, 4.1:384–390, citation 387; Howgill, "Heart of New-England Hardened," 306.

86. Shurtleff, *Records of Massachusetts Bay*, October 18, 1659, 4.1:389–390, citation 390.

87. Isaac Penington, *An Examination of the Grounds or Causes, Which Are Said to Induce the Court of Boston in New England to Make That Order or Law of Banishment against the Quakers* (London, 1660), 38–39. For an engaging, perceptive analysis of Quakers' intersectional theological and political goals, see Goodman, *Banished*, 86–114.

88. *Declaration of the General Court of Massachusetts* (1659).

89. Shurtleff, *Records of Massachusetts Bay*, October 14, 1656, 3:417–418.

90. Norton, *Heart of New England Ren*.

91. Pestana, *Quakers and Baptists*, 25–43, provides an exceptional introduction to the activities and the official response to this growing community. While I am discussing only the cases that came before the General Court, much of the disciplinary action was taken by county courts, in the case of Salem, Essex County.

92. Bishop, *New England Judged*, 43, 57–60. The pages following deal with the torture meted out to Brend and Leddra. This meeting also came to the attention of Essex County Court, May 1658, where twenty-two residents were brought to court, sent to the house of correction, or fined for attending a Quaker meeting and failing to attend church meeting on the Lord's Day. Dow, *Records of Essex County*, May 1658, 103–105; July 1658, 110.

93. Shurtleff, *Records of Massachusetts Bay*, October 19, 1658, 4.1:349; May 11, 1659, 4.1:366. Bishop, *New England Judged*, 109, noted that the court tried to sell them "not among yourselves, but into other Plantations; not a Servants in your Houses, but as Slaves to others." He noted that no ships would carry them. The General Court records do not include the phrase "as slaves," indicating that the two would have been bound as servants, a dire enough fate.

94. Shurtleff, *Records of Massachusetts Bay*, November 12, 1659, 4.1:406–407. "Ingenious" should probably be read "ingenuous."

95. Dow, *Records of Essex County*, July 1658, 2:109–110; June 1660, 2:219; June 1661, 2:314. Phelps's fine was paid by William Flint.

96. Burrough, *Declaration of the Persecution*, 17–20, citations 17, 19, 18. Bold face type is in the original. The aged couple was probably Laurence and Cassandra Southwicke, whose age and reputation are mentioned frequently in the print materials.

97. Burrough, *Declaration of the Persecution*, 18. Bold face type is in the original.

98. Fox, *To the Parliament*, 1.

99. *New England a Degenerate Plant* (London, 1659), citing actions by the General Court in May and October 1658. These actions can be found in Shurtleff, *Records of Massachusetts Bay*, May 19, 1658, 4.1:321; October 19, 1658, 4.1:345–346.

100. *New England's Ensign* (London, 1659), 7; see also Fox, *To the Parliament*, 1–2; Bishop, *New England Judged*, 12.

101. *New England's Ensign*, 12.

102. Thomas Underhill, *Hell Broke Loose, or the History of the Quakers* (London, 1660), as quoted in Howgill, *Dawnings of Gospel-Day*, 289, 296.

103. Joseph Grove, "Preface" to Bishop, *New England Judged*.

104. General Court, October 1658, as cited in R. A. Lovell, *Sandwich a Cape Cod Town* (Sandwich, MA. Town of Sandwich, 1984), 91. The fast day is also discussed in Frederick Freeman, *The History of Cape Cod: The Annals of Barnstable County and of Its Several Towns* (Boston, 1860), 1:229.

105. Extract from *Mercurius Politicus* 341, no. 2 (1656), in Frederick Gay Lewis Collection, Massachusetts Historical Society.

106. Bishop, *New England Judged*, 102, noted discomfort with these decisions, including twelve deputies dissenting about the law setting up a special jury of three magistrates. According to Bishop, they wanted a standard trial by jury.

107. Shurtleff, *Records of Massachusetts Bay*, November 27, 1661, 4.2:34.

108. Record of the examination before the General Court, in Frederick Gay Lewis Collection, Massachusetts Historical Society.

109. "Report of the Trial," in Hall, *Antinomian Controversy*, 372.

110. From Mary Traske and Margaret Smith to John Endicott and others, December 21, 1660, Massachusetts State Archives, photostat copy, Massachusetts Historical Society.

Chapter 7

1. Hutchinson's self-revelation can be found in Winthrop, *Short Story*, 268–273, and "Examination of Hutchinson," in Hall, *Antinomian Controversy*, 336–338, citations 268, 272.

2. Romans 11:33. From *Geneva Bible*, NT leaf 73.

3. The clearest articulation of this system is found in Morgan, *Puritan Family*.

4. Again, this is the experiential piety explored in Perry Miller's illuminating early chapters in his *New England Mind: The Seventeenth Century*, 3–108.

5. Avery, *Scripture Prophecies Opened*, 21.

6. Hutchinson, cited in Winthrop, *Short Story*, 268; Dyer, Petition to the General Court, 1659.

7. See, for example, Taylor, *Works*, 152–153; Gouge, *Of Domesticall Duties*, 44–46, 273–278, 346–348; Gataker, *Marriage Duties Briefely Couched*, 8–14, 33–34; Rodgers, *Matrimonial Honour*, 162, 253–255. Barker-Benfield, "Anne Hutchinson," provides an excellent outline of the changing Puritan focus from Christ the Bridegroom to God the Father.

8. Introduction to "An Excellent Song Which Was Salomons," *Geneva Bible*, OT leaf 280.

9. John Cotton, *A Brief Exposition with Practical Observations upon the Whole Book of Canticles* (London, 1655); Hooker, *The Unbelievers Preparing*, 72; Shepard, *God's Plot*, 1st ed., 45. Porterfield, *Female Piety*, has identified a superfluity of these sexual allusions in the writings of Cotton, Hooker, and Shepard.

10. John Lilburne, *A Work of the Beast* (1638), 8 as cited in Mack, *Visionary Women*, 49.

11. Trapnel, "Poetical Addresses," 348–349; Trapnel, *Report and Plea*, 47, 9.

12. Winthrop, *Short Story*, 273, also quoted in "Examination of Hutchinson," in Hall, *Antinomian Controversy*, 337; Parr, *Susanna's Apology*, 21; Anne Wentworth, *A Vindication of Anne Wentworth* ([London], 1677), 9, similar reference on 4.

13. Bradstreet, "Meditations Divine and Moral," no. 67, in *Works of Anne Bradstreet*, 288; Bradstreet, "As Weary Pilgrim Now at Rest," August 31, 1669, in *Works of Anne Bradstreet*, 295.

14. Edward Taylor, "Meditation. Cant. 4.8. My Spouse," in *Poems of Edward Taylor*, 39.

15. Bynum, *Jesus as Mother* and *Fragmentation and Redemption*, 35.

16. Again, Porterfield, *Female Piety*, 40–79, points up the importance of the language of male/divine aggression and female/human humiliation in religious discourse.

17. Ironically, most studies of Puritan piety do not discuss female piety, despite the predominance of women among sectarians. While Thomas, "Women and the Civil War Sects," Mack, "Women as Prophets," and Mary Dunn, "Saints and Sisters: Congregational and Quaker Women in the Early Colonial Period," *American Quarterly* 30 (1978), 582–601, have focused essays upon female religious activity in old and New England, few historians have incorporated female experience into general studies. Exceptions include Foster, "New England," and Gura, *Glimpse of Sion's Glory*; Porterfield, *Female Piety*; and, most recently, Traister, *Female Piety*.

18. I have identified more than thirty prophetic or preaching women who either had their writings published or were identified by name in the publications of others; many more have been identified in church records and the polemical literature, and this does not include the more than one hundred women who were known as prophets, missionaries, and writers among Quakers. A fairly complete list of female prophets can be found in Mack, *Visionary Women*, appendix, 413–420. See also Ludlow, "Arise and Be Doing."

19. Niclaes, *Terra Pacis*, 123; see also Niclaes, *Prophecy of the Spirit* and Niclaes, *Revelatio Dei*.

20. *A Discovery of 29 Sects Here in London* (London, 1641), 4. For similar comments on familists, see Pagitt, *Heresiography*, 82–87.

21. Draper, *Plain and Faithfull Discovery*, 4.

22. Eaton, *Most Dangerous Dead Faith*, 119–120.

23. Samuel Yarb, *A New Sect of Religion Descryed, Called Adamites* (n.p., 1641); *A Nest of Serpents Discovered* (n.p., 1641); *The Routing of the Ranters* (n.p., [1641]), 2; *Strange News from Newgate and the Old Baily* (London, 1651), 4.

24. John Cotton's admonition, "Report of the Trial," in Hall, *Antinomian Controversy*, 372.

25. *The Anatomy of the Separatists* (London, 1642), 3; Edward Harris, *A True Relation of a Company of Brownists* (n.p., 1641), 1. See also *The Brownist Haeresies Confuted, Their Knavery Anatomized* (n.p., 1641); *The Brownist Synagogue* (n.p., 1641); *The Brothers of the Separation* (London, 1641).

26. "Report of the Trial," in Hall, *Antinomian Controversy*, 372.

27. Puritan radicalism crossed class as well as gender lines, and the extensive literature on English radicalism has been far more deeply engaged with class than gender. Moreover, when gender is raised, the evidence is usually considered as an episode apart from the narrative about class. The separation of class and gender into two interpretive categories is a mistake. Not only can one discuss both groups within the broad political language of disfranchised communities; but sexualized language was one of the rhetorical tools used to dismiss the lower classes. In describing the lower classes as vulgar, uncontrolled, irrational, and oversexed, the attackers were portraying the lower classes as women. On gender as the primary language of power and authority in seventeenth-century English culture, see Brown, *Good Wives, Nasty Wenches*. On religious radicalism and class, see Hill, *World Turned Upside Down*; Morton, *World of the Ranters*; Capp, *Fifth Monarchy Men*; McGregor and Reay, *Radical Religion*; Hill, Reay, and Lamont, *World of the Muggletonians*; Dow, *Radicalism in the English Revolution*; Barry Reay, *The Quakers and the English Revolution* (London: Palgrave Macmillan, 1985).

Chapter 8

1. *New York Times*, September 18, 1930, 24.

2. S. E. Morison, "Review," *New England Quarterly* 3 (1930), 358–361. The three biographies include Rugg, *Unafraid*; Curtis, *Anne Hutchinson*; Augur, *American Jezebel*.

3. Winthrop, *Short Story*; Cotton, *Way of Congregational Churches*.

4. Johnson, *Wonder-Working Providence*, 95–112, citation 100.

5. Cotton Mather, *Magnalia Christi Americana, or, the Ecclesiastical History of New-England*, 2 vol. (1702; Hartford: Silas Andres and Son, 1853). His account takes up four pages, 2:517–520, with the citations on 2:517. The Priscilla (Acts 18) reference is in Winthrop, *Short Story*, 268.

6. Revelation 2:20, *Geneva Bible*, NT leaf 115.

7. Hutchinson, *History of the Colony*, 3 vols 1:380–532, citations 1: 382, 395.controversy covers 55–57, 60–75, citation, 55.

8. Hawthorne, "Mrs. Hutchinson."

9. Charles Francis Adams, *Three Episodes of Massachusetts History* (Boston: Houghton Mifflin, 1892), 380–532, citations 382, 395.

10. George Bancroft, *The History of the United States from the Discovery of the American Continent* (1855; Open Access: Palala Press, 2015), 385–394, citations 388, 391.

Bibliography

Manuscripts Sources

Belknap Papers, Massachusetts Historical Society.

Cotton Family Papers, Prince Collection, Boston Public Library.

Frederick Gay Lewis Collection, Massachusetts Historical Society.

Greenough Collection, Massachusetts Historical Society.

Holder, Christopher. "Warning to Massachusetts." 1659. Massachusetts Historical Society.

Hutchinson Papers, Massachusetts State Archives.

Keayne, Robert. Notebook; Sermon Notes 1627–1628; 1639–1642, Massachusetts Historical Society.

Winthrop Papers, Massachusetts Historical Society.

Miscellaneous Papers, Massachusetts State Archives and the Massachusetts Historical Society.

Published Editions of Manuscript Sources

Adams, Charles Francis ed., *Antinomianism in the Colony of Massachusetts Bay, 1636–1638.* Boston: Prince Society, 1894.

Bartlett, John Russell, ed. *Records of the Colony of Rhode Island and Providence Plantation, in New England.* Providence, RI, 1857.

Bradford, William. *History of Plimoth Plantation.* Boston: Wright & Potter, 1896.

Chapin, Harvard M. *The Documentary History of Rhode Island.* Providence, RI: Preston and Rounds, 1916.

Cott, Nancy F., ed. *Roots of Bitterness: Documents of the Social History of American Women.* New York: Dutton, 1972.

Demos, John, ed. *Remarkable Providences.* New York: G. Braziller, 1972.

Dyer, William. *Two Letters of William Dyer of Rhode Island, 1656–1660.* Facsimile of transcript. Cambridge, MA, n.d.

Hall, David D., ed. *The Antinomian Controversy, 1636–1638: A Documentary History.* 1968; Durham, NC: Duke University Press, 1990.

Hess, Karen, ed. *Martha Washington' Booke of Cookery.* New York: Columbia University Press, 1981.

Holder, Christopher. "A Warning from the Spirit of the Lord. To the Governor & Magistrates: & People of the Massachusetts Bay." 1659. *Transactions of the Colonial Society of Massachusetts* 8:72, 1903.

Hutchinson, Thomas. *History of the Colony and Province of Massachusetts Bay.* 2 vols. Boston, 1767.

Keayne, Robert. *The Apologia of Robert Keayne.* Ed. Bernard Bailyn. New York: Harper, 1965.

Kors, Alan Charles, and Edward Peters, eds. *Witchcraft in Europe, 400–1700: A Documentary History*. 2nd ed. Philadelphia: University of Pennsylvania Press, 2001.

Norton, Humphrey to John Endecott. Ed. Frederick E. Tolles. Reprint, from *Publick Intelligencer, Communicating te Chief Occcurencs and Proceedings within the Dominions of Englnd, Scotland, and Ireland,* 165 (February 21–28, 1659), 251–253. *Huntington Library Quarterly* 14 (1951), 415–421.

Plymouth Church Records, 1620–1859. Baltimore: Genealogical Publishing, 1975.

Records and Files of the Quarterly Courts of Essex County, Massachusetts, 1636–1683, 8. vols. Ed. George Francis Dow. Salem, MA: Essex Institute, 1911–21.

Records of the Colony of Rhode Island and Providence Plantations, in New England. Ed. John Russell Bartlett. Providence, RI: A. Crawford Greene and Brother, 1857.

Records of the Court of Trials of the Colony of Providence Plantations, 1647–1662. Providence, RI, 1920.

Records of the First Church in Boston, 1630–1868. Ed. Richard D. Pierce. Boston: Colonial Society of Massachusetts, 1961.

Records of the First Church of Salem, 1629–1736. Ed. Richard. D. Pierce. Salem, MA: Essex Institute, 1974.

Records of the Governor and Company of the Massachusetts Bay in New England. Ed. Nathaniel B. Shurtleff. Boston: W. White, 1853–54.

Records of Suffolk County Court, 1671–1680. Boston: Colonial Society of Massachusetts, 1933.

Selement, George, and Bruce C. Woolley, eds. *Thomas Shepard's Confessions.* Boston: Colonial Society of Massachusetts, 1981.

Sewall, Samuel. *Diary of Samuel Sewall.* Ed. M. Halsey Thomas. New York: Farrar, Straus and Giroux, 1973.

Shepard, Thomas. *God's Plot: The Paradoxes of Puritan Piety.* Ed. Michael McGiffert. Amherst: University of Massachusetts Press, 1972.

Testimony of the Hartford Quakers. n.p., 1676.

Town Records of Salem, Massachusetts. 2 vols. Salem, MA: Essex Institute, 1868, 1913.

Winthrop Papers. 5 vols. Boston: Massachusetts Historical Society, 1929–47; New York: Russell & Russell, 1968.

Winthrop, John. *The Journal of John Winthrop, 1630–1649.* Ed. Richard S. Dunn, James Savage, and Laetitia Yeandle. Cambridge, MA: Harvard University Press, 1996.

Winthrop, John. *A Modell of Christian Charity* (1630). In *The Puritans: Sourcebook of Their Writings,* ed. Perry Miller and Thomas H. Johnson. 1938; New York: Harper and Row, 1963.

Pamphlets and Books

Allein, Toby. *Truths Manifest.* London, 1658.

Allein, Toby. *Truths Manifest Revived.* London, 1659.

The Anatomy of the Separatists. London, 1642.

Anti-quakerism, or, A Character of the Quakers Spirit. London, 1659.

Aspinwall, William. *A Brief Description of the Fifth Monarchy, or Kingdome, That Shortly Is to Come into the World.* London, 1653.

Aspinwall, William. *The Legislative Power is Christ's Peculiar Prerogative—Proved from the 9th of Isaiah, Vers. 6.7.* London, 1656.

Aspinwall, William. *Thunder from Heaven against Back-Sliders, and Apostates of the Times. In Some Meditations on the 24 Chapter of Isaiah.* London, 1655.

Askew, Anne. *The First Examinacyon of Anne Askew, Lately Martyred in Smythfelde by the Romysh Popes Upholders, with Elucydacyon of Johan Bale.* Wesel, 1546.

Askew, Anne. *The Lattre Examinacion of the Worthye Servaunt of God Mastres Anne Askewe.* Wesel, 1547.

Avery, Elizabeth. *Scripture Prophecies Opened.* London, 1647.

[Aylett, R.] *Susanna, or the Arraignment of the Two Unjust Elders.* London, 1654.

Aylett, R. *A Wife, Not Ready Made but Bespoken.* London, 1653.

Baillie, Robert. *Anabaptism.* London, 1647.

Baillie, Robert. *A Dissuasive from the Errours of the Time.* London, 1645.

Barrett, R. *A Companion for Midwives.* London, 1699.

Bastwick, John. *The Storming of the Anabaptists Garrisons.* London, 1647.

Bastwick, John. *The Utter Routing of the Whole Army of All the Independents & Sectaries.* London, 1646.

Bewick, John. *Answer to a Quaker's Seventeen Heads of Queries; Containing in Them Seventy-Seven Questions.* London, 1660.

Bewick, John. *An Antidote against Lay-Preaching.* London, 1642.

Biddle, Esther. *The Trumpet of the Lord Sounded Forth unto These Three Nations.* London, 1662.

Biddle, Esther. *A Warning from the Lord God of Life and Power, unto Thee, O City of London.* London, 1660.

Bishop, George. *New England Judged, by the Spirit of the Lord. In Two Parts.* 1661, 1667, reprint, London, 1703.

Blackborow, Sarah. *A Visit to the Spirit in Prison.* London, 1658.

Bourgeois, Louise. *Observations diverses . . .sur les accouchments, maladies des femmes, et des nouveaux naiz.* Paris, 1609.

[Bradshaw, William.] *English Puritanism.* [London], 1641.

Bradstreet, Anne. *The Works of Anne Bradstreet.* Ed. Jeannine Hensley. Cambridge, MA: Harvard University Press, 1967.

A Brief Narration of the Practices of the Churches in New-England. London, 1647.

Brightmans Predictions and Prophesies. n.p., 1641.

Brinsley, John. *A Looking-Glasse for Good Women.* London, 1645.

Brinsley, John. *Mystical Implantation: or, The Great Gospel Mystery of the Christian's Union and Communion with and Conformity to Jesus Christ.* London, 1652.

The Brothers of the Separation. London, 1641.

Brownist Haeresies Confuted, Their Knavery Anatomized. n.p., 1641.

The Brownist Synagogue. n.p., 1641.

The Brothers of the Separation. London, 1641.

Bulkeley, Peter. *The Gospel Covenant; or the Covenant of Grace Opened.* London, 1651.

Bullinger, Henrich. *The Christian State of Matrimonye.* Trans. Miles Coverdale. Translation of London, 1541.

[Burrough, Edward.] *A Declaration of the Sad and Great Persecution and Martyrdom of the People of God, Called Quakers, in New England.* n.p., [1660].

C., T. *Schismatickes Sifted through a Sieve of the Largest Size.* London, 1646.

Carter, Richard. *The Schismatic Stigmatized.* London, 1641.

Cary, Mary. *The Little Horns Doom and Downfall: Or a Scripture-Prophesie of King James, and King Charles, and of the Present Parliament Unfolded.* London, 1651.

Cary, Mary. *The Resurrection of the Witness.* London, 1648.

Channel, Elinor. *A Message from God, by a Dumb Woman to His Highness*. n.p., 1654.

Cheynell, Francis. *A Plot for the Good of Posterity*. London, 1646.

Chidley, Katherine. *Good Counsell, to the Petitioners for Presbyterian Government That They May Declare Their Faith before They Build Their Church*. London, 1645.

[Chidley, Katherine.] *The Humble Petition of Divers Wel-affected Women*. London, 1649.

Chidley, Katherine. *The Justification of the Independent Churches of Christ. Being an Answer to Mr. Edwards His Booke, Which Hee Hath Written against the Government of Christ's Church, and Toleration of Christs Publike Worship*. London, 1641.

Chidley, Katherine. *A New-Yeares Gift, or a Brief Exhortation to Mr. Thomas Edwards*. n.p., 1645.

Clark, John. *Ill Newes from New-England: or A Narative of New-Englands Persecution*. London, 1652; printed in *Collections of the Massachusetts Historical Society*, 4th series. Boston: Massachusetts Historical Society, 1854.

Clinton, Elizabeth. *The Countesse of Lincolnes Nurserie*. Oxford, 1622.

The Coblers End, or His (Last) Sermon. London, 1641.

Coddington, William. *A Demonstration of True Love unto You the Ruleres of the Colony of the Massachusets in New England*. London, 1674.

Cogan, Thomas. *The Haven of Health: Chiefly Gathered for the Comfort of Students, and Consequently of All Those That Have a Care of Their Health*. London, 1584.

Collins, Anne. *Divine Songs and Meditations*. 1653; Los Angeles: Clark Library, 1961.

A Confession of Faith of Seven Congregations. London, 1646.

Constantia Munda (pseud.). *The Worming of a Mad Dogg*. London, 1617.

Cotton, John. *The Bloudy Tenent Washed, and Made White in the Bloud of the Lambe*. London, 1647.

Cotton, John. *A Brief Exposition with Practical Observations upon the Whole Book of Canticles*. London, 1655.

Cotton, John. *A Conference Mr. Cotton Held at Boston with the Elders of New England*. London, 1646.

Cotton, John. *A Coppy of a Letter of Mr. Cotton of Boston*. n.p., 1641.

Cotton, John. *The Covenant of Gods Free Grace*. London, 1645.

Cotton, John. *The Covenant of Grace: Discovering the Great Work of a Sinners Reconciliation to God*. London, 1655.

Cotton, John. *Of the Holinesse of Church Members*. London, 1643.

Cotton, John. *A Reply to Mr. Williams His Examination*. London, 1647.

Cotton, John. *The Saints Support and Comfort*. London, 1658.

Cotton, John. *The Way of Congregational Churches Cleared*. London, 1648.

Cotton, Priscilla and Mary Cole. *To the Priests and People of England*. London, 1655.

The Country House-wives Garden, Containing Rules for Hearbs and Seeds of Common Use. 1637; Milford, CT: Rosetts E. Clarkson, 1940.

The Country House-wives Garden, Containing Rules for Hearbs and Seeds of Common Use . . . Together, with the Husbandry of Bees, Published with Secrets Very Necessary for Every House-wife. 1637; Milford, CT: Rosetta E. Clarkson, 1940.

Culpeper, Nicholas. *Culpeper's Directory for Midwives*. First and Second Parts. 1651; London, 1675/76.

Culpeper, Nicholas. *A Physical Directory*. London, 1651.

Dawson, Thomas. *The Good Huswifes Jewell* and *The Second Part of the Good Huswives Jewell*. London, 1596/97 bound together; facsimile, Norwood, NJ: Walter J. Johnson, 1977.

Deacon, John. *The Grand Imposter Examined*. London, 1657.

A Declaration of the General Court of Massachusetts. Boston, 1659.

A Declaration of the Present Sufferings of above 140 Persons of the People of God Called Quakers. London, 1659.

A Description of the Sect Called the Familie of Love. London, 1641.

A Discovery of 29 Sects Here in London. London, 1641.

A Discoverie of Six Women Preachers. [London], 1641.

A Discovery of a Swarme of Separatists. London, 1641.

Dod, John, and Robert Cleaver. *A Plaine and Familiar Exposition of the Ten Commandements.* London, 1615.

Dod, John, and William Hinde. *Bathshebas Instructions to her Sonne Lemuel.* London, 1614.

[Douglas], Eleanor. *Apocalypse, Chap. 11. Yt Accomplishment shewed from the Lady Eleanor.* n.p., [164–].

Douglas, Eleanor. *Appeale to the High Court of Parliament* and, especially, *Apocalypse Ch. 11 Yt Accomplishment Shewed from the Lady Eleanor.* n.p., 1641.

Douglas, Eleanor. *The Blasphemous Charge against Her.* n.p., 1636.

Douglas, Eleanor. *The Crying Charge.* n.p., 1649.

Douglas, Eleanor. *The Day of Judgments Modell.* n.p., 1646.

Douglas, Eleanor. *The Everlasting Gospel.* n.p., 1649.

Douglas, Eleanor. *The Excommunication out of Paradise.* [London], 1647.

Douglas, Eleanor. *The Gatehouse Salutation from the Lady Eleanor.* n.p., 1646.

Douglas, Eleanor. *Given to the Elector Prince Charles of the Rhyne.* Amsterdam, [1648]; reprinted in 1651 with notes regarding the fulfillment of the prophecy.

Douglas, Eleanor. *Hells Destruction.* n.p., 1651.

Douglas, Eleanor. *The Lady Eleanor, Her Appeale to the High Court of Parliament.* n.p., 1641.

[Douglas, Eleanor.] *The Mystery of General Redemption.* n.p., 1647.

Douglas, Eleanor. *The New Jerusalem at Hand.* n.p., 1649.

Douglas, Eleanor. *The Restitution of Prophecy; That Buried Talent to Be Revived.* n.p., 1651.

Douglas, Eleanor. *The Serpents Excommunication.* n.p., 1651.

[Douglas, Eleanor.] *The Writ of Restitution.* n.p., 1648.

Draper, Edward. *A Plain and Faithfull Discovery of a Beame in Master Edwards His Eye.* London, 1646.

Eaton, John. *The Discovery of the Most Dangerous Dead Faith.* London, 1641.

Eaton, John. *The Honey-combe of Free Justification by Christ Alone.* London, 1642.

Edwards, Thomas. *Antapologia: Or, A Full Answer to the Apologeticall Narration.* London, 1646.

Edwards, Thomas. *The Casting Down of the Last and Strongest Hold of Satan, or a Treatise against Toleration.* London, 1647.

Edwards, Thomas. *Gangraena.* 3 vols. London, 1646.

Edwards, Thomas. *Reasons against the Independent Government of Churches.* n.p., 1641.

Eighteen New-Court-Quaeries. London, 1659.

Elborow, John. *Euodias and Syntyche: Or, The Female Zelots of the Church of Philippi.* London, 1637.

Ellis, Humphrey. *Pseudochristus.* London, 1650.

Ester Sowerman (pseud.). *Ester Hath Hang'd Haman.* London, 1617.

False Prophets and False Teachers Described. n.p., [1652].

The Fanatick History: Or An Exact Relation and Account of the Old Anabaptists, and New Quakers. London, 1660.

Farmer, Ralph. *Sathan Inthron'd in His Chair of Pestilence.* London, 1657.

Fell, Margaret. *A Call to the Universall Seed of God.* n.p., 1665.

Fell, Margaret. *The Daughter of Sion Awakened.* n.p., 1677.

F[ell], M[argaret]. *A Declaration and an Information from Us the People of God Called Quakers.* London, 1660.

Fell, Margaret. *An Evident Demonstration to Gods Elect.* London, 1660.

Fell, Margaret. *A Letter Sent to the King.* n.p., 1666.

F[ell], M[argaret]. *A Paper Concerning Such as Are Made Ministers.* London, 1659.

Fell, Margaret. *The Standard of the Lord Revealed.* n.p., 1667.

[Fell, Margaret.] *This to the Clergy.* London, 1660.

Fell, Margaret. *A Touch-Stone, or, A Perfect Tryal by the Scriptures.* London, 1667.

Fell, Margaret. *A True Testimony from the People of God.* London, 1660.

Fell, Margaret. *Women's Speaking Justified, Proved and Allowed of by the Scriptures.* London, 1667.

Fell, Margaret, and George Fox. *The Examination and Tryall of Margaret Fell and George Fox.* n.p., 1664.

Five Strange and Wonderfull Prophesies and Predictions. n.p., [1642].

Fox, George. *Cain against Abel, Representing New-England's Church Hirarchy, in Opposition to Her Christian Protest Dissenters.* n.p., 1675.

Fox, George. *A Collection of Many Select and Christian Epistles.* London, 1698.

Fox, George. *Concerning Revelation, Prophecy, Measure, and Rule.* 1676.

Fox, George. *A Declaration of the Ground of Error and Errors.* London, 1657.

Fox, George. *Gospel Family-Order.* n.p., 1676.

Fox, George. *Possession above Profession.* n.p., 1675.

Fox, George. *Primitive Ordination and Succession of Bishops, Deacons, Pastors, and Teachers in the Church of Christ.* n.p., 1675.

Fox, George. *Saul's Errand to Damascus.* London, 1653.

Fox, George. *To the Parliament of the Commonwealth of England.* n.p., [ca. 1659].

Fox, George. *A Warning to the World.* London, 1655.

Fox, George. *The Woman Learning in Silence.* London, 1656.

Fox, George, and John Burnyeat. *A New-England-Fire-Brand Quenched.* London, 1678.

Fox, George, and John Burnyeat. *A New-England-Fire-Brand Quenched. The Second Part.* London, 1678.

Foxe, John. *The Acts and Monuments of John Foxe.* Ed. Josiah Pratt. 8 vols. London: George Seeley, 1870.

Gardiner, Richard. *Profitable Instructions for the Manuring, Sowing and Planting of Kitchin Gardens.* London, 1603; facsimile Norwood, NJ: Walter J. Johnson, 1973.

Gargill, Anne. *Warning to All the World.* London, 1656.

Gataker, Thomas. *Antinomianism Discovered and Confuted: And Free Grace as It Is Held Forth in Gods Word.* London, 1652.

Gataker, Thomas. *A Good Wife Gods Gift; And, A Wife Indeed.* London, 1623.

Gataker, Thomas. *Marriage Duties Briefely Couched.* London, 1620.

Gataker, Thomas. *A Mariage Praier.* London, 1624.

The Geneva Bible: A Facsimile of the 1560 Edition. Introduction by Lloyd E. Berry. Madison: University of Wisconsin Press, 1969.

Gerbier, Charles. *Elogium Heroinum: Or, the Praise of Worthy Women.* London, 1651.

A Godly Forme of Household Government: For the Ordering of Private Families According to the Direction of Gods Word. London, 1598.

Goodwin, John. *An Apologesiates Antapologias.* London, 1646.

Goodwin, John. *Cretensis.* London, 1646.

Goodwin, Thomas, Philip Nye, Sedrach Simpson, Jeremiah Burroughs, and William Bridge. *An Apologeticall Narration.* London, 1643.

Gorton, Samuel. *Simplicities Defence against Seven-headed Policy.* London, 1646.

Gouge, William *Of Domesticall Duties, Eight Treatises.* London, 1622.

[Grey, Elizabeth]. *A Choice Manuall, of Rare and Select Secrets in Physick and Chirurgery: Collected, and Practised by the Right Honourable, the Countesse of Kent, Late Deceased.* London, 1653.

G[roome], S[amuel]. *A Glass for the People of New-England.* London, 1676.

Guillemeau, Jacques. *Child-birth, or The Happy Deliverie of Women,* trans. from French. London, 1612.

H. E. *Proceedings at the Sessions.* London, 1651.

Halkett, Anne. *Instruction for Youth.* Edinburgh, 1701.

Halkett, Anne. *Meditations and Prayers upon the First Week.* Edinburgh, 1701.

H, [I.]. *A Strange Wonder or A Wonder in a Woman.* London, 1642.

Halkett, Anne. *Meditations on the Twentieth and Fifth Psalm.* Edinburgh, 1701.

Harris, Edward. *A True Relation of a Company of Brownists.* n.p., 1641.

Hendericks, Elizabeth. *An Epistle to Friends in England.* n.p., 1672.

Hilgard. *A Strange Prophecie against Bishops.* London, 1641.

Hill, William. *A New-Years Gift for Women Being a True Looking Glass.* London, 1660.

The History of the Life and Death of Hugh Peters. London, 1661.

Hollingworth, Richard. *Certain Queries.* London, 1646.

Hooker, Thomas. *The Application of Redemption.* London, 1659.

Hooker, Thomas. *The Covenant of Grace Opened.* London, 1649.

Hooker, Thomas. *The Soules Humiliation.* London, 1640.

Hooker, Thomas. *The Soules Implantation into the Naturall Olive.* London, 1640.

Hooker, Thomas. *The Soules Preparation for Christ.* London, 1632.

Hooker, Thomas. *The Unbelievers Preparing for Christ.* London, 1638.

How, Samuel. *The Vindication of the Cobler.* London, 1640.

Howgill, Francis. *The Dawnings of the Gospel-Day, and Its Light and Glory Discovered.* London, 1676.

Howgill, Francis. *The Popish Inquisition New Erected in New England Whereby Their Church Is Manifested to Be a Daughter of Mysterie-Babylon.* n.p., [1659].

Hubbard, William. *General History of New England, from the Discovery to MDCLXXX.* Cambridge, MA: Massachusetts Historical Society, 1815.

The Humble Petition of Divers Well-Affected Women. n.p., 1649.

Jocelin, Elizabeth. *The Mothers Legacie, To Her Unborne Childe.* London, 1624.

Johnson, Edward. *Wonder-Working Providence of Sions Saviour in New England.* 1654; Andover, MA: W.F. Draper, 1867.

Killen, Margret, and Patison, Barbara. *A Warning from the Lord to the Teachers and People of Plimoth.* London, 1656.

The Ladies Champion Confounding the Author of the Wandring Whore. London, 1660.

Lake, Arthur. *Sermons with Some Religious and Divine Meditations.* London, 1629.

Lay-Preaching Unmarked. London, 1644.

Leigh, Dorothy. *A Mothers Blessing.* London, 1616.

The Life of the Lady Halkett. Edinburgh, 1701.

A List of Some of the Grand Blasphemers and Blasphemies. London, 1654.

Little Non-Such. London, 1646.

Lymn, Margaret. *The Controversie of the Lord against the Priests of the Nations.* n.p., 1676.

Maddocks, John, and Henry Pinnell. *Gangraenachrestum, or, A Plaister to Alay the Tumor.* Oxford, 1646.

Mall, Thomas. *A True Account of What Was Done by a Church of Christ in Exon.* London, 1658.

Marbury, Francis. *A Fruitful Sermon Necessary for the Time.* London, 1602.

Marbury, Francis. *Notes on the Doctrine of Repentance.* London, 1602.

Marbury, Francis. "Preface" to Robert Rollock, *A Treatise of Gods Effectual Calling.* Trans. Henry Holland. London, 1603.

Marbury, Francis. *A Sermon Preached at Paules Cross.* London, 1602.

M[arkham], G[ervase]. *The English Hus-wife.* London, 1615; facsimile, Norwood, NJ: Walter Johnson, 1973.

Mather, Cotton. *Elizabeth in Her Holy Retirement.* Boston, 1710.

Mather, Cotton. *A Family Well Ordered.* Boston, 1699.

Mather, Cotton. *Magnalia Christie Americana; Or, The Ecclesiastical History of New England.* 1702; New York: F. Ungar, 1970.

Mather, Cotton. *Ornaments for the Daughters of Zion.* Boston, 1692.

The Mid-wives Just Petition. London, 1643.

Mrs. Rump Brought to Bed of a Monster. n.p., n.d.

Munda, Constantia. *The Worming of a Mad Dogge.* London, 1617.

Murther, Murther. London, 1641.

A Nest of Serpents Discovered. n.p., 1641.

New England a Degenerate Plant. London, 1659.

New England's Ensign. London, 1659.

New Preachers, New. n.p., 1641.

N[edham], M[archamont]. *Independencie No Schisme.* London, 1646.

Newcastle, Margaret Cavendish. *Orations of Divers Sorts, Accommodated to Diverse Places.* London, 1662.

Niccholes, Alex[ander]. *A Discourse of Marriage and Wyving.* London, 1615.

Niclaes, Henrik. *Evangelkium Regni. A Joyful Message of the Kingdom.* 1575; London, 1652.

Niclaes, Henrik. *An Introduction to the Holy Understanding of the Glasse of Righteousnesse.* 1575; London, 1649.

Niclaes, Henrik. *The Prophecy of the Spirit of Love.* 1574; London, 1649.

Niclaes, Henrik. *Revelatio Dei. The Revelation of God.* 1575; London, 1649.

Niclaes, Henrik. *Terra Pacis. A True Testification of the Spiritual Land of Peace.* 1575; London, 1649.

Norton, John. *The Heart of New England Rent.* London, 1660.

Now or Never: Or a New Parliament of Women. n.p., 1656.

Overton, Mary. *To the Right Honourable, the Knights, Citizens, and Burgesses of the Parliament of England . . . Petition of Mary Overton, Prisoner in Bridewell.* London, 1647.

Pagitt, Ephraim. *Heresiography.* London, 1654.

Parker, Thomas. *The Copy of a Letter . . . to . . . Elizabeth Avery.* London, 1650.

Parr, Susanna. *Susanna's Apology against the Elders.* n.p., 1659.

Pechey, J. *The Compleat Midwifes Practice Enlarged.* London, 1698.

Pennington, Isaac. *An Examination of the Grounds or Causes, Which Are Said to Induce the Court of Boston in New England to Make That Order or Law of Banishment against the Quakers.* London, 1660.

Perkins, William. *Christian Oeconomie*. London, 1609.

Perkins, William. *A Discourse of the Damned Art of Witchcraft*. Cambridge, 1608.

Peters, Hugh. *A Dying Fathers Last Legacy to an Onely Child*. London, 1660.

Poole, Elizabeth. *An Alarum of War Given to the Army*. London, 1649.

Poole, Elizabeth. *Another Alarum of War Given to the Army*. London, 1649.

Poole, Elizabeth. *A Vision, Wherein Is Manifested the Disease and Cure of the Kingdome*. London, 1648.

Pope, Mary. *A Treatise of Magistry*. [London], 1647.

The Prentises Prophecie. London, 1642.

Preston, John. *The New Covenant, or The Saints Portion*. London, 1629.

Prynne, William. *A Fresh Discovery of Some Prodigious New Wandring-Blasing-Stars, & Firebrands, Styling Themselves New Lights*. London, 1644.

Rachel Speght (pseud.). *A Mouzell for Melastomus*. London, 1617.

R[athband], W[illiam]. *A Briefe Narration of Some Courses . . . in New England*. London, 1644.

A Representation to King, and Parliament of Some of the Unparralleld Sufferings of the People of the Lord, Called Quakers in New England. n.p., 1669.

Robinson, John. *A Justification of Separation for the Church of England*. Amsterdam, 1610.

Robinson, William, and William Leddra. *Several Epistles Given Forth by Two of the Lords Faithful Servants*. London, 1669.

Rodgers, Daniel. *Matrimonial Honour: Or the Mutuall Crowne and Comfort of Godly, Loyall, and Chaste Marriage*. London, 1642.

The Routing of the Ranters. n.p., [1641].

Rueff, J. *The Expert Midwife*. London, 1637.

S., [J.] *A Brief Anatomie of Women*. London, 1653.

S., [M]. *A Looking-Glass for Sectaryes*. London, 1647.

The Saints Testimony Finishing through Sufferings. London, 1655.

Saltmarsh, John. *Free Grace: or The Glowings of Chriss Blook Freely to Sinners*. London, 1649.

Saltmarsh, John. *Groanes for Liberty*. London, 1646.

Sharp, Jane. *Compleat Midwife's Companion*, 4th ed. London, 1725.

Shepard, Thomas. *Certain Select Cases Resolved*. 1648; n.p., 1695.

Shepard, Thomas. *The Parable of the Ten Virgins*. 1660; Falkirk, 1997.

Shepard, Thomas. *The Sincere Convert*. n.p., 1646.

Shepard, Thomas. *The Sound Believer*. n.p., 1645.

A Short Relation of Some Part of the Sad Sufferings. n.p., 1640.

Spencer, John. *A Short Treatise Concerning the Lawfullnesse of Every Mans Exercising His Gift*. London, 1641.

A Spirit Moving in the Women-Preachers. London, 1645.

Stephenson, Marmaduke. *A Call from Death to Life*. London, 1660.

Strange Newes from Scotland. London, 1647.

Strange News from Newgate and the Old Baily. London, 1651.

Stubbe, Henry. *A Vindication of That Prudent and Honourable Knight, Sir Henry Vane*. London, 1659.

Stockden, John. *The Seven Women Confessors*. London, 1641.

Stucley, Lewis. *Manifest Truth: Or an Inversion of Truth's Manifest*. London, 1658.

Swetnam, Joseph. *The Arraignment of Lewd, Idle, Froward, and Unconstant Women*. 1615; London, 1637.

Sydenham, Thomas. *The Whole Works of That Excellent Practical Physician*. Trans. John Pechy. London, 1696.

T., E. *Diotrephes Detected, Corrected, and Rejected*. London, 1658.

Tattle-well, Mary, and Joane Hit-him-home (pseuds.). *The Womens Sharpe Revenge*. London, 1640.

Taylor, Edward. *The Poems of Edward Taylor*. New Haven, CT: Yale University Press, 1960.

Taylor, John. *The Brownist Conventicle*. n.p., 1641.

Taylor, John. *A Medicine for the Times*. London, 1641.

Taylor, John. *A Swarme of Sectaries, and Schismatiques*. n.p., 1641.

Taylor, John. *The Whole Life and Progresse of Henry Walker the Ironmonger*. London, 1642.

Taylor, Thomas. *The Works of That Faithful Servant of Jesus Christ, Dr. Thomas Taylor*. London, 1653.

Torshell, Samuel. *The Womans Glorie*. London, 1650.

Trapnel, Anna. *Anna Trapnel's Report and Plea, or, A Narrative of Her Journey from London into Cornwal*. London, 1654.

Trapnel, Anna. *The Cry of a Stone, or a Relation of Something Spoken in Whitehall*. London, 1654.

Trapnel, Anna. "Poetical Addresses." n.p., 1659.

A True Copie of the Petition of the Gentlewomen, and Tradesmen's Wives. London, 1641.

A True Relation of a Combustion, Hapning, at St. Anne's Church. n.p., 1641.

A Tub Lecture Preached at Watford. London, 1642/43.

Tub-Preachers Overturn'd. London, 1647.

Turner, Wylliam. *The Names of Herbes in Greke, Latin, Englishe, Duche, Frenche with the Commone Names Herbaries and Apothecaries Use*. London, 1548.

Two Strange Prophesies. London, 1642.

Vane, Henry. *A Healing Question Propounded and Resolved*. London, 1656.

Vane, Henry. *Two Treatises: An Epistle General to the Mystical Body of Christ on Earth, and the Face of the Times*. London, 1662.

Vicars, John. *The Schismatick Sifted*. London, 1646.

Vicars, John. *Speculum Scripturae Schismaticorum: Or A Scripture Looking-Glass*. London, 1649.

The Vindication of the Cobler. London, 1640.

The Virgins Complaint. London, 1642/43.

W., A. *A Booke of Cookrye, Very Necessary for All Such as Delight Therein*. London, 1591; facsimile, Norwood, NJ: Walter J. Johnson, 1976.

Wadsworth, Benjamin. *The Well-Ordered Family*. Boston, 1721.

Walker, Henry. *An Answer to a Foolish Pamphlet*. n.p., 1641.

Walker, Henry. *The Modest Vindication of Henry Walker*. London, 1642.

Walwyn, William. *An Antidote against Master Edwards His Old and New Poyson*. London: Thomas Paine, 1646.

Walwyn, William. *A Whisper in the Eare of Mr. Thomas Edwards Minster*. n.p., 1646.

Walwyn, William. *A Word More to Mr. Thomas Edwards*. London, 1646.

The Wandering Whore. London, 1660.

The Wandering Whore Continued, Second Installment. London, 1660.

The Wandering Whore Continued, Third Installment. London, 1660.

Warren, Elizabeth. *The Old and Good Way Vindicated*. London, 1646.

Warren, Elizabeth. *Spiritual Thrift, or Meditations*. London, 1647.

Warren, Elizabeth. *A Warning-Peece from Heaven*. London, 1649.

Welde, Thomas. *An Answer to W.R. His Narration of the Opinions and Practises of the Churches Lately Erected in New-England.* London, 1644.

[Welde, Thomas.] *A Brief Narration of the Practices of the Churches in New-England.* London, 1647.

Wentworth, Anne. *The Revelation of Christ.* n.p., 1679.

Wentworth, Anne. *A Vindication of Anne Wentworth.* n.p., 1677.

The Widows Lamentation for the Absence of Their Deare Children. London, 1643.

[Wheelwright, John.] *Mercurius Americanus, or Mr. Welds His Antitype.* London, 1645.

Winthrop, John. *A Short Story of the Rise, Reign, and Ruine of the Antinomians, Familists, & Libertines.* Preface by Thomas Weld. London, 1644.

White, Thomas. *A Discoverie of Brownisme.* London, 1605.

The Widows Lamentation for the Absence of Their Deare Children. London, 1643.

Willis, Thomas. *The London Practice of Physick.* London, 1685.

Yarb, Samuel. *A New Sect of Religion Descryed Called Adamites.* n.p., 1641.

Secondary Scholarship

Adams, Charles Francis. *Three Episodes of Massachusetts History.* Boston: Houghton Mifflin, 1892.

Anderson, Virginia DeJohn. "Migrants and Motives: Religion and the Settlement of New England, 1630–1640." *New England Quarterly* 58 (1985), 339–383.

Anderson, Virginia DeJohn. *New England's Generation: The Great Migration and the Formation of Society and Culture in the Seventeenth Century.* Cambridge: Cambridge University Press, 1991.

Ashton, Robert. *Conservatism and Revolution, 1603–1649.* New York: Norton, 1978.

Ashton, Robert. *Counter-revolution: The Second Civil War and Its Origins, 1646–48.* New Haven, CT: Yale University Press, 1994.

Bailyn, Bernard. *The New England Merchants in the Seventeenth Century.* New York: Harper, 1955.

Barker-Benfield, Ben. "Anne Hutchinson and the Puritan Attitude toward Women." *Feminist Studies* 1 (1972), 65–96.

Battis, Emery. *Saints and Sectaries: Anne Hutchinson and the Antinomian Controversy in the Massachusetts Bay Colony.* Chapel Hill: University of North Carolina Press, 1962.

Beilin, Elaine V. "Anne Askew's Self-Portrait in the *Examinations*." In *Silent but for the Word: Tudor Women as Patrons, Translators, and Writers of Religious Works*, ed. Margaret Patterson Hannay, 77–91. Kent, OH: Kent State University Press, 1985.

Bendroth, Margaret Lamberts. "Feminism, Anne Hutchinson, and the Antinomian Controversy, 1634–1638." *Trinity Journal* 2 (1981), 40–48.

Berkin, Carol Ruth. *Within the Conjurer's Circle: Women in Colonial America.* Morristown, NJ: General Learning Press, 1974.

Block, Sharon. *Rape and Sexual Power in Early America.* Chapel Hill: University of North Carolina Press, 2006.

Bozeman, Theodore Dwight. *The Precisionist Strain: Disciplinary Religion and Antinomian Backlash in Puritanism to 1638.* Chapel Hill: University of North Carolina Press, 2004.

Brauer, Jerald. "Types of Puritan Piety." *Church History* 56 (1987), 39–58.

Breen, Louise A. *Transgressing the Bounds: Subversive Enterprises among the Puritan Elite in Massachusetts, 1630–1692.* New York: Oxford University Press, 2001.

Bremer, Francis. *Puritanism: Transatlantic Perspectives on a Seventeenth-Century Anglo-American Faith*. Boston: Massachusetts Historical Society, 1993.

Bremer, Francis. *Troubler of the Puritan Zion*. New York: Krieger, 1981.

Briggs, Robin. *Witches and Neighbors: The Social and Cultural Context of European Witchcraft*. New York: Viking Press, 1996.

Brod, Manfred. "Politics and Prophecy in Seventeenth-Century England: The Case of Elizabeth Poole." *Albion* 31 (1999), 395–412.

Brown, Kathleen M. *Good Wives, Nasty Wenches, and Anxious Patriarchs: Gender, Race, and Power in Colonial Virginia*. Chapel Hill: University of North Carolina Press, 1996.

Buchanan, Lindal. "A Study of Maternal Rhetoric: Anne Hutchinson, Monsters, and the Antinomian Controversy." *Rhetoric Review* 3 (2006), 239–259.

Bynum, Caroline Walker. *Fragmentation and Redemption: Essays on Gender and the Human Body in Medieval Religion*. New York: Zone Books, 1991.

Bynum, Caroline Walker. *Holy Feasts Holy Fasts*. Berkeley: University of California Press, 1987.

Bynum, Caroline Walker. *Jesus as Mother: Studies in the Spirituality of the High Middle Ages*. Berkeley: University of California Pres, 1982.

Caldwell, Patricia. "The Antinomian Language Controversy." *Harvard Theological Review* 69 (1976), 345–367.

Caldwell, Patricia. *The Puritan Conversion Narrative: The Beginnings of American Expression*. Cambridge: Cambridge University Press, 1983.

Capp, Bernard. *The Fifth Monarchy Men*. London: Faber, 1972.

Chapin, Howard M. *Our Rhode Island Ancestors*. Rhode Island Historical Society. Photocopy.

Chester, Joseph Lemuel. *Notes upon the Ancestry of William Hutchinson and Anne Marbury*. Boston: D. Clapp and Son, 1866.

Chu, Jonathan. *Neighbors, Friends, or Madmen: The Puritan Adjustment to Quakerism in Seventeenth-Century Massachusetts*. Westport, CT: Greenwood Press, 1985.

Coggeshall, Charles Pierce, and Thellwell Russell Coggeshall. *The Coggesshalls in America*. Boston: C.E. Goodspeed, 1930.

Cohen, Charles Lloyd. *God's Caress: The Psychology of Puritan Religious Conversion*. New York: Oxford University Press, 1986.

Cohen, Ronald D. "Church and State in Seventeenth-Century Massachusetts: Another Look at the Antinomian Controversy." *Journal of Church and State* 12 (1970), 475–494.

Colacurcio, Michael J. "Footsteps of Ann Hutchinson: The Context of *The Scarlet Letter*." *ELH* 39 (1972), 459–494.

Cole, C. Robert, and Michael E. Moody. *The Dissenting Tradition*. Athens: Ohio University Press, 1975.

Colket, Meredith B. *The English Ancestry of Anne Marbury Hutchinson and Katherine Marbury Scott*. Philadelphia: Magee Press, 1936.

Collinson, Patrick. *The Elizabethan Puritan Movement*. Berkeley: University of California Press, 1967.

Collinson, Patrick. *From Cranmer to Sancroft: Essays on English Religion in the Sixteenth and Seventeenth Centuries*. London: Bloomsbury Academic, 2006.

Collinson, Patrick. *Godly People: Essays on English Protestantism and Puritanism*. London: Hambledon Press, 1983.

Como, David R. "Women, Prophecy, and Authority in Early Stuart Puritanism." *Huntington Library Quarterly* 61 (1999), 203–222.

Crawford, Patricia. *Women and Religion in England, 1550–1720*. London: Routledge, 1993.

Cross, Clare. *Church and People, 1450–1660: The Triumph of the Laity in the English Church*. Hassocks: Harvester Press, 1976.

Cross, Clare. "'He-Goats before the Flocks': A Note on the Part Played by Some Women in the Founding of Some Civil War Churches." *Studies in Church History* 8 (1972), 195–202.

Daston, Lorraine J., and Katharine Park. *Wonders and the Order of Nature, 1150–1750*. New York: Zone Books, 2001.

Davies, Stevie. *Unbridled Spirits: Women of the English Revolution, 1640–1660*. London: Women's Press, 1998.

Dayton, Cornelia. *Women before the Bar: Gender, Law, and Society in Connecticut, 1639–1789*. Chapel Hill: University of North Carolina Press, 1995.

Demos, John. *Entertaining Satan: Witchcraft and the Culture of Early New England*. New York: Oxford University Press, 1982.

Demos, John. *A Little Commonwealth*. New York: Oxford University Press, 1970.

Dickens, A. G. *The English Reformation*. New York: Schocken Press, 1964.

Ditmore, Michael G. "A Prophetess in Her Own Country: An Exegesis of Anne Hutchinson's Immediate Revelation." *William and Mary Quarterly* 57 (2000), 349–392.

Dolan, Frances E. *Whores of Babylon: Catholicism, Gender, and Seventeenth-Century Print Culture*. 1999; Notre Dame: University of Notre Dame Press, 2005.

Donnelly, Dorothy H. "The Sexual Mystic: Embodied Spirituality." In *The Feminist Mystic and Other Essays on Women and Spirituality*, ed. Mary E. Giles, 120–141. New York: Crossroads, 1982.

Donnison, Jean. *Midwives and Medical Men: A History of the Struggle for the Control of Childbirth*. London: Historical Publications, 1988.

Douglas, Mary. *Natural Symbols: Explorations in Cosmology*. New York: Vintage, 1973.

Douglas, Mary. *Purity and Danger: An Analysis of Concepts of Pollution and Taboo*. 1965; London: Routledge, 2002.

Douglass, Jane Dempsey. Women and the Continental Reformation." In *Religion and Sexism: Images of Woman in Jewish and Christian Traditions*, ed. Rosemary Radford Ruether, 292–318. New York: Simon and Schuster, 1974.

Dow, F. D. *Radicalism in the English Revolution, 1640–1660*. London: Blackwell, 1985.

Doyle, Patricia Martin. "Women and Religion: Psychological and Cultural Implications." In *Religion and Sexism: Images of Woman in Jewish and Christian Traditions*, ed. Rosemary Radford Ruether, 15–40. New York: Simon and Schuster, 1974.

Dunn, Mary. "Saints and Sisters: Congregational and Quaker Women in the Early Colonial Period." *American Quarterly* 30 (1978), 582–601.

Dunn, Richard S. "The Social History of Early New England." *American Quarterly* 24 (1972), 661–679.

Eccles, Audrey. *Obstetrics and Gynaecology in Tudor and Stuart England*. London: Croom Helm, 1982.

Erikson, Kai T. *Wayward Puritans: A Study in the Sociology of Deviance*. New York: Allyn and Bacon. 1966.

Ezell, Margaret J. M. "Performance Texts: Arise Evans, Grace Carrie, and the Interplay of Oral and Handwritten Traditions during the Print Revolution." *English Literary History* 76 (2009), 49–73.

Field, Jonathan Beecher. "The Antinomian Controversy Did Not Take Place." *Early American Studies* 6 (2008), 448–463.

Fletcher, Anthony. *The Outbreak of the English Civil War*. New York: New York University Press, 1981.

Foster, Stephen. *The Long Argument: English Puritanism and the Shaping of New England Culture, 1570–1700*. Chapel Hill: University of North Carolina Press, 1991.

Foster, Stephen. "New England and the Challenge of Heresy, 1630–1660: The Puritan Crisis in Trans-Atlantic Perspective." *William and Mary Quarterly* 38 (1981), 624–660.

Freeman, Frederick. *The History of Cape Cod: The Annals of Barnstable County and of Its Several Towns*. Boston, 1860.

Freeman, Thomas. "'The Good Ministrye of Godlye and Vertuouse Women': The Elizabethan Martyrologists and the Female Supporters of the Marian Martyrs." *Journal of British Studies* 39 (2000), 8–33.

Gay, Frederick. "Rev. Francis Marbury." *Proceedings of the Massachusetts Historical Society* 48 (1915), 280–291.

George, Carol V. R. "Anne Hutchinson and the Revolution Which Never Happened." In *"Remember the Ladies": New Perspectives on Women in American History. Essays in Honor of Nelson Manfred Blake*, ed. Carol V. R. George, 13–38. Syracuse, NY: Syracuse University Press, 1975.

Gildrie, Richard P. *Salem, Massachusetts, 1626–1683: A Covenant Community*. Charlottesville: University of Virginia Press, 1975.

Giles, Mary E. "The Feminist Mystic." In *The Feminist Mystic and Other Essays on Women and Spirituality*, ed. Mary E. Giles, 6–38. New York: Crossroads, 1982.

Gill, Catie. "Evans and Cheever's *A Short Relation* in Context: Flesh, Spirit, and Authority in Quaker Prison Writings, 1650–1662." *Huntington Library Quarterly* 72 (2009), 265–269.

Goodman, Nan. *Banished: Common Law and the Rhetoric of Social Exclusion in Early New England*. Philadelphia: University of Pennsylvania Press, 2012.

Greaves, Richard L. "Foundation Builders: The Role of Women in Early English Nonconformity." In *Triumph over Silence, Women in Protestant History*, ed. Richard L. Greaves, 70–81. Westport, CT: Greenwood Press, 1985.

Green, Ian. *Print and Protestantism in Early Modern England*. New York: Oxford University Press, 2000.

Greven, Philip J. *Four Generations: Population, Land, and Family in Colonial Andover, Massachusetts*. Ithaca, NY: Cornell University Press, 1972.

Gura, Philip. *A Glimpse of Sion's Glory: Puritan Radicalism in New England, 1620–1660*. Middletown, CT: Wesleyan University Press, 1984.

Hall, David D. *Worlds of Wonder, Days of Judgment: Popular Religious Belief in Early New England*. Cambridge, MA: Harvard University Press, 1990.

Hambrick-Stowe, Charles E. *The Practice of Piety: Puritan Devotional Disciplines in Seventeenth-Century New England*. Chapel Hill: University of North Carolina Press, 1982.

Hamburger, Jeffrey F., and Susan Marti, eds. *Crown and Veil: Female Monasticism from the Fifth to the Fifteenth Centuries*. Trans. Dietlinde Hamburger. New York: Columbia University Press, 2008.

Hannah, Margaret Patterson, ed. *Silent but for the Word: Tudor Women as Patrons, Translators, and Writers of Religious Works*. Chapel Hill: University of North Carolina Press, 1982.

Hawthorne, Nathaniel. "Mrs. Hutchinson." *Salem Gazette*, 1830. Retrieved November 12, 2020, from http://people.ucls.uchicago.edu/~pdoyle/bustlesandbeaux.wordpress.com-Mrs_Hutchinson_by_Nathaniel_Hawthorne1830.pdf.

Hill, Christopher. *God's Englishman: Oliver Cromwell and the English Revolution.* New York: Penguin, 1970.

Hill, Christopher. *The Intellectual Origins of the English Revolution.* Rev. ed. 1965; New York: Oxford University Press, 2001.

Hill, Christopher. *Society and Puritanism in Pre-revolutionary England.* 1958; New York: Schocken Books, 1965.

Hill, Christopher. *The World Turned Upside Down: Radicalism and Religion during the English Revolution.* New York: Viking, 1972.

Hill, Christopher, Barry Reay, and William Lamont. *The World of the Muggletonians.* London: T. Smith, 1983.

Hinds, Hilary. *God's Englishwomen: Seventeenth-Century Radical Sectarian Writing and Feminist Criticism.* Manchester, UK: Manchester University Press, 1996.

Huber, Elaine C. "'A Woman Must Not Speak': Quaker Women in the English Left Wing." In *Women of Spirit: Female Leadership in the Jewish and Christian Traditions,* ed. Rosemary Ruether and Eleanor McLaughlin, 153–182. New York: Simon and Schuster, 1979.

Huber, Elaine C. *Woman and the Authority of Inspiration.* Lanham, MD: University Press of America, 1987.

Hughes, Ann. *"Gangraena" and the Struggle for the English Revolution.* New York: Oxford University Press, 2004.

Hughes, Ann. *Gender and the English Revolution.* Abingdon, UK: Routledge, 2011.

Hutchinson, Thomas. *Anne Hutchinson in Massachusetts.* Boston: Directors of the Old South, 1907.

Johnson, Penelope D. *Equal in Monastic Profession: Religious Women in Medieval France.* Chicago: University of Chicago Press, 1991.

Jones, Rufus M. *Mysticism and Democracy in the English Commonwealth.* Cambridge, MA: Harvard University Press, 1932.

Jones, Rufus M. *The Quakers in the American Colonies.* 1911; New York: Norton, 1966.

Jones, Rufus M. *Spiritual Reformers in the Sixteenth and Seventeenth Centuries.* Boston: Beacon Press, 1914.

Kamensky, Jane. *Governing the Tongue: The Politics of Speech in Early New England.* New York: Oxford University Press, 1997.

Karlsen, Carol. *The Devil in the Shape of a Woman: Witchcraft in Colonial New England.* New York: Norton, 1987.

Kaufmann, Michael W. "Post Secular Puritans: Recent Trials of Anne Hutchinson." *Early American Literature* 45 (2010), 331–359.

Kibbey, Ann. *The Interpretation of Material Shapes in Puritanism: A Study of Rhetoric, Prejudice, and Violence.* Cambridge: Cambridge University Press, 1986.

King, David. *William Coddington. Resistance by Him and Others in Lincolnshire to the Royal Loan, 1626-7. New England Historical and Genealogical Register,* 36 (1882), 138–143.

King, David, and Sarah Birckhead. "Governor William Coddington." *Bulletin of Newport Historical Society* 5 (1913), 1–20.

Knight, Janice. *Orthodoxies in Massachusetts: Rereading American Puritanism.* Cambridge, MA: Harvard University Press, 1994.

Koehler, Lyle. "The Case of the American Jezebels: Anne Hutchinson and Female Agitation during the Years of the Antinomian Turmoil, 1636-1640." *William and Mary Quarterly* 31 (1974), 55–78.

Koehler, Lyle. *A Search for Power: The "Weaker Sex" in Seventeenth-Century New England.* Urbana: University of Illinois Press, 1980.

Kristeva, Julia. *In the Beginning Was Love: Psychoanalysis and Faith.* Trans. Arthur Goldhammer. New York: Columbia University Press, 1988.

Lake, Peter. *The Boxmaker's Revenge: "Orthodoxy," "Heterodoxy" and the Politics of the Parish in Early Stuart London.* Stanford, CA: Stanford University Press, 2001.

Lake, Peter. *Moderate Puritans and the Elizabethan Church.* Cambridge: Cambridge University Press, 1982.

Lamb, Mary Ellen. "The Cooke Sisters: Attitudes toward Learned Women in the Renaissance." In *Silent but for the Word: Tudor Women as Patrons, Translators, and Writers of Religious Works*, ed. Margaret Patterson Hannay, 107–125. Kent, OH: Kent State University Press, 1985.

Lang, Amy Shrager. *Prophetic Woman: Anne Hutchinson and the Problem of Dissent in the Literature of New England.* Berkeley: University of California Press, 1987.

Laqueur, Thomas. *Making Sex: Body and Gender from the Greeks to Freud.* Cambridge, MA: Harvard University Press, 1990.

Larner, Christina. *Witchcraft and Religion: The Politics of Popular Belief.* Oxford: Blackwell, 1984.

Lerner, Gerda. *The Majority Finds Its Past: Placing Women in History.* New York: Oxford University Press, 1979.

Lewis, I. M. *Ecstatic Religion: An Anthropological Study of Spirit Possession and Shamanism.* New York: Penguin, 1971.

Lock, Margaret. "Cultivating the Body: Anthropology and Epistemologies of Bodily Practice and Knowledge." *Annual Review of Anthropology* 22 (1993), 133–155.

Lockridge, Kenneth A. *A New England Town: The First Hundred Years.* New York: Norton, 1970.

Loewenstein, David. *Literacy in Colonial New England.* New York: Norton, 1974.

Loewenstein, David. "Scriptural Exegesis, Female Prophecy, and the Radical Politics in Mary Cary." *Studies in English Literature, 1500–1900* 46 (2006), 133–153.

Lovejoy, David. "Shun Thy Father and All That: The Enthusiasts' Threat to the Family." *New England Quarterly* 60 (1987), 71–85.

Lovell, R. A. *Sandwich a Cape Cod Town.* Sandwich, MA, 1684.

Ludlow, Dorothy Paula. "Arise and Be Doing": English "Preaching" Women, 1640–1660. PhD diss. Indiana University, 1978.

Mack, Phyllis. *Visionary Women: Ecstatic Prophecy in Seventeenth-Century England.* Berkeley: University of California, 1992.

Mack, Phyllis. "Women as Prophets during the English Civil War." *Feminist Studies* 8 (1982), 19–45.

Maclear, James Fulton. "Anne Hutchinson and the Mortalist Heresy." *New England Quarterly* 54 (1981), 74–103.

Maclear, James Fulton. "'The Heart of New England Rent': The Mystical Element in Early Puritan History." *Mississippi Valley Historical Review* 4 (1956), 621–652.

Maclear, James Fulton. "New England and the Fifth Monarchy: The Quest for the Millennium in Early American Puritanism." *William and Mary Quarterly* 32 (1975), 223–260.

McGiffert, Michael. "American Puritan Studies in the 1960s." *William and Mary Quarterly* 27 (1970), 36–67.

McGiffert, Michael. "Grace and Works: The Rise and Division of Covenant Divinity in Elizabethan Puritanism." *Harvard Theological Review* 75 (1982), 463–502.

McGregor, J. F., and Barry Reay, eds. *Radical Religion in the English Revolution*. New York: Oxford University Press, 1984.

McLaughlin, Eleanor. "Equality of Souls, Inequality of Sexes: Women in Medieval Theology." In *Religion and Sexism: Images of Woman in Jewish and Christian Traditions*, ed. Rosemary Radford Ruether, 213–266. New York: Simon and Schuster, 1974.

McLaughlin, Eleanor. "Women, Power and the Pursuit of Holiness in Medieval Christianity." In *Women of Spirit: Female Leadership in the Jewish and Christian Traditions*, ed. Rosemary Ruether and Eleanor McLaughlin, 99–130. New York: Simon and Schuster, 1979.

Middlekauf, Robert. "Piety and Intellect in Puritanism." *William and Mary Quarterly* 22 (1965), 457–470.

Miller, Perry. *Errand into the Wilderness*. New York: Harper and Row, 1956.

Miller, Perry. *The New England Mind: From Colony to Province*. Cambridge, MA: Harvard University Press, 1956.

Miller, Perry. *The New England Mind: The Seventeenth Century*. Cambridge, MA: Harvard University Press, 1939.

Mintz, Susannah B. "The Specular Self of 'Anna Trapnel's Report and Plea.'" *Pacific Coast Philology* 35 (2000), 1–16.

Moran, Gerald F. "Religious Renewal, Puritan Tribalism, and the Family in Seventeenth-Century Milford, Connecticut." *William and Mary Quarterly* 36 (1979), 236–254.

Morgan, Edmund S. "The Case against Anne Hutchinson." *New England Quarterly* 10 (1937), 633–649.

Morgan, Edmund S. "Introduction" to *Puritan Political Ideas*, ed. Edmund S. Morgan. New York: Bobbs-Merrill, 1965, xiii–xlviii.

Morgan, Edmund S. *The Puritan Dilemma: The Story of John Winthrop*. Boston: Little, Brown, 1958.

Morgan, Edmund S. *The Puritan Family: Religion and Domestic Relations in Seventeenth-Century New England*. 1956; New York: Harper & Row, 1966.

Morgan, Edmund S. *Visible Saints: The History of a Puritan Idea*. New York: New York University Press, 1963.

Morris, Richard B. "Jezebel before the Judges: Anne Hutchinson Tried for Sedition." In his *Fair Trial*, 3–32. New York: Harper & Row, 1967.

Morton, Arthur L. *The World of the Ranters: Religious Radicalism in the English Revolution*. London: Lawrence and Wishart, 1970.

Moss, Jean Dietz. *"Godded with God": Hendrik Niclaes and His Family of Love*. Philadelphia: American Philosophical Society, 1981.

Myles, Anne G. "From Monster to Martyr: Re-presenting Mary Dyer." *Early American Literature* 36 (2001), 1–30.

Nevitt, Marcus. *Women and the Pamphlet Culture of Revolutionary England, 1640–1660*. Aldershot, UK: Ashgate, 2006.

Norton, Mary Beth. "'The Ablest Midwife That Wee Know in the Land': Mistress Alice Tilly and the Women of Boston and Dorchester, 1649–1650." *William and Mary Quarterly* 55 (1998), 105–134.

Norton, Mary Beth. "The Evolution of White Women's Experience in Early America." *American Historical Review* 89 (1984), 593–619.

Norton, Mary Beth. *Founding Mothers and Fathers: Gendered Power and the Forming of American Society*. New York: Vintage Press, 1997.

Nuttall, Geoffrey F. *The Holy Spirit in Puritan Faith and Experience*. New York: Oxford University Press, 1946.

Park, Katharine and Lorraine Daston. "Monsters: A Case Study." In their *Wonders and the Order of Nature*, 173–214, 408–417. New York: Zone Books, 2001.

Park, Katharine and Lorraine Daston. "Unnatural Conceptions: The Study of Monsters in Sixteenth- and Seventeenth-Century France and England." *Past and Present* 92 (1981), 20–54.

Pestana, Carla Gardina. "The City upon a Hill under Siege: The Puritan Perception of the Quaker Threat to Massachusetts Bay, 1656–1661." *New England Quarterly* 56 (1983), 323–353.

Pestana, Carla Gardina. *Quakers and Baptists in Colonial Massachusetts*. New York: Cambridge University Press, 1991.

Pettit, Norman. *The Heart Prepared: Grace and Conversion in Puritan Spiritual Life*. New Haven, CT: Yale University Press, 1966.

Polishook, Irwin H. *Roger Williams, John Cotton and Religious Freedom*. Englewood Cliffs, NJ: Prentice Hall, 1967.

Porterfield, Amanda. *Female Piety in Puritan New England: The Emergence of Religious Humanism*. New York: Oxford University Press, 1992.

Prior, Mary. *Women in English Society, 1500–1800*. London: Methuen, 1985.

Reay, Barry. *The Quakers and the English Revolution*. London: Palgrave Macmillan, 1985.

Reis, Elizabeth. *Damned Women: Sinners and Witches in Puritan New England*. Ithaca, NY: Cornell University Press, 1999.

Richards, Jeffrey. *Sex, Dissidence and Damnation: Minority Groups in the Middle Ages*. London: Routledge, 1990.

Rogers, Horatio. *Mary Dyer of Rhode Island: The Quaker Martyr That Was Hanged on Boston Common*. Providence, RI: Preston and Rounds, 1896.

Rosenmeier, Jesper. "New England's Perfection: The Image of Adam and the Image of Christ in the Antinomian Crisis, 1634–1638." *William and Mary Quarterly* 27 (1970), 435–459.

Ross, Isabel. *Margaret Fell: Mother of Quakerism*. London: Longmans, Green, 1949.

Russell, Conrad. *The Causes of the English Civil War*. New York: Oxford University Press, 1990.

Rutman, Darrett B. *Winthrop's Boston: A Portrait of a Puritan Town, 1630–1649*. 1965; New York: Norton, 1972.

Ryan, Mary P. *Womanhood in America: From Colonial Times to the Present*. 3rd ed. New York: Franklin Watts, 1983.

Salmon, Marylynn. *Women and the Law of Property in Early America*. Chapel Hill: University of North Carolina Press, 1986.

Schiebinger, Londa. *Nature's Body: Gender in the Making of Modern Science*. Boston: Beacon Press, 1993.

Schofield, Roger. "Did Mothers Really Die? Three Centuries of Maternal Mortality in 'The World We Have Lost.'" In *The World We Have Gained: Histories of Population and Social Structures*, ed. Lloyd Bonfield, Richard M. Smith, and Keith Wrightson, 230–260. Oxford: Basil Blackwell, 1986.

Schutte, Anne Jacobson. "'Such Monstrous Births': A Neglected Aspect of the Antinomian Controversy." *Renaissance Quarterly* 38 (1985), 85–106.

Selement, George. "John Cotton's Hidden Antinomianism: His Sermon on Revelation 4:1–2." *New England Historical and Genealogical Register* 129 (1975), 278–294.

Shammas, Carole. *The Pre-industrial Consumer in England and America*. Oxford: Clarendon Press, 1990.

Smith, Nigel. *Perfection Proclaimed: Language and Literature in English Radical Religion, 1640–1660*. Oxford: Clarendon Press, 1989.

Stoever, William K. "Nature, Grace and John Cotton: The Theological Dimension in the New England Antinomian Controversy." *Church History* 44 (1975), 22–33.

Stone, Lawrence. *The Causes of the English Revolution, 1529–1642*. New York: Harper, 1972.

Stone, Lawrence. *The Crisis of the Aristocracy, 1558–1641*. New York: Oxford University Press, 1965.

Stout, Harry S. *The New England Soul: Preaching and Religious Culture in Colonial New England*. New York: Oxford University Press, 1986.

Tannenbaum, Rebecca J. *The Healer's Calling: Women and Medicine in Early New England*. Ithaca, NY: Cornell University Press, 2009.

Tarter, Michele Lise. "Quaking in the Light: The Politics of Quaker Women's Corporeal Prophecy in the Seventeenth Century Transatlantic World." In *A Centre of Wonders: The Body in Early America*, ed. Janet Lindman Moore and Michele Lise Tarter, 145–162. Ithaca, NY: Cornell University Press, 2001.

Thomas, Keith. *Religion and the Decline of Magic*. New York: Scribner's Sons, 1970.

Thomas, Keith. "Women and the Civil War Sects." *Past and Present* 13 (1958), 42–62.

Thompson, Roger. *Women in Stuart England and America: A Comparative Study*. London: Routledge and Kegan Paul, 1974.

Thwing, Walter Eliot. *History of the First Church of Roxbury, Massachusetts*. [1908.]

Tipson, Baird. "Invisible Saints: The 'Judgement of Charity' in Early New England Churches." *Church History* 44 (1975), 460–471.

Traister, Bryce. *Female Piety and the Invention of American Puritanism*. Columbus: Ohio State University Press, 2016.

Ulrich, Laurel Thatcher. *Good Wives: Image and Reality in the Lives of Women in Northern New England, 1650–1750*. New York: Knopf, 1982.

Valerius, Karyn. "So Manifest a Sign from Heaven: Monstrosity and Heresy in the Antinomian Controversy." *New England Quarterly* 83 (2010), 179–199.

Wald, Alan M. "From Antinomianism to Revolutionary Marxism: John Wheelwright & the New England Rebel Tradition." *Marxist Perspectives* 3 (1980), 44–88.

Warnicke, Retha. *Women of the English Renaissance and Reformation*. Westport, CT: Greenwood Press, 1983.

Watkins, Owen C. *The Puritan Experience: Studies in Spiritual Autobiography*. New York: Schocken Books, 1972.

Watt, Tessa. *Cheap Print and Popular Piety, 1550–1640*. New York: Cambridge University Press, 1991.

Weber, Max. *The Sociology of Religion*. Trans. Ephraim Fischoff. Boston: Beacon Press, 1963.

Westerkamp, Marilyn J. "Anne Hutchinson, Sectarian Mysticism, and the Puritan Order." *Church History* 59 (1990), 482–496.

Westerkamp, Marilyn J. "Puritan Patriarchy and the Problem of Revelation." *Journal of Interdisciplinary History* 23 (1993), 571–595.

Westerkamp, Marilyn J. *Women and Religion in Early America: The Puritans and Evangelical Traditions, 1600–1850*. London: Routledge, 1999.

Willen, Diane. "Godly Women in Early Modern England: Puritanism and Gender." *Journal of Ecclesiastical History* 43 (1992), 561–580.

Willen, Diane. "Women and Religion in Early Modern England." In her *Women in Reformation and Counter-Reformation Europe*, 140–165. Bloomington: Indiana University Press, 1989.

Williams, Selma R. *Divine Rebel: The Life of Anne Marbury Hutchinson*. New York: Henry and Holt, 1981.

Winship, Michael. *Making Heretics: Militant Protestantism and Free Grace in Massachusetts*. Princeton, NJ: Princeton University Press, 2002.

Winship, Michael. *The Times and Trials of Anne Hutchinson: Puritans Divided*. Lawrence: University of Kansas Press, 2005.

Winsser, Johan. "Mary Dyer and the 'Monster' Story." *Quaker History* 79 (1990), 20–34.

Withington, Ann Fairfax and Jack Schwartz. "The Political Trial of Anne Hutchinson." *New England Quarterly* 51 (1978), 226–240.

Ziff, Larzer. *The Career of John Cotton: Puritanism and the American Experience*. Princeton, NJ: Princeton University Press, 1982.

Zikmund, Barbara Brown. "The Feminist Thrust of Sectarian Christianity." In *Women of Spirit: Female Leadership in the Jewish and Christian Tradition*, ed. Rosemary Ruether and Eleanor McLaughlin, 206–224. New York: Simon and Schuster, 1979.

Index

For the benefit of digital users, indexed terms that span two pages (e.g., 52–53) may, on occasion, appear on only one of those pages.

Hutchinson, Anne (*cont.*)
  children of, 85, 130
  Cotton (John) and, 10, 11–12, 14, 19,
    21–22, 23–25, 27–28, 31–32, 47–48,
    52–53, 54–55, 71–72, 107, 108–9,
    137, 142, 181, 215, 229, 232–33
  death of, 26, 188
  Dudley and, 19–21, 25–26, 27, 54, 56,
    58, 71–72, 106, 107–8
  Dyer and, 25–26, 204–5
  excommunication from First Church of
    Boston of, 1–3, 9, 25–26, 53–54
  historiography of, 1, 2, 232–34
  midwifery of, 11–12, 57–58, 62, 89
  millennialism and, 179
  "monstrous births" attributed to, 130
  in New Netherland, 26, 201–2
  patriarchy and, 18–19, 57–58, 60–63,
    71–72, 76–77, 92, 97, 106, 108–9,
    110–11
  piety and, 3–4, 142, 144
  in Portsmouth, 56–58
  private religious meetings convened by,
    3–4, 6, 12, 19, 52, 54, 57–58, 71–72,
    108–9, 142–45, 147, 149, 153, 181–82
  revelations and prophesies of, 2–3, 6,
    22–24, 52, 147–48, 184–85, 194,
    195–96, 201–2, 219, 222–23, 225,
    227–28, 233
  at Rhode Island settlement, 26
  Saint Botolph's Church and, 10, 31–32
  salvation views of, 13–14, 19
  Scripture cited by, 109–10, 175–
    76, 178–79
  trial at First Church of Boston of, 25–26,
    53–54, 143–44, 175–76
  trial at General Court of, 1–3, 17–25,
    50–51, 52–53, 108, 143–44, 147, 179
  Vane and, 2–3, 6, 9, 12, 27, 49–50, 55–
    56, 108–9, 231–32
  wealth and gentry status of, 2, 31–33,
    46, 62
  Wheelwright (John) and, 2–3, 15, 18–19,
    46, 55
  Wilson and, 11–12, 15, 20–21, 53–54, 55
  Winthrop and, 1–3, 9, 16–24, 26, 27–28,
    46, 50–53, 55–58, 89, 92, 108–10,
    143–45, 175–76, 181, 231–32
Hutchinson, Edward (brother-in-law of
  Anne Hutchinson), 10–11

Hutchinson, Edward (son of Anne
  Hutchinson), 10–11
Hutchinson, Sarah, 10–11
Hutchinson, Susannah, 10–11
Hutchinson, Thomas, 233
Hutchinson, William, 9, 10–11, 26,
  31–32, 201–2

Independents, 166–67, 171–72, 174–75
Indigenous communities, 3–4, 28–29, 39,
  56, 162–63, 189

Jael (Old Testament), 94–95, 109, 171, 185
James I (king of England)
  Anglican Church and, 161–62
  ascension of, 36–37, 161–62
  Parliament and, 37, 59
  Puritans and, 34, 36–37, 59, 161–62
  Scottish church and, 37
  Williams's criticism of, 42–43
  on witchcraft, 131
Jezebel (Old Testament), 95, 109,
  128, 232–33
Job's wife (Old Testament), 95
Jocelin, Elizabeth, 65–66, 76, 86, 96–97
Joel, Book of, 167–68, 170–71, 185–86,
  197–98
Johnson, Edward, 232–33
Jones, Margaret, 133–34
Jones, Rufus, 192
Judith (Old Testament), 94–95, 109,
  177, 185
Julian of Norwich, 64–65

Kamensky, Jane, 2
Karlsen, Carol, 2, 62, 89
Keayne, Robert, 150, 243n.39
Keayne, Sarah, 148, 165
Kibbey, Ann, 2
Killin, Margret, 197–98
Knollys, Hanserd, 164
Knox, John, 155–56

Lake, Arthur, 161–62, 167–68
Larner, Christina, 131
Laud, William
  Anglican Church ritual and, 37–38,
    162–63, 172–73
  Archbishop of Canterbury
    appointment of, 38